THE ZUNI MAN-WOMAN

THE ZUNI MAN-WOMAN

WILL ROSCOE

University of New Mexico Press
ALBUQUERQUE

Library of Congress Cataloging-in-Publication Data

Roscoe, Will.
The Zuni man-woman/Will Roscoe.— 1st ed.
p. cm.
Includes bibliographical references and index.
ISBN 0–8263–1253–5
1. Zuni Indians–Social life and customs. 2.Zuni Indians–Sexual behaviour. 3. Sex role. I. Title
E99.Z9R78 1991
306.73'089974—dc20

Design by Susan Gutnik.

Second paperbound printing, 1996

Contents

PREFACE vii

ACKNOWLEDGEMENTS xix

PROLOGUE *A Death That Caused Universal Regret* 1

CHAPTER ONE *The Middle Place* 7

CHAPTER TWO *We'wha, the Celebrated Lhamana* 29

CHAPTER THREE *Among the Most Enlightened Society* 53

CHAPTER FOUR *The Country Was Full of Soldiers* 98

CHAPTER FIVE *The Rites of Gender* 123

CHAPTER SIX *Two-fold One-kind* 147

CHAPTER SEVEN *They Left This Great Sin* 170

CHAPTER EIGHT *The Berdache Tradition* 195

APPENDIX ONE *Pronunciation Guide* 215

APPENDIX TWO *The Beginning* 217

NOTES 223

BIBLIOGRAPHY 267

INDEX 291

Tables

TABLE 1. Correspondences of the Zuni Origin Myth 150

TABLE 2. Kan'a:kwe Synonymy 155

Preface

THE GENESIS OF *The Zuni Man-Woman* dates back to 1982, when I spent several months in the home of my friend and colleague Harry Hay.[1] Hay gave me access to notes and source materials from his extensive historical and cross-cultural research on homosexuality and alternative gender roles, conducted in the 1950s and early 1960s. As I discovered, Hay had come to view the American Indian berdache role as an example of a socially approved channel for the expression of a pattern of sex and gender variance that allowed individuals to make unique social, religious, and artistic contributions to their communities. In the 1960s, however, he interrupted this research to shift his energies to political organizing on behalf of American Indian causes. As a result, most of his insights and discoveries concerning this subject remain unpublished.

With Hay's encouragement, I decided to begin my own study of alternative gender roles. My approach from the outset was less theoretical than his and more in the vein of contemporary ethnohistory, which combines the methods of history and anthropology. I hoped to find specific cultural contexts with enough documentation to reconstruct not only the social and conceptual dimensions of alternative gender roles, but the lives of the individuals who occupied them as well. When I joined Hay and a small group of friends in New Mexico in 1983, however, I had not yet decided on a specific tribe to study. But after witnessing dances at four Pueblo villages, visiting the homes of Hay's friends at San Juan and San Ildefonso, clambering about ancient mesa-top ruins, and acquiring an appreciation for Pueblo art and architecture, I had little doubt regarding the direction my research would take. In this land—where the high point of the day for Indian, Hispanic, and Anglo residents alike consists of pulling up a chair to watch afternoon thunderclouds streak the horizons or the setting sun dissolve in spectacular opulence—I experienced the same awe of natural surroundings I had known while growing up in western Montana. I also found another, equally important source of inspiration in New Mexico's rich cultural diversity, the kind of diversity that had led me to resettle some years ago in the San Francisco Bay Area.

The wealth of published documentation on Zuni culture and history led me to focus my studies on that tribe. Even so, I had little inkling of the abundance of unpublished and oral sources that would enable me to tell the life story of a particular male berdache, We'wha, in remarkable detail. Nor did I foresee the extensive visual resources that would allow me to compile a slide-lecture program, "The Zuni Man-Woman," which I have since presented throughout the United States and Canada. Initially, I imagined the outcome of my research would be an article, but I soon found myself stymied by the very abundance of the resources that had led me to single out Zuni. I began pursuing separate questions in far-flung aspects of Zuni culture—analyzing locational references in myths and ceremonies; studying gender symbolism on kachinas; reconstructing the sexual politics of Zuni prehistory; compiling biographical background on key figures in Zuni history; studying the Zuni language. Gradually, as I became better acquainted with the philosophy underlying the diversity of Zuni cultural expressions, new sources began falling into familiar patterns. I also took advantage of the wealth of sources to cross-check statements by one observer with those of others. By following this procedure I was able to avoid excessive reliance on either of the two early anthropologists, Frank Hamilton Cushing and Matilda Coxe Stevenson, whose work still dominates the field of Zuni studies.

In the spring of 1984, efforts to locate the source of a photograph of We'wha led me to the collections of the Southwest Museum and my initial venture into archival research on berdaches. Subsequently, I visited the National Anthropological Archives of the Smithsonian Institution, the National Archives centers in Washington and Denver, the American Museum of Natural History and the Museum of the American Indian in New York, the Wheelwright Museum in Santa Fe, and collections at the University of New Mexico, George Washington University, the Library of Congress, and the Bancroft Library of the University of California at Berkeley. Unpublished manuscripts and notes by anthropologists and travelers; government and military records; collections of photographs; correspondence of teachers, missionaries, Indian agents, and social welfare organizations all proved valuable sources of information. For example, although certain episodes from We'wha's life, such as his trip to Washington and his confrontation with American soldiers, have long been preserved in print and in oral forms, I was able to determine the specific dates for these events only after an exhaustive survey of daily newspapers and military records.

Interviews, discussions, and correspondence with other scholars were also valuable, especially for insight into the otherwise unrecorded history of Zuni berdaches during the past fifty years. Anthropology, perhaps more than other disciplines, maintains a lively oral tradition that includes many unpublished (and unpublishable) anecdotes regarding the gender and sex practices of both natives and anthropologists. For the ethnohistorian, initiation into this informal discourse can be as valuable as access to native traditions.

Although resources for the study of berdaches are far greater in the case of Zuni than for any other North American tribe, they are finite and their quality uneven. For this reason, it was quite late in my research before the idea of a book seemed feasible. Eventually, I adopted an eclectic approach, examining my material through the successive windows of history, anthropology, religious studies, and psychology. While I believe this method has resulted in the most complete look at the male berdache role to date, it has the disadvantage of sacrificing a more unified narrative theme. Thus, the title of this work refers both to the *role* of the Zuni man-woman and to *the* Zuni man-woman, the famous nineteenth century berdache, We'wha. The chapters that follow can be divided into three parts: an introduction to Zuni society and gender roles and a biography of

We'wha in Chapters 1 to 4; a cultural and psychological exploration in Chapters 5 and 6; and a social history of the berdache role since European contact in Chapters 7 and 8. An explanation of the orthographic system for rendering Zuni terms and a guide to pronunciation appears in Appendix 1. A synopsis of the Zuni origin myth, which is referred to at various points in the main text, is included in Appendix 2.

THE FASCINATION OF ZUNI

There is an old joke that the typical Zuni household consists of a mother, father, children, and an anthropologist.[2] In fact, the Zunis are one of the most written-about tribes in the world. Anthropologists have been joined by writers and poets, artists and patrons of the arts, and political and social reformers of every stripe, all of whom sought and found in Zuni and Pueblo Indian cultures a model to be preserved and even copied. As I quickly learned, seeking answers from the Indians, whether in the form of sexual or social alternatives, is an American tradition almost as old as the seizure of Indian lands and the disruption of Indian cultures.

John Collier, Commissioner of Indian Affairs during Franklin Roosevelt's administration, considered Zuni a living example of an ideal social order—society organized into autonomous but interdependent groups, with each responsible for a particular social function but none so powerful as to dominate or control the others. Collier believed that Zuni "not merely foreshadows the democratic, pluralistic and holistic world order to come. It possesses and lives by the organizational principles which must be those of the democratic, pluralistic, holistic world order which must take form in the ages to come."[3] Anthropologist Elsie Clews Parsons, on the other hand, saw in Pueblo communities an example of "social responsibility combined with individual tolerance." A committed feminist, Parsons became a convert to anthropology after a visit to Zuni in 1915. As a result of her experiences among the Pueblos, she came to see feminism as part of an even larger goal, the freedom of individual expression.[4] Ruth Benedict, in *Patterns of Culture*, one of the most popular and enduring of all books by an anthropologist, used the example of Zuni berdaches to support her argument for tolerance of racial and individual differences. Challenging the widely accepted mental illness theory of homosexuality, she concluded, "We have only to turn to other cultures . . . to realize that homosexuals have by no means been uniformly inadequate to the social situation. . . . In some societies they have even been especially acclaimed."[5]

My interest in the legacy of intercultural relations in the Southwest grew as I realized how many of these pilgrims were, in one way or another, outcasts from Anglo-American society. As archaeologist Jacquetta Hawkes observed, "The South-West is full of American refugees from the American Way of Life. Men and women who are nonconformists in their sexual loves, in the strength of their love for history and the arts, or in their desire to be able to drive an old car in peace, are glad to live there in the sun."[6] Cushing, Stevenson, Parsons, Benedict, Bunzel, and many others who found fascination in Zuni and the Southwest lived unconventional lives. They rejected the restraints that Anglo society imposed on genders and arrived with a predisposition to find Pueblo culture somehow more organic and integrated. As Margaret Mead wrote of Benedict, "In her own search for identity, she had persistently wondered whether she would have fitted better into another period or another culture than she fitted into contemporary America."[7] For these individuals, women in particular, the Southwest offered psychological as well as geographical space, an otherness that intrigued and renewed.[8] It is to them that we owe nearly all of our knowledge of Zuni and Pueblo berdaches.

It was with genuine disappointment, then, that I came to realize how often the impact of these outsiders on the objects of their fascination has been disruptive and detrimental. Despite their admiration of the Pueblos, early anthropologists more often bolstered the image of the vanishing Indian than challenged it. As historian Curtis Hinsley, Jr., has pointed out, theirs was a legacy of both knowledge and annihilation.[9] The bitterness that many Zunis feel toward the countless investigators who have dissected their society is apparent from comments and actions recorded in a variety of sources, but most of all, in the work of anthropologist Triloki Pandey, who has devoted particular attention to the history of intercultural relations at Zuni. "Why are you studying us?" one Zuni demanded to know when Pandey first arrived in the 1960s. "Why not study those white people . . . who treat us like dogs?" And another asked, "Are we still so primitive that you anthropologists have to come to study us every summer?"[10]

Justification for these feelings is not hard to find. Stevenson, for example, candidly describes in her reports how she persuaded, tricked, and coerced Zunis into providing her information, artifacts, or other assistance, even when this caused obvious distress. In 1902, when she obtained an image of a kachina she "was compelled to give it up to prevent the woman who sold it to me receiving a severe whipping."[11] When priests or tribal leaders objected to her presence at religious ceremonies, she threatened to call on soldiers from nearby Fort Wingate. No wonder that during her later visits Stevenson had to post guards at her camp. As one Zuni woman told Pandey, "Some of the Zunis wanted to get rid of her. You cannot believe how arrogant she was. She entered the *Kivas* without asking permission of the high priests. She took pictures because the Zunis did not know what she was doing."[12]

Where Stevenson relied on bald authority, Cushing used flattery and subterfuge; nonetheless, he was equally obsessed with the goal of penetrating Zuni's secrets. "It is my conviction," he wrote in 1880, "that it is the duty of some one to record, word for word, in the original language, and with faithful translation, these prayers, ancient instructions and formulae. And that duty is more clearly my own."[13] The famous 1882 tour, in which five Zunis and a Hopi spent several months in various eastern cities, was part of a bargain that Cushing had made with Zuni leaders to provide them with an entrée to the White House in return for his initiation into the Zuni kachina society. When Cushing discovered that the bow priest or warrior society was the one group at Zuni whose members, in their role as messengers and guards, could attend the ceremonies of every other society and priesthood, he bluffed his way into its ranks.[14] Stevenson, Cushing, and others also became involved in Zuni's internal affairs by aligning themselves with opposing political interests within the tribe. Interference of this sort directly contributed to the emergence of political factions that persist to this day.[15]

The removal of religious objects from tribal possession was yet another source of dismay. The expeditions of 1879 and 1881 led by James Stevenson carried away so many irreplaceable objects that certain ceremonies had to be altered or suspended as a result.[16] Equally upsetting to the Zunis was the discovery that anthropologists were publishing descriptions of their ceremonies, including photographs of sacred paraphernalia and transcripts of prayers and other liturgy. In Zuni belief, dissemination is inimical to sacred knowledge. It not only dilutes its power, it hands over this knowledge to individuals outside Zuni religious institutions, whose motives may not include the good of all.

Early observers were convinced that the cause of science and the imminent disappearance of tribal cultures justified their actions.[17] In 1879, Cushing wrote, "My anxiety would not be so great were there not a probability that I am the last man who will have the opportunity to witness all of this in its purity." Stevenson echoed his sentiments twenty-five years later. "For this work," she lamented, "the passing hours are golden." Even Ruth Benedict was "appreciative of the privilege of getting at Zuñi before it's gone." Such predictions enact what James Clifford has termed the redemptive allegory of anthropology—the assumption that "primitive" cultures are doomed to disappear except for those artifacts "rescued" by Western scientists. Such predictions are not only self-serving—since they inflate the importance of the fieldworker's reports—they can also be self-fulfilling. They sustain and foster the idea of Indians as a vanishing race by referring only to their past.[18]

The alternative view, however, challenges many comfortable assumptions: that there are neither primitive nor civilized, inferior nor superior, simple nor advanced societies—only different ones. This view requires learning to think in "plurals"—imagining the multiple histories and cultural stories of human societies in every part of the world as parallel, equal developments intersecting without necessarily merging, and associating non-Western societies such as Zuni with the future of the planet instead of its past. We must question the assumption that change means the loss of something essential and find ways to discuss cultural differences without encasing them in value-ladened descriptions.

Avoiding these pitfalls, however, involves more than a conceptual shift executed in the comfort of one's armchair. In my own case, awareness of the unequal cultural exchange between Zunis and Anglo-Americans led me to ask two questions. At a time when

Indian writers, artists, scholars, historians, and anthropologists are coming to the fore, is there a role for non-Indian scholars in the study of Indian history and cultures? And, if so, can our study be conducted in a way that reverses the historical relationship between the advancement of Western knowledge and the disempowerment and disappearance of non-Western peoples? I have no definitive answers for either question, but I can share my personal responses, fashioned in the course of this project.

I began in 1984 by seeking out American Indians who might share my interest in berdaches and respond to my work, not as informants but as colleagues. Somewhat hesitantly, I presented myself one day before a table staffed by the Gay American Indians organization at a political rally in San Francisco. I explained that I had been collecting information on berdaches and asked if any of their members were interested in the subject. To my delight, Randy Burns, the organization's cofounder, called me a few days later and invited me to a meeting.

That was the beginning of a collaboration that continues to this day. The organization's board of directors was very interested in the traditional cultures of their tribes, especially in the role of berdaches, but they were preoccupied with more immediate social service needs in their community. So they welcomed my offer to help coordinate, under their direction, the GAI History Project. Our goal was to make information about traditional roles accessible to Indians. Under the project's auspices, a bibliography of sources on berdache roles in North America was compiled and published. I subsequently helped edit *Living the Spirit: A Gay American Indian Anthology*.[19] My role in this project was essentially one of administration; decisions regarding contents, format, and publication arrangements were made by GAI's board of directors, and contributors represented over twenty tribes throughout North America. I urge readers to consult *Living the Spirit*, where they will find sources of inspiration for this work in such authors as Maurice Kenny, Paula Gunn Allen, Beth Brant, Midnight Sun, and M. Owlfeather.

In addition to these projects in San Francisco, I also began looking for a way to make my research accountable to Zunis. I wanted to provide Zuni cultural experts with a way of giving me feedback, and, if it should prove to be the case, of criticizing my overall project. The opportunity to do so developed when two Stanford faculty members, Clifford Barnett and Rick Paul, saw my slide-lecture in late 1986 and subsequently offered advice on how to arrange a presentation at Zuni. The following spring, I received permission from the Zuni Tribal Council to give an illustrated lecture on Zuni history in the village. The council also requested that I talk to students at the Zuni High School. The lecture I prepared focused on the tribe's response to the changes of the late nineteenth century as seen through the lives of four Zuni leaders, including We'wha. This lecture was presented four times—once for the general public and three times for students at the high school in November 1987—and it was also taped and broadcast on the tribal radio station.

The Zunis are deeply interested in their cultural heritage. Individuals and organizations today are actively working to preserve this heritage for the next generation. The Zunis were among the first tribes in the United States to take over administration of their own school district, and as a result, all Zuni students are required to take courses in Zuni culture. Consequently, my talks on Zuni history, including my discussion of We'wha, were warmly received, and my desire to submit my work to Zuni critics was especially appreciated. Many older Zunis, although quite familiar with the individuals and events I described, thanked me for recovering specific dates that had been forgotten. Again, I found that when research by an outsider coincides with the goals and programs of Indian communities a common ground for exchange opens up. (Of course, the kindness of the Zuni Tribal Council in granting me permission to talk at Zuni constitutes in no way an endorsement or approval of my findings.)

That was my second trip to Zuni, first having traveled there in 1984 to attend Sha'lako, and I have returned to visit since. By sharing my work with Zunis in both written form and in lectures, I have received valuable feedback and learned many new details. Most of this information falls into the category of common knowledge—facts widely known and freely shared with outsiders—and so I report it as such, without specific attribution. As a general principle, I have tried to incorporate into this narrative, whenever possible, the voices of Zunis.

Historians, compared to anthropologists, stand an extra step removed from their subjects. Because of the sensitive nature of my research, dealing with highly charged issues in gender and sexuality, I believe this position offers one advantage. My study is based on a reconstruction of Zuni culture of a century ago—which is why I have written in the past tense, a convention that should not be taken to imply anything about the current status of Zuni culture. In my discussions of religion and ceremonialism, I do not reveal any information that has not been published previously. I have tried to avoid having to choose between reporting data I might have learned informally from Zunis and respecting the confidence and privacy of personal relationships. In short, should any aspect of *The Zuni Man-Woman* be found incorrect or inappropriate there are no Zuni "informants" to be blamed for it. I am responsible for all contents and conclusions.

"We white Americans glance wistfully at moments toward the Indians whom only a short time ago we were fighting tooth and nail," wrote author Edmund Wilson after his visit to Zuni in the 1940s. "The idealist like John Collier, once a social worker in big cities, finds in Indian life a 'wholeness' and a harmony with Nature that the specialized urban man, quite divorced from the earth for a century, is incapable even of imagining. An anthropologist like Ruth Benedict goes to the pueblos for evidence to prove to us that there are other human possibilities than our badly run industrial societies, with their murderous national phobias and their jarring individual neuroses. The aesthete in Santa Fe admires, even adores, the Indian for the vitality and the self-sufficiency that he has known how to sustain in his art. And the journalist like myself, who has reported many hateful and destructive events, wants to get a good look at the Shálako birds, bringers of happy abundance, before they shall have ceased to come."[20]

But the Sha'lakos have not ceased to come. The Zunis have survived four centuries of European–American contact, and they still maintain key social and religious institutions. They have also developed new institutions—social forms that are not traditional, but neither are they Western. And if the Zunis have been changed by their contact with Europeans and Americans, American society has been influenced by the Zunis. They helped inspire Cushing's modern conception of culture and, with it, the ideas of cultural wholeness and cultural relativism; Collier's vision of a pluralistic society; and the call by Parsons and Benedict for greater tolerance of individual differences. More recently, Dennis Tedlock has drawn from his Zuni experiences to advocate "dialogical" anthropology based on collaboration between anthropologists and native people.[21]

As the history of the fascination of Zuni reveals, the act of investigating another culture always entails a particular ethical and moral stance. Perhaps the most important corrective is this: Instead of hiding behind an illusion of objectivity, investigators should disclose their own ethical and social positions and make them accessible to criticism by the people whose lives are the subject of their studies.[22] In this regard, readers will find no attempt to hide the kinship of this book to the tradition of applying insights from American Indians to American social problems. I have written *The Zuni Man-Woman* to share what has been a profound experience in my own life—the exchange of values across cultures, leading to new images of our fuller humanity—while striving to honor that common ground where the interest of the non-Indian coincides with the interests and needs of Indians themselves.

Acknowledgements

AT THE END OF A LONG AND FRUITful project such as this one, nothing gives more pleasure than the recollection of the friendships formed, the conversations and insights shared, the kindness of colleagues, and the adventures lived in its course. Indeed, so many have helped in the past eight years that the warmth of these memories is offset by the humbling realization that one's work is really not one's own at all but that of a community of inquirers whose care for the heritage of American Indian values led them to honor me with their assistance. No less humbling is the possibility, with so many to remember, that I might neglect some one among them.

I have already mentioned how Harry Hay first sparked my interest in berdache studies. Along with his partner John Burnside, he has provided constant encouragement, criticism, insight, contacts, and friendship. I have also mentioned my collaboration with Gay American Indians. I have been genuinely honored by the trust placed in me by the GAI Board of Directors in our joint projects and their encouragement of my own research. Randy Burns, Erna Pahe, Vicki Arnau, and Bart Amarillas, in particular, extended their friendship early and patiently taught me the ways of their world. I also would like to honor the memory of Nancy Ingram, Ray Harjo, and Mark Waukchen, three openly gay American Indians who lived and died in service to their communities.

Among the scholars and colleagues who were kind enough to read portions of my manuscript or otherwise consult with me, I would like to thank John Adair, John Beebe, Anne Bolin, Clifford Barnett, Lowell Bean, T. J. Ferguson, Margaret Hardin, E. Richard Hart, Thomas Lippert, Caitlin Manning, Dennis Miles, Triloki Pandey, John Rick, Rodney Simard, Thomas Tavis, and Mitch Walker. I am especially grateful to Jonathan Batkin, Lawrence Kelly, and Luke Lyon for sharing valuable source material, while Evelyn Blackwood was instrumental in clarifying my understanding of third-gender status. For their personal as well as professional support, I thank Jack Collins, John DeCecco, Michael Lynch, Gerry Stilwell, Terry Tafoya, and David Thomas. Special thanks are also due to Mark Thompson (a friend from the beginning, who first suggested that I write a book on We'wha), Frank Brayton, Dennis Morse, Pat Gourley, and my mother Harriette Dooling.

It is not possible to thank individually all the people, and organizations, around the country who have sponsored my slide-lecture, "The Zuni Man-Woman," over the past four years and welcomed me into their homes. Suffice to say that We'wha has led me to many wonderful people and places. While I must thank them collectively here, I hope they will let me return their hospitality on a more individual basis should they ever come this way.

Today's unsung heroes of scholarship are the librarians and archivists who, despite growing financial constraints, continue to provide personal and professional attention to researchers. Without such guidance and assistance, many of the sources that made this book possible would never have been located. Particularly helpful were Kathleen Baxter of the National Anthropological Archives, Daniela Moneta at the Southwest Museum, Octavia Fellin of the Gallup Public Library, Bruce Bernstein at the Wheelwright Museum of the American Indian, and Cynthia Swanson and Christine Kehrwald at the George Washington University Library.

I am also grateful to the Ann and Erlo Van Waveren Foundation for a generous fellowship in 1987 that made it possible to present my talks at Zuni, to conduct on-site research in New Mexico, and to begin writing the first draft of this book.

Discoveries become joyous experiences when shared with another who appreciates their value. This is what my partner and colleague, Bradley Rose, has added to my experience of studying the berdache tradition. He has shared in every part of this project—from the delight of finding the first photograph of We'wha to the compilation of my slide-lecture program (and attendance at far more presentations, both near and far, than anyone has a right to expect of one's partner), to sleeping in a car next to the old Zuni mission while Sha'lako dancers slipped through the night around us, to reading, editing, re-reading, and re-editing the manuscript itself. Brad's critical and loving spirit infuses this book. It is only fitting that such dedication as his be returned by the dedication of *The Zuni Man-Woman* to him.

Prologue

A Death That Caused Universal Regret

On a December day in 1896, six great warrior-birds, the Sha'lakos, ten feet high with snapping beaks and bulging eyes, descended from the southern mesas at dusk to the outskirts of the ancient village called the Anthill at the Middle of the World. For more than an hour, they lurked in the icy blackness across the river from the stone and red adobe pueblo that clung to a small knoll overlooking a broad valley plain. Then, amid song and prayer and sacred corn meal strewn by the villagers, they came in. With another six called the Council of the Gods, their protégé the young Fire God, and the comic but holy clowns called Koyemshi, they danced in the new houses erected to receive them—for one night, all night—diving, bobbing, careening to the awe and delight of the onlookers. Thus, they bestowed their blessings of increase and health and in turn received the prayers of the people for snow and rain in the season to come.

And when the night was over and the new day arrived, these ungainly beings staged a dramatic contest in the field across the trickling river. Racing to and fro with breathtaking skill, they dramatized their role as mediators between humans and the forces of nature—supernatural couriers who carried the prayers of the villagers to the rainmakers of the six directions: north, east, south, west, up, and down. Then, as quickly as they had begun, the great birds ended their race and were gone to the mesas and mountaintops whence they came.

In the village, dances continued for another week. Outside, adobe ovens spewed columns of pungent piñon smoke as women baked loaf after loaf of heavy wheat bread; and inside, huge vats of mutton stew, fired with red chili, simmered on the hearths. Neighbors and visitors crowded into the homes of the Sha'lako hosts and enjoyed the liberal hospitality, the colorful dances, the free and easy (and sometimes raucous) social intercourse of men, women, and children. The Sha'lako festival melded all—devotion and delight, prayer and celebration, religion and drama—into a showcase of the cultural achievements of the people of the Middle Place.

Except for the presence of a few white people and selective technological borrowings such as wagons and metal implements, there was little to distinguish the annual Sha'lako ceremony of 1896 from any other observed by the Zuni Indians of New Mexico from time immemorial.[1] The Zunis and their ancestors had been living in the same location in west-central New Mexico for two thousand years or more, long enough for them to view their homeland as the veritable middle of the world. Throughout this time, the Zunis beseeched their gods, gave thanks for their harvests, blessed their houses, and entertained neighbors by observing Sha'lako, or Kokko 'A:'iya, "the gods come."

In 1896, however, one of the families selected to host a Sha'lako god included a "noted and prominent" Zuni named We'wha (WEE'wah).[2] An accomplished artist and craftsman as well as an active participant in religious and ceremonial life, We'wha had served as a cultural ambassador for the Zunis, traveling to Washington in 1886 to meet national leaders and shake hands with the president. Six years later, he spent a month in jail for resisting soldiers sent by that same government to interfere in his community's affairs. We'wha was also a berdache—to use the currently accepted anthropological term—a man who combined the work and social roles of men and women, an artist and a priest who dressed, at least in part, in women's clothes.

Hosting a Sha'lako god entailed heavy responsibilities, including participation in monthly religious observances for the entire year preceding the ceremonies, construction or refurbishing of the necessary rooms for the dances, and feeding countless guests throughout the festival. We'wha labored long and hard in preparation, carefully laying the stone floor in the large room where the bird-god would dance. Not yet fifty, We'wha nonetheless suffered from heart disease, and according to his white friend, Matilda Coxe Stevenson, these efforts proved too much. When the time came for the arrival of the god, We'wha could not attend. From then on, he was "listless and remained alone as much as possible." Yet he made no complaint of illness.

The anthropologist Stevenson—who, in the following passage, uses female pronouns to refer to We'wha—was conducting research in Zuni that fall.[3] She joined her friend of over fifteen years in his final hours.

> *When a week or more had passed after the close of the great autumn ceremonial of the Sha'lako, and the many guests had departed, the writer dropped in at sunset to the spacious room in the house of We'wha's foster father, the late Jose Palle. We'wha was found crouching on the ledge by the fire-place. That a great change had come over her was at once apparent. Death evidently was rapidly approaching. She had done her last work. Only a few days before this strong-minded, generous-hearted creature had labored to make ready for the reception of her gods; now she was preparing to go to her beloved Ko'thluwala'wa [Sacred Lake]. When the writer asked, "Why do you not lie down?" We'wha replied: "I can not breathe if I lie down; I think my heart break." The writer at once sent to her camp for a comfortable chair, and fixed it at a suitable angle for the invalid, who was most grateful for the attention. There was little to be done for the sufferer. She knew that she was soon to die and begged the writer not to leave her.*
>
> *From the moment her family realized that We'wha was in a serious condition they remained with her, ever ready to be of assistance. The family consisted of the aged foster mother, a foster brother, two foster sisters with their husbands and children, and an own brother with his wife and children. The writer never before observed such attention as every member of the family showed her. The little children ceased their play and stood in silence close to their mothers, occasionally toddling across the floor to beg We'wha to speak. She smiled upon them and whispered, "I can not talk." The foster brother was as devoted as the one related by blood. . . .*
>
> *The foster brother, with streaming eyes, prepared te'likinawe [prayer sticks] for the dying, the theurgist having*

> *said that her moments on earth were few. We'wha asked the writer to come close and in a feeble voice she said, in English: "Mother, I am going to the other world. I will tell the gods of you and Captain Stevenson. I will tell them of Captain Carlisle, the great seed priest, and his wife, whom I love. They are my friends. Tell them good-by. Tell all my friends in Washington good-by. Tell President Cleveland, my friend, good-by. Mother, love all my people; protect them; they are your children; you are their mother." These sentences were spoken with many breaks. The family seemed somewhat grieved that We'wha's last words should be given to the writer, but she understood that the thoughts of the dying were with and for her own people. A good-by was said to the others, and she asked for more light.*
>
> *It is the custom for a member of the family to hold the prayer plumes near the mouth of the dying and repeat the prayer, but this practice was not observed in We'wha's case. She requested the writer to raise the back of the chair, and when this was done she asked if her prayer plumes had been made. Her foster brother answered "Yes," whereupon she requested him to bring them. The family suppressed their sobs that the dying might not be made sad. The brother offered to hold the plumes and say the prayers, but We'wha feebly extended her hand for them, and clasping the prayer plumes between her hands made a great effort to speak. She said but a few words and then sank back in her chair. Again the brother offered to hold the plumes and pray, but once more she refused. Her face was radiant in the belief that she was going to her gods. She leaned forward with the plumes tightly clasped, and as the setting sun lighted up the western windows, darkness and desolation entered the hearts of the mourners, for We'wha was dead.*[4]

Among the Zunis, the death of a berdache like We'wha elicited "universal regret and distress." But from the Spanish and Anglo-Americans who overran the Southwest, berdaches often evoked dismay, disgust, anger, or, at the least, ridicule. Berdaches were anomalies—freaks of nature, demons, deviants, perverts, sinners, corrupters. They committed the "nefarious vice," the "abominable sin." Over the centuries, Europeans have resorted to a bewildering variety of terms to describe them—in Spanish, *sométicos* (sodomites), *amarionadas* (from Mary, meaning "effeminate"), *mujerados* (literally "made women"), *putos* (male prostitutes), and *bardajes* (from *bardaj*, Persian and Arabic for "slave" or "kept boy"), and in English, "hermaphrodites," "sodomites," "men-women," "inverts," "homosexuals," "transvestites," and "transsexuals."[5]

Today, anthropologists have settled on the term *berdache*, a version of *bardaje* used by French explorers. In fact, variations of berdache were once current in Spanish, French, English, and Italian. The Oxford English Dictionary defines "bardash" as "a boy kept for unnatural purposes." Although such a practice has very little to do with the North American berdache role, Europeans had no better terms for such a status. Their languages forced them to make a choice between labeling the gender variation of berdaches (with terms like hermaphrodite and *mujerado*) or their sexual variation (with terms like sodomite and berdache).[6]

Male and female berdaches (that is, women who assumed male roles as warriors and chiefs or engaged in male work or occupations) have been documented in over 130 North American tribes, in every region of the continent, among every type of native culture, from the small bands of hunters in Alaska to the populous, hierarchical city-states of Florida. Among the Pueblo Indians of Arizona and New Mexico, male berdaches have been recorded at Acoma, Hopi, Isleta, Laguna, Santa Ana, Santo Domingo, San Felipe, San Juan, Tesuque, and Zuni. In the various languages spoken in these pueblos they were called *kokwimu* (Keres), *hova* (Hopi), *lhunide* (Tiwa), *kwidó* (Tewa), and *lhamana* (Zuni).[7]

In traditional native societies berdaches were not anomalous. They were integral, productive, and valued members of their communities. But the European culture transplanted to America lacked any comparable roles, and the Europeans who saw berdaches were unable to describe them accurately or comprehend their place in Indian societies. Indeed, through a long span of history, European social institutions have sought to suppress the very economic, social, and sexual behaviors typical of berdaches. Few aspects of European and American Indian cultures conflicted as much as they did in this.

What is it that American Indians saw in these men and women who bridged genders that Western civilization has overlooked or denied? And what was it like to be such a person? Although the answers that follow are based on a study of the male berdache role in a single tribe, and the career of a particular berdache, it is a story that could have been told hundreds of times over when the Europeans first arrived in North America, and may yet be told again, for all the tribes that recognized this status.

But first, we will begin with a visit to the home of the Zunis, the land they call the Middle Place; for this land and their relationship to it is at the heart of what makes the Zunis different from the non-Indians who are now their neighbors.

1
The Middle Place

TIRED AND THIRSTY, HIS FACE burned and chapped by two weeks of exposure to the searing sun of New Mexico, the frail young adventurer pressed his mule ahead of the others. To the south and west he could sense the terrain opening up. The immense sky, which seemed pressed so close to the earth that he could reach up and touch it, parted just slightly, brightening at the edges, as if a crack in the horizon had let in the light of some other sun. Perhaps, through this final pass, beyond the gray and red banded mesas that now walled him in, was his long-sought destination—the ancient village of the Zuni Indians. Frank Hamilton Cushing and the other members of his small party were about to hurtle themselves into an abyss of culture and time that would forever alter their lives.

Only a few weeks earlier, Cushing had been a humble curator at the Smithsonian Institution in Washington, D.C., when the head of the Institution called him into his office one sweltering day in July 1879. "Haven't I heard you say you would like to go to New Mexico to study the cliff-houses and Pueblo Indians?"

"Yes, sir," Cushing replied earnestly.

"Very well then, be ready to accompany Colonel Stevenson's collecting party, as ethnologist, within four days. I want you to find out all you can about some typical tribe of Pueblo Indians."[1]

Ever since his childhood in upstate New York, when he had spent his days combing the woods for Indian arrowheads and artifacts, Cushing had imagined and wondered about the original inhabitants of this land. Certain that valuable secrets were locked within their mute remains, he dreamed of finding the key. Their world, the world of the ancients, was as vivid to him as that of the post–Civil War America he had grown up in—the age of manifest destiny, voracious capitalism, and narrow Victorian propriety. Although he had never been separated from the comforts of civilization, had never ridden a horse or camped under open skies, and had never seen a "wild Indian" or a gun-toting outlaw, of which New Mexico had plenty, Cushing eagerly joined the first expedition of the government's newly created Bureau of Ethnology.[2]

Cushing was not the only member of the expedition eager to reach its destination. Not far behind were James Stevenson, the expedition's official leader; photographer John K. Hillers; and Stevenson's intrepid wife, Tilly, as she was then known. Although her role at that time was merely that of an unpaid assistant, Matilda Coxe Stevenson would eventually outlive and outperform her husband as an anthropologist to become Cushing's chief rival as the leading authority on the Zuni Indians.

Born the only child of a middle-class Washington, D.C., family, Stevenson had received something few women of the nineteenth century enjoyed—a formal education. Making her debut in the dazzling milieu of Gilded Age society in the nation's capital, she learned to hold her own in the intercourse of politicians, civil servants, intellectuals, lobbyists, appointment-seekers, and businessmen.[3] But Victorian America had little to offer a young woman with an unconventional interest in science and a strong need for recognition. Her frustration over these constraints fostered a personality that has been described as aggressive, strong-willed, and dominating. She was, in the language of the times, a "formidable woman," although her friends considered her "able, self-reliant, and fearless."[4] Marriage to geologist James Stevenson afforded her some contact with scientific circles, and by joining him on his official travels in the West she discovered a setting where she did not have to stifle her freedom of movement and natural assertiveness.[5] Indeed, where Cushing was the consummate greenhorn who would complain pathetically of the rigors of field work throughout his career, Stevenson was emboldened by outdoor life.

In the years to come, Stevenson would garner a rich store of knowledge regarding the Zunis. After her husband's death in 1888, the Bureau of Ethnology would hire her to complete his studies, making her one of the first American women to receive full-time employment in the pursuit of science.[6] The massive compendium on the Zunis that she published in 1904 was, at that time, one of the most comprehensive cultural descriptions of a single American Indian society ever written. Cushing's career at Zuni took a different course. Shortly after his arrival, he decided to move in with the pueblo's governor, Balowahdiwa. When the expedition returned to Washington, he remained behind, becoming one of the first anthropologists to actually live with the people he studied. He was adopted into Balowahdiwa's family and participated in nearly every aspect of Zuni social, political, and religious life.

When Cushing next appeared in the East, with a delegation of Zunis in 1882, his transformation seemed complete. He wore an embroidered blue blouse hung with numerous small silver buttons, knee-length trousers, colored woolen garters, buckskin anklets also embroidered and hung with silver, and a buckskin belt studded with silver dollars that had been hammered and engraved. A fringed quiver filled with arrows and a heavy chain made of hammered silver coins completed the ensemble. This is how he posed for his famous portrait by Thomas Eakins. In truth, the only authentic Zuni articles of clothing were his coarse footless socks and the bandana around his head.[7] Indeed, to this day Zunis remember Cushing as a "show-off" who donned his "Indian" outfit only when other Americans visited the pueblo.

Regarding Cushing, Stevenson once wrote, "This man was the biggest fool and charlatan I ever knew. He even put his hair up in curl papers every night. How could a man walk weighted down with so much toggery?"[8] But Stevenson was no more representative of the social norms of her time than Cushing; and in this regard, the Zuni view of her is revealing. In her report, she describes an occasion when she joined a Zuni family while they planted prayer sticks in the fields as offerings to the ancestors. Men offered prayer sticks to the sun, while women offered prayer sticks to the moon. The Zunis gave Stevenson *male* prayer sticks, and they told her, "Though you are a woman you have a head and a heart like a man, and you work like a man, and you must therefore make offerings such as men make."[9] After a childless marriage and widowhood at the age of thirty-eight, Stevenson would remain single the rest of her life, her closest personal relationships with other women.[10]

Despite the differences that would emerge between them, in 1879 Cushing and Stevenson shared a common goal. Both saw in the expedition an opportunity to launch a career in the newly emerging discipline of anthropology. For Cushing, this meant a chance to make contact with spiritual values outside those of his own society. For Stevenson, it meant a chance to participate meaningfully in the very society Cushing was trying to escape, by gaining a professional stature normally reserved, in her era, for men. But for both, anthropology represented a means to a more holistic, integrated existence.

As he urged his mule onward, slowly emerging from the red and grey mesas, Cushing became the first member of the party to sight its destination.

> *Below and beyond me was suddenly revealed a great red and yellow sand-plain. It merged into long stretches of gray, indistinct hill-lands in the western distance, distorted by mirages and sand-clouds, and overshadowed toward the north by two grand, solitary buttes of rock . . .*
>
> *Out from the middle of the rock-wall and line of sand-hills on which I stood, through a gate of its own opening, flowed a little rivulet. Emerging from a succession of low mounds beneath me, it wound, like a long whip-lash or the track of an earth-worm, westward through the middle of the sandy plain and out almost to the horizon, where, just midway between the northern buttes and the opposite gray mesas, it was lost in the southern shadows of a terraced hill.*
>
> *Down behind this hill the sun was sinking, transforming it into a jagged pyramid of silhouette, crowned with a brilliant halo, whence a seeming midnight aurora burst forth through broken clouds, bordering each misty blue island with crimson and gold, then blazing upward in widening lines of light, as if to repeat in the high heavens its earthly splendor.*
>
> *A banner of smoke, as though fed from a thousand crater-*

fires, balanced over this seeming volcano, floating off, in many a circle and surge, on the evening breeze. But I did not realize that this hill, so strange and picturesque, was a city of the habitations of men, until I saw, on the topmost terrace, little specks of black and red moving against the sky.

They had arrived at the ancient pueblo of Halona:idiwana—the Anthill at the Middle of the World. The party of four Americans, citizens of a nation barely a century old, were welcomed by a community whose American roots reached back millennia. As Cushing and Stevenson would soon discover, this tribe of barely seventeen hundred people maintained social, religious, economic, and artistic traditions of remarkable complexity. The expedition had been allotted six months to conduct an exhaustive study. In fact, both anthropologists would spend the rest of their lives as students of the people of the Middle Place.

AN ANCIENT CIVILIZATION

Located near the New Mexico–Arizona border, the Zunis were one of the most isolated of the twenty communities of Pueblo Indians in the American Southwest. This diverse group of tribes spoke several distinct languages but shared a similar life-style and religious outlook. The Zunis (they called themselves 'A:shiwi) made their home in the southeastern corner of the Colorado Plateau, in a region of low mountain ranges, buttes and pinnacles, great banded mesas, and broad valleys. From an elevation over nine thousand feet in the east, where the Zuni Mountains divided the Atlantic and Pacific drainages, the landscape sloped gradually downward toward the west. Ponderosa pine, scrub oak, juniper and piñon trees gave way to sagebrush, sharp pointed yuccas, and grasses in the valley floors. The pueblo of Zuni itself was located along the Zuni River, not far from where it emerged from the forested uplands to the east into a broad plain, bounded on the northwest by the Twin Mesas and the double points of the Zuni Buttes just behind them, and on the southeast by Dowa Yalanne, Corn Mountain, a massive, sheer-faced mesa jutting a thousand feet above the valley. To the west the plain gave way to low rolling hills.

The striking beauty of the Zuni area was offset by its harsh, unpredictable climate. The region received only eleven to thirteen inches of precipitation a year, primarily in summer thundershowers. Winter storms took the form of slow drizzles lasting for days and sometimes turning into paralyzing ice storms and blizzards. Spring was the driest season of the year, a time of blinding sandstorms that could devastate livestock and crops. Even so, the feeling of the Zunis for their land was deep and reverent, the result of centuries of intimacy and a life-style based on harmonious balance with nature. They referred to plants, minerals, and geographic forms as if they were family members. The earth was "mother," corn plants were her "children," game animals were "fathers," and Zuni mythology included such figures as Salt Woman, Cotton Woman, and White Shell Woman. All represented products of the Earth Mother, her "flesh"; all were alive or, in Zuni terms, *'a:ho'i*, living beings, a term applied to both human and nonhuman subjects.[11] "The landscape is our church, a cathedral," one Zuni explained. "It is like a sacred building to us."[12] Zuni poetry and art were filled with images of nature. When addressing their ancestors, they prayed:

> *Thus on all sides you will talk together.*
> *From where you stay quietly*
> *Your little wind-blown clouds,*
> *Your fine wisps of cloud,*
> *Your massed clouds you will send forth to sit down with us;*
> *With your fine rain caressing the earth,*
> *With all your waters*
> *You will pass to us on our roads.*
> *With your great pile of waters,*
> *With your fine rain caressing the earth,*
> *With your heavy rain caressing the earth,*
> *You will pass to us on our roads.*[13]

At the time of their first contact with Europeans in 1540, the Zunis lived in six towns along a fifteen-mile stretch of the Zuni River. Their compact pueblos of stone and adobe rose as high as seven stories with numerous roof-top patios and balconies. Desert farmers, they cultivated as many as ten thousand acres, with some fields located sixty miles or more from the main villages. Men tended corn, while Zuni women cultivated a variety of vegetables in highly productive plots (called "waffle gardens") located on the periphery of the village. Men also hunted various game animals, roaming as far as the Great Plains to track down buffalo, while an extensive knowledge of plants and minerals provided resources ranging from food to medicines and cosmetics.[14]

The basic unit of traditional Zuni society was the family group that shared a household and was related through either the mother or her daughters. This group was a lifelong source of support and the center of social, economic, and ceremonial life for the individual, even after marriage. Beyond the household were the clans, extended kinship groups that included several families who traced their descent back to a common female ancestor—a system referred to as matrilineal.[15] The other important institutions of Zuni society were religious in nature. Foremost was the kachina society, to which all adult men belonged. The six subgroups of this society, each of which maintained a kiva, or ceremonial chamber, sponsored public ceremonies featuring colorful masked dances. There were also several medicine societies, open to both men and women, referred to as the "societies of the completed path," because they enabled those whose lives had been threatened by illness or other forms of physical and spiritual harm to complete their "life road."

At the head of the Zuni theocracy were six religious leaders called rain priests. These priests were charged with the welfare of all living beings, human and nonhuman. They held long retreats to pray for rainfall and other blessings, and they were responsible for overseeing the ceremonial calendar and ensuring the timely performance of all rites and observances. Because their religious duties required them to avoid any form of strife or violence, they appointed two members of the warrior society—the bow priests—to serve as their executive arm, announcing their messages and enforcing decisions. The council of priests also appointed a civil governor to serve as a go-between with Spanish and, later, American officials.[16] It was not a democratic system—there were no popular elections—but it was a system with numerous checks and balances and decentralized authority. All decision-making bodies employed the principle of consensus, and on matters of grave concern the adult men of the village met as a whole. Any official, secular or religious, could be impeached by public outcry.[17]

The Zunis were a highly creative and artistic people. Families decorated their living rooms with colorful and symbolic murals; women painted ceramics with elaborate designs that were prayers for rain; and both men and women wove, painted, and embroidered textiles. After the Zunis acquired sheep in the seventeenth century, their woolen goods gained a reputation as the finest in the Southwest. Today, Zuni jewelry and other arts are admired by collectors throughout the world. All these articles of human handiwork were also considered *'a:ho'i*, living beings, and the process by which they were created was compared to the act of giving birth.

In all their arts, the Zunis sought to express an ideal they referred to as *tso'ya*, which Barbara Tedlock has defined as "a combination of dynamic, multicolored, chromatic (in the musical sense), varied, new, exciting, clear and beautiful."[18] This aesthetic of diversity found its fullest expression in the kachina dances—and, above all, in the annual fall Sha'lako ceremony. On this occasion, the kachinas danced in homes where every wall was decked with brilliantly colored shawls and blankets, strings of jewelry, stuffed deer and elk heads with turquoise earrings and necklaces, pictures, paintings, and other artwork, as well as traditional altars and ceremonial trappings. Edmund Wilson compared this multi-media extravaganza to Diaghilev's famous dance theater, the Ballet Russe.[19]

FINDING THE MIDDLE

Considering the intricate social structure of the Zunis, the multiplicity of their arts, knowledge, and technology, and their accumulated wisdom from centuries of social living, it is no wonder that even after three years Cushing was in "despair of grasping the whole of the rich store at his disposal."[20] What held this diversity together was a complex worldview based on an all-encompassing concept of "the middle." The Zunis believed they lived at the center of the world. Great oceans encircled them in each of the four directions. Above were four upper worlds, each the realm of a different bird, and below the four underworlds from which their ancestors had emerged long ago. (This sense of centeredness remains so strong that contemporary Zunis sometimes attempt to reconcile geography with their worldview by arguing that if their village is not exactly between oceans in four directions, it must be in the middle of something.) Looking at the world from the center, the Zunis recognized six directions: north, west, south, east, up, and down. Colors, animals, gods, and seasons were assigned to each direction. There were the six kivas of the kachina society, and six rain priests. In mythology, there were six corn maidens, while Zuni farmers bred corn and beans in six different colors. And in recent years, the pueblo has had six little league baseball teams![21]

This system of directions was, in Donald Sandner's terms, a "macrocosmic mandala," a set of references applied not only to geography, but to the cycles of nature, the organization of society, and the stages of human life. Every geographic feature of the Zuni landscape and every cultural form, in one way or another, evoked this larger system, which, in turn, was a model of the universe as a whole. The Zuni word for "middle," *'idiwana*, was used to refer to the village itself, the winter and summer solstices, the ceremonies that occurred on those dates, and the point each day when the sun reached its apex—so that in Zuni thought, space and time were merged. Such linguistic practices serve to create what Erich Neumann has termed a "participation mystique" between individuals and the larger cosmos.[22]

Cushing believed that the idea of the middle influenced all Zuni institutions, and given their elaborate directional system he questioned whether they could be considered preliterate. "Mistake in the order of a ceremonial, a procession or a council is simply impossible," he concluded, "and the people employing such devices may be said to have written and to be writing their statutes and laws in all their daily relationships and utterances."[23] The Zuni idea of the middle also had social, ethical, and spiritual implications. Each individual had his or her own life road, or *'onnane*. Traditional Zunis tried to travel down the "middle" of this road, maintaining balanced relationships with the universe, the community, and themselves. As Edmund Ladd, an anthropologist and a member of the tribe, explains, "Personal conduct in this life assures a smooth and long road—that is, a long and healthy life."[24]

The Zunis did not always live at the middle, however; it had to be discovered and, once found, maintained. The Zunis' own account of this odyssey—their origin myth (which has been recorded in several versions)—is summarized in Appendix 2. As this narrative relates, the Zunis first emerged from beneath the earth somewhere in the region of the Grand Canyon or Mojave Desert and began their migrations "ever in the direction of the east, told and taught that they must seek, in the light and under the pathway of the Sun, the middle of the world, over which alone could they find the earth stable."[25] Along the way, they acquired the characteristic economic, social, and religious institutions of historic Zuni culture. In some cases, this was the result of encounters with alien people—the first corn seeds were provided by a witch in some accounts, while certain techniques of hunting were closely associated with a god-people called the Kan'a:kwe. Eventually, the ancestral Zunis reached the Zuni Valley and established the six (or seven) villages that were still occupied when Coronado arrived in 1540.

If this myth is viewed as a model of Zuni social development, rather than an attempt at chronological history, many of its details can be correlated with the archaeological record. Most archaeologists agree, for example, that historic Zuni society is an amalgamation of the prehistoric cultures of the Southwest that first emerged at the beginning of the present millennium—the Anasazi, centered in the Four Corners area north of Zuni where the present borders of Arizona, New Mexico, Colorado, and Utah meet, the Mogollon of the mountains and plains south of Zuni, and the Hohokam in southern Arizona. These cultures reached a peak beginning around A.D. 1000, when large towns with thousands of rooms and elaborate ceremonial structures were constructed at Mesa Verde, Chaco Canyon, and elsewhere. By the late 1200s, however, these sites were largely abandoned. Archaeologists point to drought, the limitations of dry land farming, and the lack of social institutions capable of integrating large settlements as the likely causes.

The historic culture of the Zunis took shape in the aftermath of this collapse. Before A.D. 1150, settlement in the Zuni River drainage was concentrated in the higher elevations east of the present village, in small settlements similar to those of the Chaco Canyon Anasazi. Following the abandonment of classic Pueblo sites, the Zuni area received an influx of population, and larger villages with hundreds of rooms organized around outdoor plazas became common. Architectural and ceramic evidence also indicates increased contact with Mogollon peoples to the south. Social instability appears to have been a problem, however, as several of these villages were abandoned after brief occupations. Then, beginning around A.D. 1375, the entire population of this area relocated west, in the Zuni Valley proper.[26]

The greater social stability of the villages founded at this time may be partly related, as mythology indicates, to the introduction of a new institution—the kachina society—by a body of immigrants arriving from the area southwest of present-day Zuni.[27] The kachina cult provided a means of coordinating not only religious but economic and social activities as well. Management of irrigation systems, maintenance of springs, direction of collective work parties, disciplining of children and adults, planting, harvesting and preparation of food, and the redistribution of goods could all be facilitated through the appearances of kachinas. Furthermore, men were randomly assigned to one of the six kivas of the kachina society according to the affiliation of the husband of the midwife who first touched them at birth. Thus, each kiva brought together men from unrelated households, and this contributed to overall social cohesion.

In 1680, after a century of harsh Spanish rule, Pueblo Indians throughout New Mexico revolted and expelled the entire Spanish colony. For the next ten years the Pueblos renewed their ancient customs and ceremonies. The Zunis participated in the revolt by fleeing to the top of Corn Mountain. After more than a century of contact with the Spaniards, diseases had reduced their numbers by half. When they came down from their mesa stronghold following Spanish reconquest in 1692, they consolidated into the single pueblo that Cushing and Stevenson found in 1879.[28]

Spanish colonization abruptly curtailed the independent course of Zuni history. But in the long run, the Zunis outlasted the Spaniards and survived the onslaught of the Americans who followed. Despite the stereotype of "primitive," nonwestern societies as unchanging, the history of the Zunis has involved rapid and continual change both before and after contact. This led them to develop sophisticated social and intellectual strategies for managing change; foremost being their directional system. New objects, people, organizations, and events were incorporated into the Zuni purview by assigning them a direction and offsetting them with traditional social forms. In this way, as McFeat concluded, the Zunis "were not only adjusted to change but they exercised some measure of control over the direction of change."[29]

THE ROLES OF MEN AND WOMEN

Although Zuni women and men specialized in separate areas of economic, social, and spiritual life they enjoyed equal prestige and status. According to Edmund Ladd, "Men are responsible for the universe. Women are responsible for the family and the tribe." These roles were distinct but complementary; both were essential to the welfare of society as a whole.[30] For example, men constructed the houses, but women plastered the outside walls. And while men were responsible for growing corn, women were responsible for storing and distributing it. Men were not even allowed to enter the granaries. Men and women also specialized in different arts and crafts. Men wove blankets, made jewelry, and manufactured their own tools. They even knitted their wives' wool leggings—a disturbing sight for the first Americans who visited the pueblo.[31] Pottery and ceramics, on the other hand, were made exclusively by women. And while weaving was usually a male craft among the Pueblos, at Zuni women also wove, usually with the smaller waist loom used to make belts and sashes.

Religion was the special concern of men. This is what Ladd referred to as being "responsible" for the universe; for in Zuni belief, religious ceremonies were necessary for the welfare of all living beings and the world itself. Some men, if they had a "good heart" and even temperament, and depending upon their clan membership, became priests. A priest or religious official, as one Zuni explained, "is not supposed to fight even though he is threatened. . . . When he is sworn in, he is supposed to love all the people and the animals."[32] Other Zuni men became warriors by defending the village or joining raiding parties. If they killed an enemy and returned with a scalp, they had to undergo initiation into the warrior society. This cleansed them from their exposure to violence and death and made them safe for contact with other Zunis.

While women's participation in Zuni religion was less institutionalized than that of men, it was no less important. Their religious roles were conceptualized as an extension of their responsibilities for "feeding" and "producing life."[33] For example, women regularly "fed" kachina masks stored in their houses by sprinkling them with sacred corn meal. Women also could join any of the medicine societies and "produce life" by learning the techniques of curing life-threatening illness and injury. Occasionally, women even joined the kachina society—Stevenson reported four female members in 1902—and women often acquired extensive knowledge regarding the kachinas. In fact, until the turn of the century, the council of rain priests included the position of Shiwanoka, the "priestess of fecundity," and one of her prerogatives, according to Stevenson, was the right to dismiss the highest religious official of Zuni, the Bekwin or Sun Priest.[34]

Many of the more striking features of Zuni life were related to the high status and economic independence of Zuni women. Through their waffle gardens, the collection of wild foods, and their role in harvesting and storing corn, women made substantial contributions to food production. In fact, the role of Pueblo women in agriculture may have been even greater in prehistoric times, with the earliest permanent settlements organized along lines similar to the historic Navajos—women and children tending nearby gardens while men roamed in small groups to hunt and retrieve distant resources. Cushing believed that traces of such a division of labor could be found in the ritual role of Zuni women in relation to corn.[35] The introduction of irrigation, however, may have been associated with a change in male and female roles. Elaborate diversion systems such as those constructed in Chaco Canyon, and the use of river and spring-fed irrigation by historic pueblos, are typically the work of organized male labor.[36]

If men did indeed take over responsibility for growing corn from women at some point during Southwest prehistory, women's status still remained high. Among the historic Zunis, this was reflected in such traditions as matrilineal descent and matrilocal residence (husbands lived with their wives' families); the ownership of houses by women, including their repair and periodic plastering; the control of the store rooms by women; and the assignment of fields by female-run households. Marriage was largely a private matter, transacted without ritual or ceremony. To divorce a husband, a woman simply set his possessions out on the doorstep. "When he comes home in the evening," Ruth Benedict explained, "he sees the little bundle, picks it up and cries, and returns with it to his mother's house. He and his family weep and are regarded as unfortunate." Kroeber noted, "The woman's title to the house is absolute. . . . When a man has built such a house, and he and his wife quarrel and separate, even for no other reason than her flagrant infidelity, he walks out and leaves the edifice to her and his successor without the least thought of being deprived of anything that is his. . . . The Zuñi does not even have an inkling of having been chivalrous in such an abandonment. His conduct is as much a matter of course as resigning oneself to anything inevitable."[37] A possessive attitude on the part of fathers toward their offspring was also absent at Zuni. Men did not "own" children—they belonged to their mothers' clans. In the case of divorce, children remained with their mother, and her next husband doted on them as if they were his own.

These practices addressed one of the fundamental questions all societies face—the welfare of children. The Zuni solution, however, did not depend on the institution of marriage. Married, divorced, or single, women always had a home. And in a matrilineal system, there was no such thing as an illegitimate child. Children only needed mothers to be ensured membership in a household and a clan. Thus, Zuni women were free to choose sexual partners without economic or moral compulsion, to practice birth control (including abortion and natural contraceptives), in short, to control their own bodies.[38] "Trysting is an accepted Zuni pattern, and premarital sexual intercourse is expected as a part of the culture," one study concluded. "Courtship is often initiated by the girl and premarital affairs take place in her home. According to one male Zuni informant: 'If a girl asks you to her house, you just sleep with her, and you leave before morning several times. Then one day you stay later and you're seen, and then everyone knows you're married.' "[39] Another anthropologist, who observed the flirtation between girls and boys every evening at the community well and the furtive comings and goings of adults, concluded that the "open-air evenings at Zuñi are magically charged . . . everybody seems to be sneaking around in a sneaking atmosphere."[40]

A telling measure of the status of Zuni women was the response of children to a test administered in the 1950s. When Zuni boys were asked who they would like to be if they could change themselves into anything else, 10 percent wanted to be their sisters or mothers. Such a high percentage cannot be explained as an epidemic of gender dysphoria, but simply as a reflection of the prestige of female roles. (It is interesting to note that no Zuni girls made cross-sex choices.)[41] In fact, Zuni folk tales and kachinas included a variety of role models for women, an indication of the range of behaviors open to them.

Benedict described the Zunis as Apollonian, "a people who value sobriety and inoffensiveness above all other virtues." According to Ruth Bunzel, "The most honored personality traits are a pleasing address, a yielding disposition, and a generous heart. All the sterner virtues—initiative, ambition, an uncompromising sense of honor and justice, intense personal loyalties—not only are not admired but are heartily deplored. The woman who cleaves to her husband through misfortune and family quarrels, the man who speaks his mind where flattery would be much more comfortable, the man, above all, who thirsts for power or knowledge, who wishes to be, as they scornfully phrase it, 'a leader of his people,' receives nothing but censure." Benedict added, "Even in contests of skill like their foot-races, if a man wins habitually, he is debarred from running. They are interested in a game that a number can play with even chances, and an outstanding runner spoils the game: they will have none of him."[42]

The Zunis referred to these ideals with the term *k'okshi*, which meant at once "be good, be obedient, be attractive."[43] For the Zunis, *k'okshi* was anything that promoted human survival and happiness. Being good, obedient, attractive was the way to live in balance and travel on the Good Road, "the way of life of the ideal cooperative and economically productive family man, who deeply desires an harmonious existence with his fellows, who is hard working, self-effacing and moderate in all things."[44] As the term suggests, moral good was also aesthetically pleasing. One Zuni might say of another, "A pretty personality [that is, *k'okshi*]; he's happy all the time and always joking."[45] This concept is easier to appreciate when we consider the kachina who portrays this ideal—Kokk'okshi (*k'okshi* with the prefix *ko-*, from *kokko* or gods)—the stately rain dancer considered the oldest and most sacred kachina. As a Zuni explained to Bunzel, "Kokokci never makes people frightened or angry. He is always happy and gentle, and he dances to make the world green. . . . During the war with the Käna·kwe they were the only ones who did not fight. They never fight, because they are always kind and gentle."[46]

These values were evident in the attitudes of Zuni men toward women. Dennis Tedlock has recorded a story told by a Zuni in which one of the trickster War Gods passes as a woman by placing a bottle-necked gourd between his legs to simulate a vagina. Although quite explicit about other details, the storyteller never used the common Zuni name for "that which gives a woman her being." When Tedlock persisted in asking why he had not been more explicit, the storyteller's son gave him a lecture "in an irritated tone of voice, not unlike the lectures that are given the young man in the story":

> *Didn't I know that the bodies of women are* tehya*—precious, valuable, guarded? No, it wasn't just a matter of sex: "That's secondary. It's their bodies that are* tehya.*" Finally, in one last effort to make me understand, he crossed the horizon of my own mythic world and said, "It's like Eve. She found she wanted to be* tehya *at that spot, so she put a big leaf to it." And so there she was, Eve as a Zuni saw her, not discovering evil and shame, but choosing to make a part of herself precious, valued, and guarded.*[47]

THE ZUNI BERDACHE

While the traditional roles of men and women were well defined, the Zunis viewed gender as an acquired rather than an inborn trait. Biological sex did not dictate the roles individuals assumed. Nor did Zuni thought limit gender to only two versions. Zuni berdaches occupied an "alternative" gender, a status anthropologists have termed berdache and the Zunis called *lhamana*.[48]

Stevenson defined berdaches as men who "do woman's work and wear woman's dress." The decision to become a lhamana was made by the boy in childhood and based on a preference for "hanging about the house." It became final at puberty when the youth adopted female dress. The women of the family "are inclined to look upon him with favor, since it means that he will remain a member of the household and do almost double the work of a woman, who necessarily ceases at times from her labors at the mill and other duties to bear children and to look after the little ones; but the ko'thlama [lhamana] is ever ready for service, and is expected to perform the hardest labors of the female department." Stevenson had known five lhamanas at Zuni. Two were among "the finest potters and weavers in the tribe."[49]

Another early, although less sympathetic, observer was Mary Dissette, who began teaching at the Presbyterian mission school at Zuni in 1888. Over thirty-five years later, Dissette recorded her recollections of Zuni berdaches in a letter preserved in the papers of the Indian Rights Association.[50] Dissette had known five lhamanas, whom she considered "victims of a religious superstition." Two died shortly after her arrival; one, named Manna, had done some weaving for her. Most interesting is her account of a younger lhamana "in course of training." Kwiwishdi ("Que-wish-ty") was the cousin of a Zuni girl named Daisy, whom Dissette had adopted. At the time that Dissette first offered him a regular meal, enrollment in the mission school, and a dollar a week for doing chores and laundry, he had not yet formally entered lhamana status—that is, he still wore male clothing. But he already manifested several traits typical of Zuni berdaches, especially his enthusiasm for hard work. As Dissette recalled, "He was so strong and so quick and willing." Kwiwishdi's blossoming as a lhamana, however, left the school teacher bewildered and dismayed:

> *He was with us a year or two and always spoken of as a boy by us and by the Inds. [Indians]. After a time he began to wear the 'Petone' [*bidonne*] or large square of cloth over the shoulders [a traditional article of women's clothing] and was in great demand at grinding bees and other female activities in the village. In another year he had quite an illness it appeared and came to tell me of it, and that he could not work for me any longer. . . . I did not see him at all that winter but in the spring [of 1890] a camping party which included Dr. Fewkes came to Zuni and hired Quewishty as cook and he came out in full female attire.*

Not long after this, Kwiwishdi formed a relationship with a young Zuni man and the couple set up housekeeping.

Dissette found Kwiwishdi's behavior incomprehensible. When

she asked him (through Daisy as interpreter) the reason he had adopted women's clothing, he replied that it was because he did women's work. "But I often do a man's work, Quewishty," she responded, "and I do not put on a man's clothes to do it." Daisy spoke to Kwiwishdi for several minutes and then told the teacher, "He say[s] you do not love all peoples in the world as much as he do[es], and that's why he do[es] that." Still confused, Dissette concluded, "This accounts for a kind of spiritual arrogance that is peculiar to those creatures."

By all indications, the berdache role was an ancient one. It has been documented in tribes in every region of North America, with every type of social and economic organization. Kroeber believed that some form of berdache practices, such as cross-dressing and homosexual relations by shamans, existed among the ancient Siberians who began migrating from Asia to North America thirty thousand years ago. In North America, however, a distinction between shamans and berdaches developed that is not apparent in Asia.[51]

Archaeological remains may provide some evidence of prehistoric berdaches. At the Zuni village of Hawikku, which was occupied until the time of the Pueblo Revolt, men and women were often buried with implements that indicated their occupations and social roles (a practice that continues to this day). Women, for example, were sometimes buried with pottery-making tools or an unfired ball of clay. A ball of clay in at least one male burial at Hawikku, therefore, may indicate the presence of a male berdache who engaged in the female craft of pottery-making. Equally suggestive are the baskets included in some male burials, another female craft, and, in one case, the burial of a woman wearing both a dress and a man's dance kilt.[52] Other clues are provided by comparing the portrayal of the Zuni berdache kachina—the subject of Chapter 6—to examples of prehistoric rock art and kiva murals. This figure has a characteristic hairstyle: one side wound around a board in a whorl, a female style, while the other side was allowed to hang straight in the male style (Figure 26). The same arrangement appears on a figure from the kiva murals at Pottery Mound some one hundred miles northeast of Zuni, dated between A.D. 1300 and 1425. Like the Zuni berdache kachina, who carries a bow and arrows in one hand and corn in the other, this figure carries a bow and arrows and a basketry plaque—male and female symbols, respectively (Figure 6).[53] A similar hairstyle appears on a figure scratched into the rocks at Indian Petroglyph State Park in the bluffs overlooking Albuquerque (Figure 7). Although both sites are in the prehistoric culture area of the Keres Indians, the Zunis' Pueblo neighbors to the east, the similarity of this iconography is suggestive.

The earliest American account of Pueblo berdaches was that of William A. Hammond, a former surgeon general of the army, published in 1882. While stationed in New Mexico in the early 1850s, Hammond had conducted medical examinations of two men dressed as women, called *mujerados*, at Acoma and Laguna.[54] "Of course the most important parts to be inspected were the genital organs," he reported, but these were normal.[55] Like many authorities of his time, Hammond believed that if an individual did not conform to the social role considered appropriate for his sex, there had to be a physiological cause—namely, hermaphroditism.

Berdaches have been referred to as hermaphrodites since the time of Columbus. In his 1881 census of the Zunis, Cushing recorded We'wha's gender as "hermaphrodite," and Alexander M. Stephen, who lived among the Hopis, noted in his 1893 journal: "We'we is a man, but of the abominable sort known to the Hopi as *ho'va*, to the Navajo as *nûtlehi*, to the Zuñi as *lah'ma* i.e. hermaphrodite." While some berdaches may indeed have been individuals born with anomalous genitals, the known incidence of such a condition is too rare to account for their numbers among the Zunis and other tribes. As Dissette observed, "While nature might make a blunder once in awhile, she did not make them systematically."[56]

In any case, the meaning of hermaphrodite, like that of berdache, has changed significantly over time. The *Oxford English Dictionary*, for example, while providing the familiar zoological and botanical definitions, also defines hermaphrodite as "an effeminate man or virile woman, a catamite," and "a person or thing in which any two opposite attributes or qualities are combined." In the late nineteenth century, slang variants of hermaphrodite—hermaphy, moff, morph, morphdite, muffie, murfidai, maphro, and so on—were used by Americans to refer to flamboyant male homosexuals.[57] The same terms were sometimes applied to berdaches. In 1892, anthropologist J. Walter Fewkes identified a Hopi man who "wore woman's clothes throughout life and performed a woman's duties," as Morphy.[58] The restriction of the term *hermaphrodite* to a physiological condition is a twentieth-century development.

Adolph Bandelier, another early investigator of the Pueblo Indians, mentioned berdaches only once in his writings, and then only in his private journal. In 1882, he made note of a "singular being" he had met in an Acoma village named "Mariano Amugereado," adding that there were four *amugereados* (compare *mujerado*) at Acoma and two, at least, at Santo Domingo. Bandelier was particularly curious about berdache sexual practices. "They have no inclination for women," he confided, "but pay men to sleep with them. When such propensities show themselves in a man, the tribe dresses him in a woman's dress and treats him kindly but still as a woman." In 1900, Sumner Matteson photographed an Acoma berdache and noted, "He is far more particular of dress than the women."[59]

Stevenson was less forthcoming when it came to the subject of sexuality. "There is a side to the lives of these men," she wrote, "which must remain untold. They never marry women, and it is understood that they seldom have any relations with them." Dissette, on the other hand, confided that "these creatures practice Sodomy." In fact, the evidence shows that lhamanas were typically homosexual, although perhaps not exclusively so. That is, they formed sexual and emotional relationships with non-berdache men, often long term in nature. One of the lhamanas Stevenson knew, for example, was among "the richest men of the village" when he "allied himself" to another man. "They were two of the hardest workers in the pueblo and among the most prosperous." Parsons also described marriages between berdache and non-berdache men. Some lhamanas, however, appear to have enjoyed more casual relations. In the 1940s, anthropologist Omer Stewart observed a lhamana whose home was the site of frequent male socializing. The Zunis joked about his ability to attract young men to his house.[60] Other lhamanas may have had sexual relations with women. In fact, Stevenson reported rumors that We'wha was a father—although there is no other evidence to confirm it, and it is more likely that children used parental kinship terms with We'wha out of respect or to acknowledge the role he played in their relationship.[61] In any case, if some berdaches were not exclusively homosexual, non-berdache men were not always heterosexual since some formed relationships with lhamanas.[62]

After Stevenson, Parsons was the next anthropologist to take an interest in Zuni berdaches. On her first visit to Zuni in 1915, she observed three adult lhamanas and a six-year-old boy considered to be a future lhamana. She described two of the adults as masculine. Kasineli had "the facial expression and stature of a man," she wrote, and Tsalatitse walked with a long, heavy stride. The lhamanas were skilled potters, plasterers, and weavers, their presence especially welcomed in households with a shortage of daughters. One, named U'k, was developmentally disabled. The Zunis considered U'k a simpleton because he spoke and acted like a child. Parsons watched him in a kachina dance during the Sha'lako festival. When he fell out of line for a moment, the audience grinned and chuckled. "She is a great joke," Parsons's host took pains to explain, "not because she is a *ła'mana*, but because she is half-witted." One of Parsons's informants had known nine lhamanas. Two had married men.[63]

Ruth Benedict and Ruth Bunzel first visited Zuni together in the summer of 1924. Although Bunzel recorded little on the subject of the lhamana, except to document the berdache kachina, Benedict used the example of Zuni berdaches in her famous book *Patterns of Culture*. Summarizing We'wha's career, she concluded, "There are obviously several reasons why a person becomes a berdache in Zuni, but whatever the reason, men who have chosen openly to assume women's dress have the same chance as any other persons to establish themselves as functioning members of the society. Their response is socially recognized. If they have native ability, they can give it scope; if they are weak creatures, they fail in terms of their weakness of character, not in terms of their inversion."[64]

Parsons was the only anthropologist to record information on the female counterpart of the male lhamana. She described a woman named Nancy, who was jokingly referred to as "the girl-man," or *katsotstsi'*.

> *Of the* katsotse *I saw quite a little, for she worked by the day in our household. She was an unusually competent worker,*

> *"a girl I can always depend on," said her employer. She had a rather lean, spare build and her gait was comparatively quick and alert. It occurred to me once that she might be a* ła'mana. *"If she is," said her employer, "she is not so openly like the others. Besides she's been too much married for one." She was, I concluded, a "strong-minded woman," a Zuñi "new woman," a large part of her male.*

Elsewhere, Parsons defined *katsotstsi'* as "mannish, . . . girl-man, a tomboy," and reported that Nancy was in demand as a worker among American employers.[65]

Nancy had been initiated into the kiva society—according to Parsons, to do "kiva work." In an important ceremony discussed in Chapter 6, she wore the mask of the berdache kachina, a mask usually worn by a male lhamana.[66] In other words, the Zunis linked both men and women who preferred the work of the other sex to the same supernatural archetype. Zunis typically referred to women who became members of the kachina society or engaged in vigorous activities, including men's work, as *'otstsi',* or manly, or with the verb *lhamanaye,* literally, "being lhamana," that is, like a berdache. Such a woman might be married and otherwise fulfill the usual roles of a woman, but at least some Zuni women, like Nancy, formally occupied lhamana status. That female lhamanas were often among those women initiated into the kachina society—and that they should be the ones, with their male counterparts, to impersonate the berdache kachina—is not surprising.[67]

The Zuni berdache role was assumed by individuals with a wide range of traits and abilities. Some were unlikable; others lazy or incompetent; still others, like U'k, limited in capacity at birth. It is the exceptional berdache, the one who enjoyed what Benedict called "native ability," that we must turn to in order to map the full scope of this role and its place in Zuni society. An examination of such a case also promises insight into the relationship of individual and social factors in the development of gender identity and sexuality. Thus, we turn to the life of We'wha, Zuni's most famous berdache and perhaps the most renowned "man-woman" in recorded American Indian history.

2

We'wha, the Celebrated Lhamana

By any standard, We'wha was a key figure in Zuni history. Matilda Coxe Stevenson described him as "the strongest character and the most intelligent of the Zuni tribe," "the most remarkable member of the tribe," and "the strongest, most active, and most progressive Indian in the tribe"; while the popular writer George Wharton James referred to him as "one of the most noted and prominent" of the Zunis. Elsie Clews Parsons called We'wha "the celebrated *lhamana*" and "a notable character." And Robert Bunker, an Indian agent at Zuni in the 1940s, wrote: "Wewha, that man of enormous strength who lived a woman's daily life in woman's dress, but remained a power in his Pueblo's gravest councils."[1] Zunis to this day still recall the adventures and exploits of this famous berdache. And well they might, for We'wha was at the center of some of the most dramatic events at Zuni in the late nineteenth century—events that shaped the course of Zuni history and left an impression that can be discerned to this day.

A NEW FAMILY

We'wha was born in 1849 in a community that had changed little in the 250 years since the arrival of the Spaniards.[2] After the abandonment of the Catholic mission at Zuni in 1821 following Mexico's independence from Spain, the Zunis were as isolated as they had been at any time in their history. They were free to practice their cherished customs and religious ceremonies—and to face their enemies, the Navajos and Apaches, on their own. "We were very poor," recalled a Zuni of We'wha's generation. "There were no white people, no Mexicans. There was no cloth, no coffee, no sugar. We slept on skins and saddle blankets. We had no shoes."[3] But in the year of We'wha's birth, the Zunis received an official visit from a new invader, the most powerful yet to enter the Southwest—the Americans. Many of the key events in We'wha's life unfold against the background of the Zunis' response to this development.

When the United States declared war on Mexico in 1846, Gen. Stephen W. Kearny quickly captured Santa Fe, the provincial capital. However, New Mexico's new military government inherited problems not so quickly solved—in particular, the warlike Navajos, Apaches, Utes, and Comanches whose bands ringed the territory. In the course of the Spanish colonial era, these Indians had developed a nomadic life-style based on raiding Pueblo and Hispanic villages. In 1846, Kearney dispatched an expedition either to frighten or force the Navajos into peace, but the treaties negotiated that season went unheeded and unratified.[4] In 1849, a second expedition was organized under the command of the territorial governor, Lt. Col. John M. Washington.

Washington's column arrived at Zuni in September. The Zunis, eager to impress the Americans with their willingness to join the war against the Navajos, staged a mock battle as the expedition approached the village. "Guns were fired, dust was thrown in the air," recalled Lt. James H. Simpson, "men on foot and on horseback could be seen running hurry-skurry hither and thither, the war-whoop was yelled, and altogether quite an exciting scene was exhibited." Simpson described the pueblo as it appeared in the year of We'wha's birth:

> *The town, like Santo Domingo, is built terrace-shaped—each story, of which there are generally three, being smaller, laterally, so that one story answers in part for the platform of the one above it. It, however, is far more compact than Santo Domingo—its streets being narrow and in places presenting the appearance of tunnels, or covered ways, on account of the houses extending at these places over them. The houses are generally built of stone, plastered with mud. . . .*

> *This is by far the best-built and neatest-looking pueblo I have yet seen, though, as usual, the ragged picketed sheep and goat pens detract not a little from its appearance. . . . These people seem further advanced in the arts of civilization than any Indians I have seen. They have large herds of sheep and horses, and extensively cultivate the soil. Being far off from any mercantile population, they will sell nothing for money, but dispose of their commodities entirely in barter.*[5]

The Americans brought more than military prowess, however. In the nineteenth century, deadly smallpox epidemics repeatedly swept the Zuni village. According to Stevenson, both of We'wha's parents died when he was an infant. This may have occurred in 1853, when smallpox erupted shortly after a party of American emigrants passed through the area. We'wha and his brother were adopted by an aunt, their father's sister. We'wha remained a member of his mother's clan, *donashi:kwe,* or Badger People, with lifelong ceremonial ties to his father's clan, who were *bichi:kwe,* or Dogwood People. His new family included two foster sisters and a brother.[6]

Zuni kinship terms grouped uncles and aunts with parents, and cousins with siblings. Maternal aunts were called "older" or "little" mother, depending on their ages. Paternal aunts performed important rites at key points in the individual's life. Practices like these facilitated We'wha's integration into his new family. According to Stevenson, "the loving gratitude he exhibited for his aunt and her grief at his death afforded a lesson that might well be learned by the more enlightened."[7]

Despite the arrival of the Americans (and sometimes because of it), intertribal conflict increased in the 1840s and 1850s. We'wha grew up with the ever-present threat of Navajo and Apache raids—enemies who would steal crops and livestock, kidnap women and children, and murder men. In 1846, when Navajos attacked thirty miles to the east, at the Zuni farming village of Pescado, and Zuni warriors went out to meet them, an even larger body of Navajos attacked the main pueblo itself. Women and children defended the village for several hours, until the Zuni warriors returned. In 1850, Navajos attacked again, laying siege to the village for sixteen days and carrying off most of the season's crops. On at least two occasions, Navajo warriors breached the main pueblo itself and had to be repelled by residents fighting from the roof tops.[8]

To defend themselves and to launch reprisals, the Zunis bolstered their own military capabilities. They built watchtowers in their corn fields and tended their crops armed while women and children stayed close to the safety of the main village. The great, multistoried pueblo incorporated many defensive features. There were no windows or doors on the ground floors; all access was by ladders that could be quickly raised or dismantled. In the plain surrounding the village, deep pits were dug and lined with stakes—deadly traps for unwary hostiles.[9]

A key element of the Zuni strategy was diplomacy. Throughout the 1850s and 1860s, the Zunis allied themselves with the Americans, hoping to secure desperately needed guns and ammunition. They provided warriors and provisions for military campaigns and outposts; they aided American surveying expeditions that passed through their lands; and they welcomed the development of better roads and communication with trade centers.[10] At the same time, their own military ventures ensured the frequent performance of the scalp dance in the pueblo's plazas. The bow priesthood, or warrior society, grew in size and stature accordingly.

A ZUNI CHILDHOOD

The events of these years, especially the violent deaths of relatives and loved ones, made a deep impression on We'wha's generation. The military demands of the times, however, did not alter traditional Zuni attitudes regarding a child like We'wha, even though the inclinations of such a youth veered away from the life of the hunter and warrior. Berdache tendencies merely indicated, in Zuni terms, a different "life road" or *'onnane*. Zuni families adapted their child-rearing practices accordingly. Berdaches enjoyed a certain place in the community, the support of their families, appropriate education and training, adult role models, mythological precedents, and the possibility of achieving prestige and respect.

At birth, of course, there was nothing to distinguish We'wha from any other infant. Before the age of five or six his parents called him simply child, or *cha'le'*, without reference to gender. Children of both sexes wore their hair in the same short style.[11] Eventually, however, boys and girls distinguished themselves in a variety of ways. In We'wha's case, a particular configuration of traits, appearing as early as the age of three or four, revealed his berdache inclinations.

The women of a family were usually the first to notice these traits. Among the Hopi Indians, the Zunis' Pueblo neighbors, women discussed their observations of young family members quite candidly. "My little grandson," one Hopi woman explained in a conversation recorded in 1965, "if he comes up here . . . and the children are playing, he'll say, 'I'll be the grandmother, you be the children.' 'She' tries to take the place of the mother, or be the sister or the grandmother. I hear 'her' so many times like that. . . . He talks like a girl. He'll be cleaning the house, and cooking the meal, and that's all he thinks about—the part of the girl." When asked if this worried her, the Hopi grandmother replied, "No. I don't care. We tease him about it, but he doesn't care either."[12]

We'wha, like the young berdache Parsons observed in 1915, may have adopted female kinship terms and other expressions at an early age. Girls, for example, used the same word to address their younger brothers and sisters (*hanni*) while boys used different terms for each (*suwe* and *'ikina*). Similarly, at three or four, girls began to wear simple cotton slips while boys wore trousers and shirts. But as Parsons and Dissette observed, young berdaches could find ways to distinguish themselves even at this age. We'wha might have worn a much longer shirt than other boys and instead of tucking it into his trousers, left it hanging out like a short skirt, or, like Kwiwishdi, he might have initially donned a single article of women's clothing at first, such as the *bidonne*, which was worn over the shoulders. And instead of playing with other boys, he likely preferred the company and pastimes of girls.[13]

Zuni children enjoyed the run of the great multistoried pueblo. They could chase each other across roof tops, clamber up and down ladders, and scamper through alleys and covered passages. They ran freely in and out of neighbors' houses as well as their own. Boys armed with toy bows and arrows persecuted the village dogs and pigs—their shrieks of delight and howls of pain ringing against the clear sky above—while girls played "bear at the spring," squealing in mock terror when the "bear" chased away the thirsty maidens.[14]

In springtime, hundreds of villagers might file out to the plains west of the pueblo for communal rabbit hunts and game drives. In the summer, children splashed about in the Zuni river and rolled in the sand hills south of the pueblo. Sneaking out to the orchards at the foot of Corn Mountain, they stole peaches left to dry on the rocks above the fields—although their elders threatened dire punishment and the revenge of ogres, cannibals, and Navajos. Boys practiced hunting skills on prairie dogs, rabbits, and birds and learned the strenuous kick-stick races of the men. Girls played with dolls made of baked clay or carved from cottonwood roots. In the fall, there were the endless activities of harvest time—feasts of corn roasted in pits dug in the fields, melons fresh from the vines, and dances to celebrate the bounty. In the winter, the Zunis trekked to nearby frozen ponds to cavort on the ice. Long nights were passed in the telling of tales and stories to entranced audiences of young and old.[15]

Throughout the year, the never-ending cycle of ceremonial activities incorporated special features for children. In the fall, the Koyemshi clowns arrived with bundles of toys and treats. Cushing relates a typical occasion:

> *Toward evening, when all the spectators are gathered in full force, the clowns take up their burdens of toys, and go searching cautiously and grotesquely amid the children as though afraid of the person they sought. When one of them finds the object of his search, he stares, wiggles, cuts capers, and dodges about, approaching nearer and nearer the wondering child and extending the toy he has selected. Finally, the half-frightened little one is induced by its mother to reach for the treasure; as it clutches the proffered gift, the clown suddenly straightens up and becomes grave, and delivers a long, loud-toned harangue. If the toy he has just handed be a bow and arrows, it is given to a boy; if a doll, to either a very little boy, or a girl.*[16]

These dolls were carved versions of kachinas and served to introduce children to the elaborate lore of that cult. Kachinas were central in the imaginative and emotional lives of children.[17]

Children shared the interest of their elders in the more dramatic aspects of Zuni religion. According to Bunzel, "They are keen observers of dances, they know songs, and give accurate and lively accounts of ceremonies which they attend; they are interested in sacerdotal gossip; and they orient their activities about great religious festivals."[18] Visits from certain kachinas were anticipated with much excitement. The Kan'a:kwe, for example, appeared only once every four years. In this ceremony, We'wha saw the mysterious berdache kachina, Kolhamana, a role he would one day perform.

As girls got older, they looked after their smaller brothers and sisters, carrying them about on their backs in blankets. They helped their mothers grind corn in work parties of female relatives, enlivened with gossip and song. At the same time, their brothers might be running wildly about the pueblo in gangs, waving long sticks with flaming balls of cotton or wool stuck on the ends. When slightly older, boys organized impromptu dances and were sometimes joined by girls.[19]

Stevenson describes the scene in a Zuni household on a typical evening:

> *The young mothers would be seen caring for their infants, or perhaps the fathers would be fondling them, for the Zuñi men are very devoted to their children, especially the babies. The grandmother would have one of the younger children in her lap, with perhaps the head of another resting against her shoulder, while the rest would be sitting near or busying themselves about household matters. When a story was told by the grandfather or some younger member of the group, intense interest would be depicted on the faces of all old enough to appreciate the recital.*[20]

Sleeping in a single large room with other family members, Zuni children became aware at an early age of adult sexual behavior. Boys and girls might engage in sex play as early as the age of six or seven. Although adolescent homosexuality has not been recorded at Zuni, there are reports of this behavior among male and female Hopis. No doubt, sexual experimentation took this form at Zuni, too. Parents discussed sexual matters freely with their children, and few young Zunis entered marriage without both knowledge and experience in this area.[21]

The most striking feature of Zuni child-rearing, as most anthropologists have noted, was the relative absence of corporal punishment and the emphasis, instead, on the use of reasoning. Parents, indeed all adults in the household, were sources of unconditional nurturing and support. At the same time, verbal admonishment, exhortation, criticism, and lengthy moral lectures were given freely, along with the threat of shame. The greatest shame was to have a personal shortcoming or error made public. As the anthropologist Li An-Che noted, "All the members of the family besides the parents cooperate to see that the child behaves well. In fact, any member of the community who happens to pass by will say something to correct some misbehavior of a child."[22] Scolded, a child might run away to the house of a relative, but faced with the united front of adults would, sooner or later, submit to their will. At the same time, children benefited from contact with numerous adult role models, male and female, and received training in diverse relationships.[23]

In the case of the occasionally incorrigible child, the Zunis had an extreme recourse in the form of scare kachinas. Given the somewhat fiery temper he became known for as an adult, young We'wha may have once been visited by 'Adoshle or Su:ke. Wearing frightful masks with fangs, bulging eyes, and stringy hair flying in every direction, these terrifying kachinas could appear at any time, at the request of parents or elders. Parsons has described one such visit:

> *In a slow, high-pitched voice, loud enough to be heard all over the village, all [kachinas] proceed to berate and lecture the terrified and often wailing children. The children . . . are terribly frightened and even the older children may be upset. "You must not mock your parents," all are instructed, "you must mind your mother." "You must not soil the floor after it has been swept up." A boy is told he must learn to look after the horses, a girl that she must look after the baby, she must learn to cook and to grind. And then the "old woman" may catch the little girl's ankles in her crook and drag her over to the grinding stone, pretending to be about to grind her up. Throwing his hair back from over his mask with his knife, the* a'Doshle *himself may threaten to cut off the children's ears. . . . If it is cleaning his face a boy has neglected, the* ko'yemshi *may take him down to the river and, cutting a hole in the ice, wash his face for him or, if so minded, souse him altogether that he may not forget in the future to wash*

> *his face early every morning in the river as all well-behaved Zuñi lads are expected to do.*[24]

The result of these practices, as Cushing observed, was the development of "admirable self-control" on the part of children. "These dear little brown-eyed, smooth-skinned mites," he wrote, "who tagged me or hung around me by the dozens, though veritable children, dirty and, when at play, noisy to the last degree, were so quaintly old-fashioned in behavior whenever I talked to them or particularly noticed them, and were so gentle to one another and especially to their elders withal, that I came to love them as I have loved no other children on earth."[25] Zuni children learned to conform to ideals of nonaggressive, mild, and cooperative behavior—to be *k'okshi*—and to avoid appearing sulky, greedy, uncooperative, impolite, or lazy, behaviors that were considered "childish." The young boy who delivered the appropriate formal speech upon a visit, the brother and sister who never fought, the youngster who never lost his temper—these were the children who received praise from adults.[26]

A key element of child-rearing, especially for boys, was the religious instruction they received to prepare them for membership in the kachina society. This process started with an initiation held every four years in which all Zuni boys participated. For We'wha, it marked the beginning of his religious career. The ceremony began with the visit of Kaklo in the company of the Koyemshi clowns. A blind bard like Homer, Kaklo was responsible for reciting the epic Zuni origin myth. He was a bustling, officious, and self-important figure, who insisted that the smallest Koyemshi carry him on his back into the village. When the entourage reached the river, the Koyemshi ignored the bridge and waded into the water, invariably dropping Kaklo in the mud and soiling his beautiful white robes. Through it all, he simply chanted his name, "Kaklo, Kaklo, Kaklo." He repeated his "talk of the first beginning" in each of the six kivas, and each telling took three or more hours. Filled with archaic language and monotonously chanted, few in the audience could follow Kaklo's esoteric version of the origin narrative. Nonetheless, should any of the boys nod or fall asleep, Kaklo struck them roundly on the head with a stuffed duck he carried with him.

Eight days afterward, a score or more kachinas entered the village from the west, led by the great horned serpent Kolo:wisi. These rites culminated in the whipping of the boys in the main plaza. With stiff wands of yucca, the kachinas struck each boy across the back four times. Although covered with several layers of blankets, the blows had their effect. Boys were urged to be brave, but many cried out.[27]

We'wha no doubt was fascinated by these proceedings. He was initiated into the *chuba:kwe kiwitsinne* or south kiva, the kiva of the husband of the midwife who had assisted at his birth.[28] After this, his religious training began in earnest, including memorization of the numerous songs, prayers, myths, and lore of the kachinas, an activity in which We'wha proved especially skilled. Beginning in his teens, he was allowed to join the masked dances. At first, he would have borrowed a mask, but later, by a combination of purchase and initiation, he obtained his own.[29]

We'wha had been adopted into an important and influential household. His foster father, José Palle, was a rain priest. Stevenson described the family as the "richest in Zuñi."[30] They occupied several large rooms in the northwestern corner of the main pueblo block. The apartment was the site not only of Palle's priestly activities, but also the ceremonial chamber of the *lhewe:kwe* or Sword People, an important medicine order.[31] These connections gave We'wha special opportunities to acquire ceremonial knowledge.

Although he received male religious training, once We'wha's berdache orientation was recognized his vocational training came under the direction of female relatives. We'wha learned all the skills necessary for a career in domestic and crafts work. Foremost among them was the endless labor of grinding and preparing corn, the basic ingredient for myriad Zuni dishes: from simple parched kernels and baked ears to gruels, dumplings, mushes, puddings, breads, and the delicate *hewe'* or paper breads, made by pouring thin batters of yellow, blue, red, white, all-color or black corn onto heated stone slabs.[32]

Assisting the women of his household, We'wha daily set out piles of *hewe'* and steaming bowls of mutton stew for an appreciative family. He learned to keep the house neat, according to fastidious Zuni standards, by spraying water on the dirt floor and sweeping it several times a day. In certain chores performed by women—

fetching wood, carrying water from the well in jugs balanced on the head, plastering the walls of houses, threshing wheat, winnowing grain and beans, and tending the waffle gardens along the banks of the river—We'wha's strength and endurance was especially advantageous.

We'wha probably received his first instruction in ceramics from a kinswoman with a reputation for skill in the art. Girls were often given lumps of clay to play with. Interest and promise were quickly rewarded. From this followed years of detailed instruction in the procedures involved in pottery-making—from obtaining clay at sites that were often family secrets, to the technique of forming vessels out of coils and painstakingly smoothing their surfaces, firing them beneath carefully stacked chips of sheep manure, and finally, painting their exteriors in elaborate geometric patterns. To master this art, We'wha had to learn more than technical skills. In decorating their ceramics, Zuni women drew on an extensive knowledge of religious symbols. Indeed, the entire process of pottery-making was surrounded with ritual. The Zunis considered clay to be the "flesh" of Mother Earth. Pots, like humans, were "made beings." Before firing, they were fed wafer bread. Prayers beseeched the success of the endeavor, and sympathetic magic warded off ill fortune. Dreams were an important source of designs for many potters.[33]

We'wha also acquired skills in weaving, learning the complex operation of both the large upright loom for making blankets and the smaller, horizontal loom used for weaving belts and sashes. This was the "classic period" of Pueblo textiles (1848–1880), when distinctive Zuni styles for shoulder blankets, mantas, kilts, breechcloths, and embroidery flourished. At the same time, Pueblo weavers (and their Navajo counterparts) were also learning to use the new materials brought by American railroads and traders. Wool replaced native cotton (beginning in the Spanish period), and commercial yarns and dyes became common. Photographs of We'wha taken in 1886 show him weaving a traditional stripe design typical of this period.[34]

When We'wha was in his teens, the Americans achieved a military victory against the Navajos that ushered in a new era for the Zunis. In 1864, as a result of Kit Carson's brutal "slash and burn" campaign, the Americans rounded up tens of thousands of Navajos and marched them to a bleak reservation in central New Mexico where they remained for four years. After the Long Walk, as the Navajos referred to the ordeal, intertribal conflict between the Zunis and their neighbors decreased.

The Zunis began to enjoy a new freedom of movement that allowed them to expand their economic and cultural horizons. The old, multistoried pueblo had been designed for defense, not convenience. The Zunis now undertook an ambitious building program. They added doors and windows to ground-floor rooms and moved down from the upper levels of the complex.[35] In 1881, when Lt. John G. Bourke visited Zuni, he found the refurbished pueblo bustling with activity. "The noises in the village are fearful; imagine a congregation of jackasses, quarrelsome dogs, and chickens, bleating lambs & kids, shrill voiced eagles, gobbling turkeys, screaming children and women mourning for two dead relatives. . . . As with the turmoil, so with the effluvia; the place is never policed and I am not going one jot beyond the limits of strict verity when I characterize Zuni as a Babel of noise and a Cologne of stinks."[36]

The Zunis took advantage of the Navajo removal to reoccupy the farming villages at Nutria and Pescado east of the main village. In the last half of the nineteenth century, most cultivation was carried out at these areas and at Ojo Caliente, fifteen miles to the southwest. Zuni families established fields at these sites and constructed summer homes so that they could spend the growing season tending their crops. During these months, the main pueblo was nearly empty.[37] We'wha's family farmed at Doya, or Nutria, fifteen miles northeast at the edge of the Zuni Mountains.[38] Fort Wingate was less than twenty miles to the north, and detachments of troops often passed by or camped in the vicinity. The Zunis constructed an elaborate irrigation system at Nutria, using ditches and hollowed logs to deliver spring water to earth-walled plots of wheat. Ditches and crops required attention throughout the summer, and young people were kept busy with many chores. We'wha may have actually worked in the fields with other boys and men. Cushing's census lists one of We'wha's occupations as "farmer"—a male role at Zuni.

By the late 1870s, as he approached the age of thirty, We'wha enjoyed a secure place within his family and his tribe. Stevenson's report provides occasional glimpses of life in We'wha's adopted family—for example, her description of a typical scene during the period of the winter solstice, when "the elder daughter has her hair dressed by the adopted son, who wears feminine dress."[39] As his foster mother got older, We'wha's domestic responsibilities increased. With his mother's eldest daughter, he helped manage household affairs. While this woman would eventually inherit the house, We'wha enjoyed a sister's right (and obligation) to remain a member of the household for the rest of his life.

A SKIRT FOR WE'WHA

Although the Zunis had forged a military alliance with the Americans, they remained culturally and socially isolated until the 1870s. Their ceremonial life flourished while they cultivated their fields and crafted goods according to the time-honored technologies of the prehistoric Anasazi. Their farms produced regular surpluses (which they sold to nearby military posts) without metal plows, draft animals, or grinding mills.[40] No Zuni could speak English; only a few knew Spanish. The average Zuni had never met an American face to face. Only one or two had ever traveled as far as the nearest white settlement. Many had not even strayed as far as Ojo Caliente.

But in the 1870s, the geographic, political, and cultural barriers that had guarded the Zunis for centuries came crashing down. The lessening of hostilities with the Navajos opened the way for a new invasion. Anglo and Hispanic herders and ranchers began to encroach on their lands; and traders, Indian agents, missionaries, teachers, and anthropologists began to interfere in their social life. In this onslaught of change, Zuni elders feared for the future of their tribe. "When the trains keep coming and the white people are here, there will be no happiness," Lina Zuni's grandfather told her. "They will build their towns close to you. They will build their houses." As Lina recalled, "We were afraid of the trains and the railroads. We cried."[41]

Formal relations between the Office of Indian Affairs and the Zunis were inaugurated in 1870, when a special agent visited the pueblo. The first American traders licensed to do business at Zuni arrived the following year.[42] In 1877, two more institutions of

American culture appeared at Zuni, the school and the church, combined in the form of a Presbyterian mission. These Protestant missionaries were the first Anglos to live at the pueblo. In the next decade, they would be joined by many others. Although these various "agents of assimilation" did not always act in concert, they shared a common philosophy: Indians must be absorbed into American society. They brought the promise of a better life, but they also demanded drastic changes. In the years to come, We'wha would play a prominent role in several key episodes of this confrontation.

The Presbyterian mission to Zuni had its origins in the so-called Peace Policy of the Grant administration. A key element of this policy was the role granted to Christian churches. They were invited to nominate Christians for positions as Indian agents, and they were encouraged to expand missionary efforts. Indian reservations were assigned to various denominations, and Congress appropriated funds to support schools operated by the churches. This policy blurred the separation of church and state, but American churches and church leaders nonetheless dominated Indian affairs until the end of the century.[43]

Although the Presbyterians had accepted responsibility for several Southwest tribes, they singled out the Zunis because of a threat as alarming to them as paganism itself. In April 1876, two Mormon missionaries had visited Zuni and performed over one hundred baptisms. The following year, a Mormon missionary colony was founded at Ramah, a few miles east of the Zuni village of Pescado. The Pueblo Indian agent, a devout Presbyterian, suspected that the Mormons were as interested in Zuni lands as they were in Zuni souls. He offered the Presbyterian Board of Home Missions six hundred dollars as an annual salary for a missionary-teacher.[44] Praying "that the Holy Spirit may so accompany our mission schools among that people, that they will cut down their sacred groves, and find the blessing of the Gentiles," the Presbyterians accepted the government's offer.[45] Thus began the first Protestant mission to the People of the Middle Place, bringing with it Christianity's double-edged sword of indoctrination to its own beliefs and eradication of the native ones.

Presbyterian minister and medical doctor Taylor F. Ealy, his wife, two daughters, and an assistant teacher arrived on October 12, 1878, to take over the day school founded the previous year. "We arrived here all very well . . . ," Ealy reported, "just at the closing exercises of a Devil's Dance. The noise was hideous."[46] Equally disappointing, all of the previous year's students had died in a smallpox epidemic.[47] The next two and a half years at Zuni proved difficult and trying for the Ealy family. In the end, their religious impact was negligible. As the editor of the Ealy journals concluded, the missionaries faced "a frustrating form of passive resistance—the Indians largely ignored the Ealys' well-meaning overtures." Perhaps some of the reverend's technological innovations, like a windmill to grind corn and two steel plows, were more appreciated.[48]

The Ealys rented rooms in the main pueblo and began teaching with only six broken-down desks and few supplies. Attendance fluctuated from two to forty pupils. The Ealys did not speak Zuni, and the Zunis did not speak English. Nonetheless, they tried to teach basic reading and writing skills, and, in the case of female students, housekeeping and sewing.[49] Other aspects of the Ealys' missionizing program targeted basic features of Zuni society, including the traditional division of labor between women and men. Mrs. Ealy wrote that "all the difficult labor, such as grinding the wheat and corn, carrying the water, etc., is done by the women, while the men do the sewing and knitting," and she concluded, "I wish to reverse their labors." When Reverend Ealy installed a windmill for grinding corn, he found the women willing to take advantage of it, but, he observed, "I do think the Indian men of Zuñi are afraid I will take away one of the drudges of the women."[50] Although these early attempts to alter gender roles at Zuni had little impact, they foreshadowed future, more serious efforts by missionaries, teachers, and government agents.

The Ealys' dreary existence at Zuni was greatly enlivened on September 19, 1879, with the arrival of the Bureau of Ethnology expedition. James Stevenson set up headquarters in two borrowed rooms in the mission, and, in Cushing's words, "day after day, assisted by his enthusiastic wife, gathered in treasures, ancient and modern, of Indian art and industry." On October 7, John Hillers took a photograph of the Ealy school (Figure 11). The pupils crouched in front of an adobe building with teacher Jennie Hammaker standing to one side of them and the Reverend Ealy to the other. The most striking figure, however, appears in the middle of the photograph, dressed like a Zuni woman, but taller than any of the other Zunis in the picture, and almost as tall as Reverend Ealy himself. This is the earliest surviving photograph of the celebrated Zuni berdache, We'wha.[51]

We do not know exactly when or how We'wha came to be associated with the Ealys, but it appears that he was already acquainted with them when the 1879 expedition arrived. The surviving portions of Mrs. Ealy's diary include two references to We'wha. In her entry for January 29, 1881, Mrs. Ealy wrote, "We made in all this week five garments; a skirt and two basques for We-Wa, a dress for Grace [a Zuni], a dress and skirt for her sister, besides one for which they found the calico." On January 31 she noted that "Jennie, We-Wa and I washed." Mrs. Ealy's daughter Ruth remembered We'wha as a "Zuni girl" who helped with housework.[52]

No doubt Mrs. Ealy, with two young daughters to look after as well as her teaching responsibilities, needed help with housework and child care. Reverend Ealy noted that when his family had arrived at Zuni, girls and women were among the first to call on them. Perhaps We'wha was among them. In any case, it is likely that We'wha received some kind of payment for his work, probably in the form of goods, like the dresses Mrs. Ealy referred to. He also may have begun to learn some English.[53] According to Zuni tradition, We'wha's role involved even more. Anthropologist John Adair was told that We'wha also served as "matron" at the mission school. Matrons were familiar figures in government Indian schools. They supervised dormitories, kitchens, and laundries; instructed girls in domestic work; and chaperoned small children. Often, they visited homes to teach Indian women Western methods of housekeeping, child care, and hygiene. We'wha may have earned this title simply by watching the children and assisting Mrs. Ealy and Jennie Hammaker in the classroom.[54]

We'wha soon discovered that his contacts with outsiders, like the Ealys, could entail drawbacks as well as benefits. In her report, Stevenson includes an account by a Zuni who was attacked by a witch resentful of the narrator's association with the missionary's wife. Anthropologist Dennis Tedlock explains the Zuni concept of witchcraft: "Some people, never one's own kin, are *a:halhikwi*, 'witches,' [sg. *halhikwi*] men and women who get sick at heart when someone has better fortune than they do, or when someone insults or even merely slights them. A witch will wish and plot the death of a person who makes him feel sick, or if that person is too strong, he will hurt him indirectly by attacking someone close to him."[55] Although Stevenson identifies the narrator simply as "a prominent member of the Badger clan," the details of the account fit We'wha:

> *I spent some days with the missionary's wife. She gave me a good bed to sleep in and blankets to keep me warm. She was very kind to me, and I was happy in her house, but after a time I grew very ill and had to return to my mother's home. A shaman was sent for and, through the power of the Beast Gods, he was enabled to discover the cause of my illness by placing pinches of sacred meal upon me, which opened to him the windows of my body. He discovered the disease and declared that I had been bewitched, and commanded the material which had been thrust into my body to come forth. He said he saw within me bits of the blankets I had slept between during my stay in the missionary's house, and bits of yarn and calico which the missionary's wife had given me. . . . I do not know, but I think it was the old one-eyed woman who bewitched me. She was jealous of the good times I had at the mission.*[56]

As a result of this incident, We'wha made a pledge to join the medicine society of the shaman who had cured him. This was the *beshatsilo:kwe*, or Bedbug People, a division of the Little Fire society. The Bedbug People treated burns, ulcers, cancers, and parasites. In their public rites they performed feats with fire, dowsing themselves with coals and walking barefoot across beds of fire unharmed.[57] Society membership provided We'wha with additional opportunities to expand his knowledge of Zuni lore and ceremony.

Whatever the full extent of We'wha's contact with the Ealys, it continued until their departure in June 1881. After this, the government and the Presbyterian church maintained "a token form of joint participation" at Zuni, but the school floundered for the rest of the decade. New teachers wondered what, if anything, previous teachers had accomplished. Not until the arrival of Mary Dissette in 1888 did the mission acquire staff whose zeal for the policy of assimilation would prove a match for the Zunis' stubborn resistance to American ways.[58]

In the meantime, as a result of his presence at the mission, We'wha made new friendships that would survive long past the departure of the Ealys, and these would lead him to experiences and places unseen and unimagined by most Zunis of his generation.

FAITHFUL AND DEVOTED FRIEND

Not long after her arrival at Zuni in 1879, Matilda Stevenson discovered that the "Zuni girl" who helped Mrs. Ealy with housework was "the most intelligent person in the pueblo." Stevenson may have observed We'wha in the role of "matron" at the mission school, for she wrote that his "strong character made his word law among both the men and the women with whom he associated. Though his wrath was dreaded by men as well as women, he was loved by all the children, to whom he was ever kind."[59] Stevenson found We'wha accomplished in Zuni lore and "conspicuous in ceremonials." He was eager to form friendships with outsiders and willing to learn English. This made him an excellent informant. So, while Cushing sought access to information by trying to adapt himself to Zuni ways, Stevenson found a Zuni willing to adapt to her ways, and she cultivated a long-term relationship with him.[60] In fact, the friendship that developed between Stevenson and We'wha grew beyond the roles of anthropologist and informant. Over the course of Stevenson's many return visits to Zuni (in 1881, 1884, 1886, 1891–92, 1895, and 1896–97), and during the months that We'wha spent in the Stevenson home in Washington, a genuine friendship emerged between these two remarkable individuals—one of America's first woman anthropologists and Zuni's most famous man-woman.

In one of the few humorous passages in her otherwise sober tome, Stevenson describes the incident that inaugurated her friendship with We'wha. During her stay in 1879, Stevenson decided to introduce soap into the pueblo, and she selected We'wha as her first pupil. Stevenson may not have known that We'wha already had washed clothes with Mrs. Ealy:

> *[We'wha] was averse to the work, and at first refused to wash. He looked on in silence for a time while the writer worked. Never having had any experience in that work herself, she soon had most of the water from the tub on the floor and was drenched to the skin. The pupil exclaimed: "You do not understand that which you would teach. You do not understand as much as the missionary's wife; she keeps the water in the tub and does not make a river on the floor. Let me take your place."*

After this, We'wha began to wash clothes for members of the expedition. But according to Stevenson, many weeks passed before he would wash and iron without constant urging. "Finally he began to realize that he was accumulating silver dollars from the members of the expedition. Then he declared that he would become a good laundryman and would go to Fort Wingate and wash for the captains' families. This man ultimately became as celebrated as a Chinese laundryman, his own cleanly apparel being his advertising card, and was called upon not only by the officers' families at the garrison, but by the white settlers near and far. Others of the tribe concluded that they, too, would wash their clothes, and consequently a great change for the better took place." Stevenson went on to observe that Zuni men and women each washed their own clothes. "Only a few work for the whites," she concluded, "the men wearing female attire being preferred to the women on account of their strength and endurance."[61] In fact, when Mary Dissette arrived in the pueblo a few years later and requested the tribal council to assign a woman to help her with laundry and housework, they "formally presented" her with the young berdache Kwiwishdi, for there were no women in the village willing to do laundry for pay.[62]

Stevenson's praise for We'wha, in more than one section of her report, contrasts sharply with the style of the detached, objective observer that she affects elsewhere. Of We'wha, Stevenson wrote,

> *She was perhaps the tallest person in Zuni; certainly the strongest, both mentally and physically. . . . She had a good memory, not only for the lore of her people, but for all that she heard of the outside world. . . . She possessed an indomitable will and an insatiable thirst for knowledge. Her likes and dislikes were intense. She would risk anything to serve those she loved, but toward those who crossed her path she*

> *was vindictive. Though severe she was considered just. . . . Owing to her bright mind and excellent memory, she was called upon by her own clan and also by the clans of her foster mother and father when a long prayer had to be repeated or a grace was to be offered over a feast. In fact she was the chief personage on many occasions. On account of her physical strength all the household work requiring great exertion was left for her, and while she most willingly took the harder work from others of the family, she would not permit idleness; all had to labor or receive an upbraiding from We'wha, and nothing was more dreaded than a scolding from her.*[63]

At the same time, We'wha's loyalty to Stevenson was apparent in the extraordinary risks he took to assist her studies. Stevenson describes one of these occasions, during the ceremonies of January 1892:

> *Although the writer occupied the upper story of the ceremonial house and her door opened upon the roof to which the members resort, on account of the superstitious dread of the powerful medicine of the fraternity, entertained by inmates of the house, great efforts were required to secure photographs on the roof and to enter the ceremonial chamber, in which the writer spent most of the time during the several days' ceremonies. We'wha, a conspicuous character of Zuni, was untiring in her efforts to detain an old father below while the writer secured photographs on the roof, and several times released her when the father had barred the door of her room with heavy stones. The wrath and distress of the old man knew no bounds, and he declared that the writer would bring calamity not only to herself but to all the household.*[64]

Remarkably, Stevenson did not discover the "truth" for some years—We'wha was a man. According to Stevenson, his sex was so carefully concealed that she believed him to be a woman "for years."[65] Yet We'wha's maleness hardly seems "concealed" in the several surviving photographs of him. His strong facial features, the musculature in his arms, his hands, his height—how could she have accepted We'wha as a woman? As Triloki Pandey puts it, there was "something opaque" about Matilda Stevenson.[66] This is all the more remarkable when we consider the circumstances of their relationship. Stevenson and her informant worked together closely and for extended periods of time. We'wha even lived with the Stevensons for six months in Washington, D.C., and, according to stories told later, moved about freely in the ladies' dressing rooms. Still, Stevenson continued to believe We'wha was a woman. In her 1904 report, she stated, "Some declared him to be an hermaphrodite, but the writer gave no credence to the story, and continued to regard We'wha as a woman." Even when Stevenson did discover We'wha's true sex, she wrote, "As the writer could never think of her faithful and devoted friend in any other light, she will continue to use the feminine gender when referring to We'wha." (In fact, as noted earlier, Stevenson used both male and female pronouns when referring to We'wha and other berdaches.)[67]

The exact nature of the relationship between Stevenson and We'wha has been the subject of speculation for many years. John Adair considered the possibility that We'wha and Stevenson were having an affair. Nancy Lurie more realistically concluded that Stevenson's "deep affection and admiration for this remarkable person were entirely that of a close and unquestioning friendship between any two women." Lurie also observed that "Mrs. Stevenson's forthright acceptance of Wé-wha illustrates a degree of scientific and personal sophistication noteworthy for her time and her sex." Indeed, if Stevenson believed We'wha was a woman, she took the berdache to be a woman of her own kind—intelligent, independent, self-confident—an equal worthy of introduction to her own social world in the East.[68]

There is no record of exactly when Stevenson discovered the "truth" about We'wha and under what circumstances. After 1886, Stevenson did not visit Zuni again until 1891 and then again in 1896, the year We'wha died. She probably learned the facts about We'wha on one of these two visits, perhaps not until she observed the preparation of his body for burial.

The irony is that We'wha's true sex was no secret among the Zunis and other white visitors—and this is revealing of Stevenson's relations with the tribe in general. George Wharton James, another visitor at Zuni in the 1890s, wrote that "it was the comments of her own friends, Zunis, that first made me 'wise' to the situation as to her sex."[69] Stevenson, however, was not the only non-Indian to be confused by the role and status of berdaches like We'wha. Despite the obvious signs that suggested otherwise, many Anglos would follow Stevenson in assuming that We'wha was a woman.

POTTER AND WEAVER

Collection of artifacts was a major goal of the expedition, and before leaving to visit the Hopi villages in early October 1879, Mrs. Stevenson commissioned We'wha to make pots that would eventually end up in the National Museum in Washington. Cushing, who had stayed behind in Zuni, wrote to James Stevenson: "The articles which you ordered from Wē Wē are not even begun. I have called on her twice relative to them since your departure. . . . I desire you to say to Mrs. Stevenson that I have done every thing I could to get Wē Wē at the work. She always says 'Si, Si We-no [*bueno*],'[70] but when we go the next time says she has not begun them, and repeats the same. Today she informed Miss Hamakin [Hammaker] it was too cold to begin."[71]

Judging from Matilda Stevenson's accounts, We'wha was an accomplished potter who shared the deeply religious attitude of Zuni women toward this art. During one of their return visits to Zuni, the Stevensons accompanied We'wha when he collected clay on Corn Mountain. We'wha followed religious protocols all along the way:

> *On passing a stone heap she picked up a small stone in her left hand, and spitting upon it, carried the hand around her head and threw the stone over one shoulder upon the stone heap in order that her strength might not go from her when carrying the heavy load down the mesa. She then visited the shrine at the base of the Mother Rock and tearing off a bit of her blanket deposited it in one of the tiny pits in the rock as an offering to the mother rock. When she drew near to the clay bed she indicated to Mr. Stevenson that he must remain behind, as men never approached the spot. Proceeding a short distance the party reached a point where We'wha requested the writer to remain perfectly quiet and not talk, saying: "Should we talk, my pottery would crack in the baking, and unless I pray constantly the clay will not appear to*

> *me." She applied the hoe vigorously to the hard soil, all the while murmuring prayers to Mother Earth. Nine-tenths of the clay was rejected, every lump being tested between the fingers as to its texture. After gathering about 150 pounds in a blanket, which she carried on her back, with the ends of the blanket tied around her forehead, We'wha descended the steep mesa, apparently unconscious of the weight.*[72]

We know about We'wha's skills in weaving primarily through a series of documentary photographs taken during his visit to Washington and the comments of George Wharton James. James traveled to Zuni in the 1890s and appears to have been a guest in We'wha's house. "On my various visits to Zuni," he wrote, "she always befriended me."[73] In 1920, he published an account and photographs of We'wha in a New Mexico travelogue:

> *She was a remarkable woman, a fine blanket and sash maker, an excellent cook, an adept in all the work of her sex, and yet strange to say, she was a man. There never has been, as yet, any satisfactory explanation given, as far as I know, of the peculiar custom followed by the Pueblos of having one or two men in each tribe, who foreswear their manhood and who dress as, act like, and seemingly live the life of, women. Wewha was one of these. . . .*
>
> *She seldom sang at her grinding, but at a word from her, I have heard as many as a half hundred voices all raised at once in one wonderful unison of melody, from all parts of the pueblo as the women ground their corn and sang simultaneously.*[74]

In a manuscript now at the Southwest Museum, he adds:

> *Wewa was the attendant at a certain shrine, and was quite a noted character. As will be seen from her picture she was of masculine build and had far more of the man in her character than the woman. Yet she excelled all other of the Zuni women in the exercise of her skill in blanket and pottery making. Her blanketry was noted far and wide, and her pottery fetched twice the price of that of any other maker. . . . Her home in Zuni was full of evidences of her skill. At the time I photographed her she was busy grinding corn meal in one of the rooms of her commodious house, and all around*

> *upon the floor were placed baskets and bowls full of vegetables and fruit which she was preparing for winter use.*[75]

James was a self-styled expert on American Indian weaving, publishing one of the first books on the subject. Regarding We'wha he wrote, "She was an expert weaver, and her 'pole of soft stuff' was laden with the work of her loom—blankets and dresses exquisitely woven, and with a delicate perception of colour-values that delighted the eye of the connoisseur. Her sashes, too, were the finest I ever saw, and proud indeed is that collector who can boast of one of her weave among his valued treasures."[76]

When Stevenson met We'wha in 1879, the Zuni berdache had just turned thirty. He had survived a turbulent childhood that included tragedy and danger as well as adventure. Raised according to the Zuni understanding of berdaches, he had been trained in domestic skills and the crafts of pottery and weaving. The accounts of Stevenson and James show him to have been especially productive and accomplished in these arts. We'wha was also known for his command of Zuni religious knowledge and practice, having mastered the dual skills of letter-perfect memorization required for learning esoteric material and extemporaneous improvisation employed in relating tales and stories.

We'wha had developed one other prominent characteristic—a combination of self-confidence and innate curiosity that led him to make friends among the Anglos who had begun to visit and live in the village—a trait that would earn him a reputation as a "conspicuous character of Zuni."[77] In 1886, this self-assurance served him well in an adventure that unfolded for him through one of these friends, Matilda Coxe Stevenson.

3

Among the Most Enlightened Society

IN 1882, FRANK CUSHING AND A delegation of five Zunis and one Hopi made a grand tour of the East Coast. Their successive appearances in Chicago, Washington, New York, Boston, and other cities proved to be a public relations bonanza. Everywhere they traveled, Cushing's "adventures at Zuni" received fresh publicity, and this, in turn, led to valuable scientific and financial contacts. As author Charles Lummis observed, Cushing's tour with the delegation was the "cleverest thing" ever "devised and carried out by a scientific student anywhere."[1] Matilda Stevenson, on the other hand, viewed these developments with alarm. The young greenhorn who had tagged along in 1879 was now threatening to eclipse the more serious work that she and James Stevenson were doing. In the ongoing battle between these pioneers of American anthropology, the next move was hers. In late 1885, after spending several months in the Southwest, James and Matilda Stevenson returned to Washington with a "carload of rare and valuable curios"—and the famous Zuni man-woman We'wha. We'wha spent the next six months as a guest in the Stevenson home.[2]

DEBUT

What was it like for a Zuni Indian who considered a summer at Nutria, twenty-five miles away, an exciting adventure to travel three thousand miles into an utterly alien world? The 1882 delegates had had each other's company and Cushing as interpreter. But We'wha journeyed to Washington alone, with a limited knowledge of English and in the company of a host whose knowledge of Zuni was equally limited. We'wha's reactions were not recorded, but he must have been deeply impressed by the sights he saw. In 1882, the Zuni delegation had prayed when they boarded the train, and when they saw the massive locomotive they declared, "The Americans are gods, only they have to eat material food." They greeted each body of water they crossed with prayers and offerings of corn meal. By the time they arrived in the East, where streams occurred every few miles, they had to pray almost constantly. They also marveled at the sprawling American cities, composed, it seemed, of countless individual pueblos, each occupying their own city block.[3]

But if traveling to Washington was an adventure for a Zuni Indian, Washingtonians were somewhat more complacent about such visits. Indian delegations were a constant feature of Washington life throughout the nineteenth century. The government brought Indians to Washington to negotiate treaties and to impress them with American power and wealth. Delegations were taken to see forts, battleships, arsenals, parades, artillery demonstrations, the Capitol, the Smithsonian, and various churches—and sometimes theaters and prostitutes. In fact, by 1886 so many delegations were arriving, usually at government expense, that the Indian Commissioner issued a circular prohibiting visits without prior authorization.[4] Cushing and Stevenson added a twist to this tradition, however, when they brought Zunis east. In addition to the goal of impressing Zunis with American culture (and cementing relationships with informants), these anthropological delegates were also intended to impress Americans with Zuni culture. In this way, both anthropologists hoped to generate public interest in their research and facilitate their efforts to secure funding.

Because Indian women rarely participated in delegations, they received special attention when they did appear.[5] This, in part, accounts for the high profile enjoyed by We'wha, who was taken to be a woman, throughout his stay. Other Indian visitors came and went and were barely mentioned in the Washington press. But We'wha was the subject of lengthy articles and feature stories, and his months in the nation's capital were filled with a wide range of social, diplomatic, and scientific activities. According to Stevenson, he "came in contact only with the highest conditions of culture, dining and receiving with some of the most distinguished women of the national capital." Another Washingtonian observed We'wha "with wonderful dignity and self-possession moving among the most enlightened society of the metropolis."

Although We'wha spoke only a little English before his visit, Stevenson noted that he "acquired the language with remarkable rapidity, and was soon able to join in conversation," while a newspaper reporter observed that "Wewha, who knew no English when she first came here, and who had never before traveled beyond the immediate neighborhood of Zuni, has rapidly learned to understand our language and to speak a little in it very distinctly." We'wha also learned to make his way about the city, taking long walks alone both day and night. He told a newspaper reporter that he found his way by following the streetcar tracks.[6]

We'wha made himself comfortable in the Stevenson home at 1913 N Street, near Dupont Circle. Industrious as always, he spent his time weaving and, as Stevenson once wrote when describing We'wha, taking "the harder work from others." According to a newspaper account,

> *The princess is an eccentric child of nature. Although she is moving at present in the highest circles of Washington and is the pet guest of Mrs. Stevenson, she yet has lapses from the conventionalities of life and goes back to the freer notion of life on the plains. During the late heavy snow fall the princess heard the Stevensons talking about the heavy load of snow on the roof. It was just beginning to thaw and they were fearful that the water would get through the roof. Some way or other through their signs she seemed to understand. A few moments afterwards she disappeared and could not be found. A little later a heavy rush on the roof and then a fall of snow in front of the house indicated where the princess was. She was found on the ridge pole hard at work clearing off the roof. The work was full of peril but the princess would not come down until she had completed it.*[7]

Determined to equal or outdo Cushing, Stevenson introduced We'wha to the same national leaders that the 1882 delegates had met. One was John Carlisle, Speaker of the House of Representatives (and later, Secretary of the Treasury), and his wife, a "majestic and intellectual woman" noted, like Stevenson, for her "vigorous mind and action that had assertion many times when gentleness would probably have served better."[8] According to Stevenson, "The Speaker and Mrs. Carlisle were very kind to We'wha, and upon her return to Zuni she found a great sack of seed which had been sent by the Speaker." On his deathbed, We'wha remembered Carlisle as the "great seed priest."[9]

Stevenson also took We'wha on the rounds of Washington's society world. A local newspaper reported this debut: "Society has had recently a notable addition in the shape of an Indian princess of the Zuni tribe. This is the princess Wawa. She is the guest of the wife of Col. Stevenson of the geological survey. Princess Wawa goes about everywhere at all of the receptions and teas of Washington wearing her native dress." The article goes on to describe We'wha's impact at a reception held by the wife of an army engineer. "The princess held a regular levee at the house of the handsome Mrs. David Porter Heap the other day. Mrs. Heap who is one of the most attractive ladies in Washington, suddenly found herself deserted on account of the rival charms of the Indian princess. The ladies crowded about the Princess Wawa and amused themselves endlessly in attempting to converse with her by signs and broken English."[10]

We'wha's tour of Washington parlors introduced him to a world as different from his own as it is from the world of today. At the time of the Civil War, Washington City, as it was called, remained a provincial town with a largely transient population (except for the one-quarter who were poor and black). Dubbed "Wilderness City" and "Capital of Miserable Huts" by the officials consigned to serve there, its developed areas were separated by large tracts of open countryside and empty streets. Elegant homes rising above grand but unpaved boulevards were interspersed with pigsties; churches adjoined saloons. In the local theaters, one might find melodrama and slapstick on stage, drunken politicians in the audience, fist fights in the balcony, and prostitutes on the third tier. Congressmen and senators carried guns to the Capitol and sometimes used them.

And in 1886, the city's newspapers carried daily notices of dead infants found in garbage cans, empty lots, and along the banks of the Potomac River—abandoned by desperate mothers in an era when birth control was illegal and social welfare unknown.[11]

After the Civil War, impetus for social improvement came from a new class of Washingtonians—professionals and intellectuals like the Stevensons, who were often employees of the federal government. They were anxious to forge a cultural identity that did not depend on wealth, but would also distinguish them from the working class and growing immigrant masses. In the 1870s and 1880s, these upwardly mobile Washingtonians formed a wide range of cultural, scientific, and educational associations in the belief that they were forging a national culture.[12] By the time of We'wha's visit, the capital was gaining a reputation as a "gay and pleasure-loving city" with an "unusually brilliant and delightful" social life. According to one writer, "There are receptions, dinners, balls, germans, afternoon teas, kettle drums, and all sorts of entertainments almost without number, from the beginning of winter until late in the spring, and few American cities have such an incessant round of gayety."[13]

The social scene centered around the families constituting "official society": the president, cabinet members and other high-level officials, senators and congressmen, Supreme Court justices, the diplomatic corps, and high-ranking army and navy officers. "Unofficial society" included junior military officers, civil servants, and professionals. In this group belonged the Stevensons. "Society" was more than a social class, however; it was also a set of practices used by that class to affirm its identity and status. "Society" had a "season" that began on New Year's Day and ended with the onset of Lent. During this season, "society people" might lunch in one place, dine in another, and dance in several homes before the end of an evening. The most important society ritual, however, was the "call." Calls were made upon friends and strangers during afternoon or evening receptions that were announced in the newspaper and open to the public. To make a call, one arrived at the door of the host and presented a small card, preferably plain, with one's name engraved or written on it. These cards were considered all-important. "To the man or woman of polite society and the world, it is either an open sesame or bolted door to much that is worth living for."[14]

Once inside, callers could indulge in pleasant conversation and refreshments, dallying for perhaps ten or twenty minutes. If other visitors arrived, the call was brought to a close. The first callers bowed to the next and then proceeded to another reception. Custom required these calls to be returned in three days, and women who returned calls in person increased their popularity and that of their husbands. As one devotee of the social scene observed, "Many a bill has been helped through Congress by the wife of a Senator or Representative who fathered it, attending punctiliously to her social obligations and paying special attention to the wives and daughters of other Senators and members whose assistance was needed." In Washington, the writer concluded, "the social and political currents not only run parallel, but often form one and the same stream."[15]

All this "calling" generated considerable hustle and bustle. "On any pleasant afternoon during the gay season the beautiful avenues in the fashionable portion of the city are alive with elegant equipages, while inside, their owners, with more cards than they can comfortably carry in their hands at once, are making their rounds of social duties, and so they regard it." We'wha decided that all Washingtonians must be rich, since they had "nothing to do but make and receive calls."[16]

In 1886, Matilda Stevenson hosted several receptions with her mother, Mrs. A. H. Evans. The *Washington Post* described an event in January as "one of the most delightful afternoon receptions on Friday last." As a lifelong Washingtonian, Stevenson was well equipped for the art of mixing social and professional life. Although her marriage to James Stevenson was, if anything, a step down the economic ladder, the couple knew how to make up for wealth by emphasizing their special knowledge and bearing as professionals. They counted among their friends Senators Henry M. Teller and John A. Logan, along with congressmen, army officers, leading scientists, and intellectuals.[17]

We'wha seems to have adapted quickly to the formalities of Washington society life. According to one reporter:

> *It is surprising how quickly she learned to know how to greet visitors when they came to Mr. Stevenson's house and to rec-*

> *ognize those whom she had met once. The writer hereof was introduced to her there at one of Mrs. Stevenson's Friday afternoon receptions, when others were calling, yet, on repeating the visit three or four weeks later, Wewha, who was alone in the parlor at the time, at once recognized the voice and stepped to the door, saying, as she held out her hand to shake hands, "How do you do? Walk in. Sit down." All was said in a cordial tone and with a very bright smile.*[18]

The article continues, "She soon began to notice the difference between her own dress and that of the fashionable ladies she met in society, but has never seemed at all embarrassed by it." At one point, however, We'wha decided to make a red satin skirt to wear when receiving calls. But when he went shopping for the fabric and discovered how much it cost, he gave up the idea. Then, one day, he overheard some women talking in English about a sale on parasols at a certain store, "never thinking that the Indian girl would understand them." A short while later, We'wha disappeared and, before long, returned holding a large red satin parasol over his head. From then on, We'wha regularly appeared in the streets of Washington with his red satin parasol.[19]

We'wha's high visibility resulted in a good deal of publicity for both himself and Stevenson. Articles appeared in the *Evening Star*, the *National Tribune*, the *Washington Chronicle*, and even the *New York World*. And throughout it all—the receptions, formal calls, meetings with national leaders, interviews with reporters—Washington continued to believe that We'wha was a woman. Of course, doubts arose. That is not surprising. What is surprising is how easily they were set aside. According to one article, "Folks who have formed poetic ideals of Indian maidens, after the pattern of Pocahontas or Minnehaha, might be disappointed in Wa-Wah on first sight. Her features, and especially her mouth, are rather large; her figure and carriage rather masculine." We'wha's manner, the reporter added, was "very gentle."[20] Another reporter wrote,

> *The general style of the princess is massive. Her broad face, her worn features and the peculiar parting of her hair give her a masculine look among the pale-faced society ladies.*
>
> *One prominent society lady the other day who saw the princess for the first time was charmed because the princess*

> *gave her a sweet smile and a low bow without the formality of an introduction. She said to a friend: "I always knew that these Indian chieftains were remarkable for their taste." She was quite disgusted when she found that the "chieftain" was a member of the other sex.*[21]

Still, throughout the spring of 1886, We'wha remained the Zuni "priestess," "princess," "maiden," and "girl."

CONTRIBUTIONS TO SCIENCE

The motives behind Stevenson's itinerary for her Zuni visitor are easily surmised. The previous year, in 1885, Stevenson had founded the first professional association for women scientists in America, the Women's Anthropological Society (WAS). Throughout this time she was preoccupied with building this organization, a task that included recruiting members and supporters, seeking publicity, preparing papers to present at meetings, and winning recognition from the male-dominated professional and scientific community. Stevenson hoped to drive a wedge for women into the field of anthropology—"to open to women new fields for systematic investigation," as the organization's original goals stated. Public curiosity about the Zuni "priestess" provided an excellent entrée for many important contacts.[22]

In organizing the WAS, Stevenson took full advantage of her society connections. Many wives and daughters of Washington politicians and scientists were ambitious and intelligent women in their own right, and Stevenson invited several to become honorary members in her new organization. Among them was Rose Cleveland, the president's sister and de facto first lady until her brother married in June 1886. Lending their names gave these "society leaders" a safe but meaningful way to help the cause of women, and it provided the fledgling society with an aura of prestige.[23] As a result of these efforts, anthropology became one of the first sciences open to American women. Even so, there were many obstacles to be overcome. None of the professional associations of scientists founded in Washington in the 1880s admitted women. In fact, the rejection of a woman's application, no doubt Stevenson's, by the (male) Washington Anthropological Society prompted the establishment of the women's organization.[24] Similarly, although the

Bureau of American Ethnology published many reports and ethnographies written by women, Stevenson was the only woman employed by that agency on a full-time basis until the 1960s.[25]

By early 1886, however, the Women's Anthropological Society had thirty-four members, including "some of the most cultured and best known ladies in Washington society." At least three senators' wives were honorary members, and one congressman's wife was an officer. Modeling itself after its male counterparts, the society held regular meetings at which papers approved by the officers were presented, and it eventually published various pamphlets and short monographs. During We'wha's stay, the society met several times at the Stevenson home.[26] Stevenson's social and political savvy was especially apparent in her orchestration of the society's "first annual reception" held at the end of March. Guests included Senator and Mrs. Dawes, Senator and Mrs. Teller, Rep. Darwin R. James, the Hawaiian Minister, anthropologists Albert S. Gatschet, Garrick Mallery, Otis T. Mason, John Wesley Powell, "and many other members of society."[27]

Throughout these months, Stevenson spent many hours interviewing We'wha on various aspects of Zuni culture. According to Otis Mason, curator of the National Museum, "For six months this woman has taught her patroness the language, myths, and arts of the Zuñis,—now explaining some intricate ceremony, at another time weaving belt or blanket under the eye of the camera."[28]

Stevenson also took We'wha to the Smithsonian Institution, where he commented on a detailed model of Zuni that the Mindeleff brothers had constructed for the National Museum as well as helping in arranging and interpreting "various masks, dance-rattles, and other objects" in the Bureau of Ethnology collections.[29] We'wha also demonstrated Zuni weaving and posed for a series of documentary photographs (Figures 18–20). These pictures, illustrating each step of the weaving process, represent one of the earliest uses of photography to record Indian arts. The series begins with two interior views of We'wha spinning wool. Then, in a back room in the Arts and Industries Building, We'wha is shown stringing warp onto a loom. Finally, the loom was suspended from a tree in the Mall in front of the Smithsonian, and more photographs were taken showing We'wha operating the loom.[30] A newspaper reporter described the scene:

> *An Indian woman, crouching before a rude loom, formed the center figure of the picture that met the eyes of a* STAR *reporter when he climbed, the other day, up the winding stairs to one of the galleries of the National Museum. It was the Zuni maiden, Wa-Wah, a priestess, and a person of importance among her own people. . . . Wa-Wah came there to weave a blanket on the loom and explain the use of the implements. She worked on silently, patiently in the stolid Indian way, apparently not noticing the spectators that gathered about her or the photographer's camera which was leveled at her.*[31]

According to the article, both the loom and photographs were destined for the National Museum.

Stevenson obviously felt she could learn more from We'wha "in close companionship in her own house" than she could at Zuni. In fact, many anthropologists studying Pueblo Indians have resorted to off-site interviews with informants reluctant to talk in the presence of their tribespeople.[32] Whether this strategy worked in We'wha's case is another question. We'wha made a distinction between information on social customs and religious secrets. In fact, when he saw some of the pictures that Stevenson was preparing for her book, he became alarmed. The anthropologist intended to illustrate some of the Zunis' most sacred objects. According to a newspaper account, "At first [We'wha] was much shocked, for the Zunis, like most other Indians, do not think it right to make pictures of such things. . . . But when she was kindly told what use Mrs. Stevenson would make of the pictures, and that they would be in a book in which her people would be most kindly mentioned, Wewha became reconciled and said: 'It is all right if it rains. If it rains I will know you have told the truth about us.' So, when shortly after the rain began, We'wha was very happy."[33]

Stevenson was not the only anthropologist We'wha worked with during his stay in Washington. He also provided a list of Zuni clan names to the linguist Gatschet, and perhaps other information contained in a file at the National Anthropological Archives.[34]

We'wha also took advantage of his time in Washington to try out activities he might not have engaged in at home. He took up knitting, a male craft among the Zunis. Although he told a reporter that he planned to give it up when he returned, he must have had some previous knowledge of the craft, and it is interesting to note that he felt free to experiment in this way.[35]

THE IDEAL PRIESTESS

In May, We'wha participated in a major society event, the annual Kirmes (or kermes). Originally a fund-raising fair or carnival, the kirmes in Washington took the form of an amateur theatrical production organized by society women to benefit charity. The 1886 production, mounted on the stage of the National Theatre, consisted of a series of dances called tableaus sharing the theme of a "gathering of the nations."

Tableaux vivants, or living pictures, were a popular art form in nineteenth-century America. Costumed actors deployed themselves in motionless depictions of dramatic scenes. The subject might come from a famous painting, a popular play, or a novel—or in the case of the kirmes, themes based on ethnic and racial stereotypes. A typical production usually included a series of tableaus. Audiences enjoyed the contrast between the choreographed hustle and bustle between scenes and the sudden freezing of the actors into the next tableau. Then, the fine points of composition, arrangement, and moral message could be savored. Tableaus were an ideal form for amateur productions.

Mrs. Stevenson volunteered for the 1886 kirmes in late March. With the wives of a congressman, a general, and a future Commissioner of Indian Affairs, Stevenson accepted responsibility for organizing the "Indian Dance." The dance itself involved twenty-five couples drawn from the ranks of the unmarried sons and daughters of Washington's elite. To choreograph the production, the "lady managers" of the kirmes hired Professor Marwig of New York. Once a week through April and early May, the professor traveled to Washington to direct rehearsals. By one estimate, the production drew on the services of over five hundred volunteers. The *Washington Post* eagerly anticipated the event: "The Indian dance will be a decided novelty, and is full of astonishingly rapid but withal graceful movements. . . . The costuming is a matter of great interest." According to the *Evening Star*, "The professor intends to make a special feature of the Indian figure, which he will elaborate as the national American dance. The Washington Kirmes will see the first representation of this national figure."[36]

We'wha attended several rehearsals with Mrs. Stevenson and took special interest in the Indian dance, making "some valuable suggestions." When invited to participate, however, We'wha demurred. As a newspaper account explained, "It required much coaxing before she gave her consent, for as a priestess in Zuni dancing is to her a religious rite, and she had conscientious scruples about being in a dance given for the amusement of spectators. So she spent three hours praying aloud to seek guidance of her gods on the day before the Kirmes, and finally consented to take part in the Indian dance. . . . When it rained the next day she felt sure she had decided aright in agreeing to be in the dance."[37]

Having accepted the invitation to appear in the kirmes, We'wha set about providing the religious and ceremonial elements that he believed it lacked. On the afternoon of the opening, he prepared a special prayer stick, probably modeled after the feathered wands carried in certain Zuni ceremonials. When he left the Stevenson home that evening, he carried his prayer stick with him and sprinkled sacred cornmeal along the way. Meanwhile, Washington society gathered at the National Theatre, filling box seats that had been purchased for two hundred dollars. "The galleries overflowed with Congressmen from every State in the Union," reported one newspaper, "judges abounded, Senators did much more abound, and the old families of Washington were largely represented." President Cleveland, with his private secretary and the Secretary of the Navy, sat in a box next to the stage, guests of Representative W. L. Scott. "The lowered gaslight fell softly upon the various qualities of silks and satins displayed; diamonds flashed in it, fans rustled through it, and the audience beguiled itself with a gentle undercurrent of conversation." Above them all, adorning the proscenium arch, a flying Cupid with wreath gazed sweetly upon the stellar assemblage.[38]

The curtain rose. "Then was presented a scene before which the doughtiest adjectives beat a hasty retreat. A riot of color, a blaze of light, a novel, beautiful spectacle. Row overtopping row upon the stage sat two hundred and eighty of Washington's young men and maidens. Their habiliments were very various, indeed; of brave colors and cunningly fashioned after the manner of different nations." The orchestra struck up an air from "Il Trovatore," and the dancers rose in unison. Filing into a long procession, they made several tours about the stage before retiring to allow the theme dances to begin.[39]

Although it was preceded by a minuet, Tyrolean dancers, Swedes, and Japanese, and followed by flower dancers and Gypsies, the Indian Dance was "the novel event of the evening":

> *The young people spared neither their good looks nor expense in their enthusiasm to look the part. They bronzed and blackened their faces and wore the most barbarous of costumes. There were buck-skin breeches, painted blankets, muskrat skins, feather head-gear, tomahawks, hatchets and bushels of beads and chains. . . . The presence of the Zuni priestess Wehweh, added to the realistic effect of the warlike spectacle. She was the central figure in several of the tableaux, being dressed in the complete costume of her tribe. The war-dance and song and peace tableaux were particularly striking.*[40]

According to another account, "the Indian dance called forth the wildest applause. It is the choicest product of Prof. Marwig's fertile brain, and its wildly exhilarated motions and thrilling situations reflected the utmost credit upon their originator, as well as upon the energetic young persons who conducted themselves in such genuine Apache style. There was the civilized version of the war cry, there was circling about a captive group, there was brandishing of tomahawks and waving of feathers, and in the midst there was a real Zuni priestess to give the thing local coloring."[41] Throughout it all, We'wha waved his prayer stick in time to the music. "Her dignified and self-possessed, though perfectly modest manner, as she stood more than once while the make-believe Indians were dancing, the central figure on the large stage stared at by hundreds of strangers, was generally the subject of praise. She looked statuesque and majestic—the ideal priestess of a barbaric people."[42]

The next morning, Washington's papers acclaimed the brilliance of the evening. "The long-anticipated event has transpired," announced the *Washington Post*. "The herculean labors of the self-sacrificing ladies of the Capital are at an end. The terpsichorean efforts of the city's gilded youth have culminated in a grand success. The Kirmes has come to pass." President Cleveland, it was reported, "greatly enjoyed the spectacle." A second performance followed and, by popular demand, a Saturday matinee, with audiences "fully as large, as enthusiastic and as fashionable." The Indian dance, in particular, received "deafening applause," and Professor Marwig and two of the dancers (perhaps We'wha) were called out to take bows. The kirmes raised over five thousand dollars for the Homeopathic Hospital.[43]

What did We'wha think of all this? According to the *Washington Post*, "she betrayed some surprise at the curious movement of the dance, and said she had not seen anything just like it among her people, but it was very nice notwithstanding."[44] We'wha naturally compared the event to the kachina dances of the Zunis, and in a sense, it was a type of ritual. In it, Washington society affirmed its stereotypes of Indians by acting them out on stage. In a "festival of nations," the Indian theme was an appropriate "national dance" for America, not because it portrayed Indians—hardly appropriate role models for Victorians—but because it portrayed the triumph of civilization over savagery. That theme, above all, was uniquely American. Unfortunately, such stereotypes had little to do with real American Indians. Yet, ironically, the women who organized the Indian Dance included members of the Women's Anthropological Society and other organizations concerned with Indian welfare and the reform of Indian policy. And their husbands, as elected officials, scientists, and civil servants, were responsible for formulating the government's policy toward the very "savages" so colorfully portrayed on the stage of the National Theatre.

THE SCIENCE OF CIVILIZATION

Beyond the brilliant parlors and ballrooms of Washington "society" lay a larger society of profound contrasts. In the spring of 1886, a major strike by the Knights of Labor, one of the first national unions, crippled the country's railroads. On May 4, the Haymarket Riot in Chicago escalated the level of violence associated with the growing labor struggle. Even in Washington, where the social season filled the streets with elegantly dressed gentleman and ladies, laborers were on strike for an eight-hour day. Meanwhile, in the West, anti-Chinese riots were sweeping through major cities, and white settlers, cattlemen, mining interests, and railroads were poised to seize the remaining legacy of the public domain—especially those lands still held by Indians.

Thus, the elaborately regulated world of Washington "society" belied an increasingly disordered larger society. But what government should do about these social problems—whether, indeed, it was government's role to do anything—was the subject of heated debate. Washington's professionals and scientists, like the Stevensons, believed that their training and specialized knowledge, grounded in a scientific outlook, qualified them to address these problems and recommend solutions for the good of all society.[45]

Indeed, in the 1880s anthropology became something of an American fad. Its findings and theories were thought to have direct bearing on current affairs, due, in large part, to the influence of Lewis Henry Morgan.[46] In *Ancient Society*, published in 1877, Morgan had defined three stages in the development of every society: savagery, barbarism, and civilization. According to Morgan, all societies went through these same three stages. His theories had a profound impact on the Victorian view of Indians as savage and primitive. As John Wesley Powell, director of the Bureau of Ethnology and a great admirer of Morgan, wrote, "Savagery is ethnic childhood."[47] This metaphor guided government policy toward American Indians from the 1870s to the 1930s.

The theory of the stages of civilization appeared at a time when industrialization and urbanization were dramatically altering American society—perhaps moving it from one "stage" to another. The question of what this next stage would be was a matter of national concern and a frequent topic of discussion in Washington's intellectual community.[48] In Europe, Karl Marx and Frederick Engels were arguing that the next stage of civilization would be socialism. If they were right, then the fledgling labor movements of Europe and America could claim that Morgan's "natural laws" of social development were on their side. On the other hand, Americans like Powell and his protégé, sociologist Lester F. Ward, argued that the coming stage of civilization was "enlightenment"—or, in Ward's terminology, "sociocracy." In this mode of social organization, the democratically run state would be the central agent for achieving social ends, and this would be accomplished through the "scientific control of social forces" on behalf of the common good—in short, state-guided social planning.[49] Widely circulated in publications, discussed incessantly at meetings of Washington's scientific and professional associations, the theory of the stages of civilization became, at the end of the century, the basis for government policies in public land management, natural resource development, and Indian affairs.

The pervasive influence of the theory of the stages of civilization helps explain Washington's fetish for etiquette and manners. The rude, often lawless behavior of the American frontier and the squalor of America's growing urban slums hardly suggested a society that had reached the epitome of social evolution. If Anglo-Americans were really more advanced than American Indians there ought to be noticeable differences in their manners and social practices—especially in the nation's capital. At the same time, this "difference" had to be American and not European.

As historian Roy Harvey Pearce observed, nineteenth-century Americans believed that they were making a new world. They were obsessed with knowing who and what they were and where they were going. One way of accomplishing this was to compare themselves with Indians. The American Indian "lived as an example of the savage life out of which civilized Americans had long grown. He was, in fact, a means to measuring that growth."[50] This made savagery an indispensable complement of civilization; neither could be defined without reference to the other. American Indians provided a past that, as a young nation, America lacked.

Popular diversions like the Indian dance of the kirmes reaffirmed the all-important distinction between savagery and civilization essential to the American sense of identity. On stage, the "stages of civilization" were reassuringly acted out. On stage, the wild savagery of the Indian—heroic, violent, primitive—was safely displayed and its relationship to civilization clearly drawn, even with We'wha incongruously placed in the center of it all, a not-man, not-warrior from a tribe of peaceful village farmers. The Indian dance of the 1886 kirmes was indeed a fitting "national dance," a true dramatization of the ideology of the day.

A CULTURAL AMBASSADOR

Throughout his stay, We'wha continued to follow Zuni religious practices. He received sacred cornmeal "by express from Zuni regularly." Morning and evening, he stepped onto the Stevensons' front porch to pray to the sun and offer cornmeal to the six directions. According to a newspaper article, "at such times she strews cornmeal all around her until the front door steps and sidewalk are much daubed with dough."[51]

We'wha was still in Washington at the time of the summer solstice on Saturday, June 19. This was an occasion when all Zunis, men, women, and children, offered prayer sticks to the gods. For We'wha, this observance was too important to miss, even if he was three thousand miles from home. He insisted on making the traditional offering, and Mrs. Stevenson determined to help him. According to an article in *Science* magazine, the Stevensons wrote to New Mexico to determine the exact day on which the Zuni ceremonies would take place. A problem arose when it came to making the prayer sticks, however, because We'wha would not use substitute materials. "Various diplomatic schemes were tried, but her heart was fixed." Eventually, the collections of the National Museum were plundered to make available shells, turquoise, and various pigments collected on Bureau of Ethnology expeditions. The museum's department of ornithology provided eagle, turkey, duck, and bluebird feathers. Freshly cut twigs were gathered from a nearby stand of cottonwoods.

We'wha completed the prayer sticks on June 18 and made his offerings the next day. "On Saturday, June 19, at two o'clock in the afternoon, in a retired garden in Washington, Wa-Wah performed the ceremony of planting the plumes. Her time was arranged so as to act simultaneously with her people at Zuñi. . . . The utmost sincerity manifested itself in every portion of this ceremony. It seemed to those who gazed in rapt silence at this simple devotion, that they were witnesses to the surviving worship of the primeval world." The prayer sticks were left undisturbed for two days; then, with We'wha's permission, they were carefully dug up and deposited in the National Museum, "perhaps the most unique object ever placed among its precious collections" (Figure 21).[52]

While We'wha was preparing his prayer sticks, Matilda Stevenson wrote to President Cleveland's private secretary:

> *Dear Sir—Wéwhá a Zuñi Indian priestess who has been spending the winter with me for the purpose of Ethnological study will in a short time leave for her far away home. She is anxious to meet the President and Mrs. Cleveland and extend to them a greeting from her people. She has a little wedding gift of her own handiwork which she wishes to present in person to Mrs. Cleveland. May I ask your kindness to arrange for a time when it will suit the convenience of the President and Mrs. Cleveland for me to present Wéwhá to them.*[53]

If We'wha was the tallest member of the Zuni tribe, Grover Cleveland was one of America's largest presidents. Robert La Follette, a key figure of the Progressive era, recalled, "My first impression of Cleveland was extremely unfavorable. . . . Cleveland's coarse face, his heavy, inert body, his great shapeless hands, confirmed in my mind the attacks made upon him during the campaign."[54] These "attacks" had to do with Cleveland's relationship years earlier with a widow that had resulted in an illegitimate child. This raised not only moral questions, but, as La Follette hints, an assumption typical of the nineteenth century: that such moral turpitude was invariably accompanied by corresponding physical degeneracy. Cleveland was still elected, however, largely because his opponent's anti-Catholic statements swung Irish voters to his side.[55]

In 1886, Cleveland had already received a variety of Indian visitors.[56] But even though We'wha's call on June 23 was a routine matter, the sight of the six-foot-tall Zuni "princess" must have made an impression. As the *Washington Post* reported, "We Wah, the Zuni princess, walked up the broad entrance to the White House yesterday, and, in company with Mrs. Col. Stevenson, was shown into the Green Room. She was dressed in her aboriginal costume, and wore a head-dress of feathers. Her conversation with the President was mainly in monosyllables, but Mrs. Stevenson and the President had quite an interesting talk."[57] And so We'wha became the first American Indian berdache on record to shake hands with an American president.

The trip had a lasting impact on We'wha and he told many stories when he returned. According to Edmund Wilson, who visited Zuni in the 1940s, "he assured his compatriots that the white women were mostly frauds, for he had seen them, in the ladies' rooms, taking out their false teeth and the 'rats' from their hair." Mary Dissette gossiped, "Wayweh had a national fame as he was taken to Wash. by Mrs. Stevenson and palmed off on an unsuspecting public as a 'Zuni Princess' and had the entree into the most exclusive cabinet social circles. She penetrated to the budoir [*sic*] of the wife of the Sec. of State [Speaker of the House of Representatives], Mrs. Carlisle, having gone on her own initiative to make her a social call. To hear Mrs. Stevenson give Waywah's description of the way a society lady in Washington 'Make herself young again' was exceedingly amusing."[58]

George Wharton James was another recipient of this lore. "So bright was she," he wrote, "that President Cleveland invited her to visit him at the White House, where she was his honoured and interesting guest for several days"![59] According to James, "On the lawn of the White House—the residence of the President of the United States—she set up her primitive loom, and there, to the infinite amazement and delight of many hundreds of people who came to witness the spectacle, she wove one of the beautiful blankets which, among the Zunis, had won for her so much renown."[60]

Stevenson noted that We'wha's skin became several shades lighter during his stay in Washington. Aside from that, he seems to have changed little as a result of his exposure to white culture. According to Stevenson, a former congressman, "desiring to aid in Christianizing and civilizing the Zunis," gave We'wha a large box of cutlery and silverware, "thinking that this Indian, having had the environment of civilization for six months, would carry back its influence to her people." But when Stevenson visited Zuni two months after We'wha's return, she found that "the steel knives had been distributed among the rain priests and others, for the purpose of fashioning te'likinawe, and that the large silver spoons were used with popcorn water, which is drunk in certain ceremonials. The forks were playthings among the children, the Indian to whom the things were given having returned to the use of her fingers in place of the knife and fork."[61]

Washington society would have been shocked to learn that We'wha was a man. Yet Stevenson published the facts fifteen years later in a report on the tribe printed by the government. For many years, jokes about the Zuni maiden who visited Washington circulated at Stevenson's expense. In 1908, Clara True, Stevenson's estranged friend in New Mexico, wrote to Stevenson's lawyer seeking "permission" to use We'wha's story as the subject of a few "squibs for popular diversion" to benefit charity. True obviously intended to threaten Stevenson with the embarrassment of publishing the story.

> *I can't think of any thing so funny as the story of "We-wha." . . . We-wha was a Zuni maiden of wonderful beauty of character who was taken to Washington on account of her extraordinary qualities. She was a brilliant social success, had an interview with President Cleveland, was entertained at Secretary Carlisle's, etc. Her crowning act in society was leading a "kirmess" charity ball in which wealth and fashion participated. She was given a beautiful bouquet and responded to an encore. She was "studied" by many scientific persons whose names are famous.*
>
> *The joke of the story is that the beautiful "We-wha" was a "bold bad man," father of a family in Zuni. The fun he had after he got back home you can imagine. The possibilities of the tale are beyond description. I should of course leave out all objectionable features for instance "We-wha" being employed as lady's maid for a time by an ethnologist and being around the dressing rooms where pompadours were being "done," which happened.*
>
> *It really is one of the best things on Washington which ever occurred, especially scientific Washington. . . .*
>
> *I have promised to be one of a band to raise a few thousand dollars for hospital purposes by the use of our few natural abilities, my part being cast for a humorous writer up of the aborigines. "We-wha" is the cream. I think she ought to buy many pills and plasters. . . . Of course I could do the*

> *story without permission of the Smithsonian but I do not wish to take liberties, more especially as Mrs. Stevenson and myself are not personal friends.*[62]

During his visit in Washington, We'wha considered himself a representative of his tribe, conveying to Americans the greetings and goodwill of his people. His comportment is best understood in light of the long-standing Zuni policy of friendship with the United States. In this period, the Zunis were especially anxious to obtain the government's assistance in protecting their shrinking land base from squatters and encroachment. Anything that kept the Zuni cause before the American public and its elected officials was a boon.

While in Washington, We'wha did just that. The image and the reputation of the Zunis—America's industrious, peaceable ally on the New Mexico frontier—were well served by that pueblo's leading berdache. Few tribes could count on the instant recognition that the name "Zuni" enjoyed in the 1880s.

FIGURE 1. Zuni pueblo in the 1880s looking southeast toward Corn Mountain. National Anthropological Archives, Smithsonian Institution.

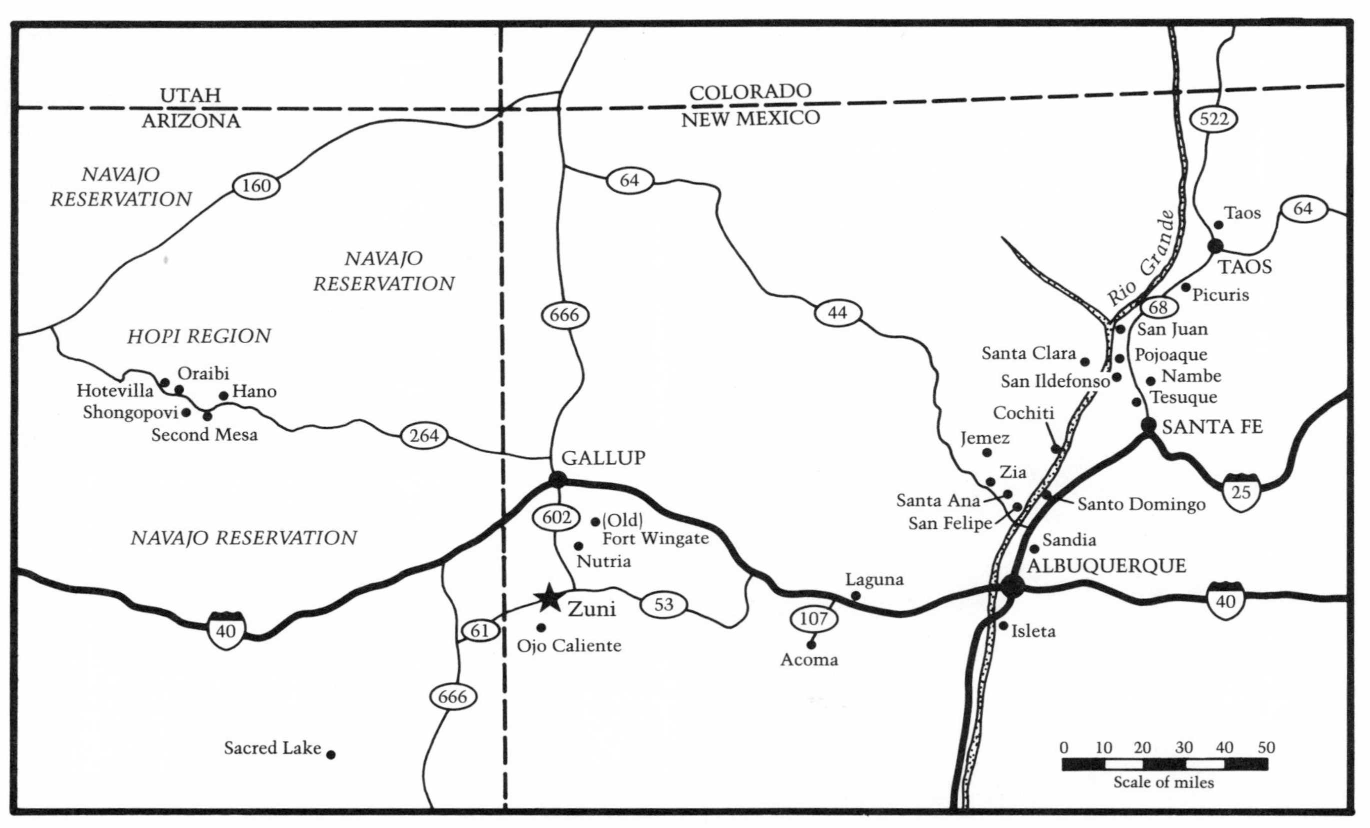

FIGURE 2. Zuni and the Pueblo Indian region. From Fox, *Pueblo Weaving and Textile Arts*. By permission.

FIGURE 3. Frank Hamilton Cushing posing as a Plains Indian warrior. National Anthropological Archives, Smithsonian Institution.

FIGURE 4. Matilda Coxe Stevenson, the Washington debutante who became one of America's first women anthropologists. National Anthropological Archives, Smithsonian Institution.

FIGURE 5. Stevenson's methods in the field earned her the distrust and resentment of the Indians she studied. This cartoon, captioned, "Cowed by a Woman: A Craven Red Devil Weakens in the Face of a Resolute White Heroine," is based on an episode that occurred among the Hopis in 1885. From *Illustrated Police News* 39(1010) [1886]: 9,15. Courtesy National Anthropological Archives, Smithsonian Institution.

FIGURE 6. Painted figure from kiva murals at Pottery Mound. The hairstyle, half-up and half-down, and the basketry plaque in one hand and the bow and arrows in the other—female and male symbols respectively—resemble the costuming of the Zuni berdache kachina, Kolhamana (Figures 26 and 27). From Hibben, *Kiva Art of the Anasazi*, fig. 49. By permission of the author.

FIGURE 7. Petroglyph figure from the Rio Grande Valley with berdache kachina hairstyle.

FIGURE 8. We'wha in the ceremonial costume of Zuni women, holding a pottery bowl with sacred corn meal. National Anthropological Archives, Smithsonian Institution.

FIGURE 9. Stevenson described We'wha's adopted family as "the richest in Zuñi." National Anthropological Archives, Smithsonian Institution.

FIGURE 10. We'wha's family lived in the northwestern corner of the old pueblo complex. National Anthropological Archives, Smithsonian Institution.

FIGURE 11. This photograph of the mission school at Zuni, taken in 1879, shows Reverend Ealy on the right, teacher Jennie Hammaker on the left, and We'wha prominently featured in the center. National Anthropological Archives, Smithsonian Institution.

FIGURE 12. According to Stevenson, We'wha was "beloved by all the children, to whom he was ever kind." National Anthropological Archives, Smithsonian Institution.

FIGURE 13. We'wha weaving with the waist loom used for making belts and sashes. National Anthropological Archives, Smithsonian Institution.

FIGURE 14. In his 1881 census, Cushing listed We'wha's occupations as "Farmer, Weaver, Potter, Housekeeper." The first two are male occupations, the second two, female. National Anthropological Archives, Smithsonian Institution.

FIGURES 15–17. These studio portraits of We'wha were taken in Washington in 1886 by John K. Hillers. National Anthropological Archives, Smithsonian Institution.

FIGURE 16.

FIGURE 17.

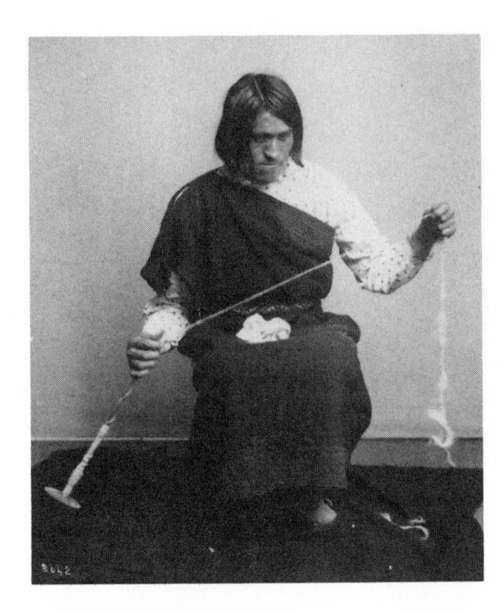

FIGURE 18. Spinning the yarn.

FIGURE 19. Stringing the warp on the loom.

FIGURES 18–20. While in Washington, We'wha documented Zuni weaving techniques in a series of photographs. National Anthropological Archives, Smithsonian Institution.

FIGURE 20. Operating the loom.

SCIENCE, July 9, 1886.

BURYING A PRAYER IN WASHINGTON: A REMNANT OF AN EXPIRING WORSHIP.

FIGURE 21. An article in *Science* magazine described We'wha's observance of Zuni summer solstice rites in the Stevensons' backyard. From Mason, "The Planting and Exhuming of a Prayer."

FIGURE 22. Nick Dumaka—the young Zuni tried for witchcraft in 1892—with his patron, trader Douglas D. Graham. Adam Clark Vroman, Seaver Center for Western History Research, Natural History Museum of Los Angeles County.

FIGURE 23. The soldiers sent to arrest the Zuni governor in 1892 were met instead by We'wha—according to Stevenson the "tallest and strongest" member of the tribe. National Anthropological Archives, Smithsonian Institution.

FIGURE 24. The army occupation of Zuni in 1897 was triggered by the events following We'wha's death. Ben Wittick, School of American Research Collections, Museum of New Mexico.

FIGURE 25. The Kan'a:kwe gods entering Zuni for their quandrennial ceremony. The berdache kachina, Kolhamana, appears sixth in line. From Stevenson, "The Zuñi Indians," Plate XLII. Courtesy National Anthropological Archives, Smithsonian Institution.

FIGURE 26. Mask of Kolhamana with hair half-up in the style of a woman and half-down in the male style. National Anthropological Archives, Smithsonian Institution.

FIGURE 27. Kolhamana wears a woman's dress with a male dance kilt over the shoulder and carries a bow and arrows (or three ears of corn) and a deer bone rattle. National Anthropological Archives, Smithsonian Institution.

FIGURE 28. Kasinelu, grandson of the bow priest Nayuchi, became a berdache in 1896, the year We'wha died. He was photographed by anthropologist John Adair in 1938. Courtesy of John Adair.

FIGURE 29. "Berdache" by Joe Lawrence Lembo. A contemporary view of a traditional role by an American Indian artist.

4

The Country Was Full of Soldiers

Although We'wha returned from Washington filled with knowledge and experience of the white world, resuming a Zuni lifestyle provoked no conflict for the berdache who had shaken hands with the president. He had tasted widely from the banquet of white ways and inventions, but he remained secure in his Zuni identity. The Zuni community as a whole, however, was losing ground against the influx of American values, possessions, and people. The U.S. Office of Indian Affairs was beginning to extend to the Pueblo Indians its policy of assimilation—that is, dismantling tribal cultures and absorbing Indians into Anglo society. The Zunis were dismayed to find their cultural autonomy under attack by the same government that they had once aided and served as allies.

In the 1890s, three arenas of contention emerged: the opposition of traditional leaders, especially the bow priests, to outside influences; the reluctance of Zuni parents to enroll their children in white-run schools; and the attempts by the government to alter the values and practices of the Zunis regarding sexuality and gender. At stake in each arena was nothing less than the survival of their community and the continued possession of their lands and resources.

We'wha appeared in the forefront of more than one of the confrontations that took place between Zunis and government officials, missionaries, traders, teachers, and soldiers—the "agents of assimilation." Although he had been a gatekeeper for the tribe in the previous decade, forming relationships with outsiders that helped in mollifying their impact, events now placed him on the other side of the gate—closing the door he had once held open.

THE DARK SIDE

The cultural and social forces sweeping through Zuni life in the 1890s were most apparent during the tribe's annual Sha'lako festival. Every year more visitors descended upon the Middle Place. Navajo, Apache, and Pueblo Indians, local Anglos and out-of-town curiosity seekers arrived from every direction to enjoy the food, hospitality, kachinas, and dances of the Zunis. "Morning brings an additional influx of visitors," Stevenson wrote in describing the Sha'lako of 1891. "Every house of any pretensions has guests, welcome or otherwise; nearly every pueblo is represented, and large numbers of Navahos are here to enjoy the lavish hospitality of the Zuñis. The house tops on the south side of the village are crowded with men, women, and children, while the streets are filled with pedestrians and equestrians."[1]

But the crush of outsiders introduced a new, ugly element—alcohol, which in 1892 would lead to a dramatic confrontation.

According to Stevenson, whiskey sales began weeks before the festival. "The liquor is usually carried in kegs, not too large to be secreted under the blanket, and gallons are brought in this way to Zuñi by the Rio Grande Indians." The Zunis bottled the whiskey and resold it to Navajos, who eagerly traded horses and valuable jewelry for a few ounces of the powerful intoxicant.[2] In her typically Victorian style, Stevenson describes the results:

> *It would be difficult to find a more revolting picture than the one presented during the day and night. The scene of debauchery in the morning is shocking, but as the day wanes it becomes disgusting in the extreme. The mad desire for drink among many of the Zuñis is too great for them to remain sober enough to observe the ceremonial of their gods, to which they have looked forward for many days. Many of these staggering Indians are not over 14 or 15 years of age. Numbers of Navahos are fighting with one another or with*

> *the Pueblos, drawing knives and pistols. The wonder is that some of the disturbers of the peace are not trampled to death, for many fall from their saddles during their quarrels; others lie motionless in the streets, too drunk to move away from approaching hoofs.*[3]

In December 1892, the drinking continued even after the visitors had departed. A Zuni named Dick Tsanahe, who was serving as governor at the time, had been left in the possession of a certain amount of whiskey.[4] Although the winter solstice observance, the Zunis' most sacred religious period, was about to begin, Tsanahe gave or sold whiskey to the young men who gathered at his house—or rather, in Zuni terms, the house of his wife, which she occupied with her sister, a young woman named Lina Zuni.

Over thirty years later, Lina Zuni vividly narrated for anthropologist Ruth Bunzel the events that unfolded that December.[5] "Many of those who liked whisky came here to my house. My sister's husband had whisky and he gave them to drink." One night, a sultry young man named Nick Dumaka came to Lina's house and began drinking Tsanahe's whiskey. Before long, he was arguing and fighting with the other young men. This was not surprising, however, for this troubled young man had been at odds with his community most of his life. Before the night was over, he would trigger a set of events that would change the course of Zuni history.[6]

Dumaka, also known as "Zuni Nick," was born in the late 1860s. As a youth, he associated closely with Americans, working as an aide for General Eugene Carr, the Civil War hero and Indian fighter who commanded Fort Wingate between 1888 and 1890, and as an assistant for Douglas D. Graham, the trader whose long career at Zuni began in 1878.[7] Dumaka learned to speak both English and Spanish, and he was one of the first Zunis to wear American clothes.[8] According to some accounts, he attended a white school, but in a narrative in his own words, Dumaka explains that he had learned English without attending school. This is what made his knowledge of the language suspicious. The only other Zunis who had learned English were four children who had been sent by Reverend Ealy to the Indian boarding school in Carlisle, Pennsylvania, in 1880. Two of these children died without ever returning, and the other two had been so traumatized that they refused to use English the rest of their lives. How was it, the Zunis wondered, that Dumaka had learned English without going to school and without harm to himself?[9]

But Dumaka's problems went deeper than language. As Benedict noted, "In a society that thoroughly distrusts authority of any sort, he had a native personal magnetism that singled him out in any group. In a society that exalts moderation and the easiest way, he was turbulent and could act violently upon occasion. In a society that praises a pliant personality that 'talks lots'—that is, that chatters in a friendly fashion—he was scornful and aloof."[10] Compounding this, Dumaka married a woman over the objections of her family. According to some accounts, she had left a well-to-do husband for Dumaka; according to others, the young couple quarreled over her insistence on following Zuni customs.[11] Worst of all, Dumaka had adopted white attitudes toward Zuni religion. This had led him "to deny and despise the teachings and superstitions of his people," as one missionary explained. Indeed, Dumaka's "continued mocking criticisms of their customs, superstitions, and religion" constituted an open challenge to the priestly hierarchy.[12] It was only a matter of time before they would respond.

Dumaka's behavior that night in December 1892 provided the priests with the excuse they needed. In fact, Dumaka later claimed they had conspired to get him drunk.[13] In any case, under the influence of Tsanahe's whiskey, Dumaka became hostile and belligerent. So, the other young men took him outside the village, and, as Lina recalled, they "beat Tumaka [Dumaka] with large stones, with black grinding stones, with rocks." He was left for dead. But when they returned later, they found him still alive—and defiant. Staggering to his feet, he taunted them.

"So you think I am going to die? So that's what you think? I won't die. For I do not have my heart where my heart is. . . . I have my heart in my toenails. Therefore, when you beat me on the body, when you beat me on the head, you do not injure me. I am wise. You will not kill me."[14]

With these words Dumaka committed his most serious affront yet. Claims such as these meant only one thing: Dumaka was a witch.

In 1882, the Zuni delegation touring the East with Cushing made a side trip to Salem, Massachusetts. Told about the seventeenth-century persecution of witches at Salem, the Zunis became excited. At a public reception, the bow priest Kiasi "thanked the good people of Salem for the service they had done the world," and he gave them some advice should witchcraft ever trouble them again. " 'Be the witches or wizards your dearest relatives or friends, consider not your own hearts,' said he, 'but remember your duty and spare them not; put them to death!' " Because the Americans had rid themselves of witches, the Zunis decided, they had become prosperous and strong.[15] Belief in witchcraft represents a darker side of Zuni life, one that contradicts the stereotype of Pueblo Indians as uniformly even tempered. While the Zunis had solved various social problems creatively and humanely, theirs was not a perfect society. Some Zunis, like Nick Dumaka, grew up at odds with themselves, their families, and the community, unable to conform to Zuni ideals and social roles. As Benedict noted, "Zuñi's only reaction to such personalities is to brand them as witches."[16]

Because the Zunis did not make the distinction, typical of European law, between behavior and intent, the wish to do harm was as bad as doing harm; psychic violence the same as physical violence. Murder, assault, theft, arson, and other crimes were all tried as forms of witchcraft.[17] However, because the Zunis considered anger, resentment, bitterness, and envy as precursors of witchcraft, sanctions were often applied before overt acts of aggression occurred. Suspected witches were subject to avoidance and criticism, and their actions were closely watched. This is why Zuni appears to have had so little crime.

Zuni folklore associated witches with everything dark, shadowy, and evil. Witches could assume the shape of animals and pass through holes and cracks to enter houses. They traveled in the form of whirlwinds and robbed the graves of the dead. For fear of witches, adult men walked in pairs wrapped in a single blanket as they passed through the deserted passages of the pueblo at night. Witches were believed to have their own clandestine organization, the *hadikanne* or Witch Society; their own sun priest and bow priest; their own kiva (to which, interestingly, *both* male and female witches belonged). To convene a meeting, a witch turned into a coyote and howled four times. "I have something to say," one witch might start. "How about that boy A:lushpa? Aren't you jealous? He has a fine wife and a fine sister and he brings in deer every day. I wish he might die." Droughts, crop failures, wind storms, insect infestations, and epidemics were all attributed to witchcraft.[18]

Witches used the religious arcana of the community for personal ends, instead of for the good of all, to get riches, revenge, or sexual favors. They attacked individuals by shooting objects into their bodies that rotted and festered, causing slow, painful deaths. Victims usually suspected specific individuals of causing their illnesses. The family called a doctor from one of the medicine societies. If treatment were successful no action against the suspect was taken, except for gossip and avoidance. But if the victim died, a trial was likely to follow.[19] Prosecution of witches was the responsibility of the bow priests, who tried "to bring them to wisdom." They seized the suspect at night and took him or her to their chambers. Witnesses both for and against the suspect, and the suspect himself, could speak. If the suspect did not confess, however, he was painfully suspended by his thumbs or with his arms tied behind his back. Hanging, with occasional respite, continued for a day. Suspects might also be hung in the large plaza, from a beam protruding from the old mission. If the suspect still remained silent after this, he was taken to the bow priests' chamber once more, "whence he never comes forth alive." Witches were not always executed, however. If the witch confessed, especially with an elaborate story of occult powers, he or she might be released, usually to live in exile.[20]

As the Zunis tried to preserve their cultural integrity against the onslaught of outside influences in the late nineteenth century, nonconformity and individualism of any form was labeled witchcraft. Zunis who associated too closely with whites; spent too much time away from the village; adopted white ways of dressing, talking, acting, or working; converted to Christianity; or failed to participate in ceremonies and dances were all suspected of witchcraft.[21]

In recent years, American Indian belief in witchcraft has been explained typically in psychological terms. Leighton and Adair concluded, "Certainly anxiety is increasingly present in a rapidly changing world in which one has to make choices where before no alternatives existed. The individual anxieties patterned by the culture are projected on to others who are believed to be witches. It is this anxiety that the shaman relieves when he 'sucks out' the object shot into the patient by a witch."[22] But the witchcraft complex also served to maintain the cooperative nature of Zuni society. Those who enjoyed less social or economic success were discouraged from harboring divisive resentments or jealousies for fear of the charge of witchcraft, while the more successful families were concerned lest they become the object of a witch's envy. So they, too, strove to be kind, generous, and humble toward others.[23]

In the early 1890s, a series of setbacks, ranging from crop failures to droughts and epidemics, brought fears of witchcraft to a peak.[24] Increasingly, Nick Dumaka, the rebel, found himself the focal point for the fears and anxieties of an entire community.

DUMAKA'S TRIAL

While Nick Dumaka lay unconscious in a field outside the village, the young men reported his words to Nayuchi, the leading bow priest. The society of warriors wasted little time. They found Dumaka and took him to their ceremonial chamber. Tying his wrists behind his back, they suspended him from the rafters.

"Now speak," the bow priests began. "It seems you are wise. . . . It seems you are a witch, and therefore you have no sense at all. Even if someone doesn't pay any attention to you, you talk to him with bad words, to make him angry. Maybe, just in order to injure the others just for something you speak evil words. You have no sense."

"Do what you yourselves want of me," Dumaka replied haughtily. Now sober, he had no memory of what he had said earlier. He asked for his wife. But when she arrived, she offered the same advice. "Well, why don't you talk?" she berated him. "It can't be helped. It seems you told them something. Everyone heard you. Why do you deny it? Have you no shame?"[25]

Dumaka now realized the seriousness of his situation. According to Lina Zuni, he appealed to his brother to seek help from his white friend at Fort Wingate. According to other accounts, however, Dumaka's brother was tried at the same time, and their Zuni father traveled to Gallup for help.[26] In any case, Dumaka was desperate: "The Zunis are going to kill me. Hurry! They are going to hang me. I shall die. . . . You will tell my friend. The soldiers will come and then I will have them all arrested."

Accounts vary regarding the role of Dumaka's patron, the trader Graham. Some versions have Graham himself—in one case, armed with twin revolvers—breaking up the trial.[27] But an Indian Office inspector who visited Zuni in 1903 noted that the trial occurred when Graham was away from Zuni.[28] This makes sense, for the bow priests would have expected Graham to intervene if he knew his assistant were on trial for witchcraft. In any case, the suspect was now released. Perhaps the bow priests took Dumaka's threats seriously, or, perhaps, Dumaka had confessed his crime.[29]

But Dumaka's "old Zuni father" was already in Gallup, begging the deputy marshal and the mayor to save his "tortured son." These men telegraphed the commander of the Arizona military department and requested the use of troops to arrest the responsible Zunis. Meanwhile, newspapers in Albuquerque and Santa Fe began printing sensational stories. "Tortured and Killed" read the headline in the *Albuquerque Morning Democrat*; "Two Zuni Indians Charged with Witchcraft Meet a Horrible Death in the Hands of the Tribe." According to the article, "the torture preceding death was of the most revolting character."[30]

On December 18, Capt. Colon Augur and Deputy Marshal Green left Fort Wingate for Zuni with a troop of twenty-five soldiers. Arriving late in the day, the soldiers bivouacked some distance outside the village, perhaps out of sight, while the captain and deputy marshal called on Nick Dumaka. Dumaka registered a string of bitter complaints: against the young men who had beaten him, the bow priests who had tried him, and Dick Tsanahe, who had given him whiskey.[31] "Let them come without fail," Dumaka said. "Let many soldiers come."

News of this spread quickly. "All over they were talking about it," Lina recalled. "I was terribly frightened." At the same time, the Zunis were beginning their observance of the winter solstice. During this ten-day period the entire population fasted from certain foods, extinguished all outdoor fires, and attended all-night religious ceremonies.

It is not likely that the captain or deputy marshal were aware of this, however. They had little reason to expect the Zunis, with their reputation for cooperation, to interfere with their duties. And so, they proceeded to the house of Dick Tsanahe, to arrest the man who had given Dumaka whiskey. But on arriving at his doorway, they found themselves facing not the governor but the governor's "younger brother." It was We'wha—according to Stevenson, one of the "tallest and strongest" members of the tribe. As Lina Zuni recalled:

> *When all the people were cutting prayersticks they came. The soldiers came for the second time. They were going to take my sister's husband. When the soldiers came we cried. "It seems that he is the valuable one, that witch," I said. We cried. His younger brother [*suwe*], although he was a man in woman's dress, got angry. He hit the soldiers. When they were going to take his brother, although he pretended to be a woman, he hit them. He was strong. He stood, holding the door posts, and would not let them come in.*[32]

An Anglo account of this confrontation adds an additional detail:

> *An officer who with the sheriff went to the Governor's house to arrest him, was bodily thrown out of doors by a woman,—or what at the time was supposed to be a woman, which amounted to the same thing. In making his exit, his coat tails caught in the door which being immediately closed held him in this position, until, thinking of the saber which until now had remained in the scabbard, he valiantly drew it, and extricated himself from his unpleasant predicament, by severing his coat tails from their attachment, becoming again, a free man.*[33]

Mary Dissette later told the *New York Times* that she was passing by the house when the incident occurred. "I saw the squaws in the house shove the Lieutenant out of the door, slam the door to, and catch the tails of his coat in it. He drew his sabre and cut off the tails of his coat with it."[34]

Captain Augur now decided to deploy his troops. But the sight of soldiers approaching the village enraged the Zunis. They greeted them just as they had greeted Coronado three and a half centuries earlier. According to one account, "Every man, woman and child in the village became armed, in an incredibly short time, with every imaginable species of weapon, from a Winchester rifle to a scythe, and but for the exercise of the discretion truly the better part of valor on this occasion, a massacre would have resulted then and there." The Zunis made "the air hideous with all sorts of demonstrations." According to George Wharton James, "The warlike Zuni, always intolerant of outside interference in their affairs . . . resisted the troops, assailed them with foul names from their housetops, led them into a trap, and there, by force of their superior numbers, well armed and dangerous, kept them until reinforcements arrived." As Lina Zuni recalled, "Some Zuni boys, some people who pretended to be brave, picked up sticks anywhere and some beat them. You know how the boys are, some of them have no sense. They beat them with sticks. Because of this they were very angry. The soldiers were very angry."[35]

Shaken, the troops withdrew. An uneasy calm settled over the village. It was the night of the solstice, the longest night of the year. Nervously, the Zunis tried to resume their ceremonies. "Next day the people planted their prayersticks," recalled Lina Zuni. "They kept their sacred fire taboo. Everyone abstained."

Captain Augur sent for reinforcements. Fort Wingate's entire command was now deployed for the purpose of arresting Dumaka's prosecutors. This included four additional troops, for a total of 193 men, "fully armed and equipped for field service," along with wagons, supplies, mules, horses, and "field pieces"—that is, artillery. The column left to relieve the beleaguered Captain Augur on December 20, 1892, arriving the next day.[36] The incident had escalated into a full-scale confrontation. The number of soldiers and guns involved, the presence of artillery, and the tense, volatile mood at Zuni created an extremely dangerous situation. Similar circumstances in 1890 had resulted in a massacre at Wounded Knee, South Dakota, when hair-trigger soldiers killed some three hundred men, women, and children. With growing horror, the Zunis watched the long line of soldiers and wagons stream into the valley and take up positions surrounding their village. Lina Zuni remembered:

> *There were so many they filled the whole long valley to the other Black Rock, the farther one, as the first ones came to Halona. There were many. Two by two in long files, the soldiers came. The Zunis cried. "We shall all die." "Impossible." "But they have enough guns as they come. A person can't live. It serves us right. We have no sense. It serves us*

right. We drink whisky. So now it is come we shall all die." The people, even the men, were crying. Their mules were many, and they carried large packs on their backs. Their food was packed in wagons and these came last. Their tents were many, and they set them up all around the village. . . . Everyone cried. There were men all around and the soldiers stood guard. No one could run away any place. Some of them watched them, so that the men could not even take their wives away, one at a time. They did not sleep, even for a little while. We were all frightened because we were going to die. However, the witch man's sisters and his mother and his father were visiting the soldiers at their camp. Because of his doing, the country was full of soldiers. The Zunis were crying, and the whole village, although they were all taboo, they left their altars and ran away. The soldiers came to the village and even though they were taboo they took their wood. They disturbed everything. These were not happy days. This is what they did to us.

The Zuni officers wrote a letter and gave their letter to the chief of the soldiers. "Be kind to us. That Zuni has no sense. He did not speak the truth. Because he was drunk he sent for you. For really he has no sense. All the people, the whole village, he treated badly. He liked whisky. He has no sense. We shall live quietly." At daybreak the Zunis took the letter over to the soldiers. It was given to the soldiers across the river. Here where the white people are living the storekeeper, Black Mustache, who was the Zunis' trader [D. D. Graham], spoke Zuni very well. He understood it. He spoke just like a Zuni. He and Jesus [Eriacho] helped one another. All night long they talked it over. They did not want a fight. Late at night, the Zunis ran away. When no one was watching they ran away. They did not sleep. "Well, all right, let us be kind to them. However, the old ones who beat him, the bow priest, and then the one who had the whisky, the one who gave him a drink, and then that one who fought with the soldiers, the one who pretended to be a woman, the lha'mana, *and her brother, and the bow priests, the one who hung the man, if these go quietly, we shall put them in jail. Just as much as they injured him, to the same extent we shall let them wear out their spirits. Then, when it is even, we shall let them go. Then at that time they will come back.*

> *You want us to be kind. If you let us take them, we shall go." Then again, the two crossed the river. They brought the message across to where the Zuni officers were meeting. "Well, let it be thus. All right, let's hope they may not die somewheres. However, it seems they will come back again. All right, go quietly. It can't be helped. They treated him badly." Now it was sunrise. So now the Zunis felt better. . . . Next day the soldiers went and they took the bow priests and the* lha'mana, *these the soldiers put into their commissary wagon, and took them with them.*

The soldiers had arrested Nayuchi, the leading bow priest, the governor, and We'wha. From the available documents, it is not clear where they were taken—to Fort Wingate or to the county jail in Gallup—nor under what authority, jurisdiction, or charges. Yet the *Albuquerque Morning Democrat* could smugly comment that the presence of the troops served "to impress the Indians with the majesty of the law."[37] According to Zuni accounts, We'wha and the others spent a month or more in jail at Fort Wingate. We do not know when or if We'wha's true sex was discovered by his jailers, but according to Dumaka, he was released before the others. He returned from Fort Wingate on foot. The forty-mile trek across the continental divide in the dead of winter was no small ordeal for the middle-aged berdache.[38]

In Albuquerque, the local paper reported Captain Augur's encounter with the Zunis and the order to dispatch reinforcements from Fort Wingate. "Although the thermometer was below zero, the gallant boys hastened to the rescue. Troop D made a forced march and Col. [George C.] Huntt followed with the remainder of the command and two pieces of artillery. The boys were aching for a little skirmish with the redskins, but Col. Huntt soon adjusted the difficulty upon arriving on the scene. He took the prisoners in charge and returned to the fort with his command in time to participate in a Xmas tree entertainment. . . . The ladies of the fort deserve the credit for the happy termination of the 'Zuni war.' "[39]

Word of the arrests spread far. In February 1893, Alexander Stephen, who was living among the Hopis, noted in his diary reports that "We'we, To'maka and four other Zuñi" were in "prison" at Fort Wingate. "We'we and others proposed hanging or destroying the witches; a general hubbub prevailed in the village for days and the soldiers interfered." In Washington, the superintendent of Indian schools noted in his annual report the trial of two Zuni Indians for witchcraft, "probably the most progressive of any people in the pueblo."[40] Ironically, the Pueblo Indian agent stationed in Santa Fe was among the last to learn of the incident. On January 19, the agent wrote to Mary Dissette at Zuni, "You speak of the Troops being there from Ft. Wingate. What has been the trouble? I read in the papers that there had been some trouble at Zuni, but not hearing of it in any other way I concluded that the News Paper article was an exaggeration. I wrote to Mr. Graham just as soon as I saw the article but did not get any reply."[41]

The Zuni conception of time does not make a sharp distinction between present and past, and the idea that "time heals all wounds" is foreign to them. Past injustices and sufferings, whether at the hands of Spaniards, Navajos, Apaches, or Americans, are kept alive through re-tellings that continue today. The events of 1892 made a particularly deep and lasting impression. When Lina Zuni related the incident, she recalled the disastrous prophecies of her grandfather. "And so indeed we suffered," she concluded. "The town was full of white soldiers. Then according to the words of my grandfather I suffered."[42]

Dumaka's revenge against Nayuchi and the bow priests was, as Ruth Benedict pointed out, "probably unique in Zuñi history."[43] But he paid a high price for his vengeance. As a result of the hanging, his shoulders were permanently crippled. And he earned the undying resentment of his community. Lina expressed what was probably the general attitude of the Zunis toward Dumaka after these events: "This man had no sense. And because of his doing, the whole great village worried. They cried. Therefore the people still hate him. Nobody likes him. Now I am this old, and he is a mature person [*ho"i ya:k'ana*, "finished person"]. And I think that perhaps he may know better. But formerly he had no sense."[44]

It is interesting to compare We'wha and Dumaka. Like We'wha, Dumaka's behavior and attitudes set him apart from average Zunis. But unlike We'wha, there was no role at Zuni that took advantage of his variation—except the anti-social role of the witch. We'wha's behavior fell within the spectrum of Zuni norms, whereas Dumaka was a rebel. In Zuni terms, We'wha was better adjusted than Dumaka—although in the white world, We'wha, not Dumaka, would have been considered the deviant.

THE SIEGE OF ZUNI

We'wha's resistance against the soldiers in 1892 was the act of a vigorous individual in the prime of life. Yet just four years later, with the Sha'lako dancing in the next room, he lay dying from heart disease. According to Stevenson, the "great theurgist" Nayuchi came three times to treat him. He quickly diagnosed the cause: bits of mutton had been "shot" into We'wha's heart by a witch. Nayuchi strove mightily to draw these out, but to no avail. We'wha died at the age of forty-nine.[45]

We'wha's death was considered a "calamity," and the January ceremonial of the *lhewe:kwe* society, which normally met in We'wha's house, was curtailed. It was a premature death, and therefore suspect. An old woman named Marita or Melita had asked We'wha for a quarter of mutton shortly before his illness, and We'wha had refused. This must have maimed the old woman's heart, as the Zunis say, and made her sick with anger—and so she resorted to witchcraft.[46] Thus, We'wha's death became the occasion for another witchcraft trial and another military intervention. This time, however, several weeks passed before the bow priests acted. With memories of 1892 still vivid, there may have been long debates over the risks of another trial.

The teacher Mary Dissette provided what became the government's official account of Marita's ordeal (no eyewitnesses ever came forward). Marita was arrested on Friday, February 19.[47] Upon learning of the trial the following Monday, Dissette began a search for the victim:

> *I found the old woman, whose name is Ma-u-ri-ta, in a little stuffy room, up two or three steps from the main floor of the house. She was lying in some filthy rags, and was badly frightened when I entered, thinking I must be some of the Indians coming to torture her again. I told her I was her friend, and had come to help her, but she did not believe me*

> *at first. I then compelled some members of her family to return to the house and care for her, after I had washed her, bandaged her lacerated arms and back, and dressed her as well as I was able. She told me that they had come for her on Friday, taken her to a corral where burros are kept, lashed her hands behind her back, and hanged her so that her feet just touched the ground. Then they beat her unmercifully time and again, until she finally confessed that she was the witch. . . . The priests charged her with having caused the death of a creature named Wa-weh, and with other misdeeds.*[48]

George Wharton James, who visited Zuni not long after these events occurred, published an even more embellished account, casting himself in a prominent role. "Melita was thus strung up," he wrote, "until the blood oozed from eyes, ears, nose, and mouth, and the blood vessels of her cheeks burst with the fearful pressure."[49]

Dissette submitted her report to the Pueblo Indian agent in Santa Fe, who notified the Office of Indian Affairs in the Interior Department. In the meantime, the office of the Pueblo Indian agent changed hands—a frequent occurrence during this period. On April 1, 1897, Capt. C. E. Nordstrom, a career army officer, assumed duties as acting agent. Within a matter of days, a letter arrived from Dissette: What was the agent planning to do in the matter of the Zuni witch hanging?[50]

Dissette's role in these developments reflected a new dimension in the conflict over witchcraft trials. When she first arrived in 1888, the Presbyterian mission at Zuni was considered "a discouraging one." But Dissette, "a woman of force and large executive ability," was determined to make the school a success.[51] When the government adopted the policy of compulsory education of Indian children in the early 1890s, Dissette wholeheartedly embraced the plan. The desire to see this policy enforced at Zuni lay behind her report of Marita's ordeal.

Compulsory education was a key element of the government's assimilation policy.[52] "When we speak of the education of the Indians," wrote Commissioner of Indian Affairs Thomas J. Morgan in 1889, "we mean that comprehensive system of training and instruction which will convert them into American citizens."[53] The government's bleak off-reservation boarding schools, organized like military academies, provided just such a "comprehensive system of training." Students were required to wear uniforms, attend church, and follow a strict daily regimen. Government regulations prohibited any use of native language, even informally. Corporal punishment was freely applied. Day schools such as the one Dissette administered at Zuni were less severe but intended to prepare young children for eventual enrollment at a boarding school.[54]

Indian parents naturally resisted placing their children in such an environment. And so, to enforce attendance, Congress authorized agents to withhold rations and annuities from families that refused to enroll their children.[55] But this leverage could not be applied to the self-sufficient Pueblo Indians. Nordstrom, Dissette, and many others in the Indian service concluded that implementing the government's policy required the use of force. Commissioner Morgan vigorously defended such tactics before a conference of policymakers and philanthropists in 1892. "Shall we allow the growth of another generation of barbarians," he asked, "or shall we compel the children to enter these schools to be trained to intelligence and industry?" The audience cheered back its affirmation of the latter.[56]

A key change in the status of Pueblo day schools occurred in 1896 when the Indian Office took over their management from the religious denominations that had been operating the schools by contract. Nordstrom inspected these schools soon after taking office and reported his conclusions in no uncertain terms: Unless mandatory attendance were enforced they might as well be closed. Only at Zuni did students attend regularly enough to make educational progress—and this was only because they were given free clothes and lunches. Pueblo parents also refused to send their children to the boarding school in Albuquerque. Nordstrom found their "selfish craving for the constant society of their offspring" exasperating and the government's "indulgence of their childish affection" incomprehensible.[57]

When Nordstrom interviewed Dissette and Marita in June, he became convinced that he could use the issue of the witchcraft trial to force the government to assert its authority over the Zunis and other Pueblo villages. "I saw the victim of this barbarism," he reported to Washington, "who bared her poor old shriveled arms and showed me where the cruel cords of the torture had cut the flesh through to the bone. As Miss Dissette, her eyes filled with sympathetic tears, her voice trembling with indignant emotion, described the particulars of this unspeakable horror, my own cheek blushed that thirty-six years of my life had been spent in the service of a Government under which such things could be done."[58] The stage was set for a new confrontation between the American government and the people of the Middle Place.

Returning to Santa Fe, Nordstrom immediately wrote to the Commissioner of Indian Affairs, recommending a show of force at Zuni.[59] But the agent's superiors were concerned with a larger picture. The official use of troops at Zuni had legal and policy ramifications reaching far beyond that remote pueblo. In 1892, troops had been used without official sanction from Washington, and the Indian Office did not have to take a stand on the practice. So, while the bureaucrats balked, Nordstrom sought even more compelling charges to lay against the Zunis. To the crimes of the bow priests and the refusal of parents to enroll their children in government schools, Nordstrom now added the charge of immorality.

Dissette had hinted of immorality in the Sha'lako ceremonies during his visit to Zuni. Hoping to uncover more, Nordstrom wrote to Graham. "Miss Dissette was not able to tell me much concerning the innermost secrets of this orgie, but from what she did say . . . I infer that this dance is, to say the least, demoralizing in its tendencies, and as such should be suppressed." He asked Graham to report "something concerning the secret mysteries, which I presume characterizes some period in the dance—such as the degree of, or tendency toward lust and licentiousness which prevails, etc. . . . being careful to make it as strong as possible."[60]

It was field matron May Faurote, however, who provided Nordstrom with the kind of information he wanted. Faurote reported the antics of the Koyemshi clowns, who sometimes imitated sexual acts to the amusement of other Zunis. "It is a shame and disgrace that they have been permitted to go on so long as they have," Nordstrom responded. "If the Department will let me I intend to abolish every thing in that dance, which have [*sic*] a tendency to debauch the old and corrupt the young." The agent forwarded

Faurote's "disgusting" report to Washington, and wrote to the matron asking her to set aside, "as far as woman's nature will allow," any sense of "false delicacy" and report even more details.[61]

Thus began the practice of using pornographic gossip for political purposes against the Zunis and other Pueblo Indians. In subsequent years, it became the resort of agents, missionaries, politicians, and local whites who had reason to compromise Indian rights or interests. Indian land, culture, family, and community were all thrown into a debate over alleged sexual practices, a debate in which Indians were not allowed to speak. Berdaches were not exempt from denunciation. As early as 1892, Dissette had written to the agent complaining about the "custom of the men wearing female dress." In 1893, the Superintendent of Indian Schools reported that at Zuni "bastardy is a frequent occurrence, occasioning no comment. Boys and girls mingle freely, out on the sands, till late at night. Married life imposes no restrictions. Men are allowed to wear women's costume, and work with the women in the house."[62]

In August, Nordstrom resubmitted his request for military intervention. He needed four troops to make the arrests and fifty men to remain indefinitely to protect witnesses. To the district attorney, he confided, "The greater the number we arrest the better effect it will have no matter what may be the ultimate result."[63] But he remained uncertain about what crime to charge the bow priests with. When the commissioner authorized only one troop, a hurried exchange of telegrams followed. The commissioner did not understand the situation, Nordstrom insisted. No less than two hundred men were needed. "This is a desperate enterprise, which will mark an epoch in the administration of Indian affairs in this Territory."[64]

Nonetheless, on September 13, 1897, only one troop left Fort Wingate—"for the purpose of assisting in the arrest of certain Indians desired by the civil authorities." When the soldiers arrived, two of the indicted bow priests surrendered immediately. The others were twenty miles away, so the first two were sent after them. All four suspects reported the next day. Nayuchi, Hadotsi, Nomase, and Kiasi were quietly taken into custody; so much for Nordstrom's "desperate enterprise."[65] Even so, the agent was exhilarated. "Three troops of cavalry and a mountain howitzer are marvelous incentives to discreet action," he reported to Washington.[66]

The prisoners were taken to Los Lunas (and, later, Albuquerque) and held on five thousand dollars bail each for grand jury action in February 1898—five months away.[67] It is not likely that there was five thousand dollars cash in the entire pueblo of Zuni, let alone that amount four times over. The *Santa Fe Daily New Mexican* reported, "This is probably the end of the much feared terrible Indian outbreak which has taken up so much space in the eastern papers the past few weeks."[68] In fact, it was just the beginning of protracted jurisdictional disputes that threatened all of Nordstrom's carefully laid plans.

At Zuni, the commanding officer refused the agent's request to remain; he saw no danger to government employees.[69] Again, Nordstrom appealed to Washington. The troops must remain. Dances in which "anything goes" must be stopped. The arrest of Nayuchi had driven a "wedge" into Zuni that would be "the beginning of the end of all these abominations." "Civilization, and barbarism," he concluded, using the terminology of Morgan's theory of the stages of civilization, "are diametrically opposed to each other, and cannot co-exist in the same community."[70] Nordstrom's plans were threatened on another front as well. On September 24, the district attorney notified him that the judge at Las Lunas was inclined to release the prisoners to save the county the expense of keeping them in jail. This action, Nordstrom believed, would reverse all his efforts to assert authority at Zuni.[71]

While Nordstrom sought to prevent the release of the Zuni prisoners, the wheels of Washington suddenly moved again. On October 2, a troop from Fort Wingate left for Zuni, "for the purpose of giving all needed protection to the civil authorities and government employees at that place." This detachment, relieved monthly, remained for the next six months, camped on the south side of the Zuni river across from the main pueblo.[72] When Andrew Vanderwagen arrived on October 9 to begin his fifty-year career as missionary and trader to the Zunis, he found the village in turmoil. Zuni leaders had been carried off to prison, fear of witchcraft was rampant, and "United States soldiers patrolled the streets."[73]

But the army still refused to enforce liquor laws, school attendance, Victorian morals, or other policies of the Indian Office. Exasperated, Nordstrom again wrote to Washington. He intended to see that all "ceremonies in their nature or tendency, the least vicious, shall, eventually, be broken up"—in particular, Sha'lako, "a period of licentious indulgence," which would begin in a few weeks. "Girls, and even married women," he raved, "are at liberty to follow the dictates of their wayward fancies, in their intercourse with the opposite sex." He must have the use of the troops, the lack of which he regretted "beyond my poor powers of expression." "It is respectfully submitted to the Department," he wrote again in late December, "that if the matter were not so grave it would be farcical. Is it thoroughly understood by the Department? I think it cannot be possible that it is!" Regulations required him as agent to enforce school attendance, but by what means? "The situation is more than humiliating—it is a disgrace, and I am ashamed. I beg, I entreat of you, Mr. Commissioner, to allow this state of things to go on no longer."[74] Still, Nordstrom found ways to take advantage of the soldiers at Zuni. He wrote to the Zuni governor that Dissette was in charge of the school "and the Pueblo," and her "commands" were to be obeyed as if they were his own. As for the opponents of the school: "Tell these obstinate old women that the place in which Nyuche and his friends are confined is full of rooms and the Sheriff of the County would like very much to fill them all with tenants from Zuni."[75]

Nordstrom's obsession with the Zunis was building toward an explosive climax when an unexpected turn of events brought the confrontation to a sudden close. On January 11, 1898, Nordstrom died in office.[76] On February 7, an acting agent assumed his duties. The next day a letter to the Commissioner of Indian Affairs requested the withdrawal of the troops at Zuni.[77] At the same time, the government's case against the bow priests was unraveling. To prevent dismissal, hearings were repeatedly postponed.[78]

With her mentor gone, Dissette's influence quickly waned. "Reports have reached this office," the acting agent wrote to the commissioner in February, "implying that Miss Dissette in charge of the school there is not managing affairs successfully and by reason of her connection with the witch hanging matter and her tyrannical ways with the children has become objectionable. . . . She is a woman of unusual nerve and ability, but circumstances seem to have conspired against her to make her further stay at Zuni undesirable." A few days later, the agent received a letter from Dick Tsanahe, complaining about Dissette's treatment of students.[79] This letter is not on file, but the charges must have been serious, for the agent wrote to the Commissioner that he had received "confidential information which leads me to call the subject to your attention in as strong a manner as possible." He recommended Dissette's transfer, hoping to avoid a formal investigation that would discredit her publicly. Over sixty years later, Zunis still harbored bitter memories of the unpopular schoolteacher.[80]

By the fall of 1898, one of the prisoners had died in jail, and the Zunis were desperate to secure the release of the others. Family members approached a trader at Laguna for assistance, and he, in turn, employed an attorney on their behalf. The lawyer confronted the authorities with the irregularities of the arrests. "An effort was made to keep them in jail," he charged, "until they would give as the price of their freedom a promise that a certain number of children from the Zuni Pueblo would be sent to the Government Indian School."[81] This is exactly what happened. When the Zunis were finally freed in November 1898—eighteen months after their arrest—the Pueblo agent reported that they had promised to place twenty-five children in the Albuquerque school and concluded that "the moral effect of this long imprisonment has been good."[82]

The "moral effect" of illegal detention and military intimidation is difficult to perceive today, and it was certainly lost on the Zunis at the time. The district attorney, Indian agents, and local and national authorities conspired to deprive the four bow priests of their most basic civil rights. While the authorities knew they lacked the evidence to win a conviction in court, they decided to punish the Zunis anyway, detaining them in jail without trial as long as possible.

Although the stated policy of Indian reformers and the Indian Office in the 1890s was to bring Indians under the same law as white Americans, thereby extending to them the political and civil rights of citizenship, the contradiction between this policy and the government's attempts to dictate to its Indian wards is revealed in the incidents of 1892 and 1897. The refusal of policymakers to perceive or make allowance for racial discrimination characterized all the programs of this period. Racism would subvert the formal extension of rights to Indians—local courts and law enforcement officials consistently would favor whites over Indians, politicians would ignore Indian needs, national policy would favor profitable development over treaty rights, and Indians would remain segregated, on their reservations, with substandard health, housing, and education. Nordstrom illustrated both sides of the nineteenth-century contradiction in Indian policy: while extending the accountabilities of white law to the Zunis, he simultaneously denied them the rights granted by that law.

"They may imprison me for one month, six months, a year, or forever," Nayuchi once told Stevenson, "but I shall hang the witch who destroys the life of my child."[83] Sadly, the old warrior could not turn back the repercussions of the events of 1892 and 1897. The intervention of the military, once by overwhelming force during a religious period and once by long-term occupation, the arrests and detention of leaders, the harsh treatment of children at government schools, and the reckless machinations of officials were part of a traumatic period in Zuni history. With the banning of witchcraft trials, the Zunis felt defenseless against enemies they considered real and dangerous. As Lina Zuni told Bunzel:

> *Long ago when we were children, whenever anyone who had any power, used magic, when they found him out and told the bow priests, they would take him. When they asked him what he had done, if he did not tell, then they would hang him. They would beat him. Then he would talk. When they made him cry out then he would tell of his power. When we were children, they fought against them that way. But that man made the soldiers come and so the witches became valuable. Therefore when any two people quarrel, one will call the other a witch. It's all right, it's good. Witches are valuable. They have soldiers. It's good for them. So he will say. Therefore they no longer strip witches of their power.*[84]

Decades later, whenever disease and illness struck, Zunis complained, "It is the white man's fault all these people are being killed. In the old days we could have hung these witches and stopped this disease."[85]

Beyond the psychological impact of these events were their long-term political and social ramifications. As Nordstrom predicted, the arrests of 1897 did indeed break the power of the bow priest society. Through their dual role as military leaders and prosecutors of witches, the bow priests had protected both the village and the collective unity that made village living possible. In their absence, the agents of assimilation could appeal directly to the hearts and minds of the Zuni people and thereby gain access to Zuni land and resources. The direct result was the development of factionalism within the tribe as individuals and families began to compete for the prestige and advantages available through alliances with outsiders. Today, tribal council politics provides an arena where factions can pursue their agendas, and individual enterprise and ambition, once suppressed as forms of witchcraft, are given free expression.[86]

WE'WHA: A RETROSPECTIVE

Throughout his career, We'wha found ways of building bridges to the white world. For better or worse, he sought to adapt and accommodate Anglo-American culture, while retaining Zuni essentials. We'wha's contributions fell into three areas: cultural preservation, economic development, and cross-cultural relations.

We'wha took a great risk by cooperating with Stevenson. Tribal members who provided information to anthropologists were viewed with suspicion and—because they received favors from their patrons—envy. In fact, many Zunis assumed that anthropological informants were "selling" Zuni religious secrets. From a Zuni point of view, this was just as bad as using secrets for malevolent or personal ends; both were forms of witchcraft.[87] In fact, Irving Goldman (citing Ruth Benedict) reported that "Mrs. Stevenson's appraisal of the attitude of the Zuni toward Wewha is not to be taken too literally."[88] But while this famous berdache was not above criticism, as far as we know he was never accused of witchcraft, and this meant that he enjoyed the trust of his community. The Zunis would say that he had a "good heart."

Normally, the kind of ceremonial knowledge We'wha had amassed over a lifetime would be passed on to a carefully trained apprentice, usually a relative or a member of one's religious society.

But as a berdache, We'wha lacked direct descendents. Perhaps he sensed the coming changes that would cause the lapse of religious societies and ceremonies and drastically reshape the berdache role. In any case, years before Native American studies and tribal cultural programs, We'wha saw a value in recording his knowledge. His insight was to perceive the use of Western technologies of inscription to record, in written and visual form, Zuni customs, crafts, and oral literature.

We'wha might be considered an "authoritative innovator," a community leader whose responsibilities included innovation. According to Tom McFeat, the continual and often rapid social change that characterizes Pueblo prehistory and history created a need for "communal philosophers—men of power, authority and prestige—for whom a speculative type of role was left open." When discrepancies between the ideal world and the world of reality emerged, the role of these philosophers was to demonstrate some significant and meaningful relationship between the two.[89] Such was the ground that We'wha explored in his contacts with the world beyond Zuni.

In addition to his efforts to preserve Zuni traditions, We'wha participated in important developments affecting native arts and crafts. In the 1880s, Indian artists, like We'wha, were beginning to refine their techniques and produce pottery, weaving, basketry, and jewelry for purchase by non-Indian collectors. We'wha was among the first Zunis to produce pottery and textiles for sale, thus helping to inaugurate a process that would lead to the emergence of traditional Indian arts as fine arts.[90] Indeed, much of the vitality of Southwest Indian societies today is due to the economic viability of native arts—a way of earning income that allows Indians to remain close to their homes and their native cultures. At Zuni, arts and crafts now provide the second largest source of income, following wage labor.[91]

We'wha's artistic career was noteworthy in one other respect, too. In Washington, he discovered a way to build a bridge to the white world through the universal appreciation of the arts. He became, in effect, a cultural ambassador for his people. By sharing the Zunis' artistic achievements—whether demonstrating weaving in the Mall, carrying his feathered wand in the Kirmes, or presenting a gift of his own making to President Cleveland—We'wha brought the insights and imagination of his people within the direct grasp of non-Indians in a way that tended to transcend the moralizing discourse of savagery and civilization. It would be in the realm of the arts that non-Indian Americans would first be able to perceive American Indians as intellectual and social equals.

If there were any doubt about We'wha's loyalties, however, the events of 1892 made it clear that he identified foremost with his family and tribe. Subject to the denunciations of teachers and agents, We'wha discovered the limits that white morality can place on friendship. Although he had engaged in a long flirtation with American culture, when he faced the soldiers in 1892 We'wha stood firmly with his community. His actions on that occasion, while reflecting his own impetuous nature, fit the Zuni pattern of shielding leaders (in this case, the governor) from outsiders. In various ways, We'wha had fulfilled such an intermediary role all his life. But while the bow priests were able to risk contact with outsiders (and witches) because they had rituals for purification, We'wha was able to engage in this contact because of the very nature of his personality as a berdache.

We'wha's achievements seem remarkable to us today because in Euro-American societies there are no avenues for individuals like We'wha to contribute to community life. To understand his career, we need to take a closer look at the psychological and spiritual dimensions of the lhamana role and Zuni attitudes and beliefs regarding gender. The next two chapters explore the double nature of the berdache personality, a configuration of skills and traits that made We'wha, in Cushing's terms, "two-fold one-kind."

5

The Rites of Gender

THE UNTIMELY DEATH OF ZUNI'S leading berdache in late 1896 was a personal loss for Matilda Stevenson and a collective loss for the tribe. Amid tears and mourning, We'wha's female relatives prepared his body for burial.

> *Blankets were spread upon the floor and the brothers gently laid the lifeless form upon them. After the body was bathed and rubbed with meal, a pair of white cotton trousers were drawn over the legs, the first male attire she had worn since she had adopted woman's dress years ago. The rest of her dress was female. The body was dressed in the finest clothing; six shawls of foreign manufacture, gifts from Washington friends, besides her native blanket wraps, and a white Hopi blanket bordered in red and blue, were wrapped around her. The hair was done up with the greatest care. Three silver necklaces, with turquoise earrings attached and numerous bangles, constituted the jewels.*
>
> *We'wha's death was regarded as a calamity, and the remains lay in state for an hour or more, during which time not only members of the clans to which she was allied, but the rain priests and theurgists and many others, including children, viewed them. When the blanket was finally closed, a fresh outburst of grief was heard, and then all endeavored to suppress their sobs, for the aged foster mother had fallen unconscious to the floor. The two brothers carried the*

remains unattended to the grave. The sisters made food offerings to the fire. The foster brother on his return prepared prayer plumes for each member of the immediate family, and also the writer. The little procession, including the foster mother, who had recovered sufficiently to accompany the others, then made its way to the west of the village and on the river bank deposited the clothing, mask, and prayer plumes in the manner heretofore described. Upon the return to the house the foster mother had the rest of We'wha's possessions brought together that they might be destroyed. All her cherished gifts from Washington friends, including many photographs, were brought out; all must be destroyed. This work was performed by the mother, who wept continually. All was sacrificed but pictures of Mr. and Mrs. Carlisle, Mr. Stevenson, and the writer. These were left in the frames on the wall. With another outburst of grief the old woman declared they must remain, saying: "We'wha will have so much with her. I can not part with these. I must keep the faces of those who loved We'wha and whom she loved best. I must keep them to look upon."[1]

THE PUZZLE OF THE PANTS OR THE DILEMMA OF THE DRESS

Stevenson's account of We'wha's death leaves us with a fascinating question. Why was We'wha dressed in pants as well as a dress before his burial? The answer to this question requires an explanation of the gender of the Zuni lhamana.

Parsons's two articles on lhamanas, one written at the beginning of her career and the other near the end, illustrate the changing definitions of the berdache in this century. In 1916, she referred to lhamanas with the English terms *man-woman, berdache,* and *hermaphrodite.* But in 1939, she published an article on the berdache Kasinelu entitled "The Last Zuñi Transvestite," employing a term that had been popularized in the intervening years.[2] *Transvestite* was coined in 1910, by the German sexologist Magnus Hirschfeld, to describe individuals with a compelling psychological need to dress in the clothes of the other sex, often for erotic pleasure.[3] Alfred Kroeber was the first anthropologist to apply this term to berdaches in 1916—reflecting his contact with psychiatrists in Europe the previous year.[4] This use of transvestite, however, was a significant departure from the original, European meaning, since berdaches cross-dressed routinely and in public without erotic motives. Nonetheless, by the time Parsons wrote her 1939 article on the lhamana, transvestite was widely used by anthropologists when referring to berdaches.

Transsexual is an even more recent term, first published in 1948 concurrently with the development of gender reassignment surgery. It, too, has been applied to berdaches. We'wha, for example, is identified as a "male transsexual" in a collection of photographs published in 1982.[5] And yet another term that has been applied to berdaches is *homosexual*. In 1940, Kroeber described berdaches as men "of homosexual trends" who became "institutionalized women."[6]

These new terms, and their variants, can be divided into two categories. On the one hand, there are transvestite and transsexual, which emphasize gender variation. On the other hand, there is homosexual, which emphasizes sexuality. In this respect, these terms perpetuate the same dualism established by the use of *hermaphrodite* and *sodomite* in the long period between the arrival of Columbus and the end of the nineteenth century.[7] After the Second World War, however, a consensus emerged that came down on the side of gender. In 1955, anthropologists Angelino and Shedd defined the berdache as "an individual . . . who assumes the role and status of the opposite sex," the meaning now associated with transsexual.[8]

Since transsexual refers to an individual who seeks to assume the social roles of the opposite sex in daily life, this would appear to be the most appropriate term in English for referring to a berdache. Didn't We'wha dress and act like a woman? Didn't other Zunis consider him a woman? This is how most anthropologists and historians who have commented on We'wha have viewed him. But the transsexual model does not explain the "puzzle of the pants" placed on We'wha before his burial. If We'wha had crossed genders to become a woman, why this final reminder of biological sex?

Parsons first tackled this question during her 1915 visit to Zuni. What was the true gender of the Zuni lhamana? She knew that the Zunis buried their dead in the plot in front of the abandoned Catholic mission in the center of the village. The Zunis had accepted this innovation at the insistence of Spanish missionaries and, after two centuries, had grown accustomed to such close proximity to their ancestors' bones. A wooden cross divided the cemetery in half. Women were buried north of the cross, men to the south. This provided Parsons with the test she needed. Approaching a Zuni elder, she asked about the lhamana, "And on which side of the graveyard will he be buried?"

"On the south side, the men's side, of course. . . . Is this not a man?" the Zuni replied with a smile.[9]

In fact, a review of We'wha's career reveals that the Zuni berdache engaged in many behaviors inconsistent with the "role and status of the opposite sex." To begin with, We'wha participated in both male and female economic pursuits. In his 1881 census, Cushing listed We'wha's occupations as "farmer, weaver, potter, housekeeper"—the first two can be considered male work roles, the last two female. It is especially significant that We'wha engaged in the male economic role of growing corn. Weaving, on the other hand, was less sex-typed at Zuni than at other pueblos, where only men wove; however, there was some tendency for Zuni men to specialize in the large blanket loom, while women used the smaller waist loom.[10] We'wha's mastery of both looms is documented in photographs and written accounts. During his stay in Washington, We'wha also took up knitting, a strictly male pastime at Zuni. He was also among the first Zunis, male or female, to sell pottery and weaving and to earn cash. Interestingly, after We'wha's venture in the laundry business, it appears that washing clothes for pay remained a berdache-specific task for some years.

In the area of religion, We'wha also participated in male roles. He was an active member of the male kachina society. He recited prayers and legends on ceremonial occasions and folk tales on informal occasions—also male roles. During his stay in Washington, he made prayer sticks, another male activity. In terms of his behavior, We'wha's self-assurance and independence were unusual for Zunis of either sex. He was among the first to make contact with the Presbyterian missionaries and the Stevenson expedition, he traveled alone across the continent to spend six months in the nation's capital, and in 1892 he single-handedly tackled two American soldiers.

While some male lhamanas adopted female names, others retained their male names.[11] The Zunis were also inconsistent in their use of kinship terms when referring to berdaches. Lina Zuni referred to We'wha, for example, as the governor's younger brother, or *suwe,* a male kinship term. Yet, while remaining a brother to his male relatives, We'wha fulfilled the duties of a sister and daughter in his adopted family's household. Practices like these led Stevenson to observe, in defense of her own confusion: "One is led into this error by the Indians, who, when referring to men dressed as women, say 'She is a man;' which is certainly misleading to one not familiar with Indian thought."[12]

The conclusion is that We'wha engaged in a combination of male and female activities. He was a specialist not just in women's work, but in cultural work in general. Although We'wha wore a dress, he did not act like a woman. To understand this paradox, we need to look at the Zuni philosophy of gender. What makes a man a man? What makes a woman a woman?

THE RAW AND THE COOKED

Cushing's adoption illustrates Zuni concepts of individual development. To be adopted, he had to be made into a Zuni, and this required that he undergo the same social and ritual procedures that all Zunis underwent in the course of their "life road." Balowahdiwa, the Zuni governor, undertook responsibility for this process shortly after Cushing moved into his house in 1879. "Little brother," he told Cushing, "you may be a Washington man, but it seems you are very poor. Now, if you do as we tell you, and will only make up your mind to be a Zuñi, you shall be rich, for you shall have fathers and mothers, brothers and sisters, and the best food in the world."[13]

Balowahdiwa proceeded to transform Cushing into a Zuni, both inside and out. "You must sleep in the cold and on a hard bed; that will harden your meat. And you must never go to the Mission, or to the trader's to eat; for I want to make a Zuni of you. How can I do that if you eat American food?"[14] The governor took away Cushing's comfortable hammock and his American clothes. Finally, Cushing was secluded in a room for ten days—the same length of time that mothers retired with newborn infants. At the end of this period, Cushing's adoptive father pierced both his ears and gave him a Zuni name. While he kneeled facing east, his head was sprinkled with water, and prayers were offered to the Sun Father.[15]

Cushing was transformed on the outside by assuming Zuni habits and wearing Zuni clothes, and he was transformed on the inside by eating Zuni food and thinking Zuni thoughts. In Zuni terms, he had come to them raw, or *k'abin*, which includes the sense of unripe, soft, and unfinished. By learning their ways he became *'akna*, cooked, ripe, and *ya:na*, finished. The Zunis used these terms as metaphors for the process of socialization, which proceeded from a "raw" to a "cooked" state. What made Zunis cooked were the cultural forms they learned, especially religion, but also economic, social, and kinship roles. By acquiring these, they became "real Zunis"—*'akna 'a:ho"i*, cooked persons—in Western terms, civilized or cultured. The *k'abin 'a:ho"i*, or raw people, on the other hand, included game, water, and prey animals; gods who had animallike characteristics; and personifications of various natural phenomena. Raw people were unfixed, could change their form easily, and had supernatural power. They were "people" in the sense that they had personality traits and distinctive patterns of behavior. But being raw they lived on raw food—or the smoke from food offerings that Zunis threw into the fire at every meal. The model underlying these concepts was the growth of plant life, especially corn.[16]

Newborn infants were considered "raw" because they were unsocialized. Their cooking was effected through initiation rites held at key points in the life of each individual. Some of these rites were fairly simple observances, conducted by the family. Others occurred as part of elaborate public ceremonies that preceded induction into religious organizations. Although the rites followed at birth and death were the same for all individuals, other rites were intended for men or women only. Anthropologist Victor Turner has identified three phases common to initiation ceremonies: *separation*, a period of withdrawal and isolation; *liminality*, a transitional period in which normal statuses and social structure are suspended, often dramatized as ritual death or a return to chaos; and *incorporation*, procedures that return the individual to society with a new identity, status, rights, or responsibilities, dramatized as a ritual rebirth.[17] The Zuni word for initiation was *'i:'bu'anaka*—from *bu"a*, to "blow on, initiate (a person), break (an object) in," a word that linked the exchange of sacred breath that occurred in all Zuni initiations ("blowing") with ceremonial whipping ("breaking in"), thereby encompassing the sense of both birth and death in a single term.[18]

In the course of each rite of passage, powerful symbols were presented to the initiates, usually within dramatic contexts so as to impress their meaning and structure upon them. These life or presentational symbols conveyed core values and concepts of the Zuni worldview and served as reminders of the ways the individual should follow in his or her life road. But more than that, the ritual use of such symbols dramatically interjected the mythical past into the present. They evoked powerful psychological responses, and this psychic energy, in turn, was used to foster growth and healing. As Balowahdiwa explained to Cushing, the ceremonial use of symbols "was only that you might be brought to the surface and see yourself in your relation with these the fathers, which you had not been aware of before."[19] The impact of such symbols presented under the dramatic circumstances of a rite of passage might be compared to that of a psychotherapist's interpretation offered at a key moment in a patient's therapy.[20]

Gender was also acquired through initiations. Zuni men and women were not born; they were made or cooked. Gender was a social, not a natural, attribute. One *became* a man or woman by learning male or female social forms and, in particular, acquiring symbols of gender during rites of passage. What initiations, then, did lhamanas undergo? If Zuni berdaches crossed genders to become women, then we could expect that they underwent female initiations, whereas completion of male initiations would point to male gender status. A review of these rites should make it possible to answer the question about the gender status of the lhamana.[21]

The rites observed at birth illustrate the basic paradigm of Zuni initiations and the use of gender-specific symbols. When a woman entered labor, she retired to a secluded, inner room to be attended by midwives and female relatives. The windows and entrance were carefully screened with blankets, and a downy white feather from an eagle's breast was posted to turn back unwanted intruders. Such prayer feathers were often tied in the hair of initiates or priests to indicate their consecrated or taboo state, referred to as *deshkwi*.[22]

When the infant was delivered, the midwife who happened to be assisting at that moment picked up the child and blew into its mouth, giving it the breath of life, or *binanne*. If the infant were male, the midwife's husband became the child's sponsor for initiation into the kachina society. Soon after birth, a large quantity of sand was brought into the house. This was heated and divided into two mounds. Depressions were made for both mother and child, and blankets were spread over the sand. Corn meal was rubbed on the head and face of the infant, and then mother and child reclined on the sand bed, facing East. If the infant were a boy, the paternal grandmother placed a perfect ear of yellow corn—a *yaboda*, which was called father—behind his head; if a girl, she received a *mik'abanne*, two ears of white corn that had grown together, which was called mother.[23] The child retained this personal symbol for the rest of his or her life. This sand bed was both therapeutic and symbolic. In its construction, it resembled the mound of earth that Zuni farmers built up around each seed of corn they planted. Thus, infants were not only cooked or hardened; they were also sprouted like seeds of corn. According to Parsons, "Creatures whose mothers are not thus treated are called uncooked, raw—they are the animals, the gods, Whites."[24]

At this time, a woman from the father's clan arrived with the infant's first article of clothing, a small woven blanket. Clothing was a frequently used symbol in Zuni initiations, representing the acquisition of a new social status. Significantly, this first article of clothing was not gender specific. The child and mother remained in seclusion for a total of ten days. During this time, infants were not yet considered human. They were referred to as "it" or "the new being."[25] Because infants were unripe and impressionable, warriors avoided contact with them for fear of imprinting them with traits of violence and aggression. On the tenth morning, the infant was wrapped in its new blanket. The mother, midwife, and female relatives sprinkled a path of corn meal before them and carried the newborn to a point east of the village where the break of dawn could be viewed. As the Sun Father rose above the horizon, the midwife held the child to the East and prayed for its health, happiness, goodness of heart, and long life.

Back inside the house, the infant's head was washed with yucca suds. The pottery bowl used in this rite, made by a female relative and decorated with water symbols, was given to the child. Similar bowls were presented to initiates in subsequent rites of passage. As female symbols, they reaffirmed the individual's link to the maternal origins of life and identity. "Is not the bowl the emblem of the Earth, our mother?," Cushing explains. "For from it we draw both food and drink, as a babe draws nourishment from the breast of its mother, and round, as is the rim of a bowl, so is the horizon, terraced with mountains, whence rise the clouds."[26] At this point, representatives of the father and mother's clans gathered while the child's ears were pierced, and he or she was given a name—the first of a series of names that individuals received upon completing each life transition.

Turner's three phases of initiation are apparent in these rites. Separation was effected by isolating the laboring mother in a darkened room. After birth came a ten-day period of liminality. Rites of incorporation followed in the form of presentation to the Sun Father, bathing the head with yucca suds, naming, and ear-piercing before clan representatives. The only symbols in these rites that acknowledged the sex of infants were the male or female ears of corn, and these were weakly differentiated—that is, both were types of corn as opposed to, say, a bow and arrows for boys and a grinding stone for girls.

The doubled, female ear of corn represents an important concept. Women were seen as naturally more complete than men. They gave birth to both males and females, and their milk sustained both. To Zuni thinking, they must therefore have the essence of both within them. According to Parsons, the double ear was thought of as mother and child.[27] It was an appropriate symbol for the mystery of two creating one and one giving birth to both male and female. This ability to create new life made women intrinsically sacred or *dehya*. As Tedlock notes, "Females are *tehya*, to a degree, by their very nature, but all boys must be initiated into the *kotikanne* 'Kachina Society' in order to 'save them' or 'make them valuable.' "[28] In other words, men had to develop the completion that came naturally to women. Indeed, the Zunis believed that male fetuses required a ten-month gestation while females needed only nine.[29] Men could eventually acquire life-creating capacities through religious knowledge, which enabled them to beseech the raw beings of the natural world for rain, plant growth, animal life, and other essential resources and blessings.

The male and female ears of corn and the gender symbols employed in subsequent rites were not simply signs of anatomical sex. In the Zuni view, the maturation of one's sex as well as the acquisition of a gender identity required cultural and ritual interventions in which symbols played an instrumental role. This began before birth, when parents made offerings at Mother Rock and other shrines to influence the infant's sex. Indeed, anatomical sex was not believed to be fixed until the moment of delivery. Should the mother take a nap during labor, for example, the sex of the child might change. After birth, the midwife massaged and manipulated the infant's face, nose, eyes, and genitals. If male, she poured cold water over its penis to prevent overdevelopment—"an act of kindness for his future wife," as Edward Curtis put it. If female, the midwife split a new gourd in half and rubbed it over the vulva to enlarge it.[30] The gradual acquisition of gender was also reflected in the Zuni use of kinship terms. Before the ages of four to six, gender was not emphasized as an attribute of the child, and parents and other relatives referred to children of both sexes with the same term, *cha'le'*, or child. In fact, *cha'le'* was applied to the offspring of any animal. Only later were children distinguished with such terms as *'aktsek'i*, young boy, and *katsik'i*, little girl.[31]

Most Zunis completed at least four initiations in the course of their lives, each employing increasingly differentiated symbols of gender. After birth, males underwent two ceremonies sponsored by the kachina society, while females experienced key transitions on the occasions of their first menstruation and first childbirth. The rites observed at death constituted a final rite of passage. In addition, many Zunis acquired other religious and ceremonial affiliations, such as membership in a medicine society, which also required initiation. And everyone in the village participated in annual and quadrennial ceremonies that served as community or collective initiations.

THE RITES OF MEN

Following birth, the next important transition for boys occurred between the ages of four and eight, when they were initiated into the kachina society in an elaborate communal ceremony. Held every four years in March, the proceedings were timed to culminate on a full moon, considered a propitious time for births.[32] The same pattern of separation, liminality, and incorporation that occurred at birth can be observed in these rites as well. The physical womb, however, was replaced by symbols of the womb and of the Earth Mother, while dramatizing birth first required returning to the condition that precedes birth—represented by chaos and ritual death. The entire community experienced such a state just before the final rites of this ceremony, when whipping kachinas chased villagers about the pueblo and smashed any pots and baskets that had been left outside. For the initiates, the experience of death was simulated by covering them in buffalo robes or deer skins to submerge them into womblike darkness and symbolize an animallike state of rawness. Their ceremonial sponsors then carried them on their backs into the sacred dance plaza and up a line of kachinas beginning with the six Salimobiya. Each kachina struck the boys four times on the back. By the end of the line, the initiates had received as many as forty-eight blows. In fact, the term used to refer to the whipping itself, *lhaknekana*, also meant killed.[33]

Having passed through the gauntlet of kachinas, the boys entered north kiva. There, a large sand painting depicted Kaklo, the Salimobiya, and the other initiating kachinas. One god was portrayed for each initiate, and a prayer feather donated by the boys' sponsors had been placed on the appropriate image. These were now tied to the boys' hair, and sand from the painting was rubbed on their bodies. The sponsors carried the boys back outside where they were again whipped, this time by the four Sayalhi"a kachinas. In contrast to the Salimobiya, who were considered beautiful kachinas and identified with agriculture, the Sayalhi"a were warriors and hunters, "hideous and terrible."[34]

Incorporation—the final phase of initiation—began that evening with a ceremonial feast with the gods in the kivas. The kachinas entered by climbing down the ladder head first and hopping around like frogs, that is, like raw beings. They exchanged lifebreath with the initiates—as midwives did with newborn infants. Then, the head of Kolo:wisi, the effigy representing the great water serpent, poked through the hatchway of the kiva. Water, drawn from Kolo:wisi's sacred spring, poured from the effigy's mouth, followed by a stream of corn seeds and then bundles of grass. Each boy had a pottery bowl given to him by a female relative of his sponsor, and these were filled with Kolo:wisi's sacred water. The boys also received a handful of seeds and grass. The boy and his family drank the water and sprinkled it on the corn stacked in their granary. The grass was also deposited in the storeroom, and the seeds were planted in the fields. The seeds, water, and grass symbolized the boys' future role as farmers.

The initiates continued to wear their prayer feathers and observe the dietary and other restrictions of *deshkwi* until the fourth morning after their whipping, when their sponsors carried them to a point east of the village. With the sun rising above the horizon, the sponsors removed the feathers from the boys' hair. These were planted in the ground, along with prayer sticks offered by the boys. The initiates also received new names.[35]

Thus, the boys crossed the threshold of the maternal sphere and entered the male world of the kivas and the fields. This separation from their mothers, however, did not entail the sharp break characteristic of initiation rites in many other societies. The boys were not isolated from their mothers or forbidden contact with females. In fact, female relatives of the boys' sponsors were prominent in the proceedings; as was a female kachina, 'Ahea'a, the great-great grandmother of the kachinas, who suckled Kolo:wisi in an act of propitiation just before the whippings in the plaza.[36] The continuity of male and female was also emphasized by the bowl, a female symbol, given to each initiate. Thus, Zuni initiation entailed a realignment of the original mother–child relationship rather than its repudiation, a broadening of the individual's social perspective from the outlook of the maternal household to that of the community as a whole.

Although the first initiation confirmed their male status, young men had to undergo a second initiation to reach full manhood. This occurred between the ages of ten and fourteen. Only the four Sayalhi"a appeared—called on this occasion Den'anikk'a, "they show them how."[37] The proceedings were less elaborate than those of the first initiation, and they occurred in the seclusion of the kivas.

While covered with a single blanket and a deer skin, the youths received four strokes from each Sayalhi"a. This whipping was far more severe than in the first initiation. According to Stevenson, "though every effort is made by the novices to keep silent, their smothered groans are pitiable to hear."[38]

Following this, the sponsors covered the eyes of the youths while the Sayalhi"a removed their masks. Upon opening their eyes, the youths discovered for the first time that the kachinas were actually men—relatives and neighbors. This knowledge had been kept from them until this moment, and the impact of the revelation was dramatic. It was followed by a powerful enactment of the psychological meaning of adulthood: switching roles, each initiate in turn donned one of the Sayalhi"a masks and whipped the four impersonators of the gods with their own yucca blades.[39]

Thus, the young men learned a profound secret: that kachinas were only real as symbols for various perceptions about humans and nature; that divinity was not external but an internal, psychological dimension of experience. Men became godlike when they donned masks to dance and observed the forms of Zuni religion. As Emory Sekaquaptewa, a contemporary Hopi, points out, the difference between the child's attitude toward the kachinas and that of an adult is not one of belief versus skepticism, but of unconscious belief versus conscious participation with "the make-believe world, the world of ideas and images."[40]

The themes of hunting and war were prominent in the second male initiation. It was held in the fall, the season of hunting; while the first male initiation was held in the spring, the season of planting. The Sayalhi"a, who directed the proceedings, portrayed the aggression, strength, and courage of warriors and hunters—behaviors considered raw, the opposite of the temperament needed for farming. Because they were initiated into the secrets of hunting and war, Zuni men could venture into the world beyond the bounds of the village and risk contact with such raw beings as game animals and members of enemy tribes. Men's mastery of the secrets of self-control and the ritual procedures for restoring and renewing life (what Zuni women knew intrinsically) enabled them to ensure the replenishment of the game animals they killed for food. As the Zunis put it, men who had been initiated "know how"—how to master fear, pain, and aggression; how to use ritual magic to preserve and sustain their own lives and the lives of others.[41]

The distinction between hunting and farming, as suggested by the separate initiations devoted to each, was important in Zuni religious and social life. Zunis believed that the behaviors and personal traits necessary for each were incompatible and had to be separated psychologically, conceptually, and seasonally. It was in the realm of hunting and war that men achieved the greatest differentiation from women. Conversely, agriculture was an area where gender differences were deemphasized, an ideal that was represented by the kachina most identified with farming, Kokk'okshi.

The nature of Kokk'okshi as an archetype or psychological model for Zuni men is apparent from his name—a combination of the word *k'okshi*, "be good, be obedient, be attractive," with the prefix *ko-*, from *kokko*, meaning "godly, supernatural." Being "good, gentle, attractive" was the Zuni ideal of personal conduct, appropriate traits for farmers. The Kokk'okshi kachinas usually appeared in large groups with a smaller number of female counterparts, the Kokkwe'lashdok'i, or Kachina Girls (portrayed by men). The Kokkwe'lashdok'i wore the same bearded masks as Kokk'okshi, although painted white.[42] This pair was one of the few examples of a complementary male and female version of a kachina. Their portrayal as complements emphasized the cooperative roles of men and women in growing, storing, and distributing food.

Thus, on a seasonal basis and over the course of their lives Zuni men alternated between the economic and psychological modes of farming and hunting. As hunters and warriors, they explored regions considered spiritually unsafe for women and children and engaged in behaviors considered raw and dangerous. But the primary foundation of male identity was the personality type portrayed by the farmer Kokk'okshi. And in the realm of agriculture—as opposed to hunting—the continuity of male and female genders was emphasized.

THE RITES OF WOMEN

Zunis considered women inherently complete or *dehya* because they created new life. Their sacredness was centered in their bodies. As a result, women, in effect, initiated themselves. Through menstruation and childbirth they apprehended the mysteries of life and death at their source and experienced their own rebirth. From the Zuni point of view, there was no need for society to intervene to induct women into religion. This has led many observers to conclude that the Zunis had no rites of passage for women and that women were excluded from religious life.[43] But, as Cushing noted, "women are the creators of being, and this is believed so profoundly that nothing which the women touch or make is supposed to lack, when it come from their hands, *life* in some form or other."[44] A closer look reveals that Zuni women were no less concerned with the supernatural, their lives no less imbued with ceremonialism than were men's.

As Paula Gunn Allen, a contemporary Laguna Indian, points out, the ceremonial life of American Indian women focused on continuity while men's ceremonies focused on change.[45] In large part, this distinction was due to the key transitions in women's lives, menstruation and childbirth, which were cyclical. Thus, the collective ceremonies concerned with female initiation occurred as part of the annual ceremonial cycle rather than as singular events—just as women repeated the initiations of menstruation and childbirth throughout their lives. Even so, the personal life transitions of women were not ignored. While the rites observed on these occasions occurred without the institutional frameworks that structured male religious life, they served a similar function in women's lives.

When a girl began menstruating, for example, she went to the house of a female relative of her father and ground corn for a day, returning in the evening with a bowl of stew. According to Eliade, learning and practicing women's crafts in seclusion is a common theme of female initiations. The Zunis believed that if girls worked hard at this time they would be free from menstrual problems in the future.[46] The rite focused on the value of corn and its transformation into food. In fact, women's role in providing food was central to Zuni religious life. All ceremonies included the distribution and consumption of food, and since women controlled food stores their tacit approval was necessary for religious observances to proceed. It would have been difficult for a man to fill any religious office without the support of the women of his household.[47]

Following the onset of puberty, the next significant threshold in women's lives was the birth of their first child. (Marriage was largely overlooked as a rite of passage.) In the ceremonies observed at birth, the mother was as much the object of attention as the infant. The physical and emotional extremes of labor stripped her of human identity and placed her in the proximity of death itself. If men were most differentiated from women in their role as warriors who took human life, women were most differentiated from men when they gave birth. Indeed, these functions were seen as mutually exclusive. Pregnant women avoided contact with whipping kachinas for fear of miscarriage, and men were required to leave the house when women went into labor. In the case of both men and women, however, experience with the extremes of life and death placed the individual in contact with the raw world; both required purification before they could resume normal social contact. The rites that mothers and their infants underwent dramatized this process. The bed of heated sand in which they were cooked prepared both for re-entry into society. Mothers also received a guardian symbol at this time, as did their infants: an ear of corn with three buds, symbolizing fecundity.[48]

The individual rites of passage for each woman were supplemented by household, public, and seasonal ceremonies also devoted to themes of female initiation. Three complexes of women's rites can be identified according to their supernatural patrons: White Shell Woman, patron of corn grinding, unmarried women, and sexuality; the Warrior Woman, patron of fertility and childbirth; and the Corn Maidens, spirits of the granary and figures of the sororal household administration.

Of these spirits, K'ohak 'Oka, or White Shell Woman, is the most elusive. Cushing refers to her as a "beautiful Goddess of the Ocean . . . younger sister of the Moon," and "that wicked, fabled Goddess of the White Shells." She was the "especial patroness of beauty and grace; who loved to number among her disciples the daughters of men, and like Hathor and Isis of the ancient Egyptians, imparted an attractiveness almost equaling her own, to those into whose hearts she deigned to breathe." She taught the "arts of women"—how to apply fine, white corn meal as a face powder, how to flirt with men while grinding, how to make perfect paper bread, and how to win "the most lingering of lovers." She was also the patron of trading—an economic form of intercourse. Stevenson identified her as the mother of the sun and "one of the greatest of beings." White Shell Woman was invoked in at least one important ceremony, the Lha:hewe', an elaborate and esoteric drama staged every four years in August, described by Parsons as a women's dance.[49]

Another deity sacred to women was Cha'kwen 'Oka—literally, Warrior Woman—the patron of fertility and childbirth.[50] Her ceremonies included several elements common to female initiations. Every four years, she led a ceremonial rabbit hunt at the time of the boys' first initiation. She entered the village "telling the people she will give to them the game of the world." Young women joined their brothers and fathers and followed Cha'kwen 'Oka and a group of other kachinas onto the plain west of the pueblo. Forming a large circle, the participants drove the rabbits out of the trees and overgrowth. Women tried to catch the rabbits with their hands while men used rabbit sticks to kill the fleeing animals. Whenever a rabbit was struck, the women ran from their places in the circle to collect it. According to Stevenson, "The first rabbit killed has its nose cut and is handed to the ᵗCha'kwena by a maiden, and the ᵗCha'kwena rubs the bleeding nose down her legs on the inner sides, that the A'shiwi (Zuñi) girls may hasten to arrive at the age of puberty and that they may be prolific in childbearing." Cha'kwen 'Oka then ran a straight course through the underbrush, so that the blood on her legs would rub off onto the vegetation and promote the fertility of rabbits. Later, the women collected the slain rabbits and presented them to the officers of the hunters' society.

Cha'kwen 'Oka spent the next four days at nadir kiva, "lounging on her bed, suggestive of a woman after accouchement" (that is, childbirth). Women who had lost infants and children stayed with her, and the goddess prepared heated sand beds for them. Each day, she left the kiva to bless the houses of the village and receive offerings of prayer sticks from men who desired luck in hunting and from women who wished to become mothers. In the evening she circled the village and planted food offerings, praying that Zuni women be prolific and pass safely through childbirth. The themes of fertility and reproduction, the participation of girls and women in the hunt, and the ceremonial lying-in of the goddess are all elements of female initiation. Cha'kwen 'Oka also appeared on the final night of the winter solstice ceremonies. Passing quickly through the pueblo, she blessed the houses while women poured live coals over her so that she might take bad luck away.

The gender role for Zuni women, and the symbolism and interpretations attached to that role, was not limited to biological reproduction. Women were also the managers of households, a responsibility shared with sisters and mothers that included the care of children, the distribution of food and other stored goods, and the administration of fields and lands used by the household. This aspect of women's lives fell under the patronage of the Corn Maidens (the 'A:dowa 'E'lashdok'i). The "cult of the Corn Maidens" included various public and domestic ceremonies focused on the sanctity of seed grain, the most precious possession of every Zuni household.[51]

The Corn Maiden drama, for example, was re-enacted every year at the end of the Sha'lako festival, in a rite called Mol'a:'iya, or "melons come." Young women were selected to participate in a race held east of the village, and the order in which they finished determined the sequence in which the Corn Maiden figures (portrayed by men) entered the plaza to present melons and seeds to the rain priests.[52] Women also observed a variety of domestic rites concerned with the protection and replenishment of the granaries. The "meeting of the children" was enacted when the first ripe ears of corn were brought from the fields. A matron brought forward a *yaboda* (father) and *mik'abanne* (mother) ear of corn from the granary, and the women of the household spoke greetings between the old and new corn. Similarly, during the winter solstice period, six perfect ears were taken from the granary for a rite called "Dancing the Corn."[53] These rites emphasized the importance of preserving seed for planting, maintaining food reserves, and, because seeds from the perfect ears used in ceremonies were planted separately, improving the genetic seed bank.

Even in their role as craft specialists, women's activities were surrounded with ritual. Pots, like prayer sticks, were considered to be living beings, and the feathers that women painted on their ceramics represented prayers for rain, like the feathered sticks made by men.[54] Indeed, all forms of making were homologized to the act of birth and the ability of women to create life. When a man made a tool, according to Cushing, "he brings it to the matron of his home, as household priestess, and presents it to her over the hearth, that she, being a mother, may breathe upon it and give it life, and therewith the ability to foster fertility in the works that it shall be used for doing."[55]

COMMUNITAS

Completion of the kachina society initiations for men and the experiences of menstruation and childbirth for women established their status as adults. However, many Zunis underwent another initiation when they joined one of the medicine societies, or *dika:-we'* (sg. *dikanne*). Society initiations employed the same paradigm and many of the same symbols as other rites of passage. Ritual death, however, took the form of a life-threatening illness or exposure to danger. When an individual was successfully cured by a society member, he or she made a pledge to join the healer's society.[56]

The universal insignia of society membership was the *mili*, bestowed upon completion of training for the curing orders of the societies. The *mili* was a *yaboda*, or male ear of corn, filled with seeds and elaborately wrapped with feathers. It represented *'a:wona:willab'ona*, "The Ones Who Hold the Roads," a universal category of supernaturals that included the Sun Father, Moon Mother, beast gods, the gods of war, and the corn spirits—a broader group than the *kokko* of the kachina society. The protection and blessing of these beings, obtained through society ceremonies, ensured the fulfillment of one's life road.[57]

Whereas men and women's religious observances generally occurred in different contexts and forms, medicine societies were one context where essentially the same rites were observed by both. Both men and women were eligible to join medicine societies, both could practice various healing arts, both could acquire esoteric lore. In initiation, they received the same symbol, the *mili*. In fact, the use of this symbol reveals the nature of the gender balance achieved through the medicine societies. When presented with this symbol, male initiates were told, "Receive your mother," while female initiates were told, "Receive your father."[58] In contrast, the ear of corn given at birth was addressed as a parent of the *same* sex. The *mili* could function in such a dual capacity because it represented a category of supernaturals that included both male and female beings. Underlying this practice of identifying the *mili* as the opposite sex of its owner was the principle of juxtaposing, and thereby balancing, gender differences.

The juxtaposition of gender differences was also linked, conceptually and ritually, to sexuality. This was especially apparent in the Zuni scalp dance, which was an initiation ceremony for men who had killed an enemy in battle. As a part of this rite of passage, new bow priests were required to have sex with a woman other than their wives before resuming marital relations. "Even if he is an old man he has to get a woman outside," Parsons was told. Throughout the public festivities accompanying the scalp dance, men and women commingled freely. According to Bunzel, "unrestrained merry-making accompanied by sexual license is indulged in by young and old of both sexes." The Zunis referred to this as *waha*, an onomatopoeic term for laughter.[59] Men were most differentiated from women in their role as warriors. But during the scalp dance this polarization was channeled toward the generation of sexual energy, which became a means of renewing social bonds. This form of sexuality, however, should not be confused with the themes of procreation and fecundity emphasized in so many other ceremonies. In the scalp dance, sexual energy was evoked simply for its value in drawing men and women together—an example of what Victor Turner calls communitas, social bonds expressed in their most rudimentary form.[60]

Sexuality was not the only means of mediating gender differences. In the kachina society, differences were often minimized or combined, as in Kokk'okshi and his female complement, while those who participated in kachina ceremonies observed long periods of sexual continence. The ceremonial calendar accommodated both of these modes of gender mediation by assigning the medicine societies to the winter months, and linking the themes of sexuality and violence associated with their rituals to the goal of renewal; while during the summer months, when the minimization of differences was part of the seasonal theme of reverence and moderation considered necessary to ensure the blessing of rain, only kachina ceremonies were performed.[61]

The procedures followed at the death of an individual constituted a final rite of passage. Paternal kinswomen prepared the body for burial—just as women of the father's clan assisted at birth and other rites of passage. But while burial rites in many ways paralleled other initiations, their intent was the opposite: they were meant to release the individual's spirit from social identity, rather than to add to that identity. The body was bathed with yucca suds and rubbed with corn meal, as was the newborn infant; but it was placed so that the deceased faced West to Sacred Lake, instead of East. A single downy eagle feather was tied to the hair and the body was dressed in new clothes as in other initiations, but a gash was cut in each garment to allow the spirit of the dead to escape.[62]

Within a few hours, male clan members buried the body at the churchyard. The family then proceeded to the river bank West of the village with various offerings—another reversal, since offerings during other rites of passage were taken East. They sprinkled sacred corn meal with the right hand and black meal with the left. This served to "darken" the road of the dead so that the spirit could not find its way back to Zuni. The family buried the deceased's personal possessions, kachina mask (if any), and prayer sticks in three excavations. Returning to the house, they all drank warm water for purification and had their heads washed with yucca suds. If the deceased owned a *mili*, it was returned to the appropriate medicine society and dismantled. The feathers were used to make a prayer-stick offering, and the seeds were distributed for planting.

The spirit, or *binanne*, of the deceased hovered about the village for four days, then proceeded to Sacred Lake. The name of the deceased was never used again. The Zunis simply said "he who was."[63] The spirits of the dead periodically returned to Zuni, however, wearing clouds as their masks. They were especially likely to visit during kachina dances. When clouds appeared on the horizon, Zunis told their children, "There goes your grandmother," or "Our grandfathers are coming." Indeed, the words for ancestors and rain were often used interchangeably. As Ladd notes, "they are only representatives of different spiritual manifestations of the total pattern."[64] Thus, as Dennis Tedlock explains, "Death, or 'the end of the light,' undoes the effects of both human and personal history, eventually returning the person to the raw world." As a raw being, the individual lost the trappings of personality acquired in the course of a lifetime. Zuni burial rites facilitated this transition from a cooked to a raw state. Death was not the end of existence but merely a change of identity.[65]

THE THIRD GENDER

As these initiations and their symbols reveal, the Zunis distinguished between biological sex and gender identity. Gender was established by specific ritual experiences and encounters with gender-specific symbols. For men, this entailed a gradual evolution out of an original maternal ground common to both males and females. For women, cooking occurred as a process of self-actualization, marked by the physiological transitions characteristic of their bodies. The three female patrons—White Shell Woman, Warrior Woman, and the Corn Maidens—indicate the range of social and psychological potentials that were open to them. Finally, certain ceremonies and religious groups provided means for both men and women to balance and, temporarily, neutralize gender differences, just as each ritual rebirth was preceded by a return to a more total, raw, and, therefore, pre-gendered, mode of being.[66]

One's identity as a Zuni could never be reduced to a fixed gender. The social and religious experiences of both men and women modulated across a range of gender positions and identities. Gender was, in many cases, situationally determined. If a medicine man were called to assist at childbirth, for example, he was temporarily referred to as "grandmother"—since men technically were not allowed to be present at births. Men could also identify with female roles by portraying female kachinas.[67] Similarly, because Stevenson fulfilled male social roles, the Zunis gave her male prayer sticks to plant.

With this in mind, ascertaining the initiations that lhamanas received holds the key to understanding their gender status. According to Parsons, boys with berdache inclinations underwent the first male initiation "just like other boys," even if they had already been identified by themselves and others as berdaches. But they did *not* receive the second male initiation. In other words, the lhamana was an "unfinished" male. Because he received the boys' first initiation, he could participate in some male activities, like kachina dancing, men's crafts work, and even farming, but not in those activities that were the theme of the boys' second initiation: warfare and hunting.[68]

At the same time, We'wha could not undergo the rites of passage specific to women because those depended on biological functions he did not possess. Even so, it is likely that he learned a certain amount of women's lore and ritual and joined female members of his household when they observed domestic rites. And since he did not give birth he was not subject to the taboos that required the periodic separation of women from men. Thus, he could move freely in both male and female social worlds. The lhamana was, in functional terms, a nonwarrior or nonaggressive male, a crafts specialist rather than a primary producer, an individual who combined elements of male and female social, economic, and religious roles.

The Zuni concepts of raw and cooked also explain the puzzle of the pants. Since individuals became raw again when they died, the pants put on We'wha beneath his dress symbolized his raw state, which was that of a biological male. The dress, over the pants, symbolized his cooked state: a man who preferred crafts and domestic work. The entire body was then wrapped in a blanket, an allusion to the nongender-specific symbol bestowed at birth. This is an example of the symbolic value of clothes among the Zunis. Clothes reflected the composite of social and economic statuses, religious affiliations, and gender identity that made an individual a cooked person. As American Indian psychologist Terry Tafoya points out, "Our clothing, hairstyle, jewelry, etc., comprise a complex communication that informs others of how we should/ought/must relate."[69] The social significance of clothing is illustrated in the many Zuni tales in which poor or lowly characters are transformed through the acquisition of fine clothes. New clothing was often given to medicine society initiates.[70] So the dress that We'wha wore in daily life, as in the case of women in general, was more a matter of social convention than personal preference. As an "unfinished male," he was not eligible to wear male symbols. But the fact that We'wha was a man was never denied by his family or community—as the pants placed on him beneath his dress illustrate.

The answer to the question "Was We'wha a man or a woman?" is "Neither." That is, the sequence of initiations and social experiences that served to "cook" berdaches did not correspond to the sequence by which either men or women were "cooked." We'wha represented a third possibility in the Zuni organization and representation of gender—a third gender status.[71] In this light, the problem of the transsexual or gender-crossing model becomes clear. The man who becomes a woman contributes to society as a woman. But the berdache made unique contributions, as we have seen in the case of We'wha and as we will see in the next chapter. Society benefited by having three, instead of two, genders.[72] Such an organization of gender geometrically increased options for individual identities and behaviors. In addition to opposite-sex and same-sex orientation, for example, some Zunis were sexually oriented toward the third gender. Similarly, variance from sex-role norms was not always a matter of imitating an "opposite" sex. Men and women who occasionally performed tasks uncharacteristic for their gender might be described as *lhamanaye*, that is, "being berdache." Having such a reference point makes it possible to recognize *combinations* of gender traits and does not require the either–or pigeonholing of a dual gender system.

Western images of men and women are not as flexible. A biological, not a social, definition of gender continues to inform both popular and scientific thinking. But being male biologically and "acting like a man" are not necessarily the same thing. In Zuni philosophy, one's status as a man, woman, or berdache was a product of culture, the result of cooking, while gender balance, the possibility of combining or temporarily adopting roles and experiences of more than one gender, was a desirable end for all Zunis. Berdaches were not branded as threats to a rigid gender ideology; rather, they were considered an affirmation of humanity's original, pre-gendered unity—representatives of a form of solidarity and wholeness that transcended the division of humans into men and women. The third gender role of the berdache was one of native North America's most striking social inventions.

6

Two-fold One-kind

ALTHOUGH ZUNI MEN AND women began from the same raw material, they differentiated as they went through life. Because some of these differences were mutually exclusive, the potential arose for too much division between genders. Yet Zuni berdaches, who represented a third gender, were both and neither men and women. In Zuni myth and religion, this paradox was represented by the kachina called Kolhamana—a name derived from the word for berdache with the prefix *ko-*, referring to the *kokko* or kachinas. This mysterious and powerful being reconciled social differences and thereby contributed to the balance of the whole community.

DANCE OF THE ENEMY ANCESTORS

Every four years in late November, the berdache kachina appeared with a special group of supernatural beings—the Kan'a:kwe. With their own priests, chiefs, and warriors, the Kan'a:kwe kachinas were distinct from the Zuni gods of Sacred Lake. Shaking their turtle shell rattles and intoning a somber chant, they arrived from the south and filed across the narrow footbridge spanning the Zuni river (Figure 25). Villagers crowded onto the housetops, eager for the first glimpse of their "enemy ancestors"—for the Kan'a:kwe had once battled the Sacred Lake kachinas in a mythological war, and their ceremony was a rite of propitiation and appeasement. It was one of the most important and elaborate of all Zuni dances.[1]

The costumes of the Kan'a:kwe were unique. They wore white ceremonial blankets tied at both shoulders to form a long robe.[2] For this reason, they were sometimes called the *kokko k'ohanna*, or White Gods. Helmet-shaped masks covered their heads, and their eyes were shaped like tadpoles. Checkered blocks of white and black, and multicolored bands, representing the Milky Way and the rainbow circled their faces. Their ears were made of corn husks, and they had pointed snouts for mouths. Collars of spruce stuffed with popped corn circled their necks.

As they crossed the footbridge, three additional figures could be seen. These were Sacred Lake kachinas, captives of the Kan'a:kwe, and first among them was the berdache kachina, Kolhamana, a role once performed by We'wha.[3] According to Stevenson,

> *He wears the woman's dress of black, embroidered in dark blue, and caught at the waist with a red woven belt. A white embroidered sash passes from the left side of the waist to the right shoulder, where it is tied, the embroidered ends falling. A piece of white commercial cotton hangs over the back. The neck and arms, which are exposed, are painted white; the hair is parted from the forehead down the back of the head, and one side is done up over a wooden form, while the other side is tied with red and blue yarn and left hanging. The mask covers only the face. A rattle of deer scapulae is carried in the right hand, and three ears of corn, tied together with yucca ribbons and te'likinawe, are carried in the left.*

Stevenson adds that Kolhamana sometimes carried a quiver of arrows on his back and, instead of corn, a bow and arrows in his left hand (Figure 27).[4] The other two captives—Sayalhi"a, a warrior god, and the Koyemshi clown, 'Itsebasha—followed.

The Kan'a:kwe and their captives circled the village and proceeded to south kiva. During the night, the Kan'a:kwe warriors administered ceremonial whippings to anyone desiring protection from bad dreams. The next morning they danced in each of the four plazas, in a double file suggestive of the U-shape formation used by Zuni hunters to drive game.[5] In fact, the Kan'a:kwe were famous for their skill as hunters. After a feast in south kiva, the gods appeared four more times in the central dance plaza. Late in the day, they returned a final time, laden with gifts of game, produce, and precious feathers. Standing face to face with the Zuni rain priests, they exchanged a series of prayers. The Koyemshi accepted their gifts and carried them to the priests. A boisterous public giveaway followed, with the Kan'a:kwe calling out, "I give, I give, I give!," as they hurled gifts of food and household goods to the eager Zunis. That evening, after the departure of the gods, the rain priests carried cooked game meat to the river, offerings to the Kan'a:kwe, "who are angry gods, and must be appeased."[6]

BIRTH OF THE BERDACHE

The berdache kachina, as the first of the captive gods, had a central role in the Kan'a:kwe ceremony. This role, along with Kolhamana's origin, are described in the Zuni origin myth. As Table 1 shows, each episode of this myth combines social, economic, and life-cycle themes that were periodically dramatized in collective and individual rites of passage. An analysis of the mythological accounts of the berdache kachina, therefore, promises insight into the religious and psychological dimensions of third-gender status. The discussion that follows examines in detail the two episodes in which the supernatural man-woman appears, beginning with the origin of this unique being.

The events resulting in the birth of the supernatural berdache occur midway in the origin myth, as summarized in Appendix 1. Up to this point, the myth has related how the Zunis' ancestors emerged through the four underworlds to the surface of the earth and were gradually "cooked" (that is, acquired cultural forms) in the course of their migrations. But now the process of differentiation from the natural, or "raw," world, creates internal, social differentiation. The episode begins as the Zunis halt their migrations, and one of their leaders asks them to choose between two eggs—one a beautiful, blue egg; the other a homely, plain egg. Half choose the blue egg and half the plain one. A brightly plumed macaw hatches from the homely egg, while an ugly, black crow, the bane of farmers, hatches from the blue one. Those who choose the macaw egg—the Macaw People—travel to the south and never return, becoming the Zunis' "lost others." Those who choose the crow egg continue the search for the Middle Place, their descendents becoming the present-day Zunis. At this stage of their development, the primordial

TABLE 1. Correspondences of the Zuni Origin Myth

Episode[a]	*Mythical Figures*	*Social Themes*	*Economic Themes*	*Life Cycle Rites*		
				Men	*Both*	*Women*
UNDERWORLD	Sun Father	Rain priests Bow priests			Birth rites	
EMERGENCE	Divine Twins Plant or insect helper	Division of tribes			Birth rites	
COOKING	Witch Corn Maidens	Matrilineal household	Agriculture		Birth rites	
BIRTH OF THE GODS	Brother and sister First-born (Kokk'okshi) Koyemshi	Kachina society	Agriculture	1st boys' initiation		Grinding
WAR OF THE GODS	War Gods Kan'a:kwe Cha'kwen 'Oka Sayalhi"a Koyemshi Kolhamana	Hunting-war societies	Hunting	2d boys' initiation		Childbirth
FINDING THE MIDDLE						
Return of the society people	Boshaya:nk'i Beast Gods	Medicine societies	Hunting		Medicine society initiation	
Testing the middle	Waterskate				Winter solstice	
Corn maidens	Corn Maidens Bayadamu		Agriculture		Mol'a:'iya Lha:hewe	
Flood	Kolo:wisi Brother and sister				Burial rites	

[a]These headings correspond to those used in the synopsis in Appendix 1.

Zunis are unable to differentiate further without splitting into separate communities.

A brother and sister, children of a rain priest, are now selected to lead the way to the Middle Place. The couple proceeds ahead of the migrating Zunis and, reaching a mountainside, stops for a rest. While the sister sleeps, the brother is seized with passion and violates her. When the sister awakens, she immediately gives birth to ten supernatural offspring. According to versions of this episode recorded by Cushing, Stevenson, and the ethnographic photographer Edward S. Curtis, the mythical man-woman is the first of this progeny. "From the mingling of too much seed in one kind," Cushing relates, "comes the two-fold one-kind, *'hlámon*, being man and woman combined."[7] The birth of the supernatural lhamana is followed by that of the nine Koyemshi clowns.

The firstborn, however, is not initially identified as Kolhamana. In fact, Stevenson and Curtis identify this figure as Kokk'okshi. The costuming of the Kolhamana kachina lends support to this association. Kolhamana wears the same blue-green half-mask as Kokk'okshi and has a Kokk'okshi dance kilt draped over the shoulder. The arms are painted white like Kokk'okshi's female counterpart, Kokkwe'lashdok'i. The implication is that Kokk'okshi, as the firstborn, represents an undifferentiated state of gender that is actually preliminary to that of the kachina berdache, whose full development is related in the next episode of the myth.[8]

The occurrence of sibling incest represents a premature, and unsuccessful, attempt to overcome difference—in this case, by a union of related or weakly differentiated opposites.[9] The outcome is a further separation of genders, achieved through the implementation of the incest taboo. The sister, enraged by her brother's assault, separates herself from him by drawing a line in the earth through which the Little Colorado River flows. She becomes Komokatsik, Old Dance Woman, and with her firstborn, she goes to live in Kachina Village beneath Sacred Lake. She is the patron of the kachinas, and the supernatural berdache serves as her deputy. The brother, on the other hand, becomes the Great Father of the nine Koyemshi and remains with his sons on the mountain opposite the site where he embraced his sister, "midway betwixt the living and the dead"—that is, between Kachina Village and Zuni. They assist the spirits of the newly dead on their journey to Sacred Lake and attend to the kachinas when they travel to Zuni. According to Cushing, the Koyemshi and their "sister elder, man-woman of the Kâ'kâ [*kokko*]," were born and "fitted" to cherish the kachina gods and other customs.[10] Thus, the episode ends, unlike the previous episode involving the choice between eggs, with the institution of a new source of social integration, the kachina society, which offsets the potential for fissure created by the growing specialization in social roles.

The placement of the sister and her berdache firstborn in the "house" of the kachinas, and the brother and his sons in the liminal realm between Sacred Lake and Zuni reflects the actual arrangement of Zuni society. Women were the guardians of the home, and berdaches, like the mythical firstborn, remained members of their mothers' households. Brothers, on the other hand, balanced responsibilities to their mothers with responsibilities to their wives. They were in an intermediate position, metaphorically between households and between the village and the raw world beyond. The specialization of Zuni men in religion reflected this arrangement. Because men were loosely bound to village and household, they were closer to the supernatural realm beyond.[11] This enabled them to intercede with the spirit world on behalf of their community and develop an outlook that transcended households to encompass the whole of society. Furthermore, through marriage and through their participation in religious institutions, men became the bond that linked otherwise independent households. This was the reverse of patrilineal (and many bilateral) societies, where the exchange of women as wives linked descent groups. Although Zuni men were not "exchanged," the Zuni tendency toward serial monogamy effectively resulted in their "circulation."[12]

In matrilineal societies like Zuni, men had a special interest in their sisters' reproduction. Her children, not his, continued the family line and ensured the economic viability of the household. This, combined with the need for ongoing cooperation in the management of their shared household, fostered close brother–sister relationships. Older brothers represented the interests of their sisters and mothers in matters of business, while sisters often consulted brothers before husbands on important decisions. Zuni children were encouraged to form relationships of mutual respect and support with opposite sex siblings from an early age.[13] In such a social organization, a psychological need arises in men for a clear distinction between interest in a sister's reproductive career and sexual interest, between thinking about a sister having children and thoughts of having sex with her. This was accomplished at Zuni through a conceptual separation of reproduction and sexuality.[14]

The offspring of the mythic brother and sister symbolize this distinction. Though nonreproductive, they are nonetheless highly sexual. As Cushing relates, "Neither man-children nor woman-children they! For look now! The first was a woman in fulness of contour, but a man in stature and brawn. From the mingling of too much seed in one kind, comes the two-fold one-kind, *'hlámon*, being man and woman combined—even as from a kernel of corn with two hearts, ripens an ear that is neither one kind nor the other, but both! . . . Not so with her brothers; in semblance of males, yet like boys, the fruit of sex was not in them! For the fruit of mere lust comes to naught, even as corn, self-sown out of season, ripens not."[15] Yet, as the farmer Kokk'okshi, the first-born stimulates fertility by cultivating fields, and the Koyemshi, although they lack the "seeds of generation" (the men who portrayed them tied strings around their foreskins to symbolize this), stimulate fertility by bringing seeds in their fawn skin pouches and by a powerful love charm that makes people crazy with lust. In their antics between kachina dances, they displayed an exhuberant pansexuality.[16] As these associations suggest, both sex and cultivation in Zuni thought were conceived of as means of stimulating the inherent and self-contained reproductivity of women and the Earth Mother. In fact, the same Zuni word, *doye*, refers both to planting and sexual intercourse.[17]

Whereas the Koyemshi are seedless and unripe, the first-born berdache is double-sexed, like a single ear of corn with "two hearts"—the *mik'abanne*, or female, ear of corn. In other words, like women, the supernatural berdache has within him the seeds of both maleness and femaleness, but unlike women, as Cushing suggests, both seeds ripen within him. The firstborn, in other words, is not half-man and half-woman, but two complete beings in a single form—the "two-fold one-kind"—with not only the psychological characteristics of a man and a woman but the physical strength of both as well. And where the clowns portray an excess of sexual energy that makes little distinction in object choice, the man-woman portrays a self-contained form of sexuality that does not need to project a heterogeneous other to find completion.[18]

The Koyemshi and berdache firstborn represent forms of sexuality and gender that are unrelated to reproduction. They are still intermediate types in the evolution of gender, however. (Two of the

Koyemshi, for example, wear simple women's mantas; the others wear male dance kilts of the same material and color.) And while they lack the female ability to create life independently, as do all men, they still retain female potency and the ability to stimulate fertility in others. Furthermore, because they manifest the pregendered wholeness of humankind's original condition, they are able to mediate as well as mark cultural differences.

Thus, the incest episode triggers a process of male differentiation only partially realized in the figures of the firstborn and the Koyemshi. Their gender status might be compared to that of the Zuni boy who has undergone the first male rite of passage, stressing the themes of farming, but not the second initiation, with its themes of hunting, warfare, and self-control. Male differentiation continues in the next episode of the origin myth, when the Koyemshi and the firstborn are supplemented by two additional, more sharply defined figures—the fully developed berdache, Kolhamana, on the one hand, and the hunter-warrior, Sayalhi"a, on the other.

WAR OF THE GODS

In a story recorded by Bunzel, a Kan'a:kwe kachina tells the priests of Zuni, "We are other people, we are dangerous."[19] The true identity of these "other people" comes into focus when we consider all the variants of the Kan'a:kwe story (see Table 2). They are, variously, the Black Corn, Black Crow, Black God people, who are sometimes called the White Gods and the White Corn people. The Zunis of the Middle Place, on the other hand, are presumably the ones who chose the crow egg and are also, therefore, *kakkakwe* or Crow People.[20] At Sacred Lake, they acquired the customs of the *kokko*, or kachinas, and became *kokkokwe* or kachina people. Then they battle the Kan'a:kwe, who are also called Crow or Raven People. In short, the Kan'a:kwe are alter egos of the Zunis themselves, as the frequent puns made by Zunis on the words *kakka* and *kokko* suggest.

The interchangeability of the Kan'a:kwe and the Zunis points to the psychological nature of the origin myth, for such ambivalence is typical of unconscious projections. The analytical psychology of Jung, who frequently drew on his studies of world mythology, provides a useful approach for interpreting such material. As Jung

TABLE 2. Kan'a:kwe Synonymy

Variant	*Translation*	*Clan*	*Village*	*Source*
Kia'nakwe, Kok'ko ko'han, Mi'kianakwe	White People, White Gods, White Corn People	Corn	Kia'makia	Stevenson, "Zuñi Indians," 36–39, 43–44, 217, 356
Kwin'nakwe	Black Corn People	Black corn	He'shota'yälla	Ibid., 44–45
Kwal'ashi kwin'na	Black Raven People		(On mountain near Sacred Lake)	Ibid., 135
	Snail People		K'iá-ma-k'ia-kwïn	Cushing, "Zuñi Fetiches," 21
Kwínikwa-kwe	Black People	Black corn	Héshotayálawa	Cushing, "Outlines," 424–25
K'yámak'ya-kwe	Snail Beings (gods of the Black People)			Cushing, "Outlines," 426
Kâ'kâ-kwe	Raven (egg) People	Winter people		Cushing, "Outlines," 386
Ky'ánaqe			(near Ojo Caliente)	Curtis, "Zuñi," 121
Kókko	Raven People		Ky'ámakya	Ibid., 173
Kyanakwe		Black corn	Heshato yalla	Parsons, "Origin Myth," 142
Kwi'nakwa		Black corn	He'cotäyalakwin	Bunzel, "Zuñi Origin Myths," 579, 582, 601
Koko a:kwinne	Black (Crow) Kachinas		(near Sacred Lake)	Ibid., 601; Bunzel, "Zuñi Katcinas," 925
Käna:kwe			Kämakä	Bunzel, *Zuni Texts*, 165–84

Notes: Heshoda Yalla, or House Mountain, is a ruin near Ojo Caliente, fifteen miles southwest of Zuni pueblo. Hanlhibinka is approximately fifteen miles west of this site. The ruin of Ka'maka (fr. "snails" or "shells") is located forty miles directly south of Zuni.

points out, "The contents of the unconscious, unlike conscious contents, are mutually contaminated to such a degree that they cannot be distinguished from one another and can therefore easily take one another's place."[21] The presence of unconscious material in the Zuni myth, from the Jungian psychological perspective, means that a process of individuation is at work—a reaching for self-awareness and self-realization that typically begins as an eruption of unconscious impulses and images. In the case of the Zuni myth, this is a "collective individuation," the self-realization of the Zunis as a people who acquire individuating forms of culture. This is described metaphorically as an emergence from the underworld of the unconscious and the raw into the light of self-awareness and the social world of cooked beings. However, the journey to the Middle Place—the Zuni mandala of wholeness—is fraught with danger. As the incest episode reveals, the primordial Zunis must find ways of incorporating and balancing the polarizing tendencies of social organization and human personality. The greatest risk is the overvaluation of consciousness and the denial of the unconscious. In Jung's words, when the separation of opposites is carried to the point "that the complementary opposite is lost sight of, and the blackness of the whiteness, the evil of the good, the depth of the heights, and so on, is no longer seen, the result is one-sidedness, which is then compensated from the unconscious without our help."[22]

In the Zuni origin myth, this danger first arises when the people are asked to choose between the two eggs. Discrimination is critical to consciousness, yet the outcome of this initial choice between opposites is a complete break. The Crow People continue to the Middle Place and the Macaw People are "lost" to the south. In psychological terms, the desirable qualities symbolized by the macaw egg are split off from the undesirable qualities of the crow egg—the unconscious with its lack of differentiation and its unholy conjunctions of good and evil. Two forms of personality result—ego or conscious identity, represented by the ideal of *k'okshi*, and the unconscious, all that is not chosen, the "lost other." But aspects of human personality consigned to the unconscious cannot be left behind. They dog the ego, becoming a "shadow," in Jung's term, that can manifest unpredictably in the form of irrational behavior and unconscious projections. "Lost others" can return, as they do in Zuni myth, in the form of menacing figures like the Kan'a:kwe, the Black Gods from the south.

The episode begins when the Zunis leave their sanctuary at Sacred Lake to renew the search for the middle. Two clowns of the

Newe:kwe society are told to go ahead and find a trail—or, in other versions, to hunt. Encountering a pair of women, they kill and scalp them, a dramatic instance of how unconscious impulse can erupt without warning. This incident points to the key moral problem of the Kan'a:kwe episode: how hunting for the purpose of obtaining food sustains human life, but in excess leads to war and death. Mediation between life and death is a central concern of the Zuni origin myth. According to anthropologist Claude Lévi-Strauss, this is a particular problem for the Zunis because they understand the origin of human life in terms of the model of plant life, or emergence from the earth, and this leads to a contradiction. "Agriculture provides food, therefore life; but hunting provides food and is similar to warfare which means death."[23] Consequently, as we have seen, hunting and farming were strictly separated, seasonally and ritually, by the Zuni ceremonial calendar.

At a psychological level, the problem is how hunters and warriors can also be *k'okshi*—good, gentle farmers who nurture and create life; how, in other words, the separation between conscious and unconscious, represented by the choice between the eggs, can now be bridged. The murder of the women results, in Lévi-Strauss's terms, from *"overstepping the boundaries of hunting"*—hunting for humans instead of animals.[24] The implication is that Zuni men, as farmers, are not properly prepared to engage in hunting. Without the lesson of self-control conveyed in the second male initiation, they become a threat to human life. Such excess occurs whenever specialization is carried too far. For example, the mythical Kan'a:-kwe, having corraled all the deer, antelope, and elk in a box canyon, are able to live easily and exclusively on game. This state of affairs negates agriculture—for if game can be "harvested" at will, why bother with growing corn in a desert? However, the myth reveals that overdependence on hunting leads to territorial conflicts and war.[25]

Upon the murder of the two women, the Kan'a:kwe attack the Zunis and a war results. Day after day the battles rage on, but neither side can win. The Zunis are unable to resume their search for the Middle Place and achieve the goal of social and psychological integration until three Sacred Lake kachinas are transformed, thereby transforming the structure of society itself. This occurs through the agency of the forbidding figure who leads the Kan'a:-kwe—Cha'kwen 'Oka, the Warrior Woman.

MOTHER TERRIBLE

Encounters with projections of the unconscious are often comparable to a battle. Conflict, sometimes a metaphorical death, precedes every growth in self-knowledge. "Confrontation with the shadow," Jung notes, "produces at first a dead balance. . . . Everything becomes doubtful."[26] The image of Cha'kwen 'Oka leading the enemy gods is an especially frightening projection. She is a "demoness," an "Ancient Woman . . . deathless of wounds in the body," who cries out shrilly as she paces before her forces.[27] Hunting was the one realm of production exclusive to Zuni men—but Cha'kwen 'Oka takes over even this field of activity, denying the primacy of agriculture.

Cha'kwen 'Oka is a female counterpart to the murderous clowns. She carries the principle of female creativity and self-sufficiency to a level of excess equal to theirs. In her, unrestrained life-giving becomes a defiance of death. Furthermore, by withholding her fertility as the "keeper of game" and closing the wombs of the creatures in her dominion, she denies life to others.[28] Just as an overemphasis on maleness results in hostility by men toward women, Cha'kwen 'Oka represents an aspect of femaleness hostile to men. She is, for all purposes, a female berdache. That is, although she appears female, she manifests male behaviors and lacks female reproductive functions. The blood of a dead animal must be rubbed on her legs to simulate menstruation. Similarly, while she assists at births, she herself does not bear offspring. She has the power, however, to stimulate the fertility of others, both animal and human.[29]

That this figure, as she appears in the Kan'a:kwe story, is a male projection of a negative mother image becomes apparent when her actual ceremonial appearances at Zuni are considered. Since, according to the myth, she was defeated by the twin War Gods, she did not appear in the quadrennial Kan'a:kwe dance. But the Warrior Woman did appear every year during the winter solstice to bless the houses and every four years to lead her ceremonial rabbit hunt. As the patron of female fertility and childbirth, she is an entirely different figure from the goddess portrayed in the Kan'a:kwe story, reflecting the divergence that can exist in male and female perceptions of an archetype within a given society.[30]

Cha'kwen 'Oka's counterparts in Western civilization include such Greek figures as Athena, a goddess of war who is also associated with the crow; Hekate, a goddess of death; and Artemis, a huntress who, like Hekate, aids women in labor. Morrigan is a related Celtic figure—a goddess of death who turned into a raven. Archaeologist Marija Gimbutas has traced many of these figures to pre-Indo-European images of the Great Goddess, who, like Cha'kwen 'Oka, encompassed childbirth, motherhood, and a manifestation Gimbutas refers to as the Mother Terrible. As Paula Allen explains, the creative power of such goddesses is intellectual and spiritual, as well as biological. "To assign this great being the position of 'fertility goddess' is exceedingly demeaning: it trivializes the tribes and it trivializes the power of women. Woman bears, that is true. She also destroys. That is true. She also wars and hexes and mends and breaks. She creates the power of the seeds, and she plants them. . . . Central to Keres theology is the basic idea of the Creatrix as She Who Thinks rather than She Who Bears, of woman as creation thinking and female thought as origin of material and nonmaterial reality."[31]

To understand the Mother Terrible aspect of Cha'kwen 'Oka, it is helpful to consider some of the social and familial experiences unique to matrilineal culture. To begin with, Zuni fathers were not authority figures for their children—a role more often filled by a maternal uncle. As a result, fathers were viewed as benevolent and affectionate figures, like the Sun Father, a passive and benign supreme being who rarely interfered in human affairs. Indeed, because the bond of husband and wife was so often temporary, fathers were interchangeable and, therefore, readily available—whether as biological fathers, stepfathers, adopted fathers, or ceremonial fathers. The bond of mother and child, on the other hand, was permanent, and both nurturing and authority were in the mother's hands. "Mother," however, was not a single individual, but a set of sisters addressed with kinship terms that meant "mother," "little mother," and "elder mother" who might even breastfeed each other's babies.[32]

Compared to patrilineal and patriarchal families, matrilineal arrangements were less likely to trigger what Freud called the

Oedipus complex and what Jung referred to as the mother complex. According to anthropologist David Schneider, "In patrilineal descent groups, the stronger the authority of the husband over his wife and the father over his children, the stronger the compensatory affective bond is likely to be between the mother and her children"—that is, the more likely the mother was to form emotionally controlling, overprotective relationships with her children and to project onto them her own ambitions and needs.[33] In such circumstances, no other choice but rejection of the mother image seems possible if psychological independence is to be achieved, especially for male children. As Nancy Chodorow has pointed out, this type of family organization creates male fear and resentment of women.[34]

In contrast, matrilineal families tend to encourage strong bonds of affection between children and fathers; and neither Zuni parent was an omnipotent figure. The fairly equal distribution of maternal care in Zuni households forestalled the inflation of the parental image that often underlies personality disorders in patriarchal families. Furthermore, as we saw in the previous chapter, adulthood for matrilineal men did not require a repudiation of the mother. Rather, as the origin myth suggests, one incarnation of the mother is replaced by another—the benevolent Kachina Mother of Sacred Lake giving way to the Warrior Woman, who, following her defeat in the war of the gods, is replaced by the Corn Maidens, representatives of the wives and sisters who were the significant others in the lives of adult men.[35] In short, the multidimensional images of women in Zuni culture allowed for more than one resolution of the encounter with the Mother Terrible and more than one form of male identity. Variations in male psychological development were supported by the various configurations of the mother archetype that might be encountered through identification and in dreams, fantasies, projections, and rituals.

Many psychologists have blamed the mother complex for such presumably pathological variations in sexuality and gender as homosexuality, transvestism, and transsexualism. An anthropological perspective allows us to see psychological dynamics as culturally specific. The Zuni approach to gender, sexuality, and child-rearing discouraged both parent and child from forming obsessive fixations, while the mother image was a broader social and psychological type. Yet variations such as berdaches still occurred. In fact, Zuni mythology reveals that berdache identity has its own inner meaning—a function, as we will see, of its connection to a powerful archetype of wholeness. Obviously, a re-evaluation of the assumed link between mother complex and sexual object choice is in order.

Nonetheless, Cha'kwen 'Oka represents dynamics in matrilineal families that hinder the development of male identity. Psychologically, the Warrior Woman must be overcome—or, rather, rendered an ally instead of a foe (for it was as an ally that Cha'kwen 'Oka appeared during her rabbit hunt and the winter solstice to bless women with fertility and men with luck in hunting). This is the significance of the captivity of the three Zuni kachinas that occurs next in the Kan'a:kwe story: it symbolizes the experience of containment by a mother who stifles growth and independence.[36] In the origin myth, the Warrior Woman is finally defeated not by superior numbers or weapons but through the wisdom of the Sun Father, who tells the War Gods the real location of her heart. Likewise, it was through the acquisition of knowledge, especially religious knowledge, that Zuni men were able to continue their psychological growth. By participating in the kachina society, they transcended the maternal household and established independent relationships to the larger community and the universe as a whole. Similarly, infantile incest fantasies were resolved by transfering sexual interest in sisters to a wife, with the close matrilineal brother–sister relationship providing a model for marriage relations.

Unlike other males, the lhamana did not leave the maternal household to marry. This does not mean that his psychological development was arrested. In a belief system that considers the female gender primary and inclusive, the occasional male who retains this wholeness is a normal occurrence. At the same time, given the special dynamics of brother–sister relations in a matrilineal society, it becomes clear that homosexual orientation was key to the smooth integration of a male "sister" in the sororal household. Any potential sexual complications of such an arrangement were avoided in the case of the homosexual berdache, who was not sexually interested in women. Psychological growth for the berdache did depend, however, on his ability to incorporate the male side of his personality in a way that did not disrupt the female domestic scene. This, in part, is the significance of the taming of Kolhamana that occurs at the climax of the Kan'a:kwe episode.

CAPTIVE GODS

Cha'kwen 'Oka blocks the progress of the migrating Zunis and produces a stand-off. Out of this crisis arise compensating and uniting symbols, unconscious at first, but ready to emerge when the opposing forces have exhausted themselves. This is the role of the three gods—Sayalhi"a, the Koyemshi clown, 'Itsebasha, and Kolhamana—captured by Cha'kwen 'Oka during the battle between the gods. They become, in effect, go-betweens. Their appearance alters the equation just enough to break the stalemate.

The capacity to mediate is a function of the pivotal positions these figures occupy within the sacred geography of the Zuni world. As hunters and warriors, the four Sayalhi"a regularly encounter aliens and raw beings in the world beyond the village. They stand at the boundaries of nature and culture, with their violent behavior only marginally socialized. The Koyemshi operate in the realm between Zuni and Sacred Lake, the living and the dead, the natural and supernatural. The berdache firstborn, assigned to live with his mother in Kachina Village, mediates the realm of social differences—the divisions of male and female, hunting and farming, sexuality and reproduction.

The double nature of these figures makes them appropriate candidates for contact with aliens—indeed, to be transported into the lair of the enemy.[37] Each is capable of communicating—and identifying—with both sides of an opposition. The two-sided nature of these gods also gives them the potential to be two-faced—to betray as well as to bridge, to do evil as well as good. The Sayalhi"a, for example, bring the meat of game animals, and this sustains human life, but as warriors they also take life. Similarly, the Koyemshis' satire can be hilarious—until one becomes the target of their jokes. While society benefits from the presence of such figures, they also represent a potential threat to social order. In the Kan'a:kwe episode, this danger is offset when each of the captives receives a symbolic scar—a metaphorical initiation that marks them as "for the collective." Such "scars of distinction," as Terry Tafoya explains, "served as teaching patterns to remind us of lessons. They maintain these 'differences' as a signal to the rest of us of how to respond to them."[38]

The scarring of the Sayalhi"a kachina is briefly described in a folk tale recorded by Benedict. Blue Kan'a:kwe captures Sayalhi"a by hitting his horn with an arrow that leaves a hole in his mask.[39] Thus, the fearsome warrior and hunter is not only wounded; he is left with a permanent mark of defeat. This compromise was reflected in the costuming of the Sayalhi"a kachina who appeared in the Kan'a:kwe ceremony. He wore a large reddish-brown deerskin, with an emblem of the Sun Father on the back, and carried a bow and arrows. Unlike his other appearances, however, he did not carry yucca for whipping. Instead, he had a turtle-shell rattle in his right hand and prayer sticks in the left, and his body was painted pink with clay from Sacred Lake.[40] These symbols of the ancestor–kachina cult served to balance Sayalhi"a's hunter–warrior temperament. At the hands of the Kan'a:kwe, the dangerous and warlike qualities of Sayalhi"a were rendered safe for inclusion in an agricultural order.

The Koyemshi clowns, on the other hand, are dangerous because they violate social norms. Their weapon is satire, the purpose of which, as Robert Graves points out, "is to destroy whatever is overblown, faded and dull, and clear the soil for a new sowing."[41] But role reversal and satire can go too far—even clowns need the lesson of self-control that is a part of the second male initiation. This is the implication behind the transformation of the captured 'Itsebasha. According to Cushing, 'Itsebasha's nature is to be "lively and cheerful," although he has also been described as "the one who is always looking for quarrels." But when captured, he begins to cry "until his eyes were dry utterly and his chin chapped to protrusion." His "mouth is still drawn with crying." This makes 'Itsebasha a sad clown; in fact, his name means "the Glum." He is a happy being with a mournful face; his satire effectively restrained.[42]

The potential for excess in the lhamana role is suggested by the bow and arrows carried by Kolhamana in conjunction with the mask of the farmer, Kokk'okshi. This constitutes a drastic reversal of the firstborn's original assignment as the deputy of the Kachina Mother at Sacred Lake. Neither lhamanas nor Kokk'okshi kachinas normally associated with the activities or symbols of hunting and warfare. But Kolhamana leaves his mother's home to join the other male kachinas in the war against the Kan'a:kwe. This adventure culminates in a dramatic face-to-face encounter with the Mother Terrible.

According to Stevenson's version, when the Kan'a:kwe require the prisoner gods to appear in a dance celebrating their capture, the firstborn defies the Warrior Woman, becoming angry and unmanageable. His behavior is contrary to the *k'okshi* ideal—in fact, it brings the entire proceedings to a halt. Bickering, arguing, infighting—all are antithetical to the proper spirit for a ceremonial occasion. And so, Cha'kwen 'Oka has Kolhamana dressed in female attire, telling him, "You will now perhaps be less angry."[43] This dressing is a domestication in two senses of the term. The dress signifies the berdache's socioeconomic status as a domestic worker and crafts specialist. At the same time, it serves to domesticate his temper by bringing him into alignment with his true self. It is interesting to imagine the impact of this story on a young lhamana. It explains the custom of adopting the dress, the supernatural origin of the status, and the assignment of berdaches within the social order. Most importantly, it contains a warning against excess and holds forth the ideal of *k'okshi* not only for men and women, but for berdaches as well.

The implication of the Stevenson and Curtis versions is that previous to this capture, the firstborn did not wear a dress. Does a specific historical development underlie the adoption of this practice? Harriet Whitehead has observed that an individual free to engage in any activity of either sex would have an enormous advantage in accumulating wealth and prestige—to grow corn *and* hunt, to assume leadership roles in religious and political life *and* in the household, to produce male *and* female crafts.[44] Stevenson's account suggests that the social imperative behind the berdache's dress is the need to circumvent the potential opportunism of his role by visibly marking his alignment with the female household and, conversely, his exclusion from the male realms of hunting and war.

Recalling that the Zuni word for initiating, *bu"a*, also means "to break (an object) in," the wounding or "breaking in" of the captives can be viewed as a rite of passage. In the case of Sayalhi"a and 'Itsebasha, initiation is administered by the Kan'a:kwe warriors. Kolhamana, however, is initiated by Cha'kwen 'Oka herself, by means of the dress she bestows, much as initiates of the medicine societies are given new clothes as part of the rite of passage. As a lesson in self-control, the dressing has an effect similar to the scars that Sayalhi"a and 'Itsebasha experience and the whippings administered in kachina society initiations: it serves to realize the full development of the berdache personality and the acquisition of an adult superego. Kolhamana emerges from this encounter bearing the sharply differentiated symbols of male and female, hunting and agriculture—powerful oppositions united in a single personality.

This completes the saga that began with the emergence of the Zunis in a raw, pre-gendered state and ends with the definition of four distinct male types, represented by the Kokk'okshi, Sayalhi"a, Koyemshi, and Kolhamana kachinas. The captives emerge from their odyssey with new capabilities for social and religious contributions to Zuni society.

By suspending the normal distinctions of age and gender, key forms of stratification in Zuni's otherwise egalitarian society, the Koyemshi and Kolhamana help to provoke states of liminality essential to the ritual expression of communitas. At the same time, they are also spirit guides capable of showing individuals and the community as a whole the way through this marginal terrain to new levels of social and psychological integration.[45] Like Joseph Campbell's hero, they become masters of two worlds, what Turner calls "liminal *personae*" or "threshold" people.[46] They appear at critical ritual and life-cycle junctures to usher the individual from one identity to another, from conscious to unconscious and back. The Sayalhi"a appeared as such in the boys' initiations, and the Koyemshi fulfilled a similar capacity when they attended to the kachinas during their dances. Then there is Kolhamana, representative of berdaches like We'wha, who could associate with men in the kivas and mix just as freely with women in the sanctum of the female household.

Kolhamana's ritual function occurred in the Kan'a:kwe dance

itself, when he carried the symbols of that drama's central oppositions. In this capacity, he was more than a role model for berdaches. As an archetype, Kolhamana was relevant to all Zunis, a ceremonial and psychological entity who could link the male and female side of every personality.[47] To men, in particular, the supernatural berdache represents the possibility of a psychological growth that does not lose touch with its female ground, just as Cha'kwen 'Oka reveals to women the ground they share with men. And while the goddess is displaced by heroic male challengers, Kolhamana wears her dress and carries her bow and arrows. He is her deputy. At the same time, Kolhamana is a more conscious being than Cha'kwen 'Oka. He is "tamed"—that is, less possessed by unconscious impulses. And where Cha'kwen 'Oka represents a single, primitive gender that seems to allow no possibility of independent male identity, in Kolhamana, male symbols are consciously brought forward and balanced against female symbols.

Out of the confrontation between shadow and consciousness, new symbols of unity emerge. The war of the gods concludes with the release of the corraled game animals, representatives of psychic energy. The Zunis tell them, "We have opened for you the doors of the world; . . . you will no longer be imprisoned within the walls, but have the whole world before you." The boon of psychological wholeness is the freeing of creativity and spontaneity. This dispersion of "animal instinct" to the six directions evokes the Zuni mandala representing the diversity of life suspended about the self, or "middle place," in dynamic equilibrium. Similarly, Kolhamana bears symbols of difference to reveal underlying unity. Bridging the interval between the maternal household and the male realm of fields and mountains, and balancing the self-indulgence of the Koyemshi with the self-control of Sayalhi"a, Kolhamana contributed a corrective influence upon the ruptures of social specialization and helped liberate individuals from the painful moral dilemma of the opposites. The result, as celebrated in the dance of the Kan'a:kwe, was a profound healing, a reconciliation of the most fundamental rift that divides human from human—gender.

ARCHETYPE AND COUNTERPART

For Jung, the archetype of the hermaphroditic or divine child, deputy of the great mother goddesses of the Old World, unites sacred and profane, god and man. The "hermaphrodite . . . represents and suffers the discord of the elements, and at the same time brings about the union of the Four and besides that is identical with the product of the union." The hermaphroditic child born of this conjunction of opposites "exactly corresponds to the psychological idea of the self, the product of conscious and unconscious."[48] But Kolhamana is no mere by-product of a male–female union of opposites. In Zuni mythology, this third principle is there at the beginning, coeval with the emergence of male and female. Although the potential for integration represented by the hermaphrodite remained for Jung merely symbolic, Zunis saw the concrete actualization of this figure in the lhamanas they encountered every day; it was an aspect of both inner and outer life.[49]

As the social counterparts of the double-sexed spirit guide, berdaches moved freely in both male and female social worlds and, as a result, helped both men and women reach greater understanding of each other and themselves. This was the role that We'wha filled—as a gatekeeper for the village who could meet outsiders on their terms yet return undaunted to the traditional values of his tribe. The high status of berdaches in Zuni society reflected the desirability of the union-that-transcends-genders. But what the lhamana achieved in social life, every Zuni could achieve in his or her psychological life—the harmonizing discourse of genders and their cross-fertilization, through cooperation in economic production, religion, sexuality, and family life.

Western civilization, in contrast, has lost almost all memory of the social counterpart of the divine-child archetype, including its potential contributions. Until quite recently, most psychological theories regarding gender and sexual variance considered traits like cross-dressing and homosexuality in isolation, as symptoms of a disturbed relationship to one's mother or to an image of women in general. The Zunis, on the other hand, attributed berdaches with a multidimensional personality that expressed important aspects of an archetype of wholeness. Adult berdaches who had undergone the sequence of life-cycle rites specific to berdaches were just as mature or "cooked" as men who became farmers and hunters. Their personalities took shape at a very young age, at about the same time that most children acquired notions of being either male or female. Certainly, the tenacity of berdache identity once crystalized was just as strong as that of male or female identity. More than a "preference" or "orientation," berdache personality entailed a complete constellation of skills, attitudes, and behaviors. And as We'wha's life illustrates, berdaches were fully capable of achieving the strong ego identity, originality, and active inner life characteristic of adult individuation and personality development.

Jung came close to the Zuni view of the third gender when he noted two exceptions to the rule that men must free themselves from the anima fascination of the mother to achieve psychological growth: artists and homosexuals. Regarding homosexuals, he wrote, "The psychological findings show that it is rather a matter of incomplete detachment from the hermaphroditic archetype, coupled with a distinct resistance to identify with the role of a one-sided sexual being. Such a disposition should not be adjudged negative in all circumstances, in so far as it preserves the archetype of the Original Man, which a one-sided sexual being has, up to a point, lost." Jung describes this personality type in terms that could be applied easily to We'wha:

> *A man with a mother-complex may have a finely differentiated Eros instead of, or in addition to, homosexuality. . . . This gives him a great capacity for friendship, which often creates ties of astonishing tenderness between men and may even rescue friendship between the sexes from the limbo of the impossible. He may have good taste and an aesthetic sense which are fostered by the presence of a feminine streak. Then he may be supremely gifted as a teacher because of his almost feminine insight and tact. He is likely to have a feeling for history, and to be conservative in the best sense and cherish the values of the past. Often he is endowed with a wealth of religious feelings, which help to bring the* ecclesia spiritualis *into reality; and a spiritual receptivity which makes him responsive to revelation.*[50]

What has Western civilization lost by its apparent lack of a counterpart to the berdache—by, indeed, bending every social institution to the task of stigmatizing gender mediation? More than the waste of individual potential that suppression entails, there is the loss of the berdache spirit guide who serves men and women alike with the insights of the intermediate position. This raises the question whether men and women today can ever achieve mutuality and wholeness as long as men who manifest qualities considered feminine, and women who do the same in male realms, are seen as deviants to be criminalized and stigmatized. Fear of being associated with this deviant status stands before every man and woman who would seek psychic integration, regardless of emotional and sexual orientation.

The matricentric archetype of the berdache represents a personality just as well adapted to its social context as the Oedipal type is to the culture of marketplace competition and individualism. But whereas the patriarchal pattern stresses the divergence of genders, projecting mother and father as exclusive categories pitted against each other, the matricentric pattern emphasizes the continuity of genders and views male individuation as an outgrowth or specialization, rather than a rejection, of the mother. Given the increasingly ominous implications of what Jung termed the hypermasculinity of the patriarchal hero, Kolhamana represents possibilities of male identity and gender reconciliation that Western societies can no longer afford to ignore.

7

They Left This Great Sin

In 1892, the Pueblo Indian agent received another in the series of missives written by Mary Dissette in her unstinting campaign for "law, order and morality" among the Zuni Indians. The only Zunis who could be hired to do laundry, she complained, were the tribe's berdaches, and "we would sooner do our own washing than have those unsexed mysterious creatures around." The agent replied sympathetically. "It is going to be quite a task to do away with their custom of the men wearing female dress, but I have made up my mind to make an effort to do so."[1] While we have few direct reports of the impact of agents, missionaries, and teachers on Zuni berdaches, the evidence makes it clear that the "disappearing" of this role was part of a larger campaign against tribal patterns of sexuality and gender. Indeed, in the history of the conquest and occupation of the New World, sexual politics have played a prominent but overlooked role, intimately tied to the transfer of native lands and resources into European and American hands.

THE SEXUAL POLITICS OF CONQUEST

In August 1550, fourteen of the Spanish empire's most eminent scholars and officials convened in the city of Valladolid to debate a moral question that had brought the machinery of conquest in the New World to a grinding halt: Were Spain's wars against the natives of America just? Fearful that the King's own Catholic conscience was in danger of moral blemish, all expeditions had been suspended until the question could be resolved.[2]

For the Spaniards, whose passion for legal and moral rectitude was unique among the European colonial powers, the question of just war against the Indians turned on the nature of the Indians themselves. Were they rational beings? Or were they intrinsically inferior, beneath the Spaniards in not only intellectual and social capacity but in moral terms as well? If the Indians were irrational, then their conquest and enslavement could be justified as an extension of the Spaniards' natural superiority, much as humans were justified in domesticating animals. Indeed, conquest would be incumbent upon good Catholics as part of their obligation to bring all pagans to the light of God's favor.

To argue these issues, two of the leading scholars of the day were called before the King's judges—Juan Ginés de Sepúlveda, renowned Latinist and historian, and Bartolomé de Las Casas, former missionary turned advocate for Indian welfare, then in his seventy-sixth year. In exhausting presentations lasting nearly a month, the question of native sexuality was a central issue. Sepúlveda argued that war against the American Indians was justified because of their patent irrationality, and as chief evidence he cited their practice of sodomy. "How can we doubt that these people—so uncivilized, so barbaric, contaminated with so much profanity and lewdness—have been justly conquered?" Sepúlveda asked, concluding, "It is not only lawful to subject them to our domination in order to bring them to spiritual health and true religion through evangelical preaching, but they can be chastised with even more severe war."[3]

Reports regarding native sexuality had been flowing back to Spain since the time of Columbus. As the debate on just war took shape, allegations of immorality, particularly sodomy, became increasingly sensational. In 1525, when a bishop and former missionary accused the Carib Indians of being "sodomites more than any other race," King Charles I condemned the entire tribe to slavery. The following year, royal historian Gonsalo Fernández de Oviedo y Valdés began publishing widely distributed treatises claiming that the "abominable sin against nature" was universal in the New World. Noting the spread of syphilis among the Indians, the author coldly observed, "See how just is what God gave him where such a thing is done." Another Spaniard, having observed berdaches in ceremonial roles, concluded, "The devil held such sway in this land that, not satisfied with making them fall into so great sin, he made them believe that this vice was a kind of holiness and religion."[4]

It was in this period that the first northward thrusts of Spanish imperialism reached the American Southwest. In 1540, when Francisco Vásquez de Coronado and Hernando de Alarcón proceeded from Mexico by land and sea, respectively, in search of the fabled seven cities of Cibola, they dutifully inventoried the sexual proclivities of the natives they encountered along the way. "At this place the old man showed me as something amazing," reported Alarcón, who visited tribes along the lower Colorado River, "a son of his dressed as a woman and used as such." Pedro de Castañeda, on the Coronado expedition, also noted the presence of berdaches and described various tribes as *grandes someticos*, or great sodomites—ammunition for a debate being staged thousands of miles away in Spain.[5]

Europeans were not only more restrictive regarding sexual expression than the New World natives they encountered, they had a long history of regulating sexual behavior for political ends. The Spaniards, in particular, during their long wars against the Moors, had come to consider themselves superior to non-Christians with respect to sexual practices. Their mores, emphasizing ascetic self-control and the limitation of sexual outlets, were a point of honor, enhancing the Spanish sense of cultural identity. By the time the Spaniards arrived in the New World, they had well-developed legal mechanisms for the suppression of homosexual behavior. According to legislation issued in 1497, sodomy was second in seriousness only to heresy and crimes against the person of the king. Conviction by circumstantial evidence was permitted, and punishment was death by burning. "Behind all this," concludes Francisco Guerra, "was the Spanish hate of Arab morals" inflamed by "the finding of *bardajes* in Moslem areas."[6]

Spanish suppression of homosexual practices in the New World took brutal forms. In 1513, the explorer Balboa had some forty berdaches thrown to his dogs—"a fine action of an honourable and Catholic Spaniard," as one Spanish historian commented. In Peru, the Spaniards burned sodomites, "and in this way they frightened them in such a manner that they left this great sin." Back in Spain, the Council of the Indies, the official body responsible for administering the colonies, promulgated special regulations for the prohibition of sodomy in the New World, while the religious orders drew up new catechisms and confessionals to help missionaries uncover and punish native homosexuality. These efforts resulted in an almost complete "disappearing" of berdaches throughout the Caribbean (where most of the native population was also eliminated), Central America, and parts of South America. As historian López de Gómara noted in 1552 while listing the benefits of conquest, "There is no longer sodomy, hateful sin."[7]

The first contact between Zunis and Europeans was marked by conflict over differing values regarding sexuality and the status of women. In 1539, Fray Marcos de Niza and Esteban, the black Moor who had accompanied Cabeza de Vaca on his trek across North America from Florida to Mexico, were sent to reconnoiter the northern frontier of New Spain. Esteban arrived at the Zuni village of Hawikku several days ahead of the friar. Though he had been welcomed by other tribes along the way, the Zunis were suspicious and hostile. According to Coronado, Esteban made the fatal error of assaulting Zuni women, "whom the Indians love better than themselves." The Zunis killed the Moor on the spot, cut his body into pieces, and sent his bones to neighboring tribes with the message that the Christians were mortal, and if any more of them appeared they should be killed. "If they did not dare to do it they should notify them [the Zunis] and they would come and do it themselves."[8]

In New Mexico, conflicts arising from the Spaniards' attitudes toward women and what they considered native licentiousness continued throughout the colonial period. Yet references to sodomy are almost entirely absent from the surviving records of the time. This is explained partly by the transformation of Spanish colonial policy that occurred in the years between Coronado's expedition and the arrival of Juan de Oñate in New Mexico in 1598 with the first Spanish colonists. After Valladolid, a consensus emerged that Indians were indeed rational beings, "not demented or mistakes of nature, nor lacking in sufficient reason to govern themselves." To wage war against them, as Las Casas argued, was "iniquitous, and contrary to our Christian religion." And so, Philip II issued a new ordinance in 1573 moderating the Spanish engine of conquest.[9] Access to Indian land and tribute was placed firmly under royal control, and a centralized, byzantine bureaucracy was devised to protect these prerogatives. These measures removed the incentive for accusing Indians of immorality.

The absence of berdaches in the official records of colonial New Mexico is also related to the cultural opaqueness that characterized the Spaniards in general. Throughout their centuries of contact with Indian communities, Spaniards remained oblivious to all forms of native culture. For them, the Indians did not represent a lower form of civilization, but the absence of civilization altogether. Their missionary program was intended to fill this void, not replace one cultural system with another.[10] Furthermore, the Spaniards were concerned with specific sexual acts, not the context in which they occurred. In many cases, it is difficult to tell whether or not their reports of sodomy involved berdaches. The fact that one partner occupied a separate gender status and dressed partly or completely in women's clothes was often overlooked or mentioned only in passing.

Even the friars who lived in or near Indian villages paid little attention to native social life. As one bishop noted after visiting New Mexico in 1730, although "there are many who have been in residence eighteen or twenty years, . . . they are as alien as if they had no dealings with the said Indians."[11] When missionaries did encounter berdaches, they were often at a loss to comprehend their behavior. Franciscans at the mission of Santa Clara in California, for example, thought berdache cross-dressing was a ruse to slip in among the women and "sin" with them. Other Spaniards assumed that cross-dressing was a form of punishment imposed upon convicted sodomites.[12]

And so, in colonial New Mexico charges of sexual immorality were more often raised by one Spaniard against another and usually in the context of conflict between civil and religious authorities.[13] This does not mean, however, that the Pueblo Indians escaped efforts to alter their marriage and sexual practices. The Franciscan missionaries persistently enforced heterosexual monogamy, resorting to whipping and other forms of corporal punishment.[14] Furthermore, whenever circumstances threatened the position of the church in New Mexico, the campaign of morals was renewed, along with demands for increased allocations of political and economic power to combat the alleged evils. Such was the case between 1659 and 1661, when Governor Bernardo López de Mendizábal began to encourage the Pueblos to resume kachina dances as a means of undermining the influence of the missionaries. The friars responded with a barrage of new charges regarding licentiousness and obscenity, and even allegations of infant sacrifice connected with these dances.[15] In fact, the severity of Spanish rule and the efforts to stamp out kachina dances were key factors in provoking the Pueblo Revolt of 1680. Following the successful expulsion of the Spaniards, the leaders of the rebellion ordered that "they burn the temples [churches], break up the bells, and separate from the wives whom God had given them in marriage and take those whom they desired."[16]

The impact of the Spanish missions is evidenced by the abandonment of matrilineal descent in several Rio Grande pueblos; by the outward conformance to various Christian rites, including marriage; and by the secrecy with which the Pueblos learned to shroud traditional religious observances, a secrecy that seems to have shielded berdaches as well. As one New Mexican noted in the early 1800s, "The doors of the estufas [kivas] are always closed to us."[17] But reliance on official documents alone can be misleading. While Spanish authorities may have overlooked berdaches, the rural Hispanic population of New Mexico was quite aware of such individuals, and they coined a term to refer to them—*mujerado* (literally, "made woman"). This term, apparently used only in the American Southwest and specifically for berdaches, reflects the either–or classification typical of a Western dual-gender system, which requires that berdaches be characterized as substitute or counterfeit women. It appears in an 1823 census of the Tewa pueblo of Tesuque in the name of a male potter—pottery being normally a female craft—one Juan Felipe Amejerado. In the 1850s, *mujerado* was in use at the Keres pueblos of Laguna and Acoma.[18]

Although the full story of the interaction between Pueblo and Hispanic culture has yet to be told, it seems clear that the Spaniards did not seriously attempt to eliminate berdache practices in New Mexico as they had done earlier in Central America. Located at the northern frontier of Spain's vast American empire, ringed by tribes of nomadic raiders, the colony's survival depended on a military and economic alliance with the Pueblos. In this compromise, Pueblo berdaches, along with religion and social customs, went "under cover," evading the crusade of morals until the late nineteenth century, when the spotlight of official concern once again focused upon them.

THE AGENTS OF ASSIMILATION

Under the Americans, the colonial discourse on native sexuality took a new form. The antislavery movement had convinced many Americans that all races were descended from Adam and Eve and, therefore, all people were equal. In this view, cultural differences were explained in terms of social evolution. Indians occupied a low position on the scale of development, while Anglo-Americans represented its pinnacle. Advancement meant that Indians had to abandon tribal customs and look and act like white Americans—and so the government implemented the policies of assimilation.

Sexual diversity was considered one sign of lower social development. In fact, the response of Victorian Americans to native sexuality, like the response of the Spaniards before them, exposed a central contradiction in their belief system. The Spaniards had used the allegation of immorality to justify what their morals otherwise prohibited—mercenary conquest. The Americans used the same charge as an excuse to adopt paternalistic and colonial policies toward their "brothers" of the red race that contradicted their beliefs in equality, autonomy, and democratic process. But in the nineteenth century no one questioned the violation of civil liberties involved in the government regulation of sexual behavior or pointed out the conflict between government-financed Christianization and the constitutional separation of church and state.

In 1883, the Office of Indian Affairs issued a set of regulations that came to be known as the Code of Religious Offenses or Religious Crimes Code. Certain ceremonies were banned outright, along with the destruction of property during mourning rites, the "purchasing" of wives or mistresses, plural marriages, and native healing practices. Indians who refused "to adopt habits of industry, or to engage in civilized pursuits or employments" were deemed vagrants subject to arrest and punishment. Until the late 1920s, Indians were jailed, penalized, and denied rations to enforce the Religious Crimes Code, while individual agents, far from Washington's supervision, often devised additional standards of their own.[19] The impact of these policies on Indian communities was traumatic and disruptive. Most North American societies were organized around kinship (as opposed to economic) relations, which were structured by a set of rules regarding gender roles and sexual behavior. By interfering with native sexuality, the agents of assimilation effectively undermined the social fabric of entire tribes. One consequence was a lowering of the status of women, especially among matrilineal and matrilocal tribes, a development that had a negative impact on berdaches as well.[20]

The Pueblo Indians, however, unlike the militarily defeated Plains tribes, were politically and economically self-sufficient. This independence limited the government's ability to impose its policies on them, explaining, in part, why the use of morals charges to justify coercion assumed such a prominent role in the history of Southwest Indian affairs. Another reason has to do with Victorian attitudes toward sexuality and privacy. While Spanish missionaries had been willing to look away when the Indians observed traditional rites and customs, the Anglo school teachers, government officials, anthropologists, traders, and settlers who began visiting and living near the Pueblos had little regard for exclusion and sanctity. Where secrecy had discouraged Spanish curiosity, it now fueled a characteristically American need to know.

As the archbishop of Santa Fe wrote in 1898, "On account of this secrecy, many have been induced to believe that these dances must be unbecoming."[21] One such critic was the historian Adolph Bandelier. In an 1890 report, Bandelier repeatedly referred to "obscene rites," "gross obscenity," and "shockingly obscene" dances among the Pueblos. The physical anthropologist Aleš Hrdlička, writing in 1908, was more specific. "There are reasons for believing that obligatory defloration of marriageable girls, promiscuous sexual intercourse, and possibly even pederasty (ceremonial) still take place occasionally in a few of the tribes."[22] Despite the fact that these "secret dances" were, by definition, secret, there was no shortage of testimony regarding what was supposed to occur in them.

The more that Anglos realized that aspects of Pueblo Indian life were hidden from them, the wilder their fantasies became. They did not doubt that Indians would do in private what they, as members of a sexually repressed culture, would do—engage in sexual activities. As a result, the phrase "secret dance" acquired sensational overtones.

This process began at Zuni in 1897, when Nordstrom and Dissette used morals charges to secure military intervention. A similar set of circumstances developed between 1914 and 1919, when Pueblo Indian Agent Philip T. Lonergan, like Nordstrom, became involved in several confrontations with native Pueblo leaders.[23] Lonergan became convinced that the traditional Pueblo governors and religious officers were obstacles to government policies and had to be replaced. Given the theocratic nature of this leadership, he knew that weakening its authority required discrediting native religion as a whole. In 1915, he began writing to local Anglos and Hispanics, soliciting statements regarding the "secret dances" of the Pueblos. "I want the entire facts stated so they will impress the Indian Office sufficient that I can get authority to put an end to these damnable doings," he instructed his informants. Elsewhere he added, "Please go into detail without any squeamishness."[24]

The eight statements collected by Agent Lonergan alleged acts "so bestial as to prohibit their description"—"a carnival of promiscuous carnal indulgence," according to one informant, in which men chased women and, according to another informant, imitated "the motions or acts of sodomy." The antics of Pueblo clowns were singled out for condemnation. In one case, Indian women had been seen pretending to kiss a clown's penis. Lonergan forwarded these letters to Washington, describing them as statements "concerning practices of secret dances." In fact, the incidents described all occurred outside the kivas and were neither secret nor, strictly speaking, even dances. Nonetheless, Lonergan requested authority and funds to use his police to "put an effectual end" to these rites. As he wrote in his annual report for 1915, "The only policy to pursue is to entirely prohibit these dances and if necessary destroy the kivas."[25] Although an inspector was dispatched and additional charges of immorality filed, the Indian Office saw little to gain by a morals campaign at this juncture, and Lonergan's report languished in Washington.[26]

Another report on Pueblo morality was compiled in 1920 and 1921, when Indian Office inspectors were sent to investigate reports of a dispute between Indians, missionaries, and government employees at Hopi.[27] One of these inspectors, E. M. Sweet, Jr., was himself a minister and clearly sided with the missionaries. With their assistance, Sweet secured a sheaf of affidavits from Christianized Hopis and government employees reviling Hopi religion and morals. "I am telling these awful things about the old ways of the Hopi Indians," one apostate Hopi testified, "only because I have become a Christian and I want these evil things known to the Government in order that they may be stopped." Again, it was alleged that dances and ceremonies were occasions for sexual license—"free love," as one Hopi was quoted as saying—and the bawdy antics of Hopi clowns were described as if the acts they mimicked actually occurred. Sweet submitted testimony in the form of four "exhibits" intended to explain the strife at Hopi and establish the existence of "unprintable and unspeakable immoralities."[28] Two exhibits contained statements from Baptist and Mennonite Hopis. One included statements from local whites. The fourth exhibit was a copy of Lonergan's 1915 report. How Sweet obtained this is not clear.

What lay behind the charges of immorality collected by Lonergan and Sweet? Those with any factual basis were, in most cases, related to the performances of Pueblo clowns. Clowns appeared at all Pueblo villages to entertain onlookers between dances in the outdoor plazas. To the Pueblos, their antics were something less than ritual but more than entertainment. Despite their best efforts to shield these performances from outsiders (by ordering all whites out of the village, posting guards, closing roads, and staging ceremonies in remote areas), Anglos sometimes saw clowns mimicking sexual acts to the hilarity of their audiences.[29] Such behavior would easily pass today's film and television censors, but in Victorian America sex was not represented in public discourse in any form, humorously or seriously.

THE SECRET DANCE FILE

In the early 1920s, political developments changed the attitude of the Indian Office toward reports on Indian morality. The Commissioner of Indian Affairs and the Secretary of the Interior began to experience the same frustrations of which field agents had long complained. No longer were their directives unquestioned, their policies exempt from public debate. And so, like Nordstrom, Lonergan, and Sweet, they turned to charges of immorality to bolster support for their assimilationist policies, resurrecting reports that had once been dismissed as the excesses of overly enthusiastic subordinates. The result was a national debate over sexual morality centered upon a mysterious collection of documents known as the "secret dance file."

This controversy originated as a result of efforts to settle longstanding land disputes in New Mexico. Since the American takeover, the Pueblo Indians had suffered a steady loss of the land granted them by the Spaniards and confirmed in treaties between the United States and Mexico. By the 1910s, Anglo and Hispanic settlers had expropriated so much Pueblo land that the economic viability of several villages was threatened. In 1922, Secretary of Interior Albert Fall, who later figured in the Teapot Dome scandal, and New Mexico Senator Holm Bursum introduced a bill intended to resolve title disputes once and for all. To their surprise, the measure met with widespread opposition from a coalition of such traditional charitable organizations as the Indian Rights Association (IRA), along with women's clubs, private philanthropists, artists, writers, anthropologists, and other "friends of the Indians," and a new organization, the American Indian Defense Association (AIDA), founded by John Collier.[30]

The campaign against the Bursum bill was the first major battle for John Collier in his career as an Indian rights activist. One of the most quixotic and influential political figures of twentieth-century America, Collier had absorbed the vision of Walt Whitman and the politics of the Russian anarchist Peter Kropotkin in his youth. In the 1910s, he plunged himself into New York's flourishing Bohemian scene, associating with artists and radicals like Emma Goldman, Margaret Sanger, Bill Haywood, Isadora Duncan, John Reed, and Lincoln Steffens and debating the latest trends in art, politics, mysticism, feminism, psychoanalysis, and sexual liberation at Mabel Dodge's famous salons. Collier became a convert to ideals of cultural pluralism and the aesthetics of primitivism after his first visit to Taos Pueblo in the winter of 1920. "Here was a reaching to the fire-fountain of life through a deliberate social action employing a complexity of many arts. . . ," he later recalled. "These men were at one with their gods."[31]

The patent unfairness of the Bursum bill made it an easy target for the publicity that Collier's forces unleashed in the fall of 1922. Equally significant was the formation of the All Pueblo Council, a body that served to unite and coordinate Pueblo response to the government. In November 1922, 121 Pueblo delegates adopted a declaration against the Bursum bill that Collier broadcast nationally. Not since the Pueblo Revolt of 1680 had the New Mexican villages acted with such concert. By February 1923, the bill was a dead issue, and Collier was looking for a way to switch from a defensive to an offensive campaign against the policies of assimilation.

The issue that provided this opportunity was rooted in a routine communication to Indian agents from Commissioner Charles Burke released over two years earlier. Devoted to the subject of "Indian dancing," Circular 1665 urged agents to control native ceremonies with "degrading tendencies" through "educational processes" or, if necessary, "punitive measures."[32] There is no evidence, however, that Burke was aware of Sweet's "exhibits" on the Hopis at this time. The circular refers only to agents' recent annual reports and the practices of Plains Indian tribes. It was little more than a routine restatement of long-standing policies, and its issuance in April 1921 passed largely unnoticed.

The "dance order" became a national controversy in February 1923, when Burke released a supplement to the circular that incorporated recommendations from a series of missionary conferences. These recommendations called for even greater restrictions on Indian dances, including a ban on participation in any dance by Indians under the age of fifty. They also suggested that "a careful propaganda be undertaken to educate public opinion against the dance." Burke quoted these recommendations and noted that they "agree in the main with my attitude outlined in Circular No. 1665." Only "lawful and decent performances free from excess" were to be allowed. To avoid the use of "arbitrary methods," however, he enclosed a "Message to All Indians" intended to explain his policy. "What I want you to think about very seriously," the Commissioner intoned, "is that you must first of all try to make your own living." Too many Indians were neglecting "home interests" by attending dances.[33] A brief reference to the Hopi snake dance reflected Burke's recent review of Sweet's exhibits.[34] The message ended on an ominous note. "I could issue an order against these useless and harmful performances, but I would rather have you give them up of your own free will," Burke wrote, adding, "If at the end of one year the reports which I receive show that you . . . reject this plea, then some other course will have to be taken."

Unlike the original circular, this supplement received widespread publicity and provoked a storm of protest—especially in New Mexico, where the local economy benefited from an annual influx of tourists eager to witness Pueblo Indian dances. Others objected on the grounds that Burke's supplement infringed on the religious freedom of Indians. The IRA, on the other hand, quickly endorsed the dance order and came to Burke's defense. Concern over Indian morality was a natural extension of its long-standing commitment to assimilation. While Burke began to equivocate under the barrage of adverse publicity, the IRA's staff—Herbert Welsh, its venerable president and founder, Matthew K. Sniffen, and Samuel M. Brosius—became preoccupied with the morality issue. "When a public official is making an earnest effort to eradicate practices that are immoral and degrading," wrote Sniffen in a pamphlet issued that May, "it is almost incomprehensible that he should be severely condemned for so doing."[35]

It was at this point, in the rush to defend the dance order, that the "secret dance file" was deployed. Soon after the supplement was issued, the Indian Office loaned the original file of Sweet's "exhibits" to the IRA.[36] The organization was quick to seize upon the publicity value of this material and copied the entire file. Over the next two years, the IRA conducted what Collier termed a campaign of "subterranean propaganda," revealing the contents of the file in private sessions with countless civic and religious leaders, elected officials, and newspaper editors throughout the country, alluding to it incessantly in correspondence and published literature, and providing copies to sympathetic associates. The Indian Office was fully aware of the IRA's use of the file and even provided additional copies upon request. Burke himself showed the file to numerous visitors to his office.[37] By mid-1923, a morality campaign—not the first or last in American history—was in full swing.

Throughout this campaign, the IRA steadfastly refused to release the secret dance file for review or verification, repeating the same excuse to each applicant: "These disclosures are of so vile a character that they are not permitted circulation in the mails."[38] Those interested in reviewing the evidence (preferably men only) could do so at the organization's Philadelphia office—which effectively prevented Collier and others from gaining access to the file for a over year. (These qualms, however, did not prevent IRA staff from mailing the file to each other and their associates when it was convenient to do so.) Allusions to and increasingly lurid claims regarding the contents of the secret dance file proliferated throughout 1923. Its existence was widely broadcast in a book published in June (with assistance from the IRA) by Indian educator and missionary G. E. E. Lindquist, which referred to "a report on file in the Indian Office concerning obscenities connected with the 'religious' rites of the more backward Pueblos, and their barbaric cruelties when inflicting punishment, that is almost beyond belief."[39]

The dance order crystalized a split that had been developing within the anti-Bursum forces. Collier's attacks on assimilation had made the IRA increasingly nervous. Endorsing the dance order provided the association a way of re-embracing familiar principles. For Collier, on the other hand, the dance order offered "peculiar opportunities" for furthering his campaign against assimilation.[40] From this time on, the IRA and Collier forces took opposite positions on most issues, and their relations became increasingly acrimonious.

Collier wanted to avoid being trapped into defending Indian morality, however, and he waited for an appropriate opportunity to join the debate. In the fall of 1923, Edith M. Dabb of the YWCA, an associate of the IRA who had seen the secret dance file, publicly defended Burke's regulations, describing Indian dances as "degrading." Such traditional observances, she claimed, "drag the young people back to the psychology of their elders"—that is, they impeded assimilation.[41] Collier responded in a lengthy letter to the *New York Times*, questioning the assumption "that there must be an immediate all-or-nothing struggle and the Indian must swiftly be denatured, stripped naked of his personality and turned into an Anglo-Saxon." He went on to relate a disturbing development in the debate on Indian affairs: the circulation of rumors, "more or less vaguely brought forward," regarding obscenity and immorality in Indian ceremonies. To avoid the appearance of defending Indian morals, however, Collier declared that "all of the Indian dance-drama ceremonials" were religious in nature. The question was not how these ceremonials rated on a scale of Christian standards, but whether Indians had the right to practice their own religion.[42]

The secret dance file received even greater exposure that December at a conference in Washington, D.C., of civic, religious, and political leaders—the Committee of One Hundred—convened by the Secretary of the Interior to advise him on Indian affairs. In the course of a heated debate on Burke's dance order, Lindquist "brandished aloft" a copy of the secret dance file and repeated the charges of immorality. This led one speaker to reply angrily, "If this Council wants to . . . abolish the communion table in the Presbyterian Church, and the altar and lights in the Roman Church, and take off the cross from the Episcopal Church, then that's the thing for them to do. But we have no right to say that a ceremony that belongs to their thousand year old faith shall be abolished."[43]

Following this conference, Collier became convinced that the religious-freedom issue deserved highest priority in the campaign against assimilation. In January 1924, he introduced the issue to the delegates of the All Pueblo Council. "There are two great questions before this meeting," he explained, "and one is the question of Pueblo land titles and the other is the question of religious freedom for all Indians." Collier described the effort "to compel the Government, the Indian Bureau and Congress, to prohibit the Indian ceremonies and dances. . . . They say that the Indian dances and religion are bad and wicked,—that they do harm to the young people,—that they make the Indians like beasts, savages, and they say the Government must forbid dances and ceremonies." Collier did not recommend any specific action at this time, however.[44]

In the spring of 1924, the controversy took a new twist when Clara D. True, Matilda Stevenson's one-time friend in New Mexico, entered the fracas. During her years as a government school teacher at Santa Clara, True had developed a small following of former students who had succumbed to her exhortations to abandon tribal customs, convert to Protestant Christianity, and challenge the traditional leadership of their pueblo.[45] These "progressive" Pueblos, as they came to be known, remained loyal to True long after her departure from Santa Clara. Now, fully aware of the controversy over the dance order, True informed the IRA (initially through her friend and companion, Mary Bryan) that conservative, "pagan" Pueblo leaders were persecuting Christian "progressives" for failing to join community work projects and, worst of all, refusing to participate in "secret dances in which the dancers are nude, both men and women." The "progressive Pueblos" never numbered more than thirty or forty individuals from a few villages, but True's charges, arriving in the middle of the IRA's morals campaign, were quickly seized upon as further evidence of the need for government intervention. Herbert Welsh directed that all other projects be halted while emergency funds were raised to send Sniffen to New Mexico to consult with True. In May, when the IRA received a grant from John D. Rockefeller, True was hired as a field representative.[46]

The alliance between the IRA and True was a strange one, however, for True and her associates in New Mexico had openly lobbied for the Bursum Bill, a measure that the IRA had ostensibly opposed.[47] Nonetheless, these interests now found common ground in their shared aversion to "Collier and Collierism" and in the advantages each saw in the morality issue. For the pro-Bursum group—including settlers holding disputed lands and their representatives, local political figures, missionaries, and Indian Office officials—the morals campaign offered a way to undercut public support for the Pueblos and their land claims. The IRA, for its part, hoped to regain its leadership among Indian welfare organizations.

In May, Collier reviewed the legal and political aspects of the religious freedom issue—"our next big struggle"—with the All Pueblo Council. "If the Indian religion dies the tribe dies," he explained, "everything falls to pieces and of course the land goes too." Collier proposed that the council adopt a declaration on the religious freedom of Indians—"a very simple document, not a fierce document"—for nationwide distribution.[48] The statement subsequently approved cited Burke's circulars and quoted a comment by the local Pueblo Indian agent: "The secret dance is perhaps one of the greatest evils. . . . I firmly believe that it is little less than a ribald system of debauchery." The Pueblo response was unequivocal: "We denounce as untrue, shamefully untrue and without any basis of fact or appearance, and contrary to the abundant testimony of White scholars who have recorded our religious customs, this statement." Burke's dance order was "an instrument of religious persecution," and the delegates appealed to the national conscience. "Will the American people not come to our rescue now, when it is proposed to take away our very souls?"[49]

Collier, however, had yet to convince the directors of his own organization, the AIDA, to support this issue. Many were not ready to consider Indian religion on equal terms with Christianity or Judaism. But Collier insisted that the religious freedom issue was "more fundamental *and practical* than the land issue." He finally received the authorization he needed in late May.[50] In the weeks that followed, hundreds of copies of the All Pueblo Council declaration were sent to newspapers throughout the country; thousands of flyers and pamphlets were printed arguing the Pueblo cause; and Collier, Charles Lummis, Frederick Hodge, Mary Austin, and others wrote letters and articles for a wide range of publications. As a result, millions of Americans became aware of Burke's dance circular, the campaign of rumors regarding native sexuality, and the plea of the Pueblos. On few occasions in American history has public attention been so focused on Indian affairs.[51] That Burke's routine restatement of a generation-old policy had become headline news reveals the dramatic changes that were occurring in American attitudes toward Indians.

Meanwhile, Sniffen, True, and Nina Otero-Warren, an Indian Office inspector, were working feverishly in New Mexico to undermine Collier and the All Pueblo Council. They urged progressive Pueblos at Santa Clara, Cochiti, and Santa Ana to organize a rival body and to file complaints with Commissioner Burke against the traditional leaders of their villages.[52] They also collected more testimony for the secret dance file. In interviews with Anglos, government employees, and progressive Pueblos, Sniffen, True, and Otero-Warren repeatedly inquired into sexual practices, although the statements they gathered added little new to the existing charges. In fact, most of the Christianized Indians denied the presence of obscenity in traditional observances or were "reluctant to give the 'disgusting details.'"[53] Local Anglos, on the other hand, were happy to repeat old rumors—that Zuni men and women imitated sodomy in a dance; that boys and girls were put together "for unrestricted sexual intercourse"; that the Taos Indians sacrificed two boys every year.[54]

Mary Dissette, still a teacher in the Indian service stationed at Santa Fe, was not idle during this campaign either. She provided the IRA with a copy of a thirteen-page letter that interjected berdaches and the charge of homosexuality into the debate for the first time. Writing to another schoolteacher, Dissette described at length her knowledge of these "peculiar victims of a religious superstition." Of the five berdaches she had known at Zuni, she noted, only one was still living—"showing pretty conclusively that 'the wages of sin is death.'" As a single woman, she had been constrained to inquire into their sexual practices; however, a government nurse told her that "these creatures practice Sodomy."[55]

By the summer of 1924, the Indian Office was fending off attacks from two directions—Collier's assault on assimilation, on the one hand, and the IRA's belligerent defense of the progressive Pueblos, on the other. Burke's reluctance to act was especially exasperating to the IRA. Herbert Welsh was "so stirred by all this iniquity, cowardice, and subterfuge" that he undertook a personal campaign to carry the cause of the progressives—and the revelations of the secret dance file—to the highest authorities. Through that summer and fall, the President of the United States, Secretary of the Interior, and Commissioner of Indian Affairs received a barrage of letters, telegrams, and appeals from the IRA, and on at least two occasions IRA representatives met directly with Burke.[56]

Hoping to turn public sentiment against Collier and the Pueblos, the IRA began leaking larger portions of the secret dance file. In July, True appealed to William E. "Pussyfoot" Johnson, a former special officer for the Indian Office responsible for suppressing the liquor traffic among Indians, for help against "an agitator named John Collier." After visiting the IRA's office in Philadelphia, where he was dutifully shown the secret dance file, Johnson wrote a letter to the *New York Times* registering some of the most sensational accusations of Indian immorality yet.[57] In fact, Pussyfoot Johnson provided the *Times* editors with a rare chance to exercise their masthead motto—"all the news that's fit to print"—for they chose not to print it. Nonetheless, this letter played a key role in the months that followed.

Johnson opened with an attack on the "well meaning ladies in pursuit of 'cult'" who supported Collier "but who really do not know what they are talking about." He denounced Pueblo "Phallic worship" and made a series of charges regarding Pueblo ceremonies: that "crowds of men and women are thrown together entirely naked"; that "boys and girls returned from Government schools are stripped naked and herded together entirely nude and encouraged to do that very worst that vileness can suggest, all in the name of 'religious liberty'"; that at Zuni (and here Johnson cited Dissette) "little girls were debauched in these dances"; that "Indian mothers, wives and daughters [are] ravished before hundreds of yelling, naked savages"; and that "little girls, too young and tender to be ravished, have been whipped naked until their little bodies were bruised and covered with purple welts." As his authority, Johnson cited "file after file of official reports" in the Indian Office and "sheafs of affidavits" at the IRA office. Most spectacular, however, was his claim that Indian boys were being withdrawn from government schools for "a two years' course in sodomy under pagan instructors." Over four hundred years had passed since the Spaniards first levied this charge against American Indians, but it had loss none of its shock value.

The refusal of the *Times* to print Johnson's letter was a minor setback. Johnson sent copies to both Burke and Sniffen, "for your information and for such use as you see fit." The IRA was ecstatic. "My man, it is one of the finest and most effective things you ever wrote," Sniffen told Johnson. Burke showed the letter to the Secretary of the Interior and informed Johnson that "we will probably see that a copy of it goes to people who are prominent." In fact, he mimeographed hundreds of copies and sought the assistance of the IRA in distributing them to the Committee of One Hundred and other national leaders.[58] Burke also provided 125 copies to Otero-Warren, noting, "It is advisable that copies . . . not be generally circulated from the Department. We of course have no objection to their being circulated by some one not connected with the Government." Otero-Warren sent her copies to the officers of the General

Federation of Women's Clubs, Collier's main base of support, and reported back to Burke that "this is according to Mr. [Edward S.] Curtis, probably the knockout of Mr. Collier." Burke's attempts to cover-up the government's role in circulating the letter were ineffectual, however. To his chagrin, Otero-Warren signed cover letters conveying copies of Johnson's missive as "Inspector, United States Indian Service."[59]

This was the sort of blunder that Collier had been waiting for, for it enabled him to directly link the Indian Office to the campaign of "subterranean propaganda." When Collier obtained a copy of Johnson's letter in September—taken from "a pile a foot deep on the desk of Burke's secretary"—he wrote gleefully, "The recklessness of the Indian Bureau is marvelous."[60] The following month, he obtained a copy of the secret dance file itself—193 photostat pages. After finally reviewing the infamous documents, Collier concluded that they contained "one charge and one only" of sexual irregularities associated with religious rites. The rest involved "such narrative as could be gathered in any American town relative to the secular behavior of loose people."[61]

In October, Herbert Welsh wrote to the *New York Times* criticizing the Indian Office for backing down from its position on Indian dances. Referring to Johnson's letter, Welsh repeated the charge of sodomy and concluded by calling for immediate federal intervention. The *Times* deleted the reference to sodomy, but published the rest of Welsh's letter. The IRA was furious. "The reliable reports on which we have based our statements . . . ," wrote Welsh in a second letter to the *Times*, "show clearly that this vice of sodomy, just as Mr. Johnson charged, is forced upon the neophytes."[62] Nonetheless, Welsh's letter was sensational enough to provoke several responses. Frederick Hodge, for example, quoted some of the less lurid accusations in Johnson's letter and observed, "It is just this kind of thing that the Indians love to pour into the eager ears of too inquisitive and gullible whites." Collier also responded, formally refuting Johnson's charges based on his own recent review of the secret dance file. This, in turn, led Sniffen to reply. Referring again to affidavits in his possession "too indecent to be printed," Sniffen challenged the cultural relativism of Hodge and Collier, reminding them that "customs must not conflict with the law of the land."[63]

Collier believed that the public would find Pussyfoot Johnson's wild charges more offensive than the possibility that they might be true, and he cited the allegation of sodomy in particular on numerous occasions.[64] In fact, this charge proved so controversial that Sniffen queried Johnson in November regarding its source, since nothing in the dance file supported it. "I had not reference to any specific cases, of course," Johnson replied lamely. "But according to the documents in your office, these pagan rites include more or less of that sort of thing."[65]

This was good enough for the IRA and, in particular, Herbert Welsh, who had become obsessed with the image Johnson had drawn of boys being instructed in sodomy. The secret dances, he concluded, "are worthy of that infamy which for hundreds and hundreds of years past had justly attached itself to those Sodomites who flourished in the days of Sodom and Gomorrah." With the Johnson letter in hand, Welsh redoubled his efforts to obtain government intervention. Repeating the sodomy charge in a letter to the Secretary of the Interior, Welsh noted, "By implication you admit the truth of that charge, otherwise your Office would not have circulated Mr. Johnson's letter."[66] When the Secretary of the Interior and the Commissioner of Indian affairs continued to balk, Welsh appealed directly to President Coolidge. After five separate pleas, he was finally granted an audience on January 24, 1925. To bring further pressure on the president, Welsh also engineered a letter-writing campaign among the country's Episcopal bishops. Referring to the Pueblos, he wrote, "They teach and practice . . . the vice of sodomy."[67]

Collier's organization countered these efforts by urging the president to resist pressures to abolish Indian religious practices and to consult with anthropological experts.[68] In the end, the president did not act. Welsh's conference at the White House marked the climax of the controversy.

The attempt to promote assimilation by maligning tribal culture had backfired, and both the IRA and the Indian Office began to retreat from their more extreme positions. In December 1924, Otero-Warren was terminated as an Indian Office inspector, and by February strained relations between True and the IRA resulted in her resignation.[69] That same month, when Sniffen asked Burke to provide additional copies of "that Secret Dance File," Burke responded obtusely. "Can not quite get your angle," he wrote. Collier was complaining "that we are doing just what the Indian Rights Association is criticizing us for not doing"—that is, distributing secret documents. "We doubt very much the wisdom of circulating the contents of what you term the Secret Dance File," he concluded.[70]

In a final fillip to its campaign of morals, the IRA published the story of the Zuni berdache We'wha, as provided by Clara True, in its February newsletter.

> *The gullibility and unreliability of some scientists . . . is illustrated in the amusing incident of "We-Wha," the Zuni Indian who passed, during several years spent in the service of some eminent representatives of the Bureau of American Ethnology, for a wonderfully intelligent Zuni woman. "We-Wha" is probably the best joke the American Indian ever played on men and women of trained minds. "We-Wha" proved to be a man, and the father of four children! . . .*
>
> *Just as much intelligence is now being displayed by a group of scientific people writing on Indian religions as was displayed in the case of "We-Wha," who was even loaded with millinery to take home to wear in Zuni! "We-Wha" was presented to President Cleveland by one of the best-known scientists of the Bureau, and introduced as a diffident female. "We-wha" led the Washington Charity Ball of that year and was given flowers by an admiring public.*[71]

That August, Collier briefed the All Pueblo Council on the contents of the secret dance file, and the Council issued a declaration denying all allegations. By then, however, the religious-freedom controversy was largely over. The secret dance file, that "budget of unprintable, pornographic allegations," mysteriously faded from the public forum.[72]

As a result of the debates of 1923 and 1924, the principle of cultural relativity was gradually introduced into the administration of Indian affairs. Although the struggle to protect the religious liberty of

American Indians continues to this day, the politically motivated use of morals charges was dropped from the government's arsenal. The Pueblos gained a new source of unity through the All Pueblo Council and some practical experience in politics. At the same time, the unwelcome spotlight of national attention led them to reinforce the barriers of secrecy surrounding their religious life.[73]

Twenty-five years later, Collier published an analysis of the controversy. "The destruction of the native religions that yet lived was viewed by the Indian Bureau as a *political* necessity," he concluded. It was "the certain way to detach the Indian's land from the Indian."[74] In fact, the Indian Office was neither as cunning nor efficient as Collier believed. Its participation in the IRA's morals campaign was as much by reflex as design. Collier was justified in holding the Indian Office responsible in one sense, however. Nordstrom, Lonergan, and Sweet collected their slanderous testimony in the sincere belief that they were advancing government policy with the tacit if not open approval of their superiors. "These are 'Pussyfoot's' words," Collier wrote in 1924, "but it is not 'Pussyfoot' who mimeographed and distributed the words."[75]

The failure of the IRA's campaign, however, did not mean that Americans were ready to acknowledge the possibility of Indians entering the mainstream of American life without shedding their tribal culture. The average American had little appreciation for the subtleties of Collier's vision of the coexistence of tradition and modernity. Indians, to the extent that they were Indian, lived in the past; to the extent that they were modern, they had to look and act like white men. For most Americans in the 1920s, cultural relativity meant allowing Indians to remain quaint and primitive if they wanted, especially if they produced native artifacts for consumption by tourists and collectors. The growing influence of racial theories at the turn of the century had convinced many that Indians were biologically incapable of competing with whites, and such a belief was not necessarily incompatible with Collier's primitivism.[76]

For the IRA the choice remained clear—as Welsh wrote, "between a wise attempt to civilize our Indians, and the reverse plan of keeping them in ancient idleness, subject to the laboratory dissections of scientific investigators or the sketches of artists and story writers." To Welsh and his peers, Collier represented the inversion of principles that had guided their generation to its proudest achievements—the settlement of the West and the emergence of the United States as a world power. As Welsh noted in a letter to the Secretary of the Interior,

> *I am convinced that at the root of the Indian dance attack is the strange wide-spread belief that affects many modern minds in literature, art, music, religion, philosophy to the effect that primitive man had more that is excellent in all the range of human mentality than the race has gained from the greatest of Christian teachers. 'Back to Nature' is their cry. It is to some a captivating theme, but there are dangerous flaws in it, as a careful perusal of the reports in your office on the secret dances will show, or a visit to the ultra impressionist picture show now going on at the Pennsylvania Academy of the Fine Arts.*[77]

True to their abolitionist roots, the assimilationists abhorred the prospect of institutionalized inequality in American society. But American racism created a self-fulfilling and self-perpetuating cycle of underdevelopment. Indians were unable to compete with whites, not because they clung to tribal culture, but because they were denied access to the resources and education necessary to compete, and this because of their assumed inferiority. Ironically, not even Collier himself, as Commissioner of Indian Affairs between 1933 and 1945, was able to put an end to the federal paternalism that contributed to this cycle. And over four centuries after the debate at Valladolid, Las Casas's bold assertion that "all the peoples of the world are men" has yet to be fully realized.[78]

THE DISAPPEARING OF THE BERDACHE

The use of morals charges as a tool of colonial administration, beginning in the 1890s, represented an important turning point in the history of American Indian affairs. Previous judgments regarding Indians had been dominated by religious values. But with the secularization of Indian policy at the end of the nineteenth century, the advocates of assimilation began to seek new justifications for intervening in native social life. The charges made by Dissette and Faurote at Zuni in 1897 reflected this development. Where Reverend Ealy's denunciations of Zuni paganism had been primarily religious in nature, their accusations targeted sexual acts—acts that were, in Dissette's words, "contrary to moral law, to the laws of the U.S. and to the laws of this Territory."[79]

Despite this transformation, a continuity in the sexual politics of colonialism can be traced from the arrival of the Spaniards to the heyday of the secret dance file. At each critical juncture in the extension of colonial control, controversy over native sexuality erupted, with the collective fantasies of non-Indians regarding the sexual behavior of Indians preempting debate over the morality of conquest. Although these customs were logically irrelevant to the rights of Indians as the original occupants of the land, this distinction was rarely observed. Perceptions of native sexuality and gender became inextricably linked to the seizure of native land and resources by Spaniards and Americans alike.

It was against this backdrop that the "disappearing" of the berdache occurred in the late nineteenth and early twentieth century. The growing level of interaction between Pueblos and Anglos made it increasingly difficult to disguise the presence of men who partly or completely dressed as women—and Stevenson's acceptance of the berdache We'wha was the exception, not the rule. Alexander Stephen, who lived among the Hopis in the 1890s, referred to We'wha as "that abominable sort," while Dissette called him a "creature" and another writer referred to him as "one of those unspeakable professional perverts connected with the Phallic ceremonies in primitive cults."[80] It comes as no surprise, therefore, that accounts of berdaches provided by the teachers True and Dissette figured in the secret dance file controversy, or that the boarding schools they worked in rigorously suppressed berdache behaviors (as related in the next chapter).

Between white intolerance and Indian reticence, memory of berdaches has been almost completely erased from the record on the Pueblo Indians. Contemporary anthropologists routinely overlook or even repudiate the documentation on Pueblo berdaches that does exist.[81] The otherwise exhaustive Southwest volume of the Smithsonian's 1979 *Handbook of North American Indians* makes no mention of them at all. In the end, berdaches were erased by silence as well as repression, their fate, like that of the victims of state terrorism known as the "disappeared ones," unacknowledged, memory of them almost lost.

8
The Berdache Tradition

In 1896, the year that We'wha died, a young Zuni named Kasinelu decided to assume the status of the lhamana. This created something of a stir in the pueblo, for Kasinelu's maternal grandfather was the famous bow priest Nayuchi, still at the height of his influence and prestige. Stevenson, the ever-inquisitive observer, was present to witness the flowering of one of Zuni's last traditional berdaches. "The mother and grandmother were quite willing that the boy should continue in the work in which he seemed interested," she reported, "but the grandfather, who was much disgusted, endeavored to shame him out of his determination to follow woman's work. He did not, however, attempt any authority in the matter, and on the boy's reaching manhood the trousers were replaced by woman's attire." Mary Dissette also witnessed the unfolding of Kasinelu's identity as a lhamana, for until the time that he assumed "full female attire" he was enrolled in her school. Despite this change, however, Kasinelu kept his male name.[1]

Given the fairly universal tendency of parents to identify with their offspring and to expect them to follow their footsteps, Nayuchi's temporary disapproval is not surprising. Such a reaction is quite different from the anger and hatred expressed toward sexual variation in Western culture, however. Nayuchi was the supreme military leader of his tribe. Yet he did not attempt to exercise his authority to block his grandson's entrance into lhamana status. When the boy's decision appeared final, Nayuchi resigned himself to it. While his initial objections sound familiar from a Western perspective, his eventual acceptance of a dress-wearing male as a member of his household is characteristically Zuni.

In fact, there is something disingenuous about Nayuchi's protests. Just five years earlier, he had assisted in the organization of the Lha:hewe, an elaborate summer ceremonial. Among the various roles called for was that of a virgin "impersonated by a male." This dancer appeared with two other virgins who were portrayed by females. "He or she," as Leslie Van Ness Denman, who witnessed this ceremony in 1932, wrote, carried a dance kilt and a hoop, male and female symbols respectively.[2] According to Stevenson, it was the responsibility of the elder bow priest to select this youth, who must be a son or grandson of a priest. Nayuchi selected his own grandson, Kasinelu. Had the boy already exhibited traits that made him an appropriate choice for such a role? If so, it is hard to accept Nayuchi's professed disappointment in 1896.

When Parsons began inquiring about Zuni berdaches in 1915, Kasinelu was in his thirties. He had become a "first-class plasterer" and was "especially good" at pottery. Like We'wha, he danced the part of Kolhamana in the quadrennial Kan'a:kwe ceremony. Parsons observed him on several occasions during a five-day rain dance.

> *Kasineli has the facial expression and the stature of a man. He has the longer stride of a man, but it is slow and ponderous like the Zuni woman's. During the rain dances he always stood on the roof top behind the old woman who is the head of his household. He did not wear the American calico petticoat so many of the Zuni women wear but his dress was in every particular as far as I could see like a woman's, and he wore his black blanket in woman fashion, up around the back of the head, irrespective of the temperature, and falling to the knees. Next to him on the roof top were standing or sitting three or four kinswomen.*[3]

By this time, however, government agents, missionaries, and teachers had effectively sensitized Zunis to white attitudes regarding sexual variation, and informants were beginning to employ the same evasiveness toward sexuality that they had learned to use in regard to religion and other privileged subjects. One of Parsons's informants, for example, was related to Kasinelu, but "to the *ła'mana* in her family she would never refer, although we talked of the subject in general from time to time and we worked together on her family genealogy. Nor would she take me to the house where he lived, the house of her father's sister where her own little son was living and where she had grown up. Her people had tried very hard to dissuade the lad from becoming a *ła'mana*, I was told, and I got the impression that in general a family would be somewhat ashamed of having a *ła'mana* among its members. In regard to the custom itself there seemed to be no reticence in general and no sense of shame."[4]

Parsons always remembered the Zuni berdache who was the grandson of a bow priest. In the summer of 1938, when John Adair, one of the anthropology students whom she encouraged, made plans to visit Zuni, Parsons asked him to look for Kasinelu and, if possible, obtain a photograph of him. Adair took two pictures of the sixty-year-old berdache, standing in the doorway of his house (Figure 28).[5] The following year, Parsons published the photographs in the *American Anthropologist*, with a brief commentary entitled "The Last Zuni Transvestite." "No boy in the last twenty years has shown any promise of transvestism," she reported, using the term introduced by psychologists. "Kasinelu, the clever potter and plasterer, is therefore the only surviving transvestite in Zuni, and almost certainly will be the last one," and she concluded, "American influence will work against the trait."[6]

Kasinelu indeed may have been the last lhamana to wear a dress, but the Zuni berdache role did not end as abruptly or as completely as Parsons had predicted. Although Zunis had become sensitive to the judgments of outsiders, traditional attitudes toward berdaches still prevailed when Omer Stewart visited the pueblo in 1940–1941. Stewart observed a berdache who "wore woman's dress and arranged his hair in the style of women, and was known in the community as providing an attractive hangout for young men. They were given food and drink and a chance to play cards and amuse themselves in the well-kept house of the berdache. The Indian governor of Zuni and other members of the community seemed to accept the berdache without criticism, although there was some joking and laughing about his ability to attract the young men to his home."[7]

Stewart may have seen Kasinelu or perhaps another berdache, unknown to Parsons.[8] In any case, Kasinelu was subsequently mentioned in a 1946 publication of the Christian Reformed church, which described the history of the Protestant mission established at Zuni by Andrew Vanderwagen. A photograph of the elder berdache is reproduced with the caption: "Kasanel, the cook. By a strange custom he wore woman's apparel all his life."[9] This is the only mention of him in the book. Apparently, Kasinelu, like We'wha and Kwiwishdi, had found employment with the local missionaries. Still, the appearance of the "last Zuni transvestite" in a missionary tract is odd, to say the least, considering the intolerance expressed in the same work toward other aspects of Zuni "paganism." Perhaps, in this particular area, the missionaries followed the example of the Zunis and adopted their traditional attitude of nonchalance regarding the "strange custom" of Kasinelu.

Despite the dramatic changes that occurred in the course of his lifetime, Kasinelu followed the life road of the lhamana until his death with a determination not so different from that of his grandfather, Nayuchi. His generation would be the last to observe the traditional forms of the berdache role, however, for in the years after World War II the most visible marker of lhamana status, the practice of cross-dressing, was abandoned.

THE END OF THE DRESS

In 1940, when Alfred Kroeber commented on the berdache role he wrote in the past tense. "While the institution was in full bloom, the Caucasian attitude was one of repugnance and condemnation," he noted. "This attitude quickly became communicated to the Indians, and made subsequent personality inquiry difficult, the later berdaches leading repressed or disguised lives."[10] At this juncture, however, an interesting question arises. Did berdaches simply disappear when boys no longer adopted the dress? Or did elements of the role persist? The case of Lasbeke, a member of the generation of Zunis that followed Kasinelu, provides a partial answer.

When Parsons first observed Lasbeke in 1915 at the age of six, he had already been identified as a lhamana because he used verbal expressions characteristic of girls. He wore boy's trousers and a shirt, but he left the shirt hanging outside his pants, like a blouse. His hair was cut in the boy's style and he wore a bead necklace. "His features are unusually fine and delicate, unusual even in a Zuñi girl, and his facial expression unusually gentle, mild of expression as is the Zuñi of either sex. Whenever I saw him playing about he was with a girl, although boys of his age begin to gang together." In 1918, Parsons saw Lasbeke again, carrying his sister on his back in a blanket, as girls and women did. Parsons quoted one Anglo's description of the youth as "a very nice looking boy, rather a sissy." But Lasbeke's development as a berdache was abruptly curtailed when he underwent the ordeal of education in an off-reservation boarding school.[11]

By the 1920s, education of Indian children had become the government's primary vehicle of assimilation. In 1922, nearly all Indian children were enrolled in government schools; 25 percent or more in off-reservation boarding schools.[12] The environment in these schools was openly hostile to all forms of traditional Indian culture. Berdache behaviors were quickly spotted and suppressed. Parsons reported the case of a young Laguna berdache who was sent to Santa Fe. "After some time he was found out at school and made to wear boy's clothes and placed with the boys." According to Parsons, he continued to wear trousers later in life but still performed women's work. In other cases, boys who cross-dressed were expelled or ran away.[13] The white teachers and government employees who operated these schools considered the behavior of berdaches a sign of debilitation and degradation, and they devised means of punishment based on these associations. At the boarding school for Hopi children, boys who ran away more than once "had their heads shaved and had to wear a dress to school." As one Hopi woman recalled, "Some of them forgot how to wear pants." This appears to have been a common punishment in Indian boarding schools. Such a practice effected a complete reversal of the attitudes toward berdaches that Indian children would have learned in traditional times.[14]

And so, when Lasbeke returned to Zuni he did not adopt the dress. Even so, he still performed "women's work" by obtaining employment as a cook for a highway construction crew. In this respect, Lasbeke followed We'wha, Kwiwishdi, and Kasinelu—all berdaches who earned money by doing domestic work.

In the 1940s, several Zunis adopted this course. As John Adair recalls, "When I was at Zuni in '47, I observed in Gallup that there were a number of Zunis that, if they had been residents of the pueblo fifty years earlier, might very well have been in the role of the lhamana, who were, again, in the job of cooks and other occupations of a similar nature."[15] In other words, while the practice of cross-dressing disappeared, individuals with the inclinations and skills of berdaches did not. But instead of a secure place in their tribes, these individuals found their social position so problematic that they resorted to self-imposed exile. This was a drastic break for any Zuni.

The abandonment of the dress occurred throughout native North America. Parsons learned of an Isleta berdache in the 1930s who had adopted men's clothes and another at San Felipe who wore men's clothing at his job in Albuquerque and women's clothing while in his pueblo. Among the Navajos, most berdaches stopped cross-dressing in the early twentieth century, and several observers have cited the impact of white ridicule. Similar accounts of berdaches giving up cross-dressing and gender-mixing have been reported for several tribes.[16] In some cases, cross-dressing and gender-mixing were actively suppressed by Indian agents (or their suppression was contemplated, as in the case of Pueblo agents in the 1890s). Many berdaches, like the Zunis observed by Adair, sought domestic and other forms of "women's work" in white communities.[17] Of course, berdaches were not alone in abandoning traditional costume. Indians who wore native clothing in the white world—male, female, or berdache—were often ridiculed. Eventually, all Indians made compromises in how they dressed, at least in white settings.

Although cross-dressing lapsed, many tribes continued to recognize preference for women's work, nonmasculine behavior, and homosexuality as berdache traits. In fact, the dress appears to have been the only trait truly "disappeared" by the impact of white culture. Still, this was a fundamental loss, for the dress had served the critical function of marking third-gender status. Among the Zunis, the dress-wearing male had a clear-cut position in the network of kinship and household relations. His daily garb signaled to others appropriate patterns of interaction. The suppression of the dress blurred the distinction between berdache and non-berdache males. Without the dress, what distinguishes a berdachelike interest in women's work from the male who occasionally performs female tasks—for example, doing the cooking for other men while in sheep camps? Or the lifelong homosexual orientation of the berdache from the bisexuality of the non-berdache men who are their casual partners? Or the bonds of two men who are *kihe*, or ceremonial friends, from the bonds of a berdache and his long-term non-berdache partner?[18] Traditional Zuni culture has no customs to guide the residence patterns and sexual practices of males who dress like men but do not fulfill the other economic, sexual, social, and kinship responsibilities of men. Even though Zunis remain willing to accommodate the behaviors traditionally associated with berdaches, new rules are needed if men who are "not-men" are to remain integrated members of their families and community.

The process by which native categories of sexuality and gender are reconciled and sometimes replaced with white categories has unfolded differently from tribe to tribe. In most cases, the real break occurred not when berdaches stopped wearing dresses but when young people stopped learning about the role. This happened when parents and elders became too ashamed of the subject to discuss it, or when children were raised away from tribal settings. With dress-wearing men no longer present in their communities, many younger Indians never learned about the berdache tradition—especially in the generation born after World War II, when white categories and white values regarding sex and gender finally replaced native practices in many tribes.

In the most extreme cases, traditional acceptance was replaced by overt hostility. As John Adair observed, Zuni World War II veterans often returned with "white GI attitudes" toward homosexuality.[19] In the 1940s, Lurie's Winnebago informants told her that "the berdache was at one time a highly honored and respected person, but that the Winnebago had become ashamed of the custom because the white people thought it was amusing or evil." When the last known berdache attempted to "put on the skirt," his brothers threatened to kill him.[20] In recent years, violent reactions to individuals with berdache inclinations have been reported even among

Pueblos.[21] In such cases, the reaction against berdache behaviors is typically linked to the degree that white values have been assimilated.

Among the Zunis, however, such a radical break with tradition has not occurred. In my discussions with experts and outsiders familiar with the tribe, including some who have been visiting the pueblo since the 1930s, and in my own experiences and conversations at Zuni, I have not encountered evidence of hostility toward nonmasculine behavior or homosexuality in that tribe. Triloki Pandey, for example, interviewed Zuni elders with vivid memories of We'wha and a respectful attitude toward the subject in the 1960s. Only in the 1970s did he detect any nervousness when the subject came up, especially among young people.[22]

Of course, television, schools, magazines and books, and contact with outsiders have made Zunis more aware than ever of Anglo attitudes and values toward sexual variation, and many have intentionally and unintentionally adopted these values. In 1987, however, I had an opportunity to discover contemporary Zuni attitudes toward the subject of the lhamana firsthand, by presenting at the pueblo a series of illustrated lectures that included a segment on We'wha. In seeking permission to make these presentations, my mention of We'wha among the subjects I intended to discuss did not seem to cause any concern. In fact, the tribal council requested that I speak to students at the Zuni High School as well as to a general audience at the tribal building. "It *was* a part of the traditional culture," declared one Zuni teacher. The warm response to these lectures and a subsequent invitation to return to speak to grade school as well as high school students indicates that the memory of We'wha and the respect accorded the lhamana role continue among that tribe.

At the same time, an interesting evolution in Zuni concepts of sexuality and gender is under way. The traditional word for berdaches, *lhamana*, is still used, for example, when referring to We'wha and, in general, to individuals who combine traits or engage in activities of both men and women, whether or not they are also homosexual. A glossary of Zuni words published by the tribe in 1973, for example, includes *lhamana* in a list of kinship and "personal terms" and defines it as "effeminate." But a new term, derived from lhamana, has been coined to refer specifically to homosexuals—*lhalha*.[23] This derivation suggests that Zunis perceive both change and continuity in berdache and homosexual roles. The divergence between these categories, however, has created confusion for many individuals. In the 1970s, when a high school teacher began offering classes in pottery-making, which had nearly lapsed at Zuni, both male and female students showed interest. Today, several potters of both sexes are gaining commercial and artistic recognition. But pottery-making was traditionally a woman's art. What does a boy's interest in this art signal today, if anything? Many Zunis themselves are uncertain. While Anglos apply the label "homosexual" primarily on the basis of sexual behavior, the assignment of lhamana status had always been based on work preference. Rules governing the use of the new term, *lhalha*, are still forming.

THE REDISCOVERY OF THE BERDACHE

"Before Alcatraz," recalls gay Mohawk poet Maurice Kenny, referring to the 1969 Indian occupation of the abandoned federal penitentiary in San Francisco Bay, "it was just about impossible to stand up and say who you were. Even in the non-Indian world, in an urban center, up until Alcatraz you just didn't talk about those things. In a nonurban situation, if you had a job you'd get fired, your family might disown you, you certainly would be ridiculed."[24] For American Indians with traits and interests that once might have been expressed through the berdache role, the postwar years were dark and lonely times. Faced with rejection by family and tribe, harassed by the agents of assimilation, it was not a period in which individuals like We'wha could flourish. For many, urban migration became the only recourse for self-preservation.

The rupture of family and community ties was especially painful. For most Indians, belonging to a tribe depends on being a member of a clan or family. But whether precipitated by a willing or an unwilling break, immersion into the white world was an act of survival. And necessity dictated that any social status that replaced berdache roles had to be viable in a white-dominated cultural milieu. It had to be a status recognized in Anglo-American culture. By and large, this was the social role of the homosexual or gay person.[25] This role, however, differed from that of the berdache in several respects. The key trait of homosexuals, according to the medical and scientific discourse that assumed responsibility for defining this status, was their sexual behavior. But in American Indian societies, sexuality was less important in defining berdaches. Most tribes allowed individuals ways to engage in homosexual behavior without altering their gender status. On the other hand, preference for work of the other sex, the key trait of berdache status from the Indian perspective, was perhaps the least important trait of the Anglo-American homosexual since white society devalued women's work anyway.

The white definition of homosexuality obscured its relationship to Indian traditions. This, and the alienation of gay and lesbian Indians from tribal communities, delayed the rediscovery of the berdache until the 1970s. By then, an entire generation of Americans, both Indian and non-Indian, had begun to challenge and reconstruct the gender roles and sexual identities of Anglo-American society and to look to other cultures, including those of native North America, for new models. Two developments in 1975 broke the silence surrounding the tradition of sexual diversity among American Indians. In San Francisco, Randy Burns and Barbara Cameron founded Gay American Indians (GAI), a social, educational, and service organization that thrives to this day; on the other side of the continent, Maurice Kenny completed his seminal essay "Tinselled Bucks: A Historical Study in Indian Homosexuality," published later that year in *Gay Sunshine* magazine. Kenny's writings, both prose and poetry, had a galvanizing effect on his audience. He reclaimed the berdache tradition in unequivocal terms. "We were special!" he declared in his poem "*Wintke*." "We had power with the people!"[26]

The invisibility that enveloped gay and lesbian Indians lifted slowly. In 1978, when Paula Gunn Allen began writing her landmark essay "Lesbians in American Indian Cultures," she knew that Indian women had been shut out of Indian organizations and physically threatened for simply calling themselves feminists, let alone lesbians.[27] Allen worked in isolation for two years before finally publishing her article in 1981. "It was really scary to put that out," she recalls. "But I finally decided that the danger was already so great that putting out the article wouldn't make things worse. . . . I can take the risk. They kicked me out years ago. But there are young people out there and they have to know about this."[28] Gradually, as a result of efforts by Kenny, Allen, and others, along with organizations like GAI memories of the berdache tradition have been recovered in many Indian communities.

In 1975, Kenny wrote, "Homosexuality is accepted if not condoned within most primal societies. In certain societies the homosexual was made a fetish or became an integral part of ceremony. The American Indian was no exception to the rule." Kenny went on to cite evidence of berdaches and native homosexuality from a wide variety of tribes, concluding his essay with a hopeful vision for the future. "Perhaps when Indians have once again regained their old cultures, languages and ceremonies, the berdache will not only be respected but will find a place in his chosen society. The current taboos against his nature will then have changed sufficiently so that he may make a contribution to and function once more in that reorganized culture."[29] By the 1980s many of these predictions were being realized. GAI has been joined by organizations of lesbian and gay Indians in Vancouver, B.C., Minneapolis, Winnipeg, Toronto, and New York City—the last naming itself after We'wha and a famous Crow Indian female berdache. As Burns declared in the preface to an anthology of historical and contemporary writing published by GAI in 1988, "We are living in the spirit of our traditional gay Indian people."[30]

Many Indians point to important differences between berdache and contemporary gay roles, however. Owlfeather, who lives on a Shoshone reservation, writes, "Berdaches had an integral place in the rigors and life-style of the tribe. The way they were viewed was not the same as the contemporary Indian gay lifestyle and consciousness that we have now—they were not fighting for a place in society and to be accepted by that society. They already had a place, a very special and sacred place." The dilemma of many contemporary gay Indians, Owlfeather observes, is that they share the vision of the berdache but have no appropriate channel for expressing themselves. "Gay Indians today grow up knowing that they are different, act in a different way, and perceive things in a different light than other Indians. They know these things, but sometimes are afraid to act or acknowledge their gayness. If they do, they try to accept and emulate the only alternative lifestyle offered to them, that of the current gay society." Having been drawn into the urban scene himself, Owlfeather describes the limitations of the white gay life-style from personal experience. "Deep inside I knew that, as an Indian, something else was needed . . . especially for a person of substance and especially for an Indian person. Most Indian people, gay or straight, have been instilled with a respect for all things, a love for the earth and all things living. The current gay lifestyle, although it is an upfront gay existence, is not an Indian way." For Owlfeather, the homosexual role of Western society lacks the spiritual component integral to the self-realization of those who are also Indian.[31]

Allen makes a similar qualification. "Simple reason dictates that lesbians did exist widely in tribal cultures, for they exist now," she notes, but "the concepts of tribal cultures and of modern, western cultures are so dissimilar as to make ludicrous attempts to relate the long-ago women who dealt exclusively with women on sexual-emotional and spiritual bases to modern women who have in common an erotic attraction for other women."[32] This observation agrees with the situation that anthropologist Walter Williams encountered among the Lakota in the early 1980s. " 'Gay' and *winkte* are different," one contemporary Lakota berdache explained. "*Winkte* is a gay with ceremonial powers." Nongay Indians recognized this distinction, as well. A Lakota woman lamented that younger gays "don't fulfill their spiritual role as *winktes*." Others, like Michael One Feather, who initially identified himself as gay without knowledge of the *winkte* tradition, eventually found older relatives who explained and instructed them in traditional berdache patterns. Today, One Feather says, "I identify both as a *winkte* and as gay."[33]

Thus, in the view of contemporary Indians the transition from traditional berdache roles to western sexual identities was not a matter of one role dying out and a second, alien role being imposed. Rather, berdache status was gradually secularized and supplemented, but not replaced. Gay American Indians today view their place in their communities as historically grounded in the berdache tradition—much as contemporary tribal officials look to the chiefs and warriors of the past as their role models. Only the recovery of the spiritual aspects of the berdache role separates them from this tradition.

CROSSCURRENTS

Of course, American Indians have not been the only ones interested in the study of berdache roles. As early as the nineteenth century, in the minor but persistent discourse that developed in opposition to the treatment of homosexuality as an illness, the example of the berdache played a key role. Karl Heinrich Ulrichs, a German homosexual, developed a theory in the 1860s that posited same-sex orientation as a third gender, and he cited North American berdaches. He was followed by Edward Westermarck, Edward Carpenter, Ferdinand Karsch, and Ruth Benedict—all citing berdaches in their theoretical formulations and in their arguments for greater social tolerance of sex and gender variance.[34] Today, berdaches have taken on particular significance in the debate over the meaning of homosexual identity.

Many of the images and interpretations of berdaches that have been deployed in these debates, however, are at odds with the conclusions of Indians themselves. Some scholars have gone so far as to deny the possibility of any connection between berdache and contemporary roles. "Why should one even begin to contemplate the notion that the *berdache* has anything at all to do with homosexuality in our terms?" asks British sociologist Kenneth Plummer—"our" presumably meaning "white." Similarly, a reviewer of GAI's anthology complained that berdaches were treated as "part of some nebulous gay history," observing that " 'homosexual' and 'gay' are, respectively, 19th-century and 20th-century historical constructs based on a Judeo-Christian tradition that was completely irrelevant to Indian cultures until it was forced upon them." Another commentator noted that "the need to claim historical validation as a foil against the oppression and distortions of the record by homophobic white society produces its own distortions." GAI's references to berdaches as "our traditional gay ancestors," he concluded, were "political distortions of the facts." My own depictions of We'wha and berdaches in general have been branded as "romantic obfuscations."[35]

Social constructionism, a theory first advanced by sociologists and historians in the 1970s to explain certain developments in modern western history, is often cited in support of such views. According to constructionism, gender roles and sexual identities are products of social influences and not the manifestation of inherent or biological drives. The identities of contemporary lesbians and gay men, for example, arose in response to efforts by various social institutions to regulate sexuality, beginning in the nineteenth century. These agencies of social control applied new labels to sexual behaviors—"homosexual," for example, instead of "sodomite." According to the theory of constructionism, when individuals accept such labels they begin to affiliate with others similarly labeled and develop characteristic life-styles and subcultures. Presumably, without social regulation and labeling there would be no identity formation and individuals would engage in heterosexual and homosexual behavior randomly, that is, as bisexuals. Many constructionists have carried this line of reasoning even farther: if different societies use different labels, then the experiences referred to must be different. The only basis for comparing such roles is when the social organization of the societies are similar. The enormous difference between Western and American Indian societies theoretically rules out any comparison of their sex and gender roles.[36]

Social constructionism is the most recent restatement of the principle of cultural relativity tentatively formulated by Cushing and refined by Parsons, Benedict, and others. This principle highlights the role of social forces in shaping human behavior, and, by pointing to the diversity of cultural forms throughout the world, it reveals the range of human psychological and social potentials. Applications of cultural relativity have made real contributions to our understanding of human behavior, to the tolerance of individual differences, and to the politics of cultural diversity. As this study of the Zuni berdache has shown, gender identity and behavior are also "constructed" through social conditioning. The evidence presented here regarding the historical, social, economic, and religious aspects of the Zuni berdache tradition, and the story of how gay American Indians have "constructed" their own contemporary identities in drawing from this tradition, supports the major contentions of constructionism. However, advocates of this theory go too far when they deny the possibility of continuity between the cultural forms of different societies and different historical periods. Before dismissing the interpretations of American Indians, first we ought to ask whether they might be seeing something that a Western point of view cannot.

The story of the Zuni berdache illustrates at least two sources of continuity between past and present identities. First is the role of individuals as social actors, who do not passively await labels to trigger their behavior, but actively participate in shaping their identities and status. The childhood development of berdaches like Kwiwishdi, Kasinelu, and Lasbeke illustrates how individual and social factors interact. The boy who showed a preference for domestic work and association with women at the age of five or six, for example, could hardly have been aware of something as abstract as lhamana identity. Rather, he expressed inclinations and skills that he experienced as intrinsic and spontaneous. His family and community, however, interpreted such expressions in terms of adult social roles, so that by the time the boy assumed the dress at the age of ten to twelve he did so aware of what his act symbolized. Clearly, both childhood interests and the presence of a formalized role were important factors in the careers of We'wha, Kasinelu, and other Zuni berdaches. Without some demonstration of berdache inclinations, Zunis were not likely to label a child as such. On the other hand, without the opportunity to develop under the sanction of a recognized social role, such traits were likely to remain indistinguishable or to manifest in distorted or anti-social ways. To the extent that a child's actual interests corresponded with the Zuni conception of berdache status, this role provided a unique opportunity for personal growth and achievement.

Thus we find that even where memory of berdache status was lost or suppressed, berdache patterns continued to appear in certain individuals. In many cases, individual Indians who had no formal knowledge of the berdache role were considered berdaches by their tribespeople, especially elders, because of these traits. Furthermore, throughout this transitional period such individuals did not simply wait for a new label to be applied to them for their lives to assume meaning; they actively searched for an appropriate social status that would allow them to express their inclinations, reaching outside their tribal communities when necessary. When Indians did adopt the sexual labels of white society, they redefined them in uniquely Indian ways, so that their sense of identity today is not reducible to the sexual definition of the homosexual role. We can conclude that while labels are necessary for discourse and self-awareness, the patterns of behavior they refer to can and do occur without them.

The overlap between berdache and gay roles among American Indians also illustrates a second source of continuity—that is, the continuity of symbols, which can be passed from one generation to another and from one culture to another. Whether in the form of cultural artifacts, metaphors, tropes, discourses, or simply a model of the world that patterns knowledge and perception in distinct ways, the referents of such signifiers can never be limited to their meaning in a specific time or place. Symbols have a way of escaping contexts to re-emerge in other contexts. Two seemingly distinct referents can become associated by sharing a signifier that has thus slipped across discourses separated in time, just as two signifiers can have the same referent. Our understanding of past terms and our definitions of present terms are both shaped by these symbolic effects. Thus, terms like *gay* and *homosexual* are not discrete categories with fixed boundaries as determined by agencies of social control. Their meaning is subject to intense dispute and negotiation within a discourse too volatile to allow prediction of the eventual consensus. Limiting these meanings to the historical contexts in which they originated, if carried to a logical conclusion, would make it impossible for contemporary American Indians to use any term from the English language to discuss traditional culture.

Coming from oral cultures in which knowledge and its interpretation are not fixed, American Indians know that tradition is subject to renewal in every generation. The symbols and concepts of the past are kept alive by giving them new meaning and new referents. Even lapsed traditions can be revived, as occurred during the Ghost Dance movement of the 1890s and during the native revivalism of the 1960s. Similarly, as M. Jane Young has found, many contemporary Zunis draw both from oral tradition and what they have read in the anthropological literature when interpreting historical symbols. If they do not always know the exact meaning of these symbols, they do not doubt that they are significant signs left by their ancestors. As one Zuni religious leader said when Young showed him a series of petroglyphs, "Do you know what this means? I think it must mean something."[37]

For gay American Indians, the berdache is not a fixed type limited to a predetermined range of dates, but a living symbol capable of endless reiterations, whether as a role model or simply as an emblem of their place in tribal life. Knowledge of the berdache tradition provides them with a sense of history that white gay men and lesbians lack. As Burns explains, "It's not just a sexual thing. It's that we have roots here in North America."[38] For Burns and other contemporary Indians, knowledge of the berdache tradition broadens their understanding of gay and lesbian identity. "Gay," in their usage, connotes a multifaceted life-style that encompasses religious, economic, and social dimensions as well as sexuality.[39]

Still, the comparison of berdache and gay roles cannot proceed in such a way that reduces them to a lowest common denominator, especially since that denominator is likely to reflect Western rather than Indian perceptions.[40] The metaphor of a family tree might be a useful way to conceptualize both the continuity and variety of alternative sex and gender roles throughout the world's cultures. The trunk of this tree would represent sex and gender variant behavior; the branches would reflect the organization of these behaviors into formal social roles. One branch might represent the combination of homosexual behavior and gender mediation in roles like that of the berdache. Another branch might represent the type of homosexuality between equals idealized by Walt Whitman and currently favored by the Western gay movement. Yet another branch might represent the age-differentiated homosexuality of the classical Greeks. Recognizing the differences between these variations is important, for they point to human and social potentials as yet unexplored in Western societies.

The single-dimensional Western category of homosexuality is an historical construct. It would be ironic indeed if this category were used to exclude data on sex and gender variance in other cultures from the current discourse on the meaning of homosexual identity. Such an approach is inherently ethnocentric, for it privileges Western definitions at the expense of non-Western insights. Rather than trying to fit berdaches into historically relative categories, our inquiries ought to use the example of the berdache to improve these categories and free them of their cultural bias.

A review of recent discussions of berdaches reveals the shortcomings of single-dimensional definitions. Many commentators, for example, feel compelled to choose between homosexuality or cross-dressing when defining their subject. If homosexuality is the outstanding trait of the homosexual, they reason, then cross-gender behavior is the dominant trait of the berdache. Thus, anthropologist Harriet Whitehead defines berdaches as "gender-crossers," while Callender and Kochems prefer the term "gender-mixing," but still view cross-dressing and the "expression of important traits of women's behavior" as the most important characteristics of the berdache role, which they consider derivative of the two "real" biological genders. Witham and Mathy would place berdaches with "transvestic homosexuals" who engage in "cross-gendering." Walter Williams rejects the cross-gender model, but falls back on the terminology of a dual gender system; his berdaches are "feminine," "effeminate," and "androgynous," and he compares them to "drag queens" in Anglo-American society.[41]

As long as perceptions are filtered through a dual gender ideology and arbitrary distinctions based on biological sex, berdache patterns cannot be appreciated for what they really are—the appropriate and intrinsic behavior of a *third* gender. From a dual gender perspective, berdaches can only imitate the behavior of one or another of the two "real" genders, an imitation invariably found inferior and somehow counterfeit. Those behaviors deemed inappropriate for an individual's biological sex, like cross-dressing, are consequently singled out. But comparisons of male berdaches to women invariably reveal more about the speaker's view of women (usually negative) than they do about berdaches. In light of the discovery of the third gender, all such accounts must be re-evaluated.

From an emphasis on the apparent cross-gender attributes of berdaches follows the denial of their homosexuality and, indeed, of any form of sexuality. The earliest European and American observers often referred to berdaches as "unsexing" themselves by donning women's clothing, an assumption deeply rooted in popular belief. Recent commentators have perpetuated these misperceptions by uncritically citing reports of sexually inactive or heterosexual berdaches and concluding that homosexuality is a secondary and derivative characteristic.[42] Berdache sexuality may appear unimportant, however, simply because berdaches were identified in childhood on the basis of traits that appeared before they were sexually active. In other cases, references to asexual and heterosexual berdaches fail to stand up to scrutiny. The rumors about We'wha's paternity reported by Stevenson, for example, are often cited as evidence of berdache heterosexuality, while the ample evidence confirming the homosexuality of other Zuni berdaches is ignored. A thorough review of the available sources does not support the view that berdaches were asexual or that they behaved like women sexually.[43] Among the Pueblos, for example, there is no evidence of women entertaining men and engaging in casual sexual encounters as has been reported for male berdaches.[44]

To account for the complex history of berdaches and their survival to the present day, social constructionism needs to adopt a multidimensional model, one that recognizes not only the sexual and gender features of these alternative roles, but their economic, religious, social, and kinship facets as well. The Zunis, for example, viewed berdache status as a unique personality configuration. They looked for an overall pattern of traits, not just a single characteristic, when deciding whether an individual was (or would become) a lhamana. Such a model accommodates subjective and individual factors in the formation of identity—the talents, interests, and motivations of the person—as well as the role of social conditioning.[45]

A multidimensional paradigm also makes it possible to specify the exact degree of similarity and difference between roles of different societies (and within societies). Although the gender-variant behavior of berdaches may be more prominent among one tribe, for example, and homosexuality in another, a multidimensional model makes it possible to trace the connection between the two roles through shared traits in other dimensions—economic or religious facets, for example. A multidimensional model also helps clarify the connections that contemporary Indians perceive between gay identity and the berdache tradition. While certain elements of the traditional configuration, such as cross-dressing, have lapsed, continuity exists in other dimensions—in work preference, sexual orientation, and gender mediation. Even though "official" definitions in Western societies do not acknowledge these traits as an aspect of homosexual orientation, many Indians find that they can be expressed through a gay identity.

That American Indians are using their knowledge of the berdache role to give meaning and purpose to their lives today makes the connection they perceive with that tradition a reality—from the Zunis' admiration of (and occasional amusement at) the exploits of We'wha in Washington to the unbroken practice of berdache customs in many tribes, to the young gay Indians who are uncovering political and social applications of gender mediation that even We'wha could not have imagined. The viability of the berdache symbol is further attested by the diverse individuals who are drawn to it, not only Indians and not only gay men and lesbians. Many contemporary Americans can appreciate the self-assured Zuni man-woman who excelled in the arts and shook hands with a president; all can take inspiration from a society where individuality and community are not always at odds.

Whether as a role model or as an archetype of wholeness, the multidimensional image of the berdache reminds us that our debates over sex and gender involve ethical choices relative to our own time and place; choices rather than the application of presumed natural or social laws. In the end, it is hard not to ask who has the greater insight into the psychological and social potentials of human diversity: Western society, which renounced the larger part of the spectrum of gender and sexuality centuries ago, or the people who live in the Anthill at the Middle of the World, who, for just as long, have ensured the representatives of diversity a place in the middle, as valued participants in their social balance?

Appendix One
Pronunciation Guide

THERE IS NO OFFICIAL OR UNIVERSALLY accepted way of transcribing the sounds of the Zuni language using the English alphabet. Despite technical advances and standardization in the field of linguistics, each generation of experts has introduced a new system, or orthography, for writing Zuni words. In the past two decades, the Zunis themselves have taken an active role in documenting their language to preserve it and teach it to their children. Therefore, while following Newman's guidelines for a practical orthography, I have also incorporated some modifications based on current Zuni preferences.[1]

a, e, i, o, u — These vowels are pronounced similar to their Continental values (for example, Spanish). Zuni vowels are sometimes lengthened—held for a slightly longer duration—and this is indicated by a colon (:) immediately following the vowel. The effect is similar to the lengthening of the vowel sounds when saying "fa-ther" or "he-elp." Consonants can also be lengthened (as in Italian), which is indicated by doubling the letters.

' — This represents the glottal stop, a sound made by closing the back of the throat, as in the exclamation "Uh-oh!" or when saying "a nice man" immediately followed by "an ice man."

b, d — These consonants (often transcribed as "p" and "t") are much softer than their counterparts in English because no air is released when they are pronounced. To practice, try saying the words "spot" and "stop" and gradually eliminating the "s" sound.

k — The Zuni "k" is pronounced farther back in the mouth than the English "k." When combined with the glottal stop (as in *k'okshi*) the sudden release of air from the back of the throat results in a slight popping sound. (Try inserting a "k" into "uh-oh" and saying "uh-k'oh.")

Before "a," "e," or "i" and before the glottal stop followed by these vowels, "k" is pronounced as "ky," similar to the "c" in "cube."

kw — This is pronounced like "q" in "quick."

lh — There is no comparable sound for this consonant in English (often transcribed as "ł"). It is pronounced by placing the tongue in the position for making an "l" sound and forcing air around the sides of the tongue as if making an "h" sound. Practice by saying "athlete" and slowing eliminating the sound represented by the "t."

Zuni words are always stressed on the first syllable.

Appendix Two
The Beginning

THE ZUNI ORIGIN MYTH, *CHIMIK'-ana'kowa*, or "that which was the beginning," is that people's most sacred literary artifact. At the beginning, the Zunis believe, were these words, so that every occasion of their retelling constitutes nothing less than a refounding of the world and the placement of the Zunis in it. The canonical version of this myth is the *kaklo an benanne*, or "the talk of Kaklo," the kachina who visits every four years at the time of the boys' initiation. As Dennis Tedlock points out, this version of the myth can be rightly called a "text" because, although it does not exist in written form, it is fixed in its ritualistic, esoteric form. This is accomplished by a radical simplification of spoken language that brings inflection, stress, and pause into a fixed relationship with the words, minimizing the potential for variation and improvisation.[1] The priests responsible for maintaining this text hold lifetime offices devoted to its painstaking memorization and flawless recitation.

Interpretation of the origin text occurs within the various priesthoods and religious societies, each of which maintains a version of the myth that features its own origins and sanctions, and within every Zuni home whenever folk tales—*delabenanne*, or "the talk of time"—are told. These tales, which are not esoteric and may be told by anyone (but usually by grandfathers), take as their starting point incidents, places, or characters from the origin myth and make them the subject of a story. In tales, interiority, subjectivity, personality, motive, and moral—absent in Kaklo's talk—are amply provided. According to Tedlock, the storyteller "does not merely quote or paraphrase the text but may even *improve* upon it, describe a scene which it does not describe, or answer a question which it does not answer. . . . What we hear from our interpreter is simultaneously something new *and* a comment on that relic, both a restoration and a further possibility."[2]

Except for Stevenson's transcription of Kaklo's chant, the other published versions of the Zuni origin myth are of this discursive, nonesoteric variety.[3] I have used all available versions following the precept put forward by Lévi-Strauss: "We define the myth as consisting of all its versions; or to put it otherwise, a myth remains the same as long as it is felt as such."[4] In fact, a reconciliation of the different versions of the origin myth would be artificial from a Zuni point of view. As Bunzel put it, "No mind in Zuñi encompasses all knowledge."[5] The synopsis that follows, therefore, is not unlike the Zuni folklorist's production. It draws from eight published versions of the origin myth, as well as the variations and elaborations of the myth contained in numerous folk tales, with special reference to those characters and incidents that shed light on the Zuni philosophy of gender and sexuality.[6]

THE UNDERWORLD

In most versions, the Zunis already exist when the narrative begins. But they live four worlds beneath the surface of the earth, in the womb of the Earth Mother, undeveloped and undifferentiated. "Everywhere were unfinished creatures, crawling like reptiles one over another in filth and black darkness, crowding thickly together and treading [upon] each other, one spitting on another or doing other indecency." The primordial Zunis are "most unfinished . . . not having even the organs of digestion."[7] Yet, the rudimentary core of Zuni society is already present, in the rain priests and their sacred bundles or fetishes.

In the sky above, the Sun Father is alone. "No one gave him prayer meal. No one gave him prayer sticks. It was a lonely place." He desires his children to emerge to the surface of the earth—"The way they are living is not what I had in mind"—where they might honor him with the proper forms of worship.[8] Through his agency, twin children are born, referred to as the Beloved Twain, Divine Ones, or simply, two Bow Priests. As intermediaries, these twins can communicate with their father above but also descend to the underworlds below, bearing his wishes to the Zunis. When the twins arrive in the fourth underworld, the rain priests convene and agree to begin the process of emergence.

THE EMERGENCE

It takes four attempts and the aid of insects or plants—trees, reeds, or prayer sticks—to move from one underworld to the next. The plants are used as ladders, which symbolize the vertical axis in the Zuni directional system that links humans to the Sun Father. The twins lead the people up through the four underworlds to the surface of the earth, where the sun is about to rise. But for the unfinished Zunis, even this dim light is too bright. "The moment they came out, they dropped to the ground. They could not bear it. Their eyes saw nothing."[9]

COOKING

The Zunis begin a series of migrations, always eastward, toward the home of the Sun Father. Although they settle in many places, internal division, encounters with outsiders, or natural disruptions like earthquakes cause them to renew their migrations. The Zunis seek the Middle of the World, that place where the natural, social, and spiritual elements of life are synchronized.

On their first migrations, they acquire agriculture and the religious rites that control precipitation. (Before this, they live on the seed of grasses.) The first corn seeds are provided by a witch, who emerges with the Zunis (or, in one version, from an alien people they encounter). The witch causes or requires the death of a child in return for the seed. Four days later, however, the child is found alive again. This is the first statement of a contradiction elaborated throughout the myth, one central to agriculture: how death yields life. When plants are harvested or animals killed for food, death sustains life. When the old die, they make available resources for the young who replace them.

As they emerge from their natural or "raw" state, the primordial Zunis are no longer able to sustain themselves on "raw" food, and so they also acquire the art of cooking, a process of mediation that makes it possible for a "raw" plant like corn to put "flesh" on "cooked" people. Cooking conceptually mediates plant and animal as well as the natural and social. Underscoring this transition, the Zunis' "natural" anatomy is also altered. The twins cut off their tails, slice their webbed hands and feet, and wash off their slime. They even provide the Zunis with mouths and anuses to allow them to eat and digest food.

In two versions of the myth, the origin of the Corn Maidens, bearers and protectors of the six differently colored seeds of corn, is also related at this juncture. The Corn Maidens represent a social element of the agricultural complex just as important as the religious role of the priests; namely, the matrilineal household, centered around the bonds of sisters and daughters who together administer the household granary.

BIRTH OF THE GODS

Having differentiated themselves from nature, the Zunis now begin to differentiate from each other. They are presented with a choice between two eggs (or between the tip of an ear of corn and its base). One of the eggs is a beautiful blue color, the other motley and unappealing. But when the blue egg hatches, a homely, unlucky crow appears—the bane of Zuni farmers—and when the motley egg hatches, a beautiful macaw emerges. The people who choose the macaw travel to the south, the land of everlasting summer, and, according to Cushing, become the "Lost Others." Those that choose the crow continue on the journey eastward.

At this point, two temporary leaders are selected: a brother and sister, children of a rain priest. They precede the main body of migrants. Reaching a mountain, they stop to rest. While the sister sleeps, the brother sexually violates her. Ten children are born of this union—the supernatural lhamana, followed by the nine Koyemshi clowns. Enraged, the sister draws a line between two mountains to separate herself from her brother. A river flows between the mountains, into a lagoon, and this becomes Sacred Lake. When the main body of Zunis reach this river, they attempt to cross it. But once in the water, the children turn into frogs, toads, and turtles (that is, raw beings) and frighten their mothers, who release them. The children swim to Sacred Lake and become the first kachina gods—young, happy, and always dancing. Sacred Lake (also called Zuni Heaven) becomes the home for all deceased Zunis.

WAR OF THE GODS

Before the Zunis renew their search for the Middle Place, the Wood Society people, who bear a snow-making fetish, separate from the main body and travel north, settling for a time in the Anasazi area of Chaco Canyon and then at Shiba:buli'ma, identified with a site in the mountains above the Rio Grande Valley. Here, the culture hero Boshaya:nk'i instructs them in the arts of medicine and curing, and introduces them to the six Beast Gods, patrons of hunters. Meanwhile, the main body of Zunis settle at Hanlhibinka, identified as a ruin some thirty miles west of the present-day village. Here, they learn the rituals of war and acquire their clan names. They also encounter an alien god-people called the Kan'a:kwe. The following account of this encounter is based primarily on the Stevenson version.[10]

When the Zunis spy smoke in the area to the East, the rain priest of the North exclaims, "Ha! There is a village. I wonder who these people are?"

"We will see," said the Divine Ones, and they ask two members of the Newe:kwe or Galaxy Society (a clown society distinct from the Koyemshi) to go ahead and "hunt" a trail. At first, the clowns refuse. "We are fighting men," they say, "and we may meet some one and kill him, and thus get you into trouble." But the Divine Ones insist, and the two leave as instructed.

Proceeding a short distance, the Newe:kwe observe two women from a nearby village washing buckskin on the bank of a stream. Without provocation, the clowns kill both women. Discovering the murders, the people of the village—the Kan'a:kwe—become enraged and attack the Zunis. Their leader is Cha'kwen 'Oka, the giant Warrior Woman. The Kan'a:kwe and Zunis fight for two days, but neither side prevails.

Meanwhile, the Sun Father causes heavy rains to fall. A nearby stream is filled suddenly with water and rushes down a mountainside in a series of cascades. Leaping joyously into the air, the water is caught in the sun's embrace and impregnated. Twin sons issue from her foam. These children of the Sun Father and Earth Mother become the Zunis' new War Gods, the 'Ahayu:da. Dwarfed, homely, eternally adolescent trouble makers, the War Gods are nonetheless powerful beings who are invulnerable to harm and capable of changing form at will.

The original Divine Ones beseech the new twins. "We have fought two days, but we can do nothing with the enemy. Many arrows have pierced the heart of the Cha'kwen 'Oka who leads the opposing forces, yet she continues to pass to and fro before her army, shaking her rattle. Until these people can be conquered or destroyed we can not proceed in our quest for the middle of the world."

"We will join you," reply the newborn gods. "We may destroy the enemy; we may not."

The fighting continues for four days. Each night, in their village, the Zunis dance and pray for rain—so that their bowstrings, made of yucca fiber (because they are farmers), might be made strong, while the bowstrings of the Kan'a:kwe, made of deer sinew (because they are hunters), might be weakened. On the third morning, the Zunis' prayers bring heavy rains as they sally forth to meet the enemy, and their ranks are swelled by the presence of the *kokko*, or Sacred Lake kachinas. But Cha'kwen 'Oka again appears before her army, shaking her rattle and stamping back and forth. She captures three of the Sacred Lake kachinas: Kokk'okshi, the Koyemshi called 'Itsebasha, and one of the Sayalhi"a warrior kachinas. A Sha'lako is also captured, but soon escapes.

Back in the Kan'a:kwe village, the prisoner gods are required to appear in a dance held in celebration of their capture. Kokk'okshi, the firstborn, is so angry and unmanageable that Cha'kwen 'Oka has him dressed in female attire, saying to him, "You will now perhaps be less angry."

The rain continues to fall, however, and on the fourth morning the bowstrings of the Kan'a:kwe become so weak that most of their shots fail. Meanwhile, after many prayers to the Sun Father, the knowledge comes to the elder War God that Cha'kwen 'Oka carries her heart in her rattle.

Carefully aiming his arrow, he pierces the rattle, and Cha'kwen 'Oka falls dead. The Kan'a:kwe forces retreat, and the Zunis capture their village, freeing the three gods, who return to Sacred Lake.

The Zunis now open the gates of the corral in which Cha'kwen 'Oka had kept all the game animals, telling them, "We have opened for you the doors of the world; now you may roam where you will, about the good grass and springs, and find good places to bear your young; you will no longer be imprisoned within the walls, but have the whole world before you." Since this time, game animals have roamed freely over the face of the earth. The episode ends when the Zunis adopt survivors of the Kan'a:kwe, who become the progenitors of the Black Corn clan.[11]

FINDING THE MIDDLE

The Zunis now establish their villages in the Zuni Valley. The Wood Society people return from the North and rejoin the tribe. Their ceremonial, enacted every January, commemorates this reunion.

But the exact location of the Middle Place is still in doubt. The rain priests ask the six-legged waterskate to help them find the true center of the world. Waterskate spreads his legs to the six directions, and the spot beneath his heart is determined to be the middle. Here the Zunis build Halona, on the south side of the Zuni river. The kiva societies are organized and initiation rites begin.

Two more crises arise before the narrative ends, however. The Corn Maidens are offended by the thoughts and/or actions of Bayadamu, the god of butterflies and music (or a bow priest, or young men in general), and they flee to the South. The people seek the aid of Newe:kwe (or Bayadamu), who "reverses" the error by using clown magic—talking backwards, speaking nonsense, and saying the opposite of what he means. The maidens finally return, and a ceremony is instituted to commemorate the occasion. The episode warns against male challenges to the female household and the danger of individual needs (Bayadamu) overriding community needs (the Corn Maidens).

A final catastrophe befalls the Zunis when they become lax in their religious observances (or because of the "error" of a priest, or because the "real" middle has not been found). A flood forces the people to take refuge atop Corn Mountain. The feathered snake, Kolo:wisi, watches from a nearby mesa. When a youth and maiden are sacrificed to the waters, the flood recedes. The Zunis now settle in a single village, Halona:idiwana, the Middle Place, in the shadow of Corn Mountain, alongside the Zuni River.

Notes

SHORT TITLES HAVE BEEN USED IN CITing works in the notes. Frequently cited manuscript collections have been identified by the following abbreviations:

CLAIR	California League for the American Indian Records, Bancroft Library, University of California, Berkeley, California.
FW	Records of the United States Army Continental Commands, Fort Wingate, New Mexico, Record Group 393, National Archives, Washington, D.C.
GWJC	George Wharton James Collection, Southwest Museum, Los Angeles, California.
HCC	Hodge–Cushing Collection, Southwest Museum.
IRAP	Indian Rights Association Papers, Historical Society of Pennsylvania, Philadelphia, Pennsylvania.
JCP	John Collier Papers, Manuscripts and Archives, Yale University Library, New Haven, Connecticut.
RBAE/LR	Records of the Bureau of American Ethnology, Letters Received, M. C. Stevenson, 1890–1906, 1908, National Anthropological Archives, Smithsonian Institution, Washington, D.C.
MCSP	Matilda Coxe Stevenson Papers, National Anthropological Archives.
PA	Records of the Pueblo and Pueblo and Jicarilla Agency, National Archives, Denver, Colorado.
RBIA	Records of the Bureau of Indian Affairs, National Archives, Washington, D.C.

PREFACE

1. On Hay's career as a labor organizer, political educator, and gay activist, see Timmons, *The Trouble with Harry Hay.*

2. L. White, "Anthropology 1964," 630.

3. Collier, *On the Gleaming Way*, 154–55.

4. Parsons, *Pueblo Indian Religion*, xiv. See also Hare, *Woman's Quest for Science*, 132–33, Chapter 6; Lurie, "Women in Early American Anthropology," 74; Spier, "Elsie Clews Parsons."

5. Benedict, *Patterns of Culture*, 262.

6. Priestley and Hawkes, *Journey Down a Rainbow*, 9. The biographer of anthropologist Alice Fletcher, a contemporary of Stevenson, similarly concluded that "one impulse behind Alice Fletcher's desire to go west and live with the Indians was a subconscious desire to explore, among a distant and foreign people and from the safe stance of scientific observer, the nature of human sexuality" (Mark, *Stranger in Her Native Land*, 65).

7. In Benedict, *Patterns of Culture*, ix.

8. Babcock and Parezo, *Daughters of the Desert*, 1. See also Bennett, "Interpretation of Pueblo Culture."

9. Hinsley, *Savages and Scientists*, 71.

10. Pandey, " 'India Man,' " 203. See also Pandey, "Factionalism," "Tribal Council Elections," "Anthropologists at Zuni," and "Images of Power."

11. Stevenson to Holmes, 22 April 1904, RBAE/LR. See also Stevenson, "Zuñi Indians," 154–55, 204, 419–20.

12. Pandey, "Anthropologists at Zuni," 326; Wilson, *Red, Black, Blond and Olive*, 21.

13. Cushing to Baird and Powell, 18 February 1880, envelope no. 47, HCC.

14. Cushing, *Zuñi*, 149–50, 153–56; Brandes, "Frank Hamilton Cushing," 67–69, 73–74.

15. On Cushing and Stevenson's role in factions, see Porter, *Paper Medicine Man*, 123; Brandes, "Frank Hamilton Cushing," 76–78; Hinsley, *Savages and Scientists*, 196; Pandey, "Anthropologists at Zuni," 328; Hart, "Factors Relating to Zuni Land."

16. Pandey, "Anthropologists at Zuni," 327; Porter, *Paper Medicine Man*, 128.

17. See Lurie, "Women in Early American Anthropology," 233.

18. Cushing to Baird, 29 October 1879, envelope no. 44, HCC; Stevenson, "Zuñi Indians," 608; Mead, *Anthropologist at Work*, 304; Clifford, "On Ethnographic Allegory," 98–121.

19. Roscoe, "Bibliography"; Roscoe, *Living the Spirit*.

20. Wilson, *Red, Black, Blond and Olive*, 67–68.

21. Mark, *Four Anthropologists*, 110–11, 114–15; Hinsley, *Savages and Scientists*, 223; D. Tedlock, *Spoken Word*, 321–38.

22. For discussions of these points, see Clifford, "On Ethnographic Allegory"; C. Martin, *American Indian and the Problem of History*.

PROLOGUE

1. The term *Zuni* is used to refer to the people, their culture, the village they live in, and their language.

2. We'wha's name has been rendered in a variety of ways. I have adopted Stevenson's spelling as the most common and recognizable form. Although some transcriptions suggest that his name may have been pronounced "WAY'wah," contemporary Zunis pronounce it "WEE'wah." A more accurate transcription, in the orthography described in Appendix 1, would be "Wi'wa."

3. Elsewhere in her 1904 monograph, Stevenson uses male pronouns when referring to We'wha and other berdaches ("Zuñi Indians," 37, 123, 310, 354, 380). The Zunis themselves were inconsistent when referring to the gender of berdaches. Since Zuni pronouns do not recognize gender, this problem was largely avoided. But even when male berdaches were referred to as if they were women, the Zunis never ignored or denied the fact that they were biologically male (see Chapter 5). In contrast, the connotation of biological sex is much stronger in the case of English pronouns, and for that reason, I use "he" when referring to We'wha to convey the Zunis' understanding that We'wha was biologically male. A somewhat closer, if less practical, approximation might be achieved by placing "she" and "her" within quotation marks when writing or speaking of Zuni berdaches.

4. Stevenson, "Zuñi Indians," 311–12.

5. Guerra, *Pre-Columbian Mind*, 43; W. N. Hammond, *Sexual Impotence*, 163–64; Courouve, "The Word 'Bardache' "; Roscoe, "Bibliography," Table 1; *Oxford English Dictionary*, s.v. "bardash."

6. Cognates include *bardaje, bardajo, bardaxo* (Spanish); *bardasso, bardascia* (Italian); *berdache* (French); bardash, berdash, burdash, bardass, bardasso, bardassa, bardachio (English). The English also used bardash to refer to a fringed sash worn by men and considered a sign of effeminacy (see listings in *Oxford English Dictionary*, s.v.)

7. See Roscoe, "Bibliography," "Glossary of Native Terms."

CHAPTER ONE

1. Cushing, *Zuñi*, 46.

2. The name was changed to the Bureau of American Ethnology in

1897 (see Judd, *Bureau of American Ethnology*). For background on Cushing, see Brandes, "Frank Hamilton Cushing"; Cushing, *Zuñi*; Fuller, "Frank Hamilton Cushing's Relations to Zuñi"; Mark, *Four Anthropologists*.

3. On Stevenson, see Lurie, "Women in Early American Anthropology" and "Matilda Coxe Evans Stevenson"; Parezo, "Matilda Coxe Evans Stevenson"; Stevenson, "From 'The Zuni Scalp Ceremonial.'" Parezo refers to five Evans children, but I have found no evidence of either brothers or sisters ("Matilda Coxe Evans Stevenson," 337). Matilda's cousin, Robley D. Evans, did join her family for a few years before the Civil War, following the death of his father, and later became a Spanish-American War hero and navy admiral (*Sailor's Log*, 10).

4. H. James, *Pages from Hopi History*, 109; Judd, *Bureau of American Ethnology*, 57; Holmes, "Matilda Coxe Stevenson," 557; Hinsley, *Savages and Scientists*, 229.

5. Stevenson had traveled with her husband prior to the 1879 Zuni expedition, conducting field work among the Ute and Arapaho Indians. (See *New York Times*, 25 June 1915; Joy McPherson, "Matilda Coxe-Stevenson Papers" (typescript, 1974), MCSP; Parezo, "Matilda Coxe Evans Stevenson," 337–38).

6. Holmes, "Matilda Coxe Stevenson," 553; McPherson, "Matilda Coxe-Stevenson Papers," MCSP; Parezo, "Matilda Coxe Evans Stevenson," 339. Stevenson's appointment became permanent in 1890.

7. Brandes, "Frank Hamilton Cushing," 94; Woodward, "Frank Cushing," 173.

8. Stevenson, in Cushing, *Zuñi*, 24; Brandes, "Frank Hamilton Cushing," 36.

9. Stevenson, "Zuñi Indians," 119. Somewhat less complimentary was the Zunis' Spanish nickname for Stevenson, *la cacique mujer*, or "woman chief" (Porter, *Paper Medicine Man*, 123).

10. At the turn of the century, Stevenson formed a close relationship with Clara True, a government school teacher at Santa Clara Pueblo. Stevenson boarded with True and her mother while conducting research at nearby pueblos, then purchased land adjoining theirs. "I liked and admired Miss True," she later wrote. In fact, Stevenson offered to take her back East "to spend the winter in fashionable society," and even considered making True her heiress (Stevenson to Renehan, 10 September 1909, F. True to Stevenson, 4 July 1908, Stevenson to Renehan, 5 July 1908, MCSP). By 1907, however, the two women had experienced a bitter falling-out and were entangled in a protracted legal dispute. In the 1910s, Elsie Clews Parsons also befriended True, only to become embroiled in similar disputes over money and land. According to Parsons, True was "in her deals and

quarrels a notorious personage far beyond her own river valley. . . . And she liked women to whom she could play the man. She was in short a feminist of the militant type, although she did not know it" (Hare, *Woman's Quest for Science*, 46, 127).

11. Cushing, "Commentary," 33, 40, 43; Bunzel, "Introduction to Zuñi Ceremonialism," 483.

12. Ferguson and Hart, *Zuni Atlas*, 51.

13. Bunzel, "Zuñi Ritual Poetry," 622.

14. Kintigh, *Settlement, Subsistence, and Society*, 19; Ferguson and Hart, *Zuni Atlas*, 37–39, 43, 45–46. See also Bohrer, "Zuni Agriculture"; Stevenson, "Ethnobotany of the Zuñi Indians."

15. I do not use the term *matriarchal* here because, technically, it means "rule by women," and there is no evidence that women ruled or governed in the prehistoric Southwest. Rather, the Pueblo Indians and their ancestors present us with examples of social balance between male and female power and prestige. *Matrifocal* or *matricentric* are more appropriate terms (see, for example, O'Kelly and Carney, *Women and Men in Society*, 42).

16. Ladd, "Zuni Social and Political Organization," 488–89.

17. See Pauker, "Political Structure"; Smith and Roberts, *Zuni Law*, 28–37.

18. B. Tedlock, "The Beautiful and the Dangerous," 255.

19. Wilson, *Red, Black, Blond and Olive*, 39.

20. Baxter, "F. H. Cushing at Zuni," 56.

21. D. Tedlock, "Zuni Religion and World View," 499; D. Tedlock, *Finding the Center*, 297; Oosterman, *The People*, 114.

22. Sandner, *Navaho Symbols of Healing*, 196; Neumann, *Great Mother*, 41, 260, 269. See also McFeat, "Some Social and Spatial Aspects."

23. Cushing, "Preliminary Notes," 158; Cushing, "Outlines," 372.

24. Ladd, "Zuni Religion and Philosophy," 26.

25. Cushing, "Outlines," 388; Ferguson and Hart, *Zuni Atlas*, 21–23.

26. Kintigh, *Settlement, Subsistence, and Society*, 110–17; Ferguson, "Emergence of Modern Zuni Culture"; Ferguson and Hart, *Zuni Atlas*, 25–27; LeBlanc, "Cultural History of Cibola."

27. Kintigh, *Settlement, Subsistence, and Society*, 115–17; E. C. Adams, "View from the Hopi Mesas," 324; Schaafsma and Schaafsma, "Evidence," 543–44. On the origin of kachina practices at Zuni and Hopi, see Anderson, "Pueblo Kachina Cult," and E. C. Adams, "View from the Hopi Mesas." It is possible that the kachina tradition adopted at Hopi and Zuni in late prehistory overtook an existing, but less developed, use of masks by the Anasazi. Schaafsma believes that this first wave of kachinas

dispersed northward to the Rio Grande Valley from the Jornada Mogollon area of southern New Mexico, where the presence of masks has been dated to A.D. 1150 (*Indian Rock Art*). However, murals recovered from prehistoric kivas at three Anasazi sites—Awatovi in the Hopi area, Pottery Mound in the Puerco Valley, and Kuaua on the Rio Grande—date to A.D. 1300 or later and include few clearly identifiable masked figures, which suggests that kachina practices were just beginning to develop at that time or that their use was limited (see Smith, *Kiva Mural Decorations*; Hibben, *Kiva Art of the Anasazi*; Dutton, *Sun Father's Way*). The kachina tradition attributed in Zuni mythology to the western immigrants appears to have been differently organized than those of this first wave, and were characterized by large, outdoor group dances in contrast to the private, kiva-oriented ceremonies typical of the historic Rio Grande pueblos. Cordell has commented on this problem ("Prehistory," 147).

Although archaeological evidence indicates that the population in the Zuni Valley was more numerous and had occupied the region continuously for several centuries, the point of view of the Zuni origin myth is that of the western immigrants. (For archaeological evidence of a late prehistoric migration into the Zuni Valley, see Ferguson, "Emergence of Modern Zuni Culture," 341; Ferguson and Hart, *Zuni Atlas*, 26–27; Haury, *Excavation of Los Muertos*, 48, 49, 200, 211; Smith, Woodbury, and Woodbury, *Excavation of Hawikuh*, 167). The origin myth associates this indigenous Anasazi population with two groups: the medicine society people, who split off from the western branch, traveled north to Chaco Canyon and the Rio Grande, then returned to build the Chaco-style villages near Nutria in the upper Zuni drainage; and the Kan'a:kwe, who are identified with either Heshoda Yala:wa, a ruin near Ojo Caliente, or Ka'maka, twenty-five miles south of Zuni (see Table 2, in chapter 6; Ferguson and Hart, *Zuni Atlas*, 20–23; Benedict, *Zuñi Mythology*, 5; Parsons, "Origin Myth," 159; Cushing, "Outlines," 343–44). Cushing attributed both Heshoda Yala:wa and Ka'-maka to ancestors of the Corn Clan (Cushing to Baird and Powell, 18 February 1880, envelope no. 47, HCC). Perhaps the subsequent importance assumed by the kachina society within Zuni culture accounts for the precedence given to the western immigrants in the origin myth.

28. Simmons, "History of Pueblo–Spanish Relations," 185; Woodbury, "Zuni Prehistory," 471–72.

29. McFeat, "Some Social and Spatial Aspects," 42. See also Young, *Signs from the Ancestors*, 228.

30. Ladd, "Zuni Religion and Philosophy," 28. Cf. Schlegel on gender complementarity among the Hopis ("Male and Female").

31. "It was quite amusing to see the men knitting stockings," wrote a

member of the Beale expedition in 1857. "Imagine Hiawatha at such undignified work" (Lesley, *Uncle Sam's Camels*, 188).

32. Smith and Roberts, *Zuni Law*, 127.

33. Young, "Women, Reproduction, and Religion," 437.

34. Stevenson, "Zuñi Indians," 65, 108, 166; Parsons, *Pueblo Indian Religion*, 137, 471, 1130; Parsons, "Zuñi Ła'mana," 527; Bunzel, "Zuñi Katcinas," 875.

35. Cushing, "Primitive Motherhood," 25, 44.

36. Wittfogel and Goldfrank, "Some Aspects of Pueblo Mythology." On Anasazi irrigation, see Kintigh, *Settlement, Subsistence, and Society*, 96–97; Plog, "Prehistory," 112; Vivian, "Inquiry." On the organization of female gardening and farming, its relationship to matrilocal and matrilineal practices, and the transition from female farming systems to male control of agriculture, see Martin and Voorhies, *Female of the Species*, 216, 277, 283; O'Kelly and Carney, *Women and Men in Society*, 38, 42, 53; Schneider and Gough, *Matrilineal Kinship*, 552, 559, 661, 670; Boserup, *Woman's Role in Economic Development*, 16, 19, 32. Such a change in the division of labor may well have been contested. Wittfogel and Goldfrank cite examples of myths from Hopi and Zia portraying tension between the sexes, some overtly referring to control of agriculture ("Some Aspects of Pueblo Mythology," 26–27). In the Kan'a:kwe episode, such conflict is suggested in the confrontation between the twin, male War Gods of the Zunis and the warrior woman Cha'kwen 'Oka, who leads the Kan'a:kwe (see chapter 6). Does the presence of the berdache kachina as a go-between in this episode reflect a memory of a role played by berdaches in the resolution of an historical conflict?

37. Benedict, *Patterns of Culture*, 74; Kroeber, *Zuñi Kin and Clan*, 89.

38. Cf. Martin and Voorhies, *Female of the Species*, 188–89, 246–47.

39. Whiting et al., "Learning of Values," 104.

40. Li An-che, "Zuñi," 74.

41. Whiting et al., "Learning of Values," 107. The researchers found no comparable responses among Anglo populations also tested.

42. Benedict, *Patterns of Culture*, 59, 99; Bunzel, "Introduction to Zuñi Ceremonialism," 480.

43. Newman, *Zuni Dictionary*, 23.

44. McFeat, "Some Social and Spatial Aspects," 18.

45. Kluckhohn, "Expressive Activities," 294.

46. Bunzel, "Zuñi Katcinas," 1012.

47. D. Tedlock, *Spoken Word*, 293. The tribe does hold a "Miss Zuni" contest every year in conjunction with the Zuni Fair, but, as Young points out, the event bears little resemblance to Anglo beauty contests. Contes-

tants appear in traditional costume, answer questions about traditional culture, and prepare traditional Zuni dishes. Needless to say, there is no swim-suit contest or equivalent (see Young, "Women, Reproduction, and Religion," 444, and *Signs from the Ancestors*, 37).

48. The etymology of this term is not certain, although it may be related to *lha*, "become large, grow," which also has the sense of "too much" (D. Tedlock, *Spoken Word*, 241). The Zuni plural form is *'a:lhamana*. For convenience, I use the Anglicized version, lhamanas.

49. Stevenson, "Zuñi Indians," 37; Parsons, "Zuñi La'mana," 527. See also Gifford, *Culture Element Distributions 12*, 66, 163. Other comments of Stevenson require clarification. She states, "The women of the family joke the fellow," and "the men of the family . . . not only discourage men from unsexing themselves in this way, but ridicule them." The distinction between "joking the fellow" and "ridicule" is not clear. Zuni fathers (and other male relatives) no doubt looked forward to training and educating their sons to follow their footsteps. To this end, they might have employed ridicule—although "joking" better describes the banter typical of Zunis. But in this regard, every Zuni was the subject of jokes, especially for idiosyncrasies in their manner or appearance (see Greenberg, "Why Was the Berdache Ridiculed?"). Violent outbursts of hatred or anger toward berdaches, comparable to expressions of Western homophobia, have never been recorded at Zuni. Perhaps the key distinction, one that will be illustrated later, is that aside from jokes older male relatives did not attempt to use authority or discipline to prevent assumption of the role.

50. Dissette to Willard, 3 March 1924, Incoming Correspondence [IC], IRAP.

51. Kroeber, "Psychosis or Social Sanction?", 210. On Siberian shamans, see Bogoras, *Chukchee*, 449–56; Jochelson, *Koryak*, 52–54.

52. Smith, Woodbury, Woodbury, *Excavation of Hawikuh*, 209, 239, 242, 243. A similar case of sex-specific burial practices was found in Chaco Canyon where feather cloths occurred exclusively in female burials, with one male exception (Akins, *Biocultural Approach to Human Burials*, 93, 99).

53. Hibben, *Kiva Art of the Anasazi*, figure 49.

54. Variants of this term were in use throughout the Spanish-speaking Southwest—*mujeringo, mojara, mojaro, amejerado, amugereado*. A dictionary of New Mexican Spanish defines *mujerero* as "fond of women or given to spending his time gossiping in the kitchen with the women," while *mujerota* is a "hard-working or brave female" (Cobos, *Dictionary*, 115).

55. W. Hammond, *Sexual Impotence*, 165. On Hammond's account, see Hay, "Hammond Report." In 1899, a doctor at Zuni also became "curious to

probe the mystery," examining Zuni berdaches to determine their sex and concluding that "there was no physical difference between them and any other man" (Dissette to Willard, IC, IRAP).

56. Cushing, "Nominal and Numerical Census," ms. 3915, National Anthropological Archives; Stephen, *Hopi Journals*, 276; Dissette to Willard, IC, IRAP. On the incidence of physical intersexuality, see Martin and Voorhies, *Female of the Species*, 87–88.

57. Rodgers, *Gay Talk*, 105–6.

58. Fewkes, "A Few Tusayan Pictographs," 11.

59. Bandelier, *Southwestern Journals*, 326; Casagrande and Bourns, *Side Trips*, 82, 229.

60. Stevenson, "Zuñi Indians," 38; Dissette to Willard, IC, IRAP; Parsons, "Zuñi La'mana," 526; Stewart, "Homosexuality among the American Indians," 13–14.

61. Dissette, for example, who lived longer at Zuni than either Cushing or Stevenson and reported other stories about We'wha, makes no reference to his alleged paternity (Dissette to Willard, 3 March 1924, IC, IRAP).

62. Another form of bonding among Zunis was the *kihe* relationship, a kind of ceremonial friendship. Two individuals, regardless of gender, might enter a *kihe* relationship for various reasons. *Kihe* relationships often included gift-giving and economic cooperation, but they could be emotionally close, and they usually lasted for the lifetime of the individuals (Goldman, "Zuni Indians," 326; Parsons, "Ceremonial Friendship at Zuñi").

63. Parsons, "Zuñi Conception and Pregnancy Beliefs," 380; Parsons, "Zuñi La'mana," 526, 528; Parsons, *Notes on Zuñi*, 295. Unfortunately, it is not possible to estimate the total number of lhamanas in the overall Zuni population (or in any other tribe, for that matter). Cushing, who lived in the pueblo and knew the tribe much more intimately than Stevenson, recorded only one berdache—We'wha—in his 1881 tally of 1,619 individuals ("Nominal and Numerical Census," ms. 3915, National Anthropological Archives). Obviously there were others in the pueblo, but Cushing must have counted them as women. No accurate count of berdaches has ever been done in any tribe. As a point of comparison, Kinsey found 4 percent of American males were predominantly or exclusively homosexual. At Zuni, with a population of 1,600 in the 1880s and assuming half were male, this would equal 32. Since Kinsey's behavioral criteria would encompass not only berdaches but the non-berdache men who were their sexual partners, it seems reasonable that Zuni might have had this many predominantly homosexual men. However, it is important to remember that this comparison overlooks the significant cultural differences between the berdache role and the homosexual role. The number of transsexuals in the United

States, on the other hand, has been estimated at .001 to .003 percent of the population. In a population of 1,600, this would account for only one case every other generation (Bolin, *In Search of Eve*, 18).

64. Benedict, *Patterns of Culture*, 264.

65. Parsons, "Zuñi La'mana," 525; Parsons, "Waiyautitsa," 159; Parsons, *Notes on Zuñi*, 246.

66. Parsons, "Zuñi La'mana," 525; Parsons, *Notes on Zuñi*, 253.

67. Stevenson's earliest report on this subject is interesting in this regard: "When a woman of the order [kachina society] becomes advanced in age she endeavors to find some maiden who will take upon herself the vows at her death. . . . After the father is spoken to, he in turn spends the night in explaining the duties of the position to his daughter and that the gods would be displeased if she should marry after joining the Kok-ko. . . . But even here in Zuñi . . . women have been guilty of desecrating their sacred office and marrying" ("Religious Life of the Zuñi Child," 555). Although the implication that women who joined the kachina society undertook vows of chastity has been contradicted by subsequent investigators, it is possible that Stevenson recorded a tradition that lapsed before it could be confirmed. It is also possible that this custom did not apply to all women who entered the kachina society but specifically to those considered lhamanas, who would wear the mask of the berdache kachina. Unfortunately, the available documentation, unlike that for male berdaches, does not allow a fuller treatment of female berdaches at this time. The entire subject of female berdaches in North America is due for re-evaluation and new research (see Blackwood, "Sexuality and Gender"; Allen, "Lesbians in American Indian Cultures").

CHAPTER TWO

1. Stevenson, "Zuñi Indians," 20, 310, 380; George W. James, "Zuñi and 2 Modern Witchcraft Trials" (typescript, c. 1899), folder 210, carton 8, GWJC; Parsons, *Notes on Zuñi*, 253; Parsons, "Zuñi La'mana," 523; Bunker, *Other Men's Skies*, 99–100. Aside from Bunker's statement, there is no evidence that We'wha formally participated in Zuni political life. Smith and Roberts reported that lhamanas, like women, were not allowed to speak at the public meetings sometimes held in the large plaza (*Zuni Law*, 114). According to Zuni tradition, however, We'wha served as an interpreter for the tribe on official occasions, and this required that he take an oath of office.

2. This date is based on Cushing's estimate of We'wha's age in "Nominal and Numerical Census," ms. 3915, National Anthropological Archives.

3. Bunzel, *Zuni Texts*, 78.

4. Ferguson and Hart, *Zuni Atlas*, 63.

5. McNitt, *Navaho Expedition*, 113, 114.

6. Hart, "Brief History," 23; Stevenson, "Zuñi Indians," 37, 311; Foreman, *Pathfinder in the Southwest*, 141.

7. Stevenson, "Zuñi Indians," 37–38. On kinship terms, see Ladd, "Zuni Social and Political Organization."

8. Ferguson and Hart, *Zuni Atlas*, 60; Abel, *Official Correspondence of James S. Calhoun*, 260, 263, 274; E. Curtis, "Zuñi," 111–12.

9. Bieber, *Marching with the Army of the West*, 206–7; Ferguson and Mills, "Settlement and Growth," 249–50; Ten Broeck, "Manners and Customs," 80.

10. Hart, "Brief History."

11. Ladd, "Zuni Social and Political Organization," 484; Parsons, "Waiyautitsa," 159.

12. Duberman, *About Time*, 219.

13. Parsons, "Zuñi Ła'mana," 521–22.

14. Cushing, *Zuñi*, 58; Parsons, "Waiyautitsa," 162–63.

15. Stevenson, "Zuñi Indians," 354; Leighton and Adair, *People of the Middle Place*, 67; Benedict, *Zuñi Mythology* 1:12.

16. Cushing, *Zuñi Breadstuff*, 605.

17. Young, *Signs from the Ancestors*, 201. See also Sekaquaptewa, "Hopi Indian Ceremonies," 38.

18. Bunzel, "Introduction to Zuñi Ceremonialism," 541–42.

19. Stevenson, "Zuñi Indians," 293–94; Cushing, "Primitive Motherhood," 41.

20. Stevenson, "Zuñi Indians," 293.

21. Leighton and Adair, *People of the Middle Place*, 67; Cushing, "Primitive Motherhood," 41. On sexual experimentation among Hopi children, see Eggan, "General Problem of Hopi Adjustment," 368; Talayesva, *Sun Chief*, 103.

22. Li An-che, "Zuñi," 70.

23. Goldman, "Zuni Indians," 339; Leighton and Adair, *People of the Middle Place*, 71–72; Whiting et al., "Learning of Values," 95; Roberts, "Zuni," 304.

24. Parsons, "Zuñi A'doshle and Suuke," 343–44.

25. Cushing, *Zuñi Breadstuff*, 573; Cushing, "Primitive Motherhood," 37–38.

26. Goldman, "Zuni Indians," 338–40; Whiting et al., "Learning of Values," 108–9.

27. See Bunzel, "Zuñi Katcinas," 975–98; Stevenson, "Zuñi Indians," 102–7.

28. Cushing, "Nominal and Numerical Census," ms. 3915, National Anthropological Archives.

29. Stevenson refers to this mask as being among the personal effects buried after We'wha's death ("Zuñi Indians," 313).

30. Ibid., 354.

31. Ibid., 480, 483. In 1917, Kroeber published a map of the village, indicating current and previous locations of various religious groups as well as the clan identification of each household. He places the *lhewe:kwe* chamber in the northwestern corner of the pueblo (see *Zuñi Kin and Clan*, Map 1, "1916 Zuñi House and Clans" and Map 8, "Religious Map of Zuñi"). The same rooms can be located on Mindeleff's 1891 map (in Ferguson and Hart, *Zuni Atlas*, Map 27).

32. See Cushing's analysis of Zuni cuisine in *Zuñi Breadstuff*, 289–343.

33. Hardin, *Gifts of Mother Earth*, 11; Cushing, *Zuñi Breadstuff*, 310–16; Bunzel, *Pueblo Potter*, 54.

34. See Kent, *Pueblo Indian Textiles*, 12–14.

35. Ferguson and Mills, "Settlement and Growth," 247, 252.

36. Bloom, "Bourke on the Southwest," 200.

37. Vogt, "Intercultural Relations," 51–52.

38. Cushing, "Nominal and Numerical Census," ms. 3915, National Anthropological Archives.

39. Stevenson, "Zuñi Indians," 123.

40. Eaton, "Description," 221.

41. Bunzel, *Zuni Texts*, 80.

42. Crampton, *Zunis of Cibola*, 115–16; McNitt, *Indian Traders*, 239.

43. On the Indian policy of this period, see Dale, *Indians of the Southwest*; Fritz, *Movement for Indian Assimilation*; Mardock, *Reformers and the American Indian*.

44. Peterson, *Take Up Your Mission*, 204–7; Vogt, "Intercultural Relations," 55; Bender, *Missionaries, Outlaws, and Indians*, 80.

45. Sheldon Jackson, in Bender, *Missionaries, Outlaws, and Indians*, 83.

46. Ibid., 84. Missionary Andrew Vanderwagen was similarly "appalled" by the Sha'lako dances he witnessed during his first visit to Zuni (Kuipers, *Zuni Also Prays*, 110).

47. Pandey, "Factionalism," 59; Bender, *Missionaries, Outlaws, and Indians*, 81.

48. Bender, *Missionaries, Outlaws and Indians*, 163, 126.

49. Ibid., 90, 96, 198.

50. Ibid., 105, 138.

51. Cushing, *Zuñi*, 59; Bender, *Missionaries, Outlaws and Indians*, 121,

124. I am indebted to Danella Moneta of the Southwest Museum for pointing out We'wha in this photograph (personal communication, 4 April 1985).

52. Bender, *Missionaries, Outlaws, and Indians,* 153, 214. Basques were close-fitting bodices.

53. Ibid., 87. According to Dissette, We'wha and Nick Dumaka were the only Zunis who could speak any English when she arrived in 1888 (Dissette to Willard, 3 March 1924, IC, IRAP).

54. John Adair, personal communication, 29 September 1986; U.S. Office of Indian Affairs, *Rules,* 12–13; Dale, *Indians of the Southwest,* 166.

55. D. Tedlock, "American Indian View of Death," 257.

56. Stevenson, "Zuñi Indians," 394. It is interesting to note that We'wha speaks of the missionary's house as if it belonged to his wife, which would be a correct assumption from a Zuni point of view.

57. Triloki Pandey, personal communication, 17 April 1985; Parsons, "Zuñi Ła'mana," 528; Cushing, *Zuñi,* 96. Cushing does not list a medicine society for We'wha in his census. However, individuals often postponed formal initiation for years, until they could afford the expense of the necessary feasts and gifts.

58. Bender, *Missionaries, Outlaws, and Indians,* 164–65. For the date of Dissette's arrival at Zuni, see Dissette to Willard, 3 March 1924, IC, IRAP (cf. Crampton, *Zunis of Cibola,* 150–51).

59. Stevenson, "Zuñi Indians," 37.

60. Ibid.; Pandey 1972, "Anthropologists at Zuni," 327. Washington Matthews ridiculed James Stevenson's claim that Matilda Stevenson had learned both Zuni and Spanish. "The Indians are just unbosoming themselves to her," he wrote sarcastically to Cushing (Hinsley, *Savages and Scientists,* 199). His doubts about Mrs. Stevenson's language skills were well founded, as evidenced by her confusion of the term *lhamana* and the name of the mythical berdache kachina, Kolhamana—that is, "ko'thlama."

61. Stevenson, "Zuñi Indians," 380.

62. Dissette to Willard, 3 March 1924, IC, IRAP.

63. Stevenson, "Zuñi Indians," 310–11.

64. Ibid., 463.

65. Ibid., 310.

66. Triloki Pandey, personal communication, 17 April 1985.

67. Stevenson, "Zuñi Indians," 310. Stevenson was no doubt referring to Cushing who identified We'wha as an hermaphrodite in his 1881 census. Despite her disclaimer, Stevenson also may have thought, at least for a time, that We'wha was an hermaphrodite. According to Dissette, "Mrs. S. tried to make me believe that Way-weh was an 'Hermaphrodite' but I think she knew better" (Dissette to Willard, 3 March 1924, IC, IRAP).

68. John Adair, personal communication, 29 September 1986; Lurie, "Women in Early American Anthropology," 57. Stevenson's relationship with Clara True was formed on much the same basis (see chapter 1, note 10).

69. G. James, *New Mexico*, 63–64.

70. This last word is partially illegible, but elsewhere Cushing explained that the Zunis pronounced the Spanish *bueno* as "we-no" (*Zuñi*, 59). This suggests that We'wha could speak at least rudimentary Spanish.

71. Cushing to J. Stevenson, 15 October 1879, envelope no. 69, HCC.

72. Stevenson, "Zuñi Indians," 374.

73. G. James, *New Mexico*, 63. See also G. James, *Our American Wonderlands*, 143.

74. G. James, *New Mexico*, 64.

75. G. James, "Zuñi and 2 Modern Witchcraft Trials," GWJC.

76. G. James, *New Mexico*, 64.

77. Stevenson, "Zuñi Indians," 463.

CHAPTER THREE

1. Quoted in Brandes, "Frank Hamilton Cushing," 86. On this trip, see Baxter, "Aboriginal Pilgrimage"; Cushing, *Zuñi*, 407–25; and Ober, "How a White Man Became the War Chief of the Zunis."

2. Powell, "Annual Report," xviii, xxi, xxiv–xxv; *New York Times*, 15 February 1886. We'wha may have stayed longer than six months. A meeting of the Women's Anthropological Society held in late November 1885 likely was attended by Stevenson (*Organization and Historical Sketch*, 17). We'wha was still in Washington as of late June 1886 when the *Evening Star* reported, "Wa-wah will go back to her home when some one, who can act as her escort, is going her way" (12 June 1886).

3. Baxter, "Aboriginal Pilgrimage," 527–28.

4. Viola, *Diplomats in Buckskin*, 52. On Indian delegations to Washington, see also K. Turner, *Red Men Calling*.

5. Viola, *Diplomats in Buckskin*, 76–77.

6. Stevenson, "Zuñi Indians," 130, 310; Mason, "Planting and Exhuming of a Prayer," 24; *National Tribune*, 20 May 1886.

7. *Washington Chronicle*, 18 April 1886.

8. Barnes, *John G. Carlisle*, 156.

9. Stevenson, "Zuñi Indians," 312. Carlisle had sent a similar gift to Pedro Pino, the retired governor of Zuni, after his visit in 1882 (Carlisle to Pino, 5 April 1882, Pedro Pino Correspondence 1882, envelope no. 35, HCC).

10. *Washington Chronicle*, 18 April 1886.

11. Lee, Meersman, and Murphy, *Stage for a Nation*, 34, 59; *Evening Star*, 24 July 1886. On abandoned infants, see the *Evening Star* for 4, 5, 7, and 8 January, 22 and 23 May, and 25, 28, and 30 June—all in 1886. Child abuse and youth prostitution were related problems (see *Evening Star*, 21 November 1885 and 17 July 1886).

12. See Flack, "Formation of the Washington Intellectual Community."

13. Moore, *Picturesque Washington*, 242.

14. Dickinson *Social Mirror*, 120.

15. Hinman, *Washington Sketch Book*, 41. See also Dickinson, *Social Mirror*, 108; Moore, *Picturesque Washington*, 243–44.

16. Hinman, *Washington Sketch Book*, 41; *Evening Star*, 12 June 1886.

17. *Washington Post*, 24 January 1886. On family friends, see obituaries of James Stevenson in the *New York Times*, 27 July 1888 and *National Tribune*, 2 August 1888.

18. *National Tribune*, 20 May 1886.

19. Ibid.

20. *Evening Star*, 12 June 1886.

21. *Washington Chronicle*, 18 April 1886.

22. On the founding of the WAS, see Croly, *History of the Woman's Club Movement*, 341–43; Flack, "Formation of the Washington Intellectual Community," 189–92; Lurie, "Women in Early American Anthropology"; *Organization and Historical Sketch*; Parezo, "Matilda Coxe Evans Stevenson."

23. Rose Cleveland was credited with suggesting the name of Stevenson's organization (*Evening Star*, 13 February 1886). Described by one historian as "a formidable lady, large and aggressive," Cleveland's passionate friendships with other women have become the subject of historical interest in recent years (Tugwell, *Grover Cleveland*, 99; Katz, "President's Sister and the Bishop's Wife").

24. *Evening Star*, 13 February 1886. Lurie was not aware of this when she wrote that "as far as records show, no women put in an appearance [at the Washington Anthropological Society], nor, in the next few years, did it seem to have occurred to women to request membership in the group." Consequently, she downplayed the feminist motives behind the founding of the Women's Anthropological Society (Lurie, "Women in Early American Anthropology," 35). On the feminist character of women's organizations in the late nineteenth century see, Blair, *Clubwoman as Feminist*.

25. Parezo, "Matilda Coxe Evans Stevenson," 339.

26. *Washington Post*, 24 January 1886, 31 January 1886; *Evening Star*, 20 January 1886, 1 February 1886.

27. *Washington Post*, 1 April 1886; *Evening Star*, 31 March 1886.

28. Mason, "Planting and Exhuming of a Prayer," 24. Mason included a retouched version of one of these photos in *Woman's Share in Primitive Culture.*

29. *National Tribune*, 20 May 1886; *Evening Star*, 12 June 1886. On the model of Zuni, see Judd, *Bureau of American Ethnology*, 63–64; Brandes, "Frank Hamilton Cushing," 76; Hinsley, *Savages and Scientists*, 197. Efforts to locate it in recent years have been unsuccessful (Bender, *Missionaries, Outlaws, and Indians*, 208).

30. Basso, "History of Ethnological Research," 19; Stevenson, "Dress and Adornment of the Pueblo Indians" (typescript, 1911), p. 194, ms. 2093, National Anthropological Archives. According to the records of the National Anthropological Archives, these photographs, along with a series of portraits of We'wha, were taken by John K. Hillers.

31. *Evening Star*, 12 June 1886.

32. *National Tribune*, 20 May 1886. Cushing, Bandelier, Parsons, Goldfrank, White, and members of the Harvard Values Project, among others, have used this strategy.

33. *National Tribune*, 20 May 1886. It is interesting to note that two years before James Stevenson's death, the "book" on Zuni was already described as Matilda's project.

34. Gatschet, "Notes on Clans," ms. 895, National Anthropological Archives.

35. *National Tribune*, 20 May 1886.

36. *Washington Post*, 21 March 1886, 4 April 1886, 11 April 1886; *Evening Star*, 31 March 1886.

37. *National Tribune*, 20 May 1886.

38. *Washington Post*, 9 May 1886, 14 May 1886.

39. *Washington Post*, 14 May 1886; *Evening Star*, 14 May 1886.

40. *Evening Star*, 14 May 1886.

41. *Washington Post*, 14 May 1886.

42. *National Tribune*, 20 May 1886.

43. *Washington Post*, 14 May 1886, 16 May 1886, 15 May 1886, 30 May 1886; *Evening Star*, 15 May 1886.

44. *Washington Post*, 14 May 1886.

45. Cf. Hinsley, *Savages and Scientists*, 145–47.

46. Flack, "Formation of the Washington Intellectual Community," 166ff.; Hinsley, *Savages and Scientists*, 57.

47. Powell, in Darrah, *Powell of the Colorado*, 262. On Powell's debt to Morgan, see Hinsley, *Savages and Scientists*, 133ff.

48. See, for example, the exchange summarized in Darrah, *Powell of the*

Colorado, 264–65. The Washington Anthropological Society was a key forum for these debates (see Flack "Formation of the Washington Intellectual Community," 175–78, 192–93).

49. Darrah, *Powell of the Colorado*, 356; Hinsley, *Savages and Scientists*, 133ff; Chugerman, *Lester F. Ward*, 326–27. Equally interesting were Ward's ideas on sexual freedom and women's rights. Ward considered sexuality "the sublimest and most exalted as well as the purest and noblest of impulses." Regarding feminism he wrote, "Civilization demands this revolution." Ward considered women originally superior to men. In fact, his philosophy of gender has much in common with the Zuni view: "Woman is the unchanging trunk of the great genealogic tree, while man, with all his vaunted superiority is but a branch, a grafted scion" (Chugerman, *Lester F. Ward*, 372, 378). Although few remember Ward's contributions today, his work influenced such early twentieth-century sexologists and feminists as Havelock Ellis and Charlotte Perkins Gilman (ibid., 379). Perhaps Ward's most influential admirer was John Collier, the muckraking reformer who became Commissioner of Indian Affairs in the 1930s (Philp, *John Collier's Crusade*, 8, 237). The ideal of social planning through democratic process was a constant theme in Collier's career. While he renounced the evolutionism of Morgan and Powell in favor of cultural relativity and pluralism, Collier always believed that the democratic will was innate among people and had only to be released—an assumption not so different from Powell's and Ward's belief in a steady evolution of society toward democracy and enlightenment.

50. Pearce, *Savagism and Civilization*, 200.

51. *National Tribune*, 20 May 1886.

52. Mason, "Planting and Exhuming of a Prayer," 24–25.

53. Stevenson to Lamont, 18 June 1886, microfilm series 2, reel 35, Grover Cleveland Papers, Library of Congress.

54. La Follette, *La Follette's Autobiography*, 24.

55. John A. Logan, running mate of Cleveland's opponent, was under fire during the campaign for his alleged involvement in a scheme to seize Zuni lands in the Nutria area (see Brandes, "Frank Hamilton Cushing," chapter 5; W. Curtis, *Children of the Sun*, chapter 3; Fuller, "Frank Hamilton Cushing's Relations to Zuñi," 74–83).

56. See, for example, visits reported in *Washington Post*, 23 January 1886, 30 April 1886; *Evening Star*, 18 December 1885.

57. *Washington Post*, 24 June 1886.

58. Wilson, *Red, Black, Blond and Olive*, 20; Dissette to Willard, 3 March 1924, IC, IRAP.

59. G. James, *New Mexico*, 63; *Our American Wonderlands*, 143.

60. George W. James, "Zuñi and 2 Modern Witchcraft Trials" (typescript, c. 1899), folder 210, carton 8, GWJC.

61. Stevenson, "Zuñi Indians," 130.

62. True to Renehan, 16 December 1908, RBAE/LR, National Anthropological Archives. Attitudes toward cross-dressing in Victorian America were not always frivolous. Non-Indians who cross-dressed did so at great risk, as the *Evening Star* reported on 1 January 1886 in an article headlined, "In Female Attire. A Man Caught Masquerading in Woman's Garb Sent to the Workhouse."

> *The first case called in the Police Court this morning was that of William Sherman. When the name was called the tall form of a colored man appeared in the dock. The prisoner was a man of thirty years, and was in female attire. He wore a pink dress trimmed with white lace, with stockings and undergarments to match. Patent leather slippers covered his feet, while he had thrown around his shoulders a black silk shawl and a white fascinator over his head. "That's Miss Maud," said the officer as he passed the reporter's table.*
>
> *"There's a man's name on this paper," said the clerk; "that's the wrong prisoner."*
>
> *"That's a man," said Officer Penny, who arrested the prisoner when the latter was returning from a "drag."*
>
> *Presently the judge's attention was attracted to the prisoner, and he admired his stylish appearance. "Has she been arraigned?" the judge asked.*
>
> *"It's a he," said the officer.*

Sherman pleaded guilty to the charge of vagrancy and was sentenced to three months in jail.

Jonathan Katz has published a brief notice from an 1893 medical journal regarding this "convocation of negro men called the drag dance, which is an orgie of lascivious debauchery. . . . Among those who annually assemble in this strange libidinous display are cooks, barbers, waiters and other employes of Washington families, some even higher in the social scale—some being employed in the Government departments" (*Gay American History*, 42–43).

CHAPTER FOUR

1. Stevenson, "Zuñi Indians," 256.
2. Ibid., 253. See also Porter, *Paper Medicine Man*, 127.
3. Stevenson, "Zuñi Indians," 256.

4. G. James, *New Mexico*, 90. He was also known as Zuni Dick (Pandey, "Factionalism," 101; Kroeber, *Zuñi Kin and Clan*, 180).

5. Bunzel, *Zuni Texts*, 44–52. Quoted material in this section is from this source unless otherwise cited. Bunzel published this text in both Zuni and English.

6. A variety of dates have been reported for the events described here, and they have often been conflated with events that occurred in 1897 (see, for example, Smith and Roberts, *Zuni Law*, 45–48). The arrest of the bow priests in 1892 has also been confused with the arrest of two Zunis that summer for the murder of a Mexican boy (e.g., Hart, "Factors Relating to Zuni Land," 2756). "Chin Boton" and "Liloklil" were acquitted in March 1898 (see letters of Agent Robertson, 20 August 1892, 3 October 1892, 4 October 1892, 15 October 1892, Letters Sent [LS], Entry 1, PA; *Albuquerque Evening Citizen*, 2 March 1893; *Albuquerque Morning Democrat*, 3 March 1893).

7. J. King, *War Eagle*, 233; Crampton, *Zunis of Cibola*, 153. Various sources report that Dumaka was raised by whites—by officers at Fort Wingate or by Graham—but these accounts cannot be confirmed. According to Pandey, he worked for Carr as a child, but by the time of Carr's tenure at Fort Wingate, Dumaka was in his twenties (Pandey, "Factionalism," 141; see also Kuipers, *Zuni Also Prays*, 141).

8. Stevenson, "Zuñi Indians," 382; Bunzel, *Zuni Texts*, viii; Saunders, *Indians of the Terraced Houses*, 134.

9. E. Curtis, "Zuñi," 111; Bender, *Missionaries, Outlaws, and Indians*, 74, 140, 165, 216; Triloki Pandey, personal communication, 17 April 1985.

10. Benedict, *Patterns of Culture*, 260–61.

11. E. Curtis, "Zuñi," 111; Dolfin, *Bringing the Gospel*, 306; G. James, *New Mexico*, 87.

12. Dolfin, *Bringing the Gospel*, 306.

13. E. Curtis, "Zuñi," 111.

14. Bunzel, *Zuni Texts*, 45–46, 81.

15. Baxter, "Aboriginal Pilgrimage," 533.

16. Benedict, *Patterns of Culture*, 261.

17. Cushing, *Zuñi*, 125–27.

18. Benedict, *Zuñi Mythology* 2:151–52. See also Benedict, *Zuñi Mythology* 1:191–92, 233, and 2:133, 163, 151–52; Bunker, *Other Men's Skies*, 126; Bunzel, "Introduction to Zuñi Ceremonialism," 492; Leighton and Adair, *People of the Middle Place*, 72–75, 79; Parsons, "Witchcraft among the Pueblos"; D. Tedlock, "Zuni Religion and World View," 506; Stevenson, "Zuñi Indians," 392–406.

19. Stevenson, "Zuñi Indians," 393.

20. Cushing, *Zuñi*, 124–26. See also Bunzel, "Introduction to Zuñi Ceremonialism," 526; Hrdlička, *Physiological and Medical Observations*, 169; Parsons, *Notes on Zuñi*, 280; Stevenson, "Zuñi Indians," 406.

21. See Pandey, "Factionalism," 148–49; Leighton and Adair, *People of the Middle Place*, 142.

22. Leighton and Adair, *People of the Middle Place*, 54. See also Whiting at al., "Learning of Values," 124.

23. See, for example, Pandey, "Flora Zuni," 221; Leighton and Adair, *People of the Middle Place*, 73.

24. Bullis to Commissioner, 17 May 1895, LS, PA; Dolfin, *Bringing the Gospel*, 306; G. James, *New Mexico*, 87–88.

25. Bunzel, *Zuni Texts*, 47.

26. *Santa Fe Daily New Mexican*, 21 December 1892; *Albuquerque Morning Democrat*, 20 December 1892; "Report of the Commissioner of Indian Affairs," 52d Cong., 2d sess., 1893, 555.

27. Dolfin, *Bringing the Gospel*, 307; G. James, *New Mexico*, 90; Kuipers, *Zuni Also Prays*, 141.

28. Journal of Mrs. Frank G. Churchill, "Kansas City to Keams Canyon, December 5, 1903 to December 21, 1903," vol. 1 (photocopy), Wheelwright Collection.

29. Parsons, *Notes on Zuñi*, 270; "Report of the Commissioner of Indian Affairs," 52d Cong., 2d sess., 1893, 555; Kuipers, *Zuni Also Prays*, 141.

30. *Albuquerque Morning Democrat*, 20 December 1892.

31. Record of Events, December 1892, Returns from U.S. Military Posts, FW (microfilm publication M617; cited hereafter as "Returns"); Orders No. 165, 17 December 1892, FW; *Albuquerque Morning Democrat*, 20 December 1892; Bunzel, *Zuni Texts*, 48.

32. Zuni pronouns do not reflect gender. Bunzel, however, translates pronouns referring to We'wha as both "he" and "she." Most interesting is Lina Zuni's use of a male kinship term (*suwe*, "younger brother") to refer to We'wha. The term translated as "although he was a man," *'otstsi'nte*, might be rendered more accurately as "although a male"—for *'otstsi'* refers specifically to physiological sex as opposed to social gender (Newman, *Zuni Dictionary*, 16). The phrase "in woman's dress," *yadonabba*, refers to the manta or Pueblo woman's dress worn over one shoulder. Thus, the passage is better rendered as "his younger brother, although a manta-wearing male." The translation of Lina's second characterization of We'wha, "although he pretended to be a woman," *'oka yashenande*, can also be improved. Newman defines the verb stem of this phrase, *'ashe*, as "be dead, act thoughtlessly, act without restraint" (*Zuni Dictionary*, 10). The concept implied, congruent with the Zuni understanding of death, is the loss or

absence of consciousness. With this in mind, the phrase is better rendered as "unconsciously acted like a female," with the connotation that this behavior was spontaneous—a natural expression of We'wha's character—which is quite different from the connotation of "pretending to be a woman."

33. Nordstrom to Commissioner, 30 August 1897, Letters to the Commissioner of Indian Affairs, Entry 2 [LC], PA.

34. Rouse, "War and Witchcraft," 4. An army officer quoted in the same article questioned this detail, pointing out that the army uniforms of that time did not have tails and officers did not carry sabres (p. 5).

35. Nordstrom to Commissioner, 30 August 1897, LC, PA; George W. James, "Zuñi and 2 Modern Witchcraft Trials" (typescript, c. 1899), folder 210, carton 8, GWJC; Bunzel, *Zuni Texts*, 49. See also Leupp, *Notes of a Summer Tour*, 15.

36. Returns, 1892 December, FW; Orders no. 165 and 167, FW. See also Rafferty to Assistant Adjutant General, 13 January 1893, Letters Sent, FW.

37. *Albuquerque Morning Democrat*, 23 December 1892.

38. E. Curtis, "Zuñi," 111; Pandey, "Factionalism," 101.

39. *Albuquerque Morning Democrat*, 28 December 1892.

40. Stephen, *Hopi Journals*, 276; "Report of the Commissioner of Indian Affairs," 52d Cong., 2d sess., 1893, 555.

41. Robertson to Dissette, 19 January 1893, LS, PA.

42. Bunzel, *Zuni Texts*, 81.

43. Benedict, *Patterns of Culture*, 261.

44. Bunzel, *Zuni Texts*, 51. One of his rivals described Dumaka as "the most hated, distrusted, and comical character in Zuni history" (Pandey, "Factionalism," 141). Nonetheless, the course of his subsequent life was not what might be expected. After a period of exile, Dumaka returned to Zuni, established his own business as a trader, and earned enough money to build a Sha'lako house. Eventually, he joined at least three medicine societies and acquired an immense store of religious knowledge, hoping to make himself indispensable to Zuni ceremonial life—and he largely succeeded. His facility with English and eagerness to befriend Anglos made him an excellent informant; Stevenson, Kroeber, Boas, Parsons, Benedict, and Bunzel all worked with Dumaka. Bunzel formed an especially close and poignant relationship with him. He died in 1927. See Benedict, *Zuñi Mythology* 1:xxxix; Bunzel, "Introduction to Zuñi Ceremonialism," 494, "Zuñi Katcinas," 876, *Chichicastenango*, xix–xx; E. Curtis, "Zuñi," 111; Fawcett and McLuhan, "Ruth Leah Bunzel," 30–32; Goldman, "Zuni Indians," 349–50; Kuipers, *Zuni Also Prays*, 72, 140–43; Pandey, "Factionalism," 141–47; Saunders, *Indians of the Terraced Houses*, 154–55; Stevenson, "Ethnobotany of the Zuñi Indians," 38.

45. Stevenson, "Zuñi Indians," 312.

46. Ibid., 312, 313, 483. Marita was a member of the same medicine society We'wha belonged to, and her family farmed at Nutria, as did We'wha's (Cushing, "Nominal and Numerical Census," ms. 3915, National Anthropological Archives). A Ben Wittick photograph from 1897 shows her seated amidst a display of pottery and native textiles (Museum of New Mexico, neg. no. 16216). A photograph of a woman identified as Dumaka's mother in Beets bears a remarkable resemblance to Marita (*Toiling and Trusting*, 209). If Marita was indeed Dumaka's mother, this would link the incidents of 1892 and 1897 even more closely.

47. G. James, "Zuñi and 2 Modern Witchcraft Trials," GWJC.

48. Rouse, "War and Witchcraft," 4.

49. G. James, *Our American Wonderlands*, 143. The construction of James's yarn can be traced by comparing various versions in his manuscripts. The earliest, dated 8 January 1898, is a printed broadside entitled "Zuñi and the Zuñians." Here, he merely describes his interview with Marita and concludes, "As soon as the agent knew of it he sent officers to arrest the chiefs" (folder 155, carton 6, GWJC). Another version appears in a typescript entitled "Zuñi and 2 Modern Witchcraft Trials," written sometime after 1899. Here, James describes the trial in greater detail and reports, "When, a week later, I arrived at Zuñi . . . I went up to her room" (folder 210, carton 8, GWJC). But in the two versions James published, he claimed to have arrived "just as she was in the final stages of her hanging, between life and death." He nursed her wounds and notified "white friends" (*Our American Wonderlands*, 143–44; *New Mexico*, 91–92).

50. Rouse, "War and Witchcraft," 4; "Report of the Commissioner of Indian Affairs," 55th Cong., 2d sess., 1897, 62–63.

51. "Proceedings of the Sixth Annual Lake Mohonk Conference," 50th Cong., 2d sess., 1888, 812; "Report of the Board of Indian Commissioners," 53d Cong., 3d sess., 1895, 1033.

52. See Dale, *Indians of the Southwest*, Chapter 12; Hoxie, *Final Promise*; Spicer, *Cycles of Conquest*, 348–49; Szasz, *Education and the American Indian*.

53. Morgan, in Prucha, *Americanizing the American Indians*, 222.

54. On Zuni experiences in government schools, see Ladd, "Zuni Education"; Napetcha, "Education at Zuni"; Parsons, "Franciscans Return to Zuni," 338.

55. Dale, *Indians of the Southwest*, 182; Hoxie, *Final Promise*, 65; Szasz, *Education and the American Indian*, 10–11.

56. Morgan, in Prucha, *Americanizing the American Indians*, 253–54.

57. Nordstrom to Superintendent of Indian Schools, 31 May 1897, LS,

PA. See also "Report of the Commissioner of Indian Affairs," 55th Cong., 2d sess., 1897, 199.

58. "Report of the Commissioner of Indian Affairs," 55th Cong., 2d sess., 1897, 199.

59. Nordstrom to Commissioner, 25 June 1897, LC, PA.

60. Nordstrom to Graham, 13 August 1897, LS, PA.

61. Nordstrom to Faurote, 23 August 1897, LS, PA.

62. Robertson to Dissette, 19 August 1892, LS, PA; "Report of the Commissioner of Indian Affairs," 52d Cong., 2d sess., 1893, 552.

63. Nordstrom to Commissioner, 18 August 1897, LC, PA; Nordstrom to Finical, 21 August 1897, LS, PA.

64. Nordstrom to Commissioner (letter and telegram), 30 August 1897, LC, PA.

65. Returns, September 1897, FW; Rouse, "War and Witchcraft," 5. Other sources report that three troops were sent to Zuni ("Report of the Commissioner of Indian Affairs," 55th Cong., 2d sess., 1897, 63; Nordstrom to Commissioner, 22 September 1897, LC, PA). The *New York Times* reported that 15,000 Zunis, including 3,500 "well-armed warriors" (the total population of the village was only 1,700), were holed up in "a veritable mud fortress," predicting "a battle will follow the invasion by the troops" (9 September 1897).

66. Nordstrom to Commissioner, 22 September 1897, LC, PA.

67. "Report of the Commissioner of Indian Affairs," 55th Cong., 2d sess., 1897, 63.

68. *Santa Fe Daily New Mexican*, 20 September 1897.

69. Godfrey to Nordstrom, 18 September 1897, Letters Received [LR], PA; Telling, "New Mexican Frontiers," 134.

70. Nordstrom to Commissioner, 22 September 1897, LC, PA.

71. Finical to Nordstrom, 24 September 1897, LR, PA; Nordstrom to Commissioner, 25 September 1897, 6 October 1897, LC, PA.

72. Returns, October 1897–March 1898, FW.

73. DeKorne, *Navaho and Zuni for Christ*, 52.

74. Nordstrom to Commissioner, ? November 1897, 18 November 1897, 25 November 1897, 27 December 1897, LC, PA. See also Telling, "New Mexican Frontiers," 134.

75. Nordstrom to Zuni Governor, 13 November 1897, LS, PA.

76. Heitman, *Historical Register*, 750.

77. Taggart, 8 February 1898, LC. It took two more letters and over a month before the troops were finally withdrawn on March 14 (Cooper to Commissioner, 23 February 1898, 14 March 1898, LC, PA; Returns, March 1898, FW).

78. Finical to Cooper, 17 February 1898, and Finical to Walpole, 10 October 1898, LR, PA.

79. Taggart to Commissioner, 18 February 1898, LC, PA; Cooper to Zuni Dick, 23 February 1898, LS, PA. It is not clear if Tsanahe wrote in an official capacity—that is, as governor. Roman Luna was serving as governor in late 1897.

80. Cooper to Commissioner, 21 February 1898, LC, PA; Pandey, "Factionalism," 61. Dissette blamed her dismissal on certain "petty snobs in uniforms" at Fort Wingate with whom she had become enemies. She returned to Zuni briefly in late 1898 to assist during the smallpox epidemic in which over three hundred Zunis died (Crampton, *Zunis of Cibola*, 151; Pandey, "Factionalism," 61; Telling, "New Mexican Frontiers," 164; Dissette to Welsh, 25 April 1898, 18 August 1898, Incoming Correspondence, IRAP). She later became an Indian school inspector.

81. Rodey to Walpole, 18 December 1898, LR, PA.

82. Walpole to Greason, 13 October 1898, Day School Letters, PA; "Report of the Governor of New Mexico," 56th Cong., 1st sess., 1899, 432.

83. Stevenson, "Zuñi Indians," 406.

84. Bunzel, *Zuni Texts*, 51–52.

85. Woodward, "Concerning Witches," 186.

86. On the development and function of factions in Zuni tribal politics, see the various articles by Pandey cited here in the Bibliography.

87. See, for example, Pandey, "Flora Zuni," 221.

88. Goldman, "Zuni Indians," 344.

89. McFeat, "Some Social and Spatial Aspects," 22, 42–43.

90. Kent, *Pueblo Indian Textiles*, 44; Nancy Fox, personal communication, 24 October 1986. Despite these early sales of textiles and efforts by Douglas Graham and the Hyde Exploring Expedition to develop markets for pottery at the turn of the century, silversmithing eventually became the primary commercial art of the Zunis (Telling, "New Mexican Frontiers," 105; Kuipers, *Zuni Also Prays*, 82–83; Ladd, "Zuni Economy"). Recently, however, both women and men have begun producing ceramics for sale (see Hardin, *Gifts of Mother Earth*).

91. Ladd, "Zuni Economy," 495–98.

CHAPTER FIVE

1. Stevenson, "Zuñi Indians," 312–13.

2. Parsons, "Zuñi Ła'mana," "Last Zuni Transvestite." Parsons's earliest comments on berdaches appear in *Religious Chastity* 310–11.

3. See D. King, "Gender Confusions."

4. A. Kroeber, "Thoughts on Zuni Religion," 272; T. Kroeber, *Alfred Kroeber*, 97–98.

5. Scherer, *Indians* 163.

6. A. Krooeber, "Psychosis or Social Sanction?", 209.

7. See Roscoe, "Bibliography."

8. Angelino and Shedd, "Note on Berdache," 125.

9. Parsons, "Zuñi Ła'mana," 528. See also Parsons, "A Few Zuni Death Beliefs," 252–53.

10. Fox, *Pueblo Weaving*, 17, 31.

11. Parsons, "Last Zuni Transvestite," 338.

12. Stevenson, "Zuñi Indians," 37.

13. Cushing, *Zuñi*, 68.

14. Ibid., 90.

15. Ibid., 93–94; Cushing, "Primitive Motherhood," 35.

16. D. Tedlock, "American Indian View of Death," 265; D. Tedlock, "Zuni Religion," 499. Zuni concepts of the raw and the cooked led Lévi-Strauss to search for similar categories in native societies throughout North and South America (*Origin of Table Manners*, 495, 479; see also *The Raw and the Cooked*, 1, 64). The Zunis consciously used these terms as metaphors. *Cooked* and *raw* served to distinguish not only Zuni from non-Zuni and adult from child, but such statuses as core household members (cooked) and in-marrying affines (raw) (Vogt and Albert, "Comparative Study," 20).

17. V. Turner, *Ritual Process*, 94–95. See also Gennep, *Rites of Passage*; Eliade, *Rites and Symbols of Initiation*.

18. Bunzel, "Zuñi Katcinas," 975; Newman, *Zuni Dictionary*, 35.

19. Cushing, *Zuñi*, 421.

20. See Sandner, *Navaho Symbols of Healing*, 12–20; Neumann, *Great Mother*, 8, 295; Young, *Signs from the Ancestors*, 153.

21. The following analysis is based on practices reported in the ethnographic literature for the late nineteenth century. Although there has been a reduction of ceremonial intensity in the past century and various religious groups and ceremonials have lapsed, the core elements of the rites described in this chapter are still observed in many Zuni households, especially birth and death rites. The two versions of the male initiation ceremony are still held, although the age of initiation is variable. Several medicine societies are also active.

22. The following account of Zuni birth rites is based on Cushing, "Primitive Motherhood"; Leighton and Adair, *People of the Middle Place*, 60–61; Parsons, "Mothers and Children"; Parsons, "Waiyautitsa," 167–69; Stevenson, "Zuñi Indians," 297–302.

23. See Cushing, *Zuñi Breadstuff*, 167–68.

24. Parsons, "Waiyautitsa," 168.

25. Cushing, *Zuñi*, 205. The period of lying-in could vary from four to eight, ten, or twelve days, according to family custom (Parsons, "Waiyautitsa," 168).

26. Cushing, *Zuñi Breadstuff*, 24. See also Parsons, "Ceremonial Friendship," 2; Neumann, *Great Mother*, 39, 133.

27. Parsons, "Waiyautitsa," 168.

28. D. Tedlock, "Zuni Religion," 502.

29. Stevenson, "Zuñi Indians," 296.

30. E. Curtis, "Zuñi," 108. See also Parsons, "Waiyautitsa," 167; Parsons, "Zuñi Conception and Pregnancy Beliefs," 379–80; Parsons, "Mothers and Children," 168; Stevenson, "Zuñi Indians," 294–95, 299.

31. Schneider and Roberts, *Zuni Kin Terms*, 4; Ladd, "Zuni Social and Political Organization," 484.

32. Bunzel, "Zuñi Katcinas," 976; Parsons, "Zuñi Tales," 35. The following account of the boys' first initiation is based on Bunzel, "Zuñi Katcinas," 975–98; Cushing, *Zuñi Breadstuff*, 612–16; Leighton and Adair, *People of the Middle Place*, 68–71; Stevenson, "Religious Life of the Zuñi Child," 547–53; Stevenson, "Zuñi Indians," 94–102.

33. Parsons, "Zuñi Tales," 35. Blows on the back would have "knocked the breath" out of the initiates. This was an effective simulation of death since the Zunis considered breath synonymous with life.

34. Bunzel, "Introduction to Zuñi Ceremonialism," 522, "Zuñi Katcinas," 980.

35. On naming, see Parsons, "Zuñi Names."

36. Bunzel, "Introduction to Zuñi Ceremonialism," 516, "Zuñi Katcinas," 986–88; Young, "Women, Reproduction, and Religion," 439.

37. Bunzel, "Zuñi Katcinas," 1000.

38. Stevenson, "Zuñi Indians," 103.

39. Ibid., 104.

40. Sekaquaptewa, "Hopi Indian Ceremonies," 39.

41. Whiting et al., "Learning of Values," 101. For an account of attitudes toward hunting by a contemporary Zuni, see Ukestine, "Ancestral Homecoming."

42. Bunzel, "Zuñi Katcinas," 1012–14.

43. See, for example, Goldman, "Zuni Indians," 341; Leighton and Adair, *People of the Middle Place*, 74; Bunzel, "Introduction to Zuñi Ceremonialism," 541, 543. Cf. Young, "Women, Reproduction, and Religion."

44. Cushing, "Primitive Motherhood," 42.

45. Allen, *Sacred Hoop*, 101, 267.

46. Stevenson, "Zuñi Indians," 303; Eliade, *Rites and Symbols of Initiation*, 45. This rite appears to be a condensed version of the female puberty rites common to the Navajos and several of the hunting and gathering tribes of the Southwest and Great Basin.

47. Parson, "Waiyautitsa," 161. Schlegel has made a similar observation regarding the position of Hopi women ("Male and Female," 255–56).

48. Stevenson, "Zuñi Indians," 299–300.

49. See Bunzel, "Introduction to Zuñi Ceremonialism," 513; Cushing, *Zuñi Breadstuff*, 306–10, 317, 336; Cushing, "Zuñi Social, Mythic, and Religious Systems," 191; Cushing, "Commentary," 33; Parsons, *Pueblo Indian Religion*, 675, 880; Stevenson, "Ethnobotany," 87. The name was the plural form of *lha'ha*, or rabbit skin blanket, which, according to Stevenson, signified "fecundity"—also the theme of Cha'kwen 'Oka's rabbit hunt. Only Stevenson has described this ceremony ("Zuñi Indians," 180–204), although Cushing (*Zuñi Breadstuff*, 631) and James claimed to have seen it ("Strange Customs of the NA Indians" [manuscript, c. 1915], folder 97, carton 4, GWJC). Leslie Van Ness Denman published a brief account in 1955 (*Pai-ya-tu-ma*).

50. The following account of Cha'kwen 'Oka's ceremonial appearances is based on Bunzel, "Zuñi Katcinas," 931–35; Parsons, *Pueblo Indian Religion*, 464, 758–61; Parsons, "Zuni Conception and Pregnancy Beliefs," 380–81; Stevenson, "Zuñi Indians," 89–94. English-speaking Zunis refer to her as "the Warrior Woman." Her personal name was Ku'yabalitsa (Stevenson, "Zuñi Indians," 89; cf. Kuyabalitsa, the "deer girl," in a tale summarized by Parsons, *Winter and Summer Dance Series*, 203). Cha'kwen 'Oka should not be confused with the Cha'kwen group dancers, who were male warrior kachinas.

51. I would add the rites of the Corn Maidens to the six cults identified by Bunzel (the cults of the sun, the rainmakers, kachinas, kachina priests, war gods, and beast gods) ("Introduction to Zuñi Ceremonialism," 511).

52. Stevenson, "Zuñi Indians," 277–83; Bunzel, "Zuñi Katcinas," 913–14. Running by young women, also an element of the ceremonial rabbit hunt, was an important feature of female initiations among the Navajos, Apaches, and Paiutes. The Lha:hewe' ceremony was another, more elaborate, enactment of the Corn Maiden drama.

53. Cushing, *Zuñi Breadstuff*, 170; Bunzel, "Introduction to Zuñi Ceremonialism," 495, 497. Parsons referred to such observances as part of the numerous "little rites peculiar to the women in Zuñi ceremonialism" ("Waiyautitsa," 161).

54. Bunzel, *Pueblo Potter*, 106.

55. Cushing, "Primitive Motherhood," 43.

56. Kroeber, *Zuñi Kin and Clan,* 156–57; D. Tedlock, "Zuni Religion and World View," 503.

57. Stevenson, "Zuñi Indians," 416–18; Bunzel, "Introduction to Zuñi Ceremonialism," 486, 491, 529. Stevenson uses the singular form, *'a:wona:-wil'ona,* "The One Who Holds the Roads." Because this term refers to beings of both genders, however, she mistakenly interpreted it as a reference to a single bisexual supreme deity (D. Tedlock, "Zuni Religion and World View," 499).

58. Stevenson, "Zuñi Indians," 420.

59. Parsons, *Pueblo Indian Religion,* 637, 624–25; Bunzel, "Zuñi Ritual Poetry," 674. See also Benedict, *Zuñi Mythology* 1:33. Cf. *we'a* in Newman (*Zuni Dictionary,* 45) and *háha* in Cushing ("Outlines," 414). According to Parsons, *waha* was a feature of all the Zuni "big dances"—the *lhewe:kwe* or sword-swallowers dance, the ceremonies of the bow priest society, the Owinahaye or harvest dance, Sha'lako, and the saint day's dance (*Pueblo Indian Religion,* 42).

60. V. Turner, *Ritual Process,* 96–97. On sexual license as an aspect of rites of passage, see Gennep (*Rites of Passage,* 115, 170).

61. See Ortiz, "Ritual Drama," 150–51, 155. While the origin of the kachina society is associated with a brother–sister, or weakly differentiated, pair, the origin stories of several medicine societies feature a husband–wife couple as founders (see Stevenson, "Zuñi Indians," 408, 409, 444–45).

62. This account of Zuni death rites is based on Leighton and Adair, *People of the Middle Place,* 78–79; Parsons, "Waiyautitsa," 169–70; Parsons, "A Few Zuni Death Beliefs"; Stevenson, "Zuñi Indians," 305–7, 418; D. Tedlock, "American Indian View of Death."

63. Parsons, "A Few Zuni Death Beliefs," 254.

64. Parsons, "Waiyautitsa," 170; Ladd, "Zuni Ethno-ornithology," 28.

65. D. Tedlock, "American Indian View of Death," 265. Zunis considered senility in old age a symptom of the encroaching rawness of death (Vogt and Albert, "Comparative Study," 20). This rawness could also entail a loss of gender differentiation, as suggested by the scare kachinas 'Adoshle, whose name has been translated as "Old Lady Granduncle," and Suuke, who was considered an 'Adoshle lhamana (D. Tedlock, *Spoken Word,* 66; Parsons, *Notes on Zuñi,* 173).

66. See Eliade, *Rites and Symbols of Initiation,* 25–26.

67. Cushing, "Primitive Motherhood," 31; Young, "Women, Reproduction, and Religion," 439.

68. From this point of view, Stevenson's designation of the male initiations as "involuntary" and "voluntary," which others have questioned,

makes sense. All boys, including berdaches, received the first initiation, hence, it was involuntary or mandatory. But the berdache did not undergo the second initiation—for him, it was voluntary or elective. From the perspective of non-berdache youths, however, both initiations were required.

69. Terry Tafoya, personal communication, February 1988.

70. Stevenson, "Zuñi Indians," 471, 485, 508, 566.

71. Cf. Martin and Voorhies, who used berdaches as an example of a "supernumerary sex," (*Female of the Species*, Chapter 4). See also Blackwood, "Review"; Jacobs, "North American Berdache"; and Roscoe, "Bibliography."

72. In other tribes the presence of female berdaches, referred to with terms distinct from those for male berdaches, establishes a fourth gender (see Blackwood, "Review").

CHAPTER SIX

1. Stevenson, "Zuñi Indians," 218.

2. This robe is essentially a woman's dress without a belt tied around the waist. Hodge excavated human remains at Hawikku dressed in similar robes made of native cotton (*History of Hawiku*, 110), and the early Spanish explorers of the Southwest also described this garb (Hammond and Rey, *Narratives*, 68). Cha'kwen 'Oka wears a robe in this style, and both Stevenson and Parsons reported that such robes were the traditional clothing of the ancient Zunis (Stevenson, "Zuñi Indians," 90; Parsons, *Pueblo Indian Religion*, 384). The kilt worn by most Sacred Lake kachinas, on the other hand, was the customary dress of the western branch of the Zunis, the immigrants who arrived in late prehistory (Cushing, "Outlines," 358; see chapter 1, n. 27). In other words, the robe was a costume of the Anasazi branch of the Zunis' ancestors.

The counterparts of the Kan'a:kwe kachinas at the nearby Keres pueblos of Acoma and Laguna—the Storoka—also wore robes, but tied on only one shoulder, in the fashion of the historic woman's manta, and beneath this men's trousers or leggings. The Keres considered the entire race of Storoka to be *kokwimu* or berdaches (Gunn, *Schat-Chen*, 173–75; Parsons, *Notes on Ceremonialism at Laguna*, 98). The Hopi counterpart of the Kan'a:kwe were called Korosta (First Mesa), Ota (Second Mesa), and Kwasaitaka (Third Mesa) (see Colton, *Hopi Kachina Dolls*, 46, 60). They wore white robes in the manta style, and they were also considered *hova* or berdache (Titiev, *Hopi Indians*, 214–15), although no corresponding myth has been recorded. The masks of all these variants—the Kan'a:kwe,

Storoka, and Hopi counterparts—share similar features: rainbow and/or checkered bands circling the face, tadpole (also called pothook) eyes, pointed snouts for mouths, and spruce collars.

3. According to Edward Curtis, this captive is portrayed in the Kan'a:-kwe ceremony "by a character called Ká-hlanna ('god big'), a man who dresses and comports himself as a woman" ("Zuñi," 122). This confusion is due to a mistranslation of "Kolhamana." The Zuni word *lha* means "big" or "in excess."

4. Stevenson, "Zuñi Indians," 219. The Kolhamana kachina is illustrated in Stevenson, "Zuñi Indians," plate 44; Bunzel, "Zuñi Katcinas," plate 33c; Bunzel, *Zuñi Katcinas,* color plate 13; Wright and Dishta, *Kachinas of the Zuni,* plate 20h; and Harmsen, *Patterns and Sources,* 75.

5. See Trotter, *From Feather, Blanket and Tepee,* 130.

6. Stevenson, "Zuñi Indians," 226; Bunzel, "Zuñi Katcinas," 1010.

7. Cushing, "Outlines," 401. It is not clear whether Cushing's term *lhamon* is transcribed in noun or adjective form. Most likely, it is the stem of *lhamana.* Newman defines "*lhajmana*" as a verb form, "to be a transvestite, to behave like a woman" (*Zuni Dictionary,* 27). Bunzel renders the term as *lhahman'ona, -ona* being a suffix meaning "the one who," which she translates simply as "the *lha'mana*" (*Zuni Texts,* 51). A more technical translation might be "the one who was being *lhaman.*" In what may be a preliminary draft of material intended to supplement his "Outlines of Zuñi Origin Myths," Cushing briefly commented on the firstborn, noting: "amplified fruit" and "instance hermaphrodites" ("Notes for Zuni Creation Myths" [manuscript], envelope no. 221, HCC).

8. The Stevenson and Curtis versions relate the birth of the firstborn as well as that figure's subsequent role in the war with the Kan'a:kwe (Stevenson, "Zuñi Indians," 32, 37, "Religious Life," 541, and "Zuñi Ancestral Gods," 35–36; E. Curtis, "Zuñi," 119, 122). Cushing describes only the birth of the berdache, while Parsons and Benedict relate only the Kan'a:kwe appearance (Cushing, "Outlines," 401; Parsons, "Origin Myth," 142, and *Pueblo Indian Religion,* 224; Benedict, *Zuñi Mythology* 1:6–8.) Parsons reports, however, that one of her informants identified Komokatsik "with *kolhahma,* god hermaphrodite" ("Origin Myth," 139). In a footnote in her 1904 report, Stevenson commented that "the firstborn was normal in all respects," presumably to correct an "error" in an earlier publication where she reported that "the tKō·thlā-ma (hermaphrodite) is the offspring of this unnatural union" ("Zuñi Indians," 32; "Religious Life," 541). Apparently, she meant that the firstborn was not a physical hermaphrodite but an anatomically normal male. Cushing's version and those that do not mention the firstborn merely indicate that the Kokk'okshi dance is the original

kachina performance. Parsons, Bunzel, and Benedict concluded that Stevenson erred in identifying Kokk'okshi as the firstborn (Parsons, "Zuñi La'mana," 524–25; Bunzel, "Zuñi Katcinas," 1012; Benedict, *Zuñi Mythology* 1:260.) In fact, one of Bunzel's informants told her, the Kokk'okshi were the only kachinas who did not fight during the war with the Kan'a:kwe ("Zuñi Katcinas," 1012). There are reasons, however, for not dismissing the Stevenson–Curtis version. We'wha was one of Stevenson's primary informants, and the additional detail in Stevenson's account could be attributable to him. As a lhamana, he would have had an interest in lore regarding the supernatural man-woman, and as a member of south kiva he would have had access to the particular lore of the Kan'a:kwe, who were always portrayed by members of that kiva. If We'wha elaborated the role of Kolhamana and drew conclusions that others had not made, this would only be typical of Zuni storytellers. Hastiin Klah, the famous Navajo berdache, also elaborated accounts of his tribe's berdache deity (see Roscoe, "We'wha and Klah"). The strongest evidence supporting the Stevenson version, however, is the costuming of the berdache kachina, which incorporates the Kokk'okshi mask. For a more technical analysis of gender symbolism in the costuming of Kolhamana and other Zuni kachinas, see Roscoe, "Semiotics."

9. See Jung, *Mysterium Coniunctionis*, 78, 359–60, 466.

10. Cushing, "Outlines," 400, 410, 413; Stevenson, "Zuñi Indians," 33.

11. See Young, "Women, Reproduction, and Religion"; Schlegel, "Male and Female."

12. See Martin and Voorhies, *Female of the Species*, 222.

13. See Whiting et al., "Learning of Values," 86, 95–96.

14. Schneider and Gough, *Matrilineal Kinship*, 13.

15. Cushing, "Outlines," 401.

16. See Stevenson, "Zuñi Indians," 32; Bunzel, "Introduction to Zuñi Ceremonialism," 521; Bunzel, "Zuñi Katcinas," 946–47, 951; Parsons, *Pueblo Indian Religion*, 748.

17. Newman, *Zuni Dictionary*, 43.

18. This is the psychological phenomenon that therapist Mitch Walker refers to as the projection of the Double. Where heterosexual orientation is based on the opposite-sex projections of anima/animus, homosexual orientation is based on projection of a same-sex image, or Double, a dynamic Walker also calls "Magickal Twinning" ("Visionary Love").

19. Bunzel, *Zuni Texts*, 176.

20. See Cushing, "Outlines," 386.

21. Jung, *Mysterium Coniunctionis*, 462–63.

22. Ibid., 333–34.

23. Lévi-Strauss, *Structural Anthropology*, 221.

24. Ibid., 223.

25. See tales recorded by Benedict (*Zuñi Mythology* 1:6ff.), Bunzel ("Zuñi Katcinas," 925ff.), E. Curtis ("Zuñi," 173ff.), and Cushing ("Zuñi Fetiches," 21ff.). Reflecting this correlation of hunting and agriculture, the Zunis believed that when hunters killed deer, the animals' spirits became kachinas at Sacred Lake. Hunters prayed over their game to ensure this, inhaling the last breath from the mouth of the dying animal—a reversal of the rite of blowing breath into infants at birth. When kachinas died, however, they returned as deer (D. Tedlock, "American Indian View of Death," 268–69).

26. Jung, *Mysterium Coniunctionis*, 497.

27. Cushing, "Outlines," 424–25.

28. Stevenson, "Zuñi Indians," 38–39.

29. The costuming of the Hopi warrior maiden He-e-e, shares features with both Cha'kwen 'Oka and Kolhamana, while her mask, with its horsehair beard and fearsome mouth, is akin to the male Cha'kwen or warrior kachinas.

30. Cushing recorded a story in which the relationship between these two incarnations of Cha'kwen 'Oka is explained. Although vanquished by the twin War Gods, she does not die. "Far away to the northward, her spirit entered the clear waters of a spring, near a city of the children of men; and when she again came forth on earth it was as the benevolent leader of warriors against evil things and the elements, that mankind might be blessed with rain" (*Nation of the Willows*, 13).

31. Gimbutas, *Goddesses and Gods*, 152, 196–200, 214; Allen, *Sacred Hoop*, 14, 15. See also Neumann, *Great Mother*, 148, 164–65.

32. Kroeber, *Zuñi Kin and Clan*, 66; Leighton and Adair, *People of the Middle Place*, 62, 64.

33. Schneider and Gough, eds., 23. See also Benedict, *Patterns of Culture*, 101; Kardiner, *Individual and His Society*, 114–16.

34. Chodorow, *Reproduction of Mothering*.

35. Indicative of their role in male psychological development, the Cha'kwen 'Oka, Komokatsik, and, interestingly, Kolhamana kachinas always danced at the head of the male kachina line instead of the female when they appeared in group dances (Bunzel, "Zuñi Katcinas," 896).

36. See Neumann, *Great Mother*, 65.

37. The presence of a Sha'lako god in versions of this incident recorded by Stevenson ("Zuñi Indians," 37) and Cushing ("Zuñi Fetiches," 21ff) is interesting. The Sha'lakos are compound beings. As birds, they fly in the realm of the Sun Father. Yet they have horns and buffalo manes like ani-

mals. They bear prayers to the rain makers, and are sometimes referred to as the bow priests of the kachinas (Parsons, *Hopi and Zuñi Ceremonialism*, 99). As a supernatural courier, the captured Sha'lako would be an ideal go-between to inaugurate an exchange of messages or gestures leading to a resolution. But the Sha'lako escapes capture. The resolution must go deeper; it must be structural in nature, resulting in a transformation of both sides—and this requires the creation of more highly evolved mediators who can not only bear messages but actually unite opposites.

38. Terry Tafoya, personal communication, February 1988.

39. Benedict, *Zuñi Mythology* 1:263.

40. Stevenson, "Zuñi Indians," 219.

41. Graves, *White Goddess*, 446.

42. Cushing, "Outlines," 402; Goldman, "Zuni Indians," 351; Benedict, *Zuñi Mythology* 1:263.

43. Stevenson, "Zuñi Indians," 37.

44. Whitehead, "The Bow and the Burden Strap," 111.

45. On the significance of such status reversals, see Hieb, "Meaning and Mismeaning," 167; Ortiz, "Ritual Drama," 148–49.

46. Campbell, *Hero with a Thousand Faces*; V. Turner, *Ritual Process*, 95.

47. It would be interesting to have evidence of the appearance of kachinas in the dreams, fantasies, and other unconscious representations of individual Zunis. Did Kolhamana ever appear in the dreams of non-berdache men, for example, and, if so, how do these appearances compare to the psychic material of berdaches? Judging from reports on the Hopis, kachinas were frequent figures in Pueblo Indian subjective life (see Sekaquaptewa, "Hopi Indian Ceremonies," 38; Eggan, "Personal Use of Myth"). As archetypes, however, versions of Kolhamana and Cha'kwen 'Oka also can be sought in the unconscious material of contemporary individuals. Jungian therapist Don Kilhefner, for example, finds that a "Black Queen of the South" is a common spirit-guide figure in the dreams of gay men; Cha'kwen 'Oka is, of course, the leader of a "Black People" who come from the south (in Thompson, *Gay Spirit*, 246). Robert Hopcke reports similar material (*Jung, Jungians, and Homosexuality*, chapter 8).

48. Jung, *Mysterium Coniunctionis*, 422, 371. For a discussion of the relationship between berdaches and the so-called eunuch priests of ancient Mediterrenean goddess religions, see Roscoe, "What Child Is This?"

49. On the relationship between "sex-role plans" contained in etiological myths and actual social relations, see Sanday, *Female Power*.

50. Jung, "Concerning the Archetypes," 71, and "Psychological Aspects," 86–87. For an overview of Jungian thinking on this subject, see Hopcke, *Jung, Jungians, and Homosexuality*.

CHAPTER SEVEN

1. Crampton, *Zunis of Cibola*, 150; Dissette to Brearly, 7 April 1894, Incoming Correspondence [IC], Series I, IRAP; Robertson to Dissette, 19 August 1892, Letters Sent [LS], PA.

2. See Hanke, *Spanish Struggle for Justice*.

3. Menendez y Pelayo, *Tratado*, 113, 117 (my translation).

4. Guerra, *Pre-Columbian Mind*, 261, 52, 53, 56–57, 91.

5. Hammond and Rey, *Narratives*, 130, 147, 248–49. Cf. Winship, "Coronado Expedition," 156, 157, 251, 253.

6. Guerra, *Pre-Columbian Mind*, 221–22, 227. According to New Mexican Archbishop Salpointe, the Spanish monarchs also issued schedules against sodomy in 1523 and 1543 (*Soldiers of the Cross*, 8). In Spain, these laws were ruthlessly, if sometimes sporadically, enforced (see Perry, "Nefarious Sin").

7. Guerra, *Pre-Columbian Mind*, 48, 190, 156, 241, 87. See also Katz, *Gay American History*, 286–87.

8. Hammond and Rey, *Narratives*, 178, 160. In 1703, the Zunis killed three Spanish soldiers stationed at their village for similar behavior (Robinson, "Troubles at Zuni," 110).

9. In Hanke, *Aristotle and the American Indians*, 17, 39. On efforts to regulate conquest and settlement in the New World, see Tyler, *Spanish Laws*, and "Zuni Indians."

10. Spicer, *Cycles of Conquest*, 282, 309, 314.

11. E. B. Adams, *Bishop Tamaron's Visitation*, 103.

12. Palou, *Life and Apostolic Labors*, 214–15; Guerra, *Pre-Columbian Mind*, 130, 155.

13. According to France Scholes, this "evil tradition" of conflict between state and church hampered the colony's development throughout the 1600s. Governors and priests regularly accused each other of immorality, usually with Indian women (see Scholes, "Church and State," and "Troublous Times"). In one of the few charges of sodomy on record for the period 1590–1820, the Taos Indians accused their friar of homosexual behavior (Scholes, "Church and State" 11(4):328; Hodge, Hammond, and Rey, *Fray Alonso*, 283).

14. See Spicer, *Cycles of Conquest*, 159, 325; Scholes "Church and State" 11(1):21, and "Troublous Times" 12(2):140, 147 and 12(4):409; Schroeder, "Rio Grande Ethnohistory," 51–52, 55, 60. The missionaries at Hawikku suppressed kachina practices and destroyed kivas (Smith, Woodbury, and Woodbury, *Excavation of Hawikuh*, 42–44; Smith and Roberts, *Zuni Law*, 29, 155).

15. See Hackett, *Historical Documents*, 133–34, 152, 158, 207, 209; Scholes, "Troublous Times" 12(4), 407–8, 438.

16. Hackett and Shelby, *Revolt of the Pueblo Indians*, 247. On causes of the revolt, see Benevides, in Hodge, Hammond, and Rey, *Fray Alonso*, 168ff.

17. Carroll and Haggard, *Three New Mexico Chronicles*, 29. See also Spicer, *Cycles of Conquest*, 166–67; Ortiz, "San Juan Pueblo," 284; Simmons, "History of Pueblo–Spanish Relations," 181.

18. Olmstead, *Spanish and Mexican Colonial Censuses*, 156; Hammond, *Sexual Impotence*; Bandelier, *Southwestern Journals*, 326. The census entry lists this individual as male, which poses an interesting question. Either Tewa berdaches had abandoned cross-dressing by this time, or the census-taker was aware of the sex of the individual and, therefore, of the berdache custom. In support of the former, it is worth noting that Jacobs's contemporary Tewa informants do not list cross-dressing as a berdache trait ("Comment").

19. Kvasnicka and Viola, *Commissioners*, 175, 199–200, 214.

20. See Allen, *Sacred Hoop*, 30–42; Martin and Voorhies, *Female of the Species*, 186, 297; O'Kelly and Carney, *Women and Men in Society*, 61. Although allotment was not seriously attempted among the Pueblos, changing land-use patterns (from agriculture to sheep and cattle grazing) have shifted control of resources once allocated with the consensus of female household members and, especially, family and clan matrons, to all-male groups. As Parsons predicted, anything tending to undermine the traditional food-exchange system administered by Pueblo women weakens their overall position in society (*Pueblo Indian Religion*, 1130).

21. Salpointe, *Soldiers of the Cross*, 118. Cf. Defouri, *Historical Sketch*, 20.

22. Bandelier, *Final Report*, 152, 286, 295, 299, 308, 313; Hrdlička, *Physiological and Medical Observations*, 47. See also Bandelier, *Southwestern Journals*, 341, 367, 374.

23. Kelly, *Assault on Assimilation*, 193–94. See also Dissette to Willard, 3 March 1924, IC, IRAP.

24. Lonergan to Mitchell, 14 May 1915 and Lonergan to McDonald, 22 September 1915, entry 90, General Correspondence File [GCF], Southern Pueblo Agency [SPA], PA.

25. See Meritt to Lonergan, 15 September 1915, McDonald to Lonergan, 11 May 1915, Casaus to Lonergan, 6 November 1915, Darnold to Lonergan, 19 May 1915, and Lonergan to Commissioner, 7 December 1915, Pueblo Day School File 101064-1915-063 [PDS], RBIA; Lonergan to Commissioner, 28 May 1915, Exhibit D, "Hopi," ms. 7070, National Anthropological

Archives. Copies of these documents also can be found in the "no date" file for 1920, IC, IRAP. Several are reprinted in Duberman, "Documents."

26. Lonergan to Commissioner, 2 March 1916, Sells to Lonergan, 11 March 1916, PDS, RBAI. The report by Inspector Traylor is mentioned in Kelly (*Assault on Assimilation*, 303), Crane (*Desert Drums*, 255), and "Annual Report of the Superintendent for the Southern Pueblos Indian Agency," 1920, GCF, SPA, PA. See also annual reports for 1919 and 1921 in the same file. Lonergan's successor, Leo Crane, complained, "I have bitterly excoriated the 'secret' dances of the Pueblo Indians of New Mexico but could never get sufficient backing from the Department to end them" (*Indians*, 209).

27. Background on these developments can be found in the Monthly Reports of the Washington Agency [MR], 30 October 1920 and 27 November 1920, IRAP. For the history of Protestant missions at Hopi and the conflicts between Hopis and the government in these years, see Spicer, *Cycles of Conquest*, 203, 207, 521, and H. James, *Pages from Hopi History*.

28. Talasnimtiwa and Hongeva in Exhibit A (also in Duberman, "Documents," 109), Sweet to Layne, 6 February 1921, and Sweet to Burke, 6 July 1921, "Hopi," ms. 7070, National Anthropological Archives.

29. Among the Rio Grande pueblos in general, kachinas only appeared in the kivas—these were the so-called secret dances. According to ethnographic accounts of the Tewa, sexual pantomime was sometimes a feature of these ceremonies (see Laski, *Seeking Life*; W. W. Hill, *Ethnography of Santa Clara*).

30. On the controversy over Pueblo land claims and the Bursum Bill, see Kelly, *Assault on Assimilation*, chapter 6.

31. Collier, *Indians of the Americas*, 19–20.

32. "Circular No. 1665," item 270, part I, JCP.

33. See typescript of the minutes, "Utilizing the American Indian Survey," March 1922, IC, IRAP; "Supplement to Circular No. 1665," 14 February 1923, and "A Message to All Indians," 24 February 1923, item 270, part I, JCP.

34. See Burke to Sniffen, 10 May 1923, IC, IRAP.

35. Matthew K. Sniffen, *Timely Indian Facts* (Philadelphia: Indian Rights Associate, 1923), 3 (item B124, Printed Matter, Series II, IRAP).

36. Welsh credited Assistant Commissioner Meritt with this "great favor" (Welsh to Elliot, 2 August 1923, IC, IRAP. See also Sniffen to Brosius, 5 April 1923, IC, IRAP, and Welsh to Kroeber, 26 September 1924, Letterpress Copy Book [LCB], IRAP).

37. See Brosius to Welsh, 6 December 1923, Burke to Sniffen, 10 May 1923, and Brosius to Sniffen, 29 May 1923, IC, IRAP. A single, complete

copy of all the secret dance file material has not been located (Lawrence Kelly, personal communication, May 1987). However, a review of materials in four collections—Pueblo Indian Agency records in the National Archives in Denver, the Bureau of Indian Affairs records in the National Archives in Washington, D.C., the National Anthropological Archives of the Smithsonian Institution, and the papers of the Indian Rights Association—makes it possible to reconstruct its contents. The original file appears to have included Sweet's 1921 exhibits, with Exhibit D being a copy of Lonergan's 1915 report. The file in the collections of the National Anthropological Archives consists of 206 pages, including the original, signed copies of Sweet's affidavits. A photostatic copy of this file is also in the IRA papers. I was unable to locate a copy of Traylor's report of April 1916, reported to consist of some one hundred pages (see n. 26, above). The transcripts from the interviews conducted by Sniffen, Otero-Warren, and True in May 1924 comprise another fifty-three pages. Copies of these are in Bureau of Indian Affairs records at the National Archives and the Indian Rights Association Papers. The IRA Papers include a few statements collected at Zuni that are not in the RBIA file.

38. Indian Rights Association, *Forty-first Annual Report*, 20.

39. Lindquist, *Red Man*, 268. On the IRA's contribution to this book, see Lindquist to Sniffen, 22 June 1922, IC, IRAP.

40. Collier to Austin, 29 March 1923, "Indian Defense Assoc. . . . General Correspondence 1923," carton 4, CLAIR.

41. "Indian Dances Degrading Says Y.W.C.A. Leader," *New York Tribune*, 25 November 1923 (item 269, part I, JCP).

42. *New York Times*, 16 December 1923 (item 269, part I, JCP).

43. Untitled typescript, 3, item 270, part I, JCP; "Minutes of the National Advisory Council on Indian Affairs, 12–14 December 1923" (typescript), 94, IC, IRAP.

44. "Proceedings of the Pueblo Indian Council Held at the Pueblo of Santo Domingo" (typescript, 17 January 1924), 2–3, item 252, part I, JCP.

45. True to Welsh, 19 April 1922, and True to Sniffen, 4 January 1925, IC, IRAP. See also Governors of San Juan, Santa Clara, Cochiti, and Santo Domingo [to Progressives], "Pueblo Ind. Miscell. Corresp. Prior to 1926," carton 1, CLAIR; *Indian Truth* 1(5):2; Kelly, *Assault on Assimilation*, 231–32, 311. Collier considered True a serious threat and went to the trouble of investigating her background, uncovering her lengthy legal disputes with Stevenson and others ("Memo as to Miss Clara D. True," n.d., item 279, part I, JCP; also in "Indian Rights Association. Corresp. Documents," carton 2, CLAIR).

46. Bryan to Welsh, 5 April 1924, IC, IRAP; Welsh to Bryan, 26 March

1924, and Sniffen to Bryan, 16 April 1924, LCB, IRAP; Sniffen to True, 24 May 1924, IC, IRAP.

47. These associates included lawyer A. B. Renehan, Edgar L. Hewitt, director of the Museum of New Mexico, photographer Edward S. Curtis, Adelina Otero-Warren, sister of a former territorial governor, and Father Fridolin Schuster of the Catholic Mission Board.

48. Collier to Ortiz, 1 May 1924, "Ind. Religious Pers. Corresp.—Indian (Declarations, etc.)," carton 1, CLAIR; "Statement made by John Collier to the Pueblo Indians in Council at Santo Domingo, New Mexico, May 5, 1924" (typescript), 5, Master File-General Services File 65731-1924-816 [GSF], RBIA.

49. "Declaration of All Pueblo Council," 5 May 1924, "Pueblo. Council of All the Pueblos: Meetings, Declarations, Etc.," carton 1, CLAIR.

50. See Berle to Collier, 3 May 1924 and Asher to Collier, 29 May 1924, "Pueblo Ind. Religious Pers. Corresp. Collier-Gen.," carton 1, CLAIR; Collier to Board of Directors, 22 May [1924], item 277, part I, JCP.

51. See collections of clippings, pamphlets, and other materials in carton 1, CLAIR, and items 269 and 270, JCP.

52. *Indian Truth* 1(4):3. On Otero-Warren, see Kelly, *Assault on Assimilation*, 279; Wilson to Sniffen, 30 October 1923, IC, IRAP.

53. Sniffen to Welsh, 30 April 1924, IC, IRAP.

54. Transcripts of these interviews are in GSF, RBIA and May 1924, IC, IRAP.

55. Dissette to Willard, 3 March 1924, IC, IRAP. In the hope of obtaining more conclusive evidence on berdache sexuality for "this war against bestiality," Dissette also wrote to Mrs. Vanderwagen at Zuni (7 March 1924, IC, IRAP).

56. *Indian Truth* 1(7):5; Welsh to Bryan, 26 March 1924, LCB, IRAP. For Welsh's letter-writing campaign, see correspondence between May 1924 to January 1925, in IC and LCB, IRAP.

57. Johnson to *Times*, [August 1924], GSF, RBIA (also in IC, IRAP); Raschke to Sniffen, 23 July 1924, LCB, IRAP; Johnson to Sniffen, 4 August 1924, IC, IRAP. For background on Johnson, see Kvasnicka and Viola, *Commissioners*, 238–39.

58. Johnson to Burke, 4 August 1924, GSF, RBIA; Johnson to Sniffen, 4 August 1924, IC, IRAP (also in GSF, RBIA); Sniffen to Johnson, 20 August 1924, IC, IRAP; Burke to Johnson, 14 August 1924, GSF, RBIA; Burke to Brosius, 14 August 1924, IC, IRAP; Sniffen to Burke, 28 August 1924, GSF, RBIA; Burke to Sniffen, 3 September 1924, GSF, RBIA (also in IC, IRAP); Welsh to Burke, 10 September 1924, LCB, IRAP.

59. Burke to Warren, 21 August 1924, Otero-Warren to Burke, 6 Septem-

ber 1924, Bear et al. to Officers of the General Federation of Women's Clubs, 30 August 1924, Burke to Otero-Warren, 10 September 1924, GSF, RBIA.

60. Collier to Sherman, 16 September 1924, item 280, part I, JCP (also in "Pueblo Ind. Religious Pers. RE-'Pussyfoot,'" carton 1, CLAIR).

61. Collier, "The Religion of the Pueblos," *New York Times*, 16 November 1924 (in "Publicity. Pueblo Religious Controversy," carton 1, CLAIR). See also typescripts (16 pp. and 9 pp.), item 270, part I, JCP; typescript (11 pp.), in "Manuscripts. Collier. General–Indian Problems," carton 2, CLAIR; Collier, *Indians of the Americas*, 255.

62. Welsh, "The Pueblo Indian Rites," *New York Times*, 19 October 1924 (item 269, part I, JCP; "Pueblo Ind. Relig. Pers. New Releases . . . ," carton 1, CLAIR); Welsh to Finley, 25 October 1924, LCB, IRAP.

63. Hodge, "Rites of the Pueblo Indians," *New York Times*, 26 October 1924 (item 269, part I, JCP); Collier, *New York Times*, 16 November 1924; Sniffen, "Secret Dances of the Pueblos," *New York Times*, 1 November 1924 (item 269, part I, JCP).

64. See, for example, "Are the Pueblo Indians Saints or Moral Lepers?" *Sunset*, November 1924, 50.

65. Johnson to Sniffen, 28 November 1924, IC, IRAP.

66. Welsh to Members and Friends, 19 November 1924, IC, IRAP; Welsh to Work, 16 September 1924, IC, IRAP.

67. Welsh to Episcopal Bishops, 26 January 1925, LCB, IRAP; Welsh to Reese, 26 January 1925, IC, IRAP.

68. Asher to Coolidge, 4 December 1924, GSF, RBIA.

69. *Indian Truth* 1(10):3; Welsh to True, 14 February 1925, Welsh to Board of Directors, 16 February 1925, Sniffen to True, 20 February 1925, IC, IRAP; Asher to Collier, 3 April 1925, "Ind. Def. Assoc., Inc. (Amer) N.Y.C. Asher–Collier Corresp. 1925," carton 2, CLAIR.

70. Burke to Sniffen, 10 February 1925, GSF, RBIA (also in IC, IRAP).

71. *Indian Truth* 2(2): 2–3. See also True to Hodge, 9 February 1925, IC, IRAP.

72. "From the Pueblo Indians of New Mexico . . . ," 31 August 1925, item 254, part I, JCP; *American Indian Life*, June 1928 (item 274, part I, JCP).

73. Sando, *Pueblo Indians*, 81.

74. Collier, *Indians of the Americas*, 255; untitled typescript (9 pp.), item 270, part I, JCP.

75. Collier to Sherman, 16 September 1924, item 280, part I, JCP.

76. See Hoxie, *Final Promise*, 94–113.

77. Welsh, "Why Indian Dances are Bad," *New York Herald*, 22 August 1924 (item 269, part I, JCP); Welsh to Work, 9 May 1923, IC, IRAP.

78. Hanke, *Spanish Struggle for Justice*, 125.

79. Dissette to "My dear friend," 14 March 1896, IC, IRAP.

80. Stephen, *Hopi Journals*, 276; Dissette to Willard, 3 March 1924, and Ryan to Sniffen, 16 September 1924, IC, IRAP.

81. Richard Clemmer, for example, has stated that "there is no berdache role" among the Hopis ("Hopi Indian Redux," 182–83). For sources on Hopi berdaches, see Roscoe, "Bibliography," 96.

CHAPTER EIGHT

1. Stevenson, "Zuñi Indians," 38, 317; Dissette to Willard, 3 March 1924, IC, IRAP; Parsons, "Zuñi Ła'mana," 522–23; Parsons, "Last Zuni Transvestite." His name has been rendered as Kasineli, Kasanel, and Kasinaloo.

2. Stevenson, "Zuñi Indians," 181–82, 198; Denman, *Pai-ya-tu-ma*, 27. For the significance of the hoop symbol at Hopi, see Schlegel, "Male and Female," 257, 268.

3. Parsons, "Zuñi Ła'mana," 522–23, 525.

4. Ibid., 523.

5. Adair, personal communication, 9 July 1984, 29 September 1986.

6. Parsons, "Last Zuni Transvestite," 338.

7. Stewart, "Homosexuality among the American Indians," 13–14. Parsons described an Isleta berdache in the 1930s with a similar reputation. Boys "could not keep away from him," she was told ("Isleta," 246). See also the account of "Arnie" (in E. White, *States of Desire*, 99–101), a gay Tewa man whom I met in 1983.

8. Stewart's account implies that this berdache lived alone, while Adair believes that Kasinelu was a member of a household (personal communication, 20 June 1986).

9. Kuipers, *Zuni Also Prays*, 35.

10. Kroeber, "Psychosis or Social Sanction?", 209.

11. Parsons, "Zuñi Ła'mana," 521–22; Parsons, "Last Zuni Transvestite," 338. Parsons also rendered his name as "Laspik." He was named after Las Vegas, New Mexico.

12. See Spicer, *Cycles of Conquest*, 174, 176, 349, 477.

13. Parsons, "Isleta," 246. As late as 1912 and 1915, Zuni leaders were jailed for refusing to enroll their children in government schools (Parsons, *Notes on Zuñi*, 267, 284). Older Zunis today recall hiding with their families at the farming villages to avoid enrollment.

14. Udall, *Me and Mine*, 137; Trotter, *From Feather, Blanket and Tepee*, 28. A similar experience is narrated in the film, *Trouble at Big Mountain*.

15. John Adair, personal communication, 20 June 1986.

16. Parsons, "Isleta," 247; Roscoe, "We'wha and Klah," 135. For other accounts of the abandonment of the dress, see (California) Essene, *Culture Element Distributions 21*, 65; (Kwakiutl) Ford, *Smoke from Their Fires*, 129–30; (Lakota) Laubin and Laubin, *Indian Dances*, 366–67; (Winnebago) Lurie, "Winnebago Berdache"; (Omaha) Mead, "Cultural Determinants," 1452; (Klamath) Spier, *Klamath Ethnography*, 52; (Great Basin) Steward, *Culture Element Distributions 13*, 253.

17. See, for example, Landes, *Prairie Potawatomi*, 196ff; Lowie, *Notes on Shoshonean Ethnography*, 283; Steward, *Ethnography of the Owens Valley Paiute*, 238.

18. On *kihe* relationships, see Parsons, "Ceremonial Friendship."

19. John Adair, personal communication, 9 July 1984.

20. Lurie, "Winnebago Berdache," 708.

21. Harry Hay, personal communication, 4 March 1983; Williams, *Spirit and the Flesh*, 209.

22. Triloki Pandey, personal communication, 17 April 1985.

23. *Glossary of Common Zuni Terms*, 10. Newman defines *lhalha* as "lace." The stem *lha*, as Tedlock points out, has connotations of "important, or even *too* important, *too* much," which, in the reduplicative form of *lhalha*, has an almost campy sense (Newman, *Zuni Dictionary*, 27; D. Tedlock, *Spoken Word*, 241).

24. Maurice Kenny, interview, 23 July 1985.

25. Some berdaches at Zuni and elsewhere may indeed have identified more with female roles than with either male or third-gender status, although their inclinations were still accommodated by the berdache role. These berdaches, unlike We'wha and Kasinelu, really did attempt to appear and act like the women of their tribe. In the postwar period, with the lapse of the berdache role, they sometimes turned to transsexual status. Robert Stoller has described a male Indian from a Yuman-speaking tribe seeking gender reassignment who had never heard of his tribe's third-gender tradition, although his community was not hostile toward him. Like a berdache, he excelled at women's crafts and had engaged in homosexual activity at an early age. According to Stoller, he was in a relationship with a man who would marry him only if he obtained a sex change. Stoller considered him "neuter" rather than feminine or masculine and felt more comfortable using the pronoun "he" than "she" ("Two Feminized Male American Indians"). One cannot help but feel that if the berdache tradition had not been forgotten by this individual's tribe, he could have made a successful adjustment without radical surgery. According to a more recent report, at least two other nonmasculine men in his tribe have adopted openly homosexual

life-styles (Whitham and Mathy, *Male Homosexuality*, 84). I have heard reference to one case of transsexualism at Zuni.

26. Gengle, "Gay American Indians," 332–34; Roscoe, "Living the Tradition"; Kenny, "*Winkte*," in Roscoe, *Living the Spirit*, 153–54.

27. Allen, "Lesbians"; reprinted as "*Hwame, Koshkalaka*, and the Rest: Lesbians in American Indian Cultures," in *Sacred Hoop*, 245–61.

28. Paula Gunn Allen, interview, July 1985.

29. Kenny, "Tinselled Bucks," 31.

30. Burns, in Roscoe, *Living the Spirit*, 2.

31. Owlfeather, "Children of Grandmother Moon," 100, 103.

32. Allen, *Sacred Hoop*, 255.

33. Williams, *Spirit and the Flesh*, 217, 226. In an unpublished paper presented at the New Gender Scholarship conference in 1987, entitled "Native Perspective of the Siouan Term: Winkte," Bea Medicine argued that recent claims regarding the spiritual dimensions of Plains Indian berdache status have been overstated by contemporary *winkte* who have elaborated the role in ways she termed "self-serving." By such a standard, however, the entire movement of native revivalism since the 1960s would have to be judged "self-serving." Medicine overlooked numerous historical references to *winkte* religious roles in reaching her conclusion (see Roscoe, "Bibliography," 94).

34. For Ulrichs, Lombardi, personal communication, 21 August 1986; Westermarck, *Origin and Development*; Carpenter, *Intermediate Types*; Karsch, *Das Gleichgeschlechtliche*; Benedict, *Patterns of Culture*.

35. Plummer, *Making of the Modern Homosexual*, 48; Burke, "Native Voices," 21; Bailor, "Native Americans," 26–27; Gutíerrez, "Must We Deracinate Indians," 67.

36. See Foucault, *History of Sexuality*, 43, 101; Weeks, "Construction of Homosexuality"; Plummer, *Making of the Modern Homosexual*. Other exponents of social constructionism with recently published works include Jonathan Katz, John D'Emilio, David Greenberg, and David Halperin. For an expanded critique of social constructionism, see Roscoe, "Making History."

37. Young, *Signs from the Ancestors*, 230.

38. Roscoe, "Living the Tradition," 71.

39. See Williams, *Spirit and the Flesh*, 223.

40. At the same time, we must strive for awareness of our valuation of difference or we risk creating a "noble berdache," a variation on the image of the "noble savage." According to one recent article, for example, "Among nature societies, where ritual transvestism and gay sex were inseparably linked to the worship of androgynous deities, cultures invoked and com-

muned with the numinous through dancing and 'by obliterating opposites through trance, drugs and sex, and by appearing in both sexes simultaneously'" (Clarke, "Native American Berdache," 23). Such romanticized images have more in common with Western utopianism than they do with Indian realities. Other writers have gone to the opposite extreme, however, in using unquestioned Western assumptions and value judgments to create extremely negative portrayals of berdaches. Ramón Gutíerrez, for example, has defined berdache status as "that social arrangement whereby a man or group of men press another male into impersonating a female, forcing him to perform work generally associated with women, offering passive sexual service to men, and donning women's clothes," and he claims that "men who were pressed into berdache status were there primarily to service and delight the chiefs" ("Must We Deracinate Indians," 61, 63). Both extremes point to the need for investigators to examine their own concepts and value judgments before attempting to interpret the sex and gender roles of other societies.

41. Whitehead, "The Bow and the Burden Strap"; Callender and Kochems, "Men and Not-Men"; Whitham and Mathy, *Male Homosexuality*; Williams, *Spirit and the Flesh*. Williams distinguishes "drag queens" from gay men, whom he considers indistinguishable from heterosexual men. But drag, in gay social contexts, is a form of entertainment and recreation. It is not a life-style, an erotic experience, or an expression of gender identity, and there are no reliable indicators that identify gay men as "drag queens" when they are not in drag. Of course, some gay men are identifiably nonmasculine and perhaps they are indeed closer in temperament to the berdache personality. However, Williams's categories are too subjective and undefined to provide the basis for reliable generalizations. For discussions of Williams's study, see Roscoe, "Indian Berdache"; Rose, "In Search of the Noble Homosexual"; and Blackwood, "Review."

42. See, for example, Whitehead, "The Bow and the Burden Strap," 96; Callender and Kochems, "North American Berdache," 449–51, 454–55, and "Men and Not-Men," 167. For further discussion, see Roscoe, "Bibliography," 158ff.

43. Early observers invariably filtered what they saw through Western categories and values. Yet many recent discussions of berdaches have been based on cursory reviews of this literature for evidence to support preformulated theories and hypotheses. This approach is especially susceptible to error. Correcting the bias of a given source requires using all other available sources. Only then can the validity of reports be weighed and bias corrected. This calls for comprehensive, in-depth studies of berdaches within specific tribes.

44. In other words, berdache sexual practices were berdache-specific

and not an imitation of heterosexuality. This contradicts Rubin's finding that universal "compulsory heterosexuality" requires that even its transformations, such as homosexuality, adopt its forms and follow its rules. While this may hold true for dual gender societies, it does not apply to the third-gender system of the Pueblos ("Traffic in Women").

45. On the uses of a multidimensional model, see Roscoe, "Making History."

APPENDIX ONE

1. Newman, *Zuni Dictionary*, and "Practical Zuni Orthography." I have also referred to Cook, *Zuni Language Learning Manual*, and D. Tedlock, *Finding the Center*, xxxiv–xxxv. The orthography used here is essentially the same as that in Young, *Signs from the Ancestors*, xix.

APPENDIX TWO

1. D. Tedlock, *Spoken Word*, 233–34.

2. Ibid., 236.

3. Stevenson, "Zuñi Indians," 73–88.

4. Lévi-Strauss, *Structural Anthropology*, 217, 218.

5. Bunzel, "Zuñi Origin Myths," 548.

6. Cushing, "Outlines"; Stevenson, "Zuñi Indians"; E. Curtis, "Zuñi,"; Parsons, "Origin Myth"; Bunzel, "Zuñi Origin Myths"; Benedict, *Zuñi Mythology*, vol. 1; Quam, *Zunis*; D. Tedlock, *Finding the Center*. I have also consulted an outline of the origin narrative as currently taught in classes at the Zuni High School.

7. Cushing, "Outlines," 381; Cushing, *Zuñi Folk Tales*, 401.

8. Bunzel, "Introduction to Zuñi Ceremonialism," 489; D. Tedlock, *Finding the Center*, 229.

9. D. Tedlock, *Finding the Center*, 256.

10. Stevenson, "Zuñi Indians," 34–38.

11. In keeping with the interchangeable nature of the Black Gods and the Zunis themselves (see chapter 6), one version has the Kan'a:kwe as the victors (Benedict, *Zuñi Mythology* 1:7).

Bibliography

MANUSCRIPT SOURCES

California League for the American Indian Records, Bancroft Library, University of California, Berkeley, Calif.

George Wharton James Collection, Southwest Museum, Los Angeles, Calif.

Grover Cleveland Papers, Library of Congress, Washington, D.C. Microfilm edition.

Hodge–Cushing Collection, Southwest Museum, Los Angeles, Calif.

Indian Rights Association Papers, 1868–1968. Historical Society of Pennsylvania, Philadelphia, Pa. Glen Rock, N.J.: Microfilming Corporation of America, 1974.

John Collier Papers, Manuscripts and Archives, Yale University Library, New Haven, Conn. Sanford, N.C.: Microfilming Corporation of America, 1980.

National Anthropological Archives, Smithsonian Institution, Washington, D.C.

- Records of the Bureau of American Ethnology, Letters Received, M. C. Stevenson, 1890–1906, 1908.
- Ms. 895, A. S. Gatschet, "Notes on Clans," 1886.
- Ms. 2093, Matilda Coxe Stevenson, "Dress and Adornment of the Pueblo Indians," 1911.
- Ms. 3915, Frank H. Cushing, "Nominal and Numerical Census of the Gentes of the Ashiwi or Zuni Indians," n.d. [1881].
- Acc. 4689, Matilda Coxe Stevenson Papers.
- Ms. 7070, "Hopi."

Records of the Bureau of Indian Affairs, Record Group 75, National Archives, Washington, D.C.
Records of the Pueblo and Pueblo and Jicarilla Agency, Records of the Bureau of Indian Affairs, Record Group 75, National Archives, Denver, Colo.
Records of United States Army Continental Commands, Fort Wingate, New Mexico, Record Group 393, National Archives, Washington, D.C.
Wheelwright Collection, Wheelwright Museum of the American Indian, Santa Fe, N.M.

GOVERNMENT DOCUMENTS

U.S. Congress. House. "Proceedings of the Sixth Annual Lake Mohonk Conference." In *Report of the Secretary of Interior*. Vol. 2. 50th Cong., 2d sess., 1888. H. Ex. Doc. 1, pt. 5. Vol. 11.
U.S. Congress. House. "Report of the Board of Indian Commissioners." In *Report of the Secretary of the Interior*. Vol. 2. 53d Cong., 3d sess., 1895. H. Ex. Doc. 1, pt. 5. Vol. 15.
U.S. Congress. House. "Report of the Commissioner of Indian Affairs." In *Report of the Secretary of the Interior*. Vol 2. 52d Cong., 2d sess., 1893. Ex. Doc. 1, pt. 5. Vol. 13.
U.S. Congress. House. "Report of the Commissioner of Indian Affairs." In *Annual Reports of the Department of the Interior*. 55th Cong., 2d sess., 1897. H. Doc. 5.
U.S. Congress. House. "Report of the Governor of New Mexico." In *Annual Reports of the Department of the Interior, Miscellaneous Reports, Part II*, 315–642. 56th Cong., 1st sess., 1899. H. Doc. 5. Vol. 2.
U.S. Office of Indian Affairs. *Rules for the Indian School Service, 1900*. Washington, D.C.: Government Printing Office, 1900.

NEWSPAPERS AND PERIODICALS

Albuquerque Evening Citizen, 1893.
Albuquerque Morning Democrat, 1892.
Evening Star (Washington, D.C.), 1886.
Indian Truth (Philadelphia), 1924–1925.
National Tribune (Washington, D.C.), 1886, 1888.
New York Herald, 1924.
New York Times, 1883, 1886, 1888, 1897, 1915, 1923–1924.
New York Tribune, 1923.
Santa Fe Daily New Mexican, 1892, 1897.

Sunset, 1924.
Washington Chronicle, 1886.
Washington Post, 1886.

PUBLISHED WORKS

Abel, Annie H., ed. *The Official Correspondence of James S. Calhoun While Indian Agent at Santa Fe and Superintendent of Indian Affairs in New Mexico.* U.S. Office of Indian Affairs. Washington, D.C.: Government Printing Office, 1915.

Adams, E. Charles. "The View from the Hopi Mesas." In *The Protohistoric Period in the North American Southwest*, edited by David R. Wilcox and W. Bruce Masse, 321–35. Arizona State University Anthropological Research Paper no. 24. Tempe: Arizona State University, 1981.

Adams, Eleanor B. *Bishop Tamaron's Visitation of New Mexico, 1760.* Historical Society of New Mexico, Publications in History 15. Albuquerque, 1954.

Akins, Nancy J. *A Biocultural Approach to Human Burials from Chaco Canyon, New Mexico.* Reports of the Chaco Center, No. 9. Santa Fe: Branch of Cultural Research, U.S. Department of the Interior, National Park Service, 1986.

Allen, Paula Gunn. "Lesbians in American Indian Cultures." *Conditions* 7 (1981): 67–87.

———. *The Sacred Hoop: Recovering the Feminine in American Indian Traditions.* Boston: Beacon Press, 1986.

Anderson, Frank G. "The Pueblo Kachina Cult: A Historical Reconstruction." *Southwestern Journal of Anthropology* 11(4) (1955): 404–19.

Angelino, Henry, and Charles L. Shedd. "A Note on Berdache." *American Anthropologist* 57(1) (1955): 121–26.

Babcock, Barbara A., and Nancy J. Parezo. *Daughters of the Desert: Women Anthropologists and the Native American Southwest, 1880–1980.* Albuquerque: University of New Mexico Press, 1988.

Bailor, Perry A. "Native Americans." Review of Walter L. Williams, *The Spirit and the Flesh: Sexual Diversity in American Indian Culture. New York Native*, 13 April 1987, 26–27.

Bandelier, Adolph F. *Final Report of Investigations among the Indians of the Southwestern United States, Carried on Mainly in the Years from 1880 to 1885, Part I.* Papers of the Archaeological Institute of America, American Series 3. Cambridge, Mass.: John Wilson and Son, 1890.

———. *The Southwestern Journals of Adolph F. Bandelier, 1880–1882*, edited by Charles H. Lange and Carroll L. Riley. Albuquerque and

Santa Fe: University of New Mexico Press, School of American Research, 1966.

Barnes, James A. *John G. Carlislė: Financial Statesman*. New York: Dodd, Mead and Co., 1931.

Basso, Keith H. "History of Ethnological Research." In *Handbook of North American Indians*, edited by Alfonso Ortiz, 14–21. Vol. 9. Washington, D.C.: Smithsonian Institution, 1979.

Baxter, Sylvester. "F. H. Cushing at Zuni." *The American Architect and Building News* 11(319) (1882): 56–57.

———. "An Aboriginal Pilgrimage." *Century Illustrated Monthly* 24 (1882): 526–36.

Beets, Henry. *Toiling and Trusting: Fifty Years of Mission Work of the Christian Reformed Church among Indians and Chinese . . .* Grand Rapids, Mich.: Grand Rapids Printing Co., 1940.

Bender, Norman J., ed. *Missionaries, Outlaws, and Indians: Taylor F. Ealy at Lincoln and Zuni, 1878–1881*. Albuquerque: University of New Mexico Press, 1984.

Benedict, Ruth. *Patterns of Culture*. 1934. Reprint. Boston: Houghton Mifflin, 1959.

———. *Zuñi Mythology*. 2 vols. Columbia University Contributions to Anthropology, vol. 21. New York, 1935.

Bennett, John W. "The Interpretation of Pueblo Culture: A Question of Values." *Southwestern Journal of Anthropology* 2(4) (1946): 361–74.

Bieber, Ralph P., ed. *Marching with the Army of the West, 1846–1848*. Glendale, Calif.: Arthur H. Clark Co., 1936.

Blackwood, Evelyn. "Sexuality and Gender in Certain Native American Tribes: The Case of Cross-gender Females. *Signs: Journal of Women in Culture and Society* 10(1) (1984): 27–42.

———. Review of Walter L. Williams, *The Spirit and the Flesh: Sexual Diversity in American Indian Culture*. *Journal of Homosexuality* 15(3–4) (1988): 165–76.

Blair, Karen J. *The Clubwoman as Feminist: True Womanhood Redefined, 1868–1914*. New York: Holmes and Meier, 1980.

Bloom, Lansing Bartlett, ed. "Bourke on the Southwest." *New Mexico Historical Review* 11(2) (1936): 188–207.

Bogoras, Waldemar G. *The Chukchee*. Memoirs of the American Museum of Natural History, vol. 11, pt. 2. Leiden: E. J. Brill, 1907.

Bohrer, Vorsila L. "Zuni Agriculture." *El Palacio* 67(6) (1960): 181–202.

Bolin, Anne. *In Search of Eve: Transsexual Rites of Passage*. South Hadley, Mass.: Bergin and Garvey, 1988.

Boserup, Ester. *Woman's Role in Economic Development*. New York: St. Martin's Press, 1970.

Brandes, Raymond S. "Frank Hamilton Cushing: Pioneer Americanist." Ph.D. diss., University of Arizona, 1965.

Bunker, Robert. *Other Men's Skies*. Bloomington: Indiana University Press, 1956.

Bunzel, Ruth L. "Introduction to Zuñi Ceremonialism." In *Forty-seventh Annual Report of the Bureau of American Ethnology, 1929–1930*, 467–544. Washington, D.C.: Government Printing Office, 1932.

———. "Zuñi Origin Myths." In *Forty-seventh Annual Report of the Bureau of American Ethnology, 1929–1930*, 547–609. Washington, D.C.: Government Printing Office, 1932.

———. "Zuñi Ritual Poetry." In *Forty-seventh Annual Report of the Bureau of American Ethnology, 1929–1930*, 611–835. Washington, D.C.: Government Printing Office, 1932.

———. "Zuñi Katcinas." In *Forty-seventh Annual Report of the Bureau of American Ethnology, 1929–1930*, 837–1086. Washington, D.C.: Government Printing Office, 1932.

———. *Zuni Texts*. Publications of the American Ethnological Society, vol. 15. New York, 1933.

———. 1952. *Chichicastenango, a Guatemalan Village*. Publications of the American Ethnological Society, vol. 22. Locust Valley, N.Y., 1952.

———. *The Pueblo Potter: A Study of Creative Imagination in Primitive Art*. 1929. Reprint. New York: Dover, 1972.

———. *Zuñi Katcinas*. 1932. Reprint. Glorieta, N.M.: Rio Grande Press, 1984.

Burke, Robert. "Native Voices." Review of *Living the Spirit: A Gay American Indian Anthology*, edited by Will Roscoe. *San Francisco Sentinel*, 23 September 1988, 21–22.

Callender, Charles, and Lee M. Kochems. "The North American Berdache." *Current Anthropology* 24(2) (1983): 443–70.

———. "Men and Not-Men: Male Gender-Mixing Statuses and Homosexuality." In *The Many Faces of Homosexuality*, edited by Evelyn Blackwood, 165–78. New York: Harrington Park Press, 1986.

Campbell, Joseph. *The Hero with a Thousand Faces*. Bollingen Series, vol. 17. 1949. Reprint. Princeton: Princeton University Press, 1972.

Carpenter, Edward. *Intermediate Types among Primitive Folk: A Study in Social Evolution*. New York: Mitchell Kennerley, 1914.

Carroll, H. Bailey, and J. Villasana Haggard, eds. and trans. *Three New Mexico Chronicles: The "Exposición" of Don Pedro Bautista Pino; the "Ojeada" of Lic. Antonio Barreiro, 1832; and the Additions of*

Don José Agustín de Escudero, 1849. Albuquerque: Quivira Society, 1942.

Casagrande, Louis B., and Phillips Bourns. *Side Trips: The Photography of Sumner W. Matteson 1898–1908*. Milwaukee: Milwaukee Public Museum and the Science Museum of Minnesota, 1983.

Chodorow, Nancy. *The Reproduction of Mothering: Psychoanalysis and the Sociology of Gender*. Berkeley, Calif.: University of California Press, 1978.

Chugerman, Samuel. *Lester F. Ward: The American Aristotle*. Durham, N.C.: Duke University Press, 1939.

Clarke, J. Michael. "The Native American Berdache: A Resource for Gay Spirituality." *RFD* 40 (Fall 1984): 22–30.

Clemmer, Richard O. "Hopi Indian Redux." *Radical History Review* 24 (1980): 177–87.

Clifford, James. "On Ethnographic Allegory." In *Writing Culture: The Poetics and Politics of Ethnography*, edited by James Clifford and George E. Marcus, 98–121. Berkeley: University of California Press, 1986.

Cobos, Rubén. *A Dictionary of New Mexico and Southern Colorado Spanish*. Santa Fe: Museum of New Mexico Press, 1983.

Collier, John. *The Indians of the Americas*. New York: W. W. Norton, 1947.

———. *On the Gleaming Way: Navajos, Eastern Pueblos, Zunis, Hopis, Apaches, and Their Land; and Their Meanings to the World*. Chicago: Sage Books, 1962.

Colton, Harold S. *Hopi Kachina Dolls, with a Key to Their Identification*. Rev. ed. Albuquerque: University of New Mexico Press, 1959.

Cook, Curtis D. *Zuni Language Learning Manual*. Gallup, N.M.: Gallup–McKinley County Schools, 1974.

Cordell, Linda S. "Prehistory: Eastern Anasazi." In *Handbook of North American Indians*, 131–51. *See* Basso.

Courouve, Claude. "The Word 'Bardache.'" *Gay Books Bulletin* 8 (1982): 18–19.

Crampton, C. Gregory. *The Zunis of Cibola*. Salt Lake City: University of Utah Press, 1977.

Crane, Leo. *Indians of the Enchanted Desert*. Boston: Little, Brown, and Co., 1926.

———. *Desert Drums: The Pueblo Indians of New Mexico, 1540–1928*. Boston: Little, Brown, and Co., 1928.

Croly, Jane Cunningham. *The History of the Woman's Club Movement in America*. New York: H. G. Allen and Co., 1898.

Curtis, Edward S. "Zuñi." In *The North American Indian*, edited by Frederick W. Hodge, 83–167. Vol. 17. 1926. Reprint. New York: Johnson Reprint Corp., 1970.

Curtis, William E. *Children of the Sun*. 1883. Reprint. New York: AMS, 1976.

Cushing, Frank H. "The Zuñi Social, Mythic, and Religious Systems." *Popular Science Monthly* 21 (1882): 186–92.

———. "Zuñi Fetiches." In *Second Annual Report of the Bureau of Ethnology, 1880–1881*, 9–45. Washington, D.C.: Government Printing Office, 1883.

———. "Preliminary Notes on the Origin, Working Hypothesis, and Primary Researches of the Hemenway Southwestern Archaeological Expedition." In *Seventh Congrès International des Américanistes*, 151–94. 1888. Reprint. Nendeln/Liechtenstein: Kraus Reprint, 1968.

———. "Commentary of a Zuni Familiar." In Edna Dean Proctor, *The Song of the Ancient People*, 27–49. Boston: Houghton Mifflin, 1893.

———. "Outlines of Zuñi Creation Myths." In *Thirteenth Annual Report of the Bureau of Ethnology, 1891–1892*, 321–447. Washington, D.C.: Government Printing Office, 1896.

———. "Primitive Motherhood." In *Work and Words of the National Congress of Mothers, First Annual Session*, 21–47. New York: D. Appleton and Co., 1897.

———. *Zuñi Folk Tales*. 1901. Reprint. New York: Alfred A. Knopf, 1931.

———. *The Nation of the Willows*. 1882. Reprint. Flagstaff: Northland Press, 1965.

———. *Zuñi Breadstuff*. Indian Notes and Monographs, vol. 8. 1920. Reprint. New York: Museum of the American Indian, Heye Foundation, 1974.

———. *Zuñi: Selected Writings of Frank Hamilton Cushing*, edited by Jesse Green. Lincoln: University of Nebraska Press, 1979.

Dale, Edward Everett. *The Indians of the Southwest*. Norman: University of Oklahoma, 1949.

Darrah, William C. *Powell of the Colorado*. Princeton: Princeton University Press, 1951.

Defouri, James H. *Historical Sketch of the Catholic Church in New Mexico*. San Francisco: McCormick Bros., 1887.

DeKorne, John C., ed. *Navaho and Zuni for Christ: Fifty Years of Indian Missions*. Grand Rapids, Mich.: Christian Reformed Board of Missions, 1947.

Denman, Leslie Van Ness. *Pai-ya-tu-ma: God of All Dance and His Customs of the Flute, Zuni Pueblo, 1932*. San Francisco: Grabhorn Press, 1955.

Dickinson, L. W. *Social Mirror: A Complete Treatise on the Laws, Rules and Usages that Govern Our Most Refined Homes and Social Circles*, with an introduction by Rose Elizabeth Cleveland. St. Louis: J. L. Hebert Publishing Co., 1888.

Dolfin, J. *Bringing the Gospel in Hogan and Pueblo*. Grand Rapids, Mich.: Van Noord Book and Publishing Co., 1921.

Duberman, Martin B. "Documents in Hopi Indian Sexuality: Imperialism, Culture, and Resistance." *Radical History Review* 20 (1979): 99–130.

———. *About Time: Exploring the Gay Past*. New York: Gay Presses of New York, 1986.

Dutton, Bertha P. *Sun Father's Way: The Kiva Murals of Kuaua*. Albuquerque and Santa Fe: University of New Mexico Press, School of American Research, Museum of New Mexico Press, 1963.

Eaton, J. H. "Description of the True State and Character of the New Mexican Tribes." In *Information Respecting the History, Condition and Prospects of the Indian Tribes of the United States*, edited by Henry R. Schoolcraft, 216–21. Vol. 4. Philadelphia: J. B. Lippincott and Co., 1856.

Eggan, Dorothy. "The General Problem of Hopi Adjustment." *American Anthropologist* 45(3) (1943): 357–73.

———. "The Personal Use of Myth in Dreams." In *Myth: A Symposium*, edited by Thomas A. Sebeok, 107–21. Bloomington: Indiana University Press, 1965.

Eliade, Mircea. *Rites and Symbols of Initiation: The Mysteries of Birth and Rebirth*. 1958. Reprint. New York: Harper Torchbooks, 1965.

Essene, Frank. *Culture Element Distributions 21: Round Valley*. University of California Anthropological Records, vol. 8, no. 1. Berkeley, 1942.

Evans, Robley D. *A Sailor's Log: Recollections of Forty Years of Naval Life*. New York: D. Appleton and Co., 1931.

Fawcett, David M., and Teri McLuhan. "Ruth Leah Bunzel." In *Women Anthropologists: A Biographical Dictionary*, edited by Ute Gacs et al., 29–36. New York: Greenwood Press, 1988.

Ferguson, T. J. "The Emergence of Modern Zuni Culture and Society: A Summary of Zuni Tribal History A.D. 1450 to 1700." In *The Protohistoric Period in the North American Southwest*, 336–53. *See* E. C. Adams.

Ferguson, T. J., and E. Richard Hart. *A Zuni Atlas*. Norman: University of Oklahoma Press, 1985.

Ferguson, T. J., and Barbara J. Mills. "Settlement and Growth of Zuni Pueblo: An Architectural History." *The Kiva* 52(4) (1987): 243–66.

Fewkes, J. Walter. "A Few Tusayan Pictographs." *American Anthropologist* 5 (1892): 9–26.

Flack, James K. "The Formation of the Washington Intellectual Community, 1870–1898." Ph.D. diss., Wayne State University, 1968.

Ford, Clellan S. *Smoke from Their Fires: The Life of a Kwakiutl Chief*. New Haven: Yale University Press, 1941.

Foreman, Grant, ed. *A Pathfinder in the Southwest: The Itinerary of Lieutenant A. W. Whipple during His Explorations for a Railway Route from Fort Smith to Los Angeles in the Years 1853 and 1854*. Norman: University of Oklahoma Press, 1941.

Foucault, Michel. *The History of Sexuality, Volume I: An Introduction*. New York: Vintage Books, 1980.

Fox, Nancy. *Pueblo Weaving and Textile Arts*. Santa Fe: Museum of New Mexico Press, 1978.

Fritz, Henry E. *The Movement for Indian Assimilation, 1860–1890*. Philadelphia: University of Pennsylvania Press, 1963.

Fuller, Clarissa P. "Frank Hamilton Cushing's Relations to Zuñi and the Hemenway Southwestern Expedition, 1879–1889." Master's thesis, University of New Mexico, 1943.

Gengle, Dean. "Gay American Indians." In Jonathan Katz, *Gay American History: Lesbians and Gay Men in the U.S.A*, 332–34. New York: Thomas Y. Crowell, 1976.

Gennep, Arnold van. *The Rites of Passage*, translated by Monika B. Vizedom and Gabrielle L. Caffee. Chicago: University of Chicago Press, 1960.

Gifford, Edward W. *Culture Element Distributions 12: Apache–Pueblo*. University of California Anthropological Records, vol. 4, no. 1. Berkeley, 1940.

Gimbutas, Marija. *The Goddesses and Gods of Old Europe, 6500–3500 BC: Myths and Cult Images*. Berkeley: University of California Press, 1982.

A Glossary of Common Zuni Terms. Zuni, N.M.: Pueblo of Zuni, 1973.

Goldman, Irving. "The Zuni Indians of New Mexico." In *Cooperation and Competition among Primitive Peoples*, edited by Margaret Mead, 313–53. New York: McGraw-Hill, 1937.

Graves, Robert. *The White Goddess: A Historical Grammar of Poetic Myth*. Rev. ed. 1966. New York: Farrar, Straus and Giroux, 1948.

Greenberg, David F. "Why Was the Berdache Ridiculed?" In *The Many Faces of Homosexuality*, 179–89. *See* Callender and Kochems, "Men and Not-Men."

Guerra, Francisco. *The Pre-Columbian Mind: A Study into the Aberrant Nature of Sexual Drives, Drugs Affecting Behaviour, and the Attitude towards Life and Death, with a Survey of Pscyhotherapy, in Pre-Columbian America*. London: Seminar Press, 1971.

Gunn, John M. *Schat-Chen: History, Traditions and Narratives of the*

Queres Indians of Laguna and Acoma. Albuquerque: Albright and Anderson, 1916.

Gutíerrez, Ramón. "Must We Deracinate Indians to Find Gay Roots?" *Out/Look* 1(4) (1989): 61–67.

Hackett, Charles W., ed. and trans. *Historical Documents Relating to New Mexico, Neuva Vizcaya, and Approaches thereto, to 1773.* Vol. 3. Papers of the Division of Historical Research, Carnegie Institute of Washington, pub. 330, 1937.

Hackett, Charles W., ed., and Charmion C. Shelby, trans. *Revolt of the Pueblo Indians of New Mexico and Otermín's Attempted Reconquest, 1680–1682.* 2 vols. Albuquerque: University of New Mexico Press, 1942.

Hammond, George P., and Agapito Rey, eds. and trans. *Narratives of the Coronado Expedition, 1540–1542.* Albuquerque: University of New Mexico Press, 1940.

Hammond, William D. *Sexual Impotence in the Male and Female.* Detroit: George S. Davis, 1887.

Hanke, Lewis. *The Spanish Struggle for Justice in the Conquest of America.* Philadelphia: University of Pennsylvania Press, 1949.

———. *Aristotle and the American Indians: A Study in Race Prejudice in the Modern World.* Bloomington: Indiana University Press, 1970.

Hardin, Margaret A. *Gifts of Mother Earth: Ceramics in the Zuni Tradition.* Phoenix: Heard Museum, 1983.

Hare, Peter H. *A Woman's Quest for Science: Portrait of Anthropologist Elsie Clews Parsons.* Buffalo, NY: Prometheus Books, 1985.

Harmsen, Bill, ed. *Patterns and Sources of Zuni Kachinas.* [Denver:] Harmsen Publishing Co., 1988.

Hart, E. Richard. "Factors Relating to Zuni Land, 1900–51." *Congressional Record.* 94th Cong., 1st sess., 1975. Vol. 121(31): 2752–63.

———. "A Brief History of the Zuni Nation." In *Zuni El Morro: Past and Present,* 19–25. Exploration, Annual Bulletin of the School of American Research. Santa Fe, 1983.

Haury, Emil W. *The Excavation of Los Muertos and Neighboring Ruins in the Salt River Valley, Southern Arizona.* Papers of the Peabody Museum of American Archaeology and Ethnology, Harvard University, vol. 24, no. 1. Cambridge, Mass., 1945.

Hay, Henry (Harry). "The Hammond Report." *One Institute Quarterly* 18 (1963): 6–21.

Heitman, Francis B. *Historical Register and Dictionary of the United States Army from Its Organization, September 29, 1789, to March 2, 1903.* Vol. 1. Washington, D.C.: Government Printing Office, 1903.

Hibben, Frank C. *Kiva Art of the Anasazi at Pottery Mound.* Las Vegas, Nev.: KC Publications, 1975.

Hieb, Louis A. "Meaning and Mismeaning: Toward an Understanding of the Ritual Clown." In *New Perspectives on the Pueblos,* edited by Alfonso Ortiz, 163–95. Albuquerque: University of New Mexico Press, 1972.

Hill, W. W. *An Ethnography of Santa Clara Pueblo, New Mexico,* edited by Charles H. Lange. Albuquerque: University of New Mexico Press, 1982.

Hinman, Ida. *The Washington Sketch Book: A Society Souvenir.* Washington, D.C.: Hartman and Cadick, 1895.

Hinsley, Curtis M., Jr. *Savages and Scientists: The Smithsonian Institution and the Development of American Anthropology 1846–1910.* Washington, D.C.: Smithsonian Institution Press, 1981.

Hodge, Federick W. *History of Hawiku, New Mexico, One of the So-called Cities of Cíbola.* Los Angeles: Southwest Museum, 1937.

Hodge, Frederick W., George P. Hammond, and Agapito Rey. *Fray Alonso de Benavides' Revised Memorial of 1634.* Albuquerque: University of New Mexico Press, 1945.

Holmes, W. H. "Matilda Coxe Stevenson." *American Anthropologist* 18(4) (1916): 552–59.

Hopcke, Robert H. *Jung, Jungians, and Homosexuality.* Boston: Shambala, 1989.

Hoxie, Frederick E. *A Final Promise: The Campaign to Assimilate the Indians, 1880–1920.* Lincoln: University of Nebraska Press, 1984.

Hrdlička, Aleš. *Physiological and Medical Observations among the Indians of Southwestern United States and Northern Mexico.* Bureau of American Ethnology Bulletin no. 34. Washington, D.C.: Government Printing Office, 1908.

Indian Rights Association. *Forty-first Annual Report of the Board of Directors of the Indian Rights Association.* Philadelphia, 1923.

Jacobs, Sue-Ellen. "Comment on 'The North American Berdache.'" *Current Anthropology* 24(4) (1983): 459–60.

———. "The North American Berdache." Unpublished manuscript.

James, George W. *Our American Wonderlands.* Chicago: A. C. McClurg and Co., 1916.

———. *New Mexico: The Land of the Delight Makers.* Boston: Page Co., 1920.

James, Harry C. *Pages from Hopi History.* Tucson: University of Arizona Press, 1974.

Jochelson, Waldemer. *The Koryak.* Memoirs of the American Museum of Natural History, vol. 10, pt. 1. Leiden: E. J. Brill, 1905.

Judd, Neil M. *The Bureau of American Ethnology: A Partial History.* Norman: University of Oklahoma Press, 1967.

Jung, Carl G. "Concerning the Archetypes, with Special Reference to the Anima Concept" and "Psychological Aspects of the Mother Archetype." In *The Archetypes and the Collective Unconscious,* 2d ed., 54–84, 85–110. Vol. 9, pt. 1, *Collected Works of C. G. Jung.* Bollingen Series, vol. 20. Princeton: Princeton University Press, 1968.

———. *Mysterium Coniunctionis: An Inquiry into the Separation and Synthesis of Psychic Opposites in Alchemy.* 2d ed. Vol. 14, *Collected Works of C. G. Jung.* Bollingen Series, vol. 20. Princeton: Princeton University Press, 1970.

Kardiner, Abram. *The Individual and His Society: The Psychodynamics of Primitive Social Organization.* New York: Columbia University Press, 1939.

Karsch, Ferdinand. *Das Gleichgeschlechtliche Leben der Naturvölker.* 1911. Reprint. New York: Arno Press, 1975.

Katz, Jonathan. *Gay American History: Lesbians and Gay Men in the U.S.A.* New York: Thomas Y. Crowell, 1976.

———. "The President's Sister and the Bishop's Wife." *The Advocate* (31 January 1989): 34–35.

Kelly, Lawrence C. *The Assault on Assimilation: John Collier and the Origins of Indian Policy Reform.* Albuquerque: University of New Mexico Press, 1983.

Kenny, Maurice. "Tinselled Bucks: A Historical Study in Indian Homosexuality." In *Living the Spirit: A Gay American Indian Anthology,* edited by Will Roscoe, 15–31. New York: St. Martin's Press, 1988.

Kent, Kate P. *Pueblo Indian Textiles: A Living Tradition.* Santa Fe: School of American Research Press, 1983.

King, Dave. "Gender Confusions: Psychological and Psychiatric Conceptions of Transvestism and Transsexualism." In *The Making of the Modern Homosexual,* edited by Kenneth Plummer, 155–83. London: Hutchinson, 1981.

King, James T. *War Eagle: A Life of General Eugene A. Carr.* Lincoln: University of Nebraska Press, 1963.

Kintigh, Keith W. *Settlement, Subsistence, and Society in Late Zuni Prehistory.* Anthropological Papers of the University of Arizona, no. 44. Tucson, 1985.

Kluckhohn, Clyde. "Expressive Activities." In *People of Rimrock: A Study of Values in Five Cultures,* edited by Evon Vogt and Ethel M. Albert, 265–98. Cambridge: Harvard University Press, 1967.

Kroeber, Alfred L. "Thoughts on Zuni Religion." In *Holmes Anniversary*

Volume: Anthropological Essays Presented to William Henry Holmes in Honor of his Seventieth Birthday, December 1, 1916, 269–77. Washington, D.C.: J. W. Bryan Press, 1916.

———. *Zuñi Kin and Clan*. Anthropological Papers of the American Museum of Natural History, vol. 18, pt. 2, 37–205. New York, 1917.

———. "Psychosis or Social Sanction?" *Character and Personality* 3(3) (1940): 204–15.

Kroeber, Theodora. *Alfred Kroeber: A Personal Configuration*. Berkeley: University of California Press, 1979.

Kuipers, Cornelius. *Zuni Also Prays: Month-by-Month Observations among the People*. Christian Reformed Board of Missions, 1946.

Kvasnicka, Robert M., and Herman J. Viola, eds. *The Commissioners of Indian Affairs, 1824–1977*. Lincoln: University of Nebraska Press, 1979.

Ladd, Edmund J. "Zuni Ethno-ornithology." Master's thesis, University of New Mexico, 1963.

———. "Zuni Social and Political Organization" and "Zuni Economy." In *Handbook of North American Indians*, 482–91, 492–98. *See* Basso.

———. "Zuni Religion and Philosophy." In *Zuni El Morro: Past and Present*, 26–31. Exploration, Annual Bulletin of the School of American Research. Santa Fe, 1983.

———. "Zuni Education." In *Zuni History*, edited by E. Richard Hart, 15. Sun Valley, Idaho: Zuni History Project and Institute of the American West, 1983.

La Follette, Robert M. *La Follette's Autobiography*. Madison: University of Wisconsin Press, 1960.

Landes, Ruth. *The Prairie Potawatomi*. Madison: University of Wisconsin Press, 1970.

Laski, Vera. *Seeking Life*. Philadelphia: American Folklore Society, 1958.

Laubin, Reginald, and Gladys Laubin. *Indian Dances of North America: Their Importance to Indian Life*. Norman: University of Oklahoma Press, 1977.

LeBlanc, Steven. "The Cultural History of Cibola." In *Zuni El Morro: Past and Present*, 2–8. Exploration, Annual Bulletin of the School of American Research. Santa Fe, 1983.

Lee, Douglas B., Roger L. Meersman, and Donn B. Murphy. *Stage for a Nation: The National Theatre, 150 Years*. Lanham, Md.: University Press of America, 1985.

Leighton, Dorothea C., and John Adair. *People of the Middle Place: A Study of the Zuni Indians*. New Haven, Conn.: Human Relations Area Files, 1966.

Lesley, Lewis B., ed. *Uncle Sam's Camels: The Journal of May Humphreys Stacey Supplemented by the Report of Edward Fitzgerald Beale (1857–1858).* 1929. Reprint. Glorieta, N.M.: Rio Grande Press, 1970.

Leupp, Francis Ellington. *Notes of a Summer Tour among the Indians of the Southwest.* Philadelphia: Office of the Indian Rights Association, 1897.

Lévi-Strauss, Claude. *Structural Anthropology.* New York: Basic Books, 1963.

———. *The Origin of Table Manners: Introduction to a Science of Mythology: 3.* Translated by John and Doreen Weightman. New York: Harper and Row, 1978.

———. *The Raw and the Cooked: Introduction to a Science of Mythology: 1.* 1969. Reprint. New York: Octagon Books, 1979.

Li An-Che. "Zuñi: Some Observations and Queries." *American Anthropologist* 39(1) (1937): 62–76.

Lindquist, Gustavus E. E. *The Red Man in the United States: An Intimate Study of the Social, Economic and Religious Life of the American Indian.* New York: George H. Doran, 1923.

Lowie, Robert H. *Notes on Shoshonean Ethnography.* Anthropological Papers of the American Museum of Natural History, vol. 20, no. 3, 183–324. New York, 1924.

Lurie, Nancy O. "Winnebago Berdache." *American Anthropologist* 55(5) (1953): 708–12.

———. "Women in Early American Anthropology." In *Pioneers of American Anthropology: The Uses of Biography*, edited by June Helm, 29–81. American Ethnological Society Monograph no. 43. Seattle: University of Washington Press, 1966.

———. "Matilda Coxe Evans Stevenson." In *Notable American Women 1607–1950: A Biographical Dictionary*, edited by Edward T. James, 373–74. Vol. 3. Cambridge, Mass.: Belknap Press of Harvard University Press, 1971.

McFeat, Tom F. S. "Some Social and Spatial Aspects of Innovation at Zuni." *Anthropologica*, n.s., 2(1) (1960): 18–47.

McNitt, Frank. *The Indian Traders.* Norman: University of Oklahoma Press, 1962.

———, ed. *Navaho Expedition: Journal of a Military Reconnaissance from Santa Fe, New Mexico to the Navaho Country Made in 1849 by Lieutenant James N. Simpson.* Norman: University of Oklahoma Press, 1964.

Mardock, Robert W. *The Reformers and the American Indian.* Columbia: University of Missouri Press, 1971.

Mark, Joan. *Four Anthropologists: An American Science in Its Early Years.* New York: Science History Publications, 1980.

———. *A Stranger in Her Native Land: Alice Fletcher and the American Indians.* Lincoln: University of Nebraska Press, 1988.

Martin, Calvin, ed. *The American Indian and the Problem of History.* Oxford: Oxford University Press, 1987.

Martin, M. Kay, and Barbara Voorhies. *Female of the Species.* New York: Columbia University Press, 1975.

Mason, Otis T. "The Planting and Exhuming of a Prayer." *Science* 8(179) (1886): 24–25.

———. *Woman's Share in Primitive Culture.* New York: D. Appleton and Co., 1898.

Mead, Margaret. "Cultural Determinants of Sexual Behavior." In *Sex and Internal Secretions,* edited by William C. Young, 1433–79. 3d ed. Vol. 2. Baltimore: Williams and Wilkins, 1961.

———, ed. *An Anthropologist at Work: Writings of Ruth Benedict.* New York: Avon Books, 1973.

Medicine, Bea. "Native Perspective of the Siouan Term: Winkte." Paper presented at the New Gender Scholarship Conference, University of Southern California, February 1987.

Menendez y Pelayo, Marcelino, trans. *Tratado Sobre las Justas Causus de la Guerra contra los Indios.* Pánuco, Mexico: Fonda de Cultura Economica, 1941.

Moore, Joseph West. *Picturesque Washington: Pen and Pencil Sketches . . .* Providence: J. A. and R. A. Reid, 1888.

Morgan, Lewis Henry. *Ancient Society or Researches in the Lines of Human Progress from Savagery, through Barbarism to Civilization.* New York: Henry Holt and Co., 1877.

Napetcha, Andrew. "Education at Zuni." In *Zuni History,* 15. *See* Ladd, "Zuni Education."

Neumann, Erich. *The Great Mother: An Analysis of the Archetype.* Bollingen Series, vol. 47. Princeton: Princeton University Press, 1963.

Newman, Stanley. "A Practical Zuni Orthography." Appendix B in *Zuni Law. See* Smith and Roberts.

———. *Zuni Dictionary.* Indiana University Research Center in Anthropology, Folklore, and Linguistics, pub. 6, and *International Journal of American Linguisitics* 24(1), pt. 2. Bloomington, 1958.

Ober, Frederick A. "How a White Man Became the War Chief of the Zunis." *Wide Awake,* June 1882, 382–88.

Olmstead, Virginia L., ed. *Spanish and Mexican Colonial Censuses of New*

Mexico: 1790, 1823, 1845. Albuquerque: New Mexico Genealogical Society, 1975.

O'Kelly, Charlotte G., and Larry S. Carney. *Women and Men in Society: Cross-Cultural Perspectives on Gender Stratification*. 2d ed. Belmont, Calif.: Wadsworth Publishing, 1986.

Oosterman, Gordon. *The People: Three Indian Tribes of the Southwest*. Grand Rapids, Mich.: William B. Eerdmans Publishing Co., 1973.

Organization and Historical Sketch of the Women's Anthropological Society of America. Washington, D.C., 1889.

Ortiz, Alfonso. "Ritual Drama and the Pueblo World View." In *New Perspectives on the Pueblos*, 135–61. *See* Hieb.

———. "San Juan Pueblo." In *Handbook of North American Indians*, 278–95. *See* Basso.

Owlfeather, M. "Children of Grandmother Moon." In *Living the Spirit*, 97–105. *See* Kenny.

Palou, Francisco. *Life and Apostolic Labors of the Venerable Father Junipero Serra*, trans. by C. Scott Williams. Pasadena: George Wharton James, 1913.

Pandey, Triloki N. "Factionalism in a Southwestern Pueblo." Ph.D. diss., University of Chicago, 1967.

———. "Tribal Council Elections in a Southwestern Pueblo." *Ethnology* 7(1) (1968): 71–85.

———. "Anthropologists at Zuni." *Proceedings of the American Philosophical Society* 116(4) (1972): 321–37.

———. " 'India Man' among American Indians." In *Encounter and Experience: Personal Accounts of Fieldwork*, edited by André Béteille and T. N. Madan, 194–213. Delhi: Vikas Publishing House, 1975.

———. "Images of Power in a Southwestern Pueblo." In *The Anthropology of Power: Ethnographic Studies from Asia, Oceania, and the New World*, edited by Raymond D. Fogelson and Richard N. Adams, 195–215. New York: Academic Press, 1977.

———. "Flora Zuni—A Portrait." In *American Indian Intellectuals: 1976 Proceedings of the American Ethnological Society*, edited by Margot Liberty, 217–25. St. Paul, Minn.: West Publishing, 1978.

Parezo, Nancy J. "Matilda Coxe Evans Stevenson." In *Women Anthropologists*, 337–43. *See* Fawcett and McLuhan.

Parsons, Elsie C. [John Main, pseud.]. *Religious Chastity: An Ethnological Study*. New York: n.p., 1913.

———. "A Few Zuñi Death Beliefs and Practices." *American Anthropologist*, 18(2) (1916): 245–56.

———. "The Zuñi A'doshle and Suuke." *American Anthropologist* 18(3) (1916): 338–47.

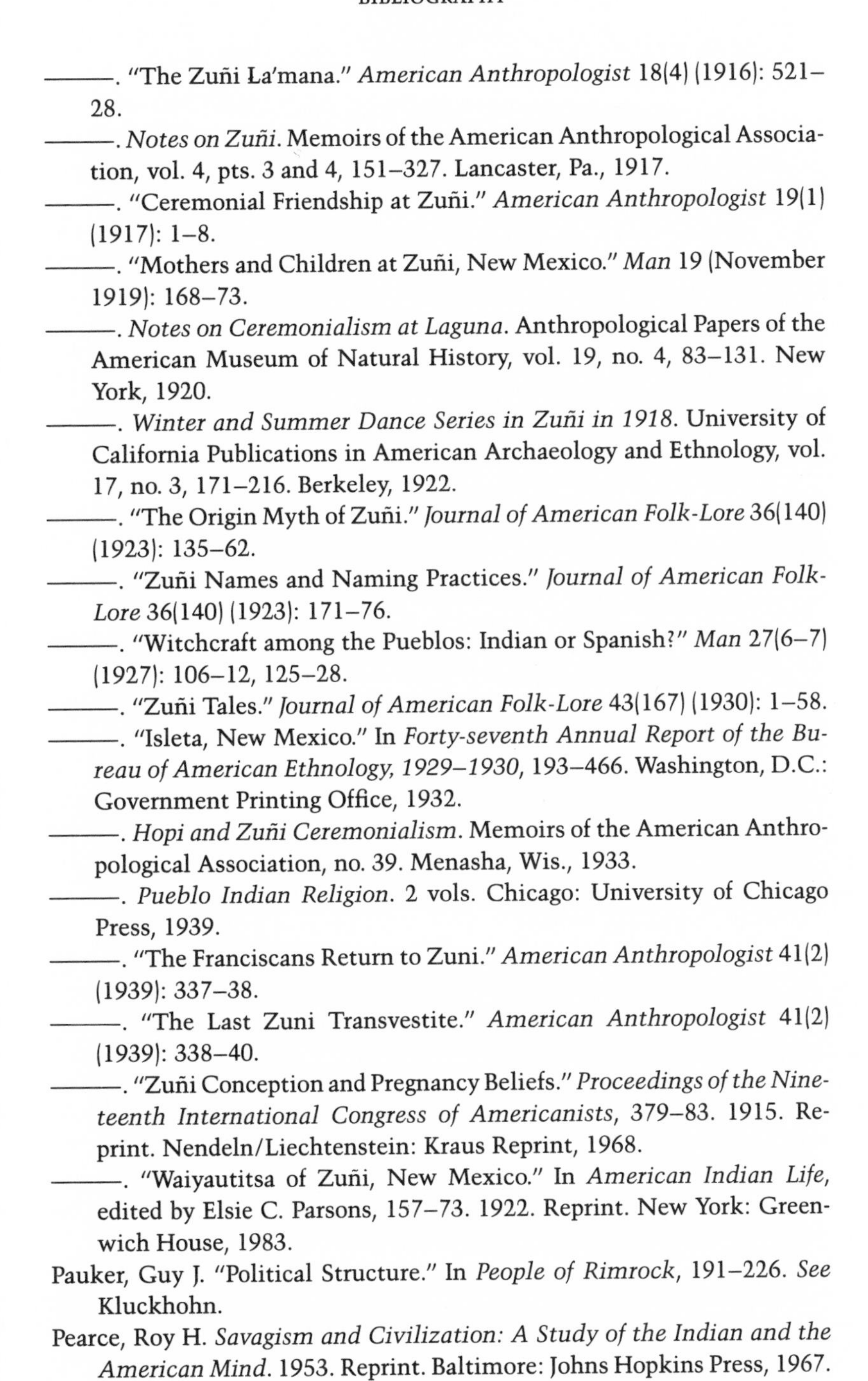

———. "The Zuñi Ła'mana." *American Anthropologist* 18(4) (1916): 521–28.

———. *Notes on Zuñi.* Memoirs of the American Anthropological Association, vol. 4, pts. 3 and 4, 151–327. Lancaster, Pa., 1917.

———. "Ceremonial Friendship at Zuñi." *American Anthropologist* 19(1) (1917): 1–8.

———. "Mothers and Children at Zuñi, New Mexico." *Man* 19 (November 1919): 168–73.

———. *Notes on Ceremonialism at Laguna.* Anthropological Papers of the American Museum of Natural History, vol. 19, no. 4, 83–131. New York, 1920.

———. *Winter and Summer Dance Series in Zuñi in 1918.* University of California Publications in American Archaeology and Ethnology, vol. 17, no. 3, 171–216. Berkeley, 1922.

———. "The Origin Myth of Zuñi." *Journal of American Folk-Lore* 36(140) (1923): 135–62.

———. "Zuñi Names and Naming Practices." *Journal of American Folk-Lore* 36(140) (1923): 171–76.

———. "Witchcraft among the Pueblos: Indian or Spanish?" *Man* 27(6–7) (1927): 106–12, 125–28.

———. "Zuñi Tales." *Journal of American Folk-Lore* 43(167) (1930): 1–58.

———. "Isleta, New Mexico." In *Forty-seventh Annual Report of the Bureau of American Ethnology, 1929–1930,* 193–466. Washington, D.C.: Government Printing Office, 1932.

———. *Hopi and Zuñi Ceremonialism.* Memoirs of the American Anthropological Association, no. 39. Menasha, Wis., 1933.

———. *Pueblo Indian Religion.* 2 vols. Chicago: University of Chicago Press, 1939.

———. "The Franciscans Return to Zuni." *American Anthropologist* 41(2) (1939): 337–38.

———. "The Last Zuni Transvestite." *American Anthropologist* 41(2) (1939): 338–40.

———. "Zuñi Conception and Pregnancy Beliefs." *Proceedings of the Nineteenth International Congress of Americanists,* 379–83. 1915. Reprint. Nendeln/Liechtenstein: Kraus Reprint, 1968.

———. "Waiyautitsa of Zuñi, New Mexico." In *American Indian Life,* edited by Elsie C. Parsons, 157–73. 1922. Reprint. New York: Greenwich House, 1983.

Pauker, Guy J. "Political Structure." In *People of Rimrock,* 191–226. *See* Kluckhohn.

Pearce, Roy H. *Savagism and Civilization: A Study of the Indian and the American Mind.* 1953. Reprint. Baltimore: Johns Hopkins Press, 1967.

Perry, Mary E. "The 'Nefarious Sin' in Early Modern Seville." *Journal of Homosexuality* 16(1/2) (1988): 67–89.

Peterson, Charles S. *Take Up Your Mission: Mormon Colonizing along the Little Colorado River, 1870–1900.* Tucson: University of Arizona Press, 1973.

Philp, Kenneth R. *John Collier's Crusade for Indian Reform, 1920–1954.* Tucson: University of Arizona Press, 1977.

Plog, Fred. "Prehistory: Western Anasazi." *In Handbook of North American Indians,* 108–30. *See* Basso.

Plummer, Kenneth, ed. *The Making of the Modern Homosexual.* London: Hutchinson, 1981.

Porter, Joseph C. *Paper Medicine Man: John Gregory Bourke and his American West.* Norman: University of Oklahoma Press, 1986.

Powell, John W. "Annual Report of the Director." In *Fifth Annual Report of the Bureau of Ethnology, 1883–1884,* xvii–liii. Washington, D.C.: Government Printing Office, 1887.

Priestley, J. B., and Jacquetta Hawkes. *Journey Down a Rainbow.* London: Heinemann-Cresset, 1955.

Prucha, Francis P., ed. *Americanizing the American Indians: Writings by the "Friends of the Indian," 1880–1900.* 1973. Reprint. Lincoln: University of Nebraska Press, 1978.

Quam, Alvina, trans. *The Zunis: Self-portrayals by the Zuni People.* Albuquerque: University of New Mexico Press, 1972.

Roberts, John M. "The Zuni." In *Variations in Value Orientations,* edited by Florence R. Kluckhohn and Fred L. Strodtbeck, 285–316. 1961. Reprint. Westport, Conn.: Freedwood Press, 1973.

Robinson, Ella L., trans. "Troubles at Zuni in 1702–03." *The Masterkey* 18(4) (1944): 110–15.

Rodgers, Bruce. *Gay Talk: A (Sometimes Outrageous) Dictionary of Gay Slang.* 1972. Reprint. New York: Paragon, 1979.

Roscoe, Will. "Indian Berdache: A Traditional Gay Role?" Review of Walter L. Williams, *The Spirit and the Flesh. The Advocate,* no. 460 (25 November 1986): 60–62, 129.

———. "Living the Tradition: Gay American Indians," in Mark Thompson, *Gay Spirit: Myth and Meaning,* 69–77. New York: St. Martin's Press, 1987.

———. "Bibliography of Berdache and Alternative Gender Roles among North American Indians." *Journal of Homosexuality* 14(3–4) (1987): 81–171.

———. "We'wha and Klah: The American Indian Berdache as Artist and Priest." *American Indian Quarterly* 12(2) (1988): 127–50.

———. "What Child Is This?" Review of Mark Thompson, *Gay Spirit* and Arthur Evans, *God of Ecstasy*. *San Francisco Jung Institute Library Journal* 8(2) (1988): 41–60.

———. "Making History: The Challenge of Gay and Lesbian Studies," *Journal of Homosexuality* 15(3/4) (1988): 1–40.

———, ed. *Living the Spirit: A Gay American Indian Anthology*. New York: St. Martin's Press, 1988.

———. "The Semiotics of Gender on Zuni Kachinas." *The Kiva* 55(1) (1990): 49–70.

Rose, Bradley. "In Search of the Noble Homosexual." Review of Walter L. Williams, *The Spirit and the Flesh*. *Gay Community News* 14(26) (18–24 January 1987): 9.

Rouse, W. J. "War and Witchcraft." *New York Times Illustrated Magazine* 47 (6 March 1898): 3–5.

Rubin, Gayle. "The Traffic in Women: Notes on the 'Political Economy' of Sex." In *Toward an Anthropology of Women*, edited by Rayna R. Reiter, 157–210. New York: Monthly Review Press, 1975.

Salpointe, Rev. J. B. *Soldiers of the Cross*. Banning, Calif.: St. Boniface's Industrial School, 1898.

Sanday, Peggy R. *Female Power and Male Dominance: On the Origins of Sexual Inequality*. Cambridge: Cambridge University Press, 1981.

Sandner, Donald. *Navaho Symbols of Healing*. New York: Harcourt Brace Jovanovich, 1979.

Sando, Joe S. *The Pueblo Indians*. 2d ed. San Francisco: Indian Historian Press, 1982.

Saunders, Charles F. *The Indians of the Terraced Houses*. 1912. Reprint. Glorieta, N.M.: Rio Grande Press, 1973.

Schaafsma, Polly. *Indian Rock Art of the Southwest*. Santa Fe and Albuquerque: School of American Research and University of New Mexico Press, 1980.

Schaafsma, Polly, and Curtis F. Schaafsma. "Evidence for the Origins of the Pueblo Katchina Cult as Suggested by Southwestern Rock Art." *American Antiquity* 39(4) (1974): 535–45.

Scherer, Joanna C. *Indians: The Great Photographs that Reveal North American Indian Life, 1847–1929, from the Unique Collection of the Smithsonian Institution*. New York: Bonanza Books, 1982.

Schlegel, Alice. "Male and Female in Hopi Thought and Action." In *Sexual Stratification: A Cross-Cultural View*, edited by Alice Schlegel, 245–69. New York: Columbia University Press, 1977.

Schneider, David M., and Kathleen Gough, eds. *Matrilineal Kinship*. Berkeley: University of California Press, 1961.

Schneider, David M. and John M. Roberts. *Zuni Kin Terms*. 1956. Reprint. N.p.: Human Relations Area Files Press, 1965.

Scholes, France V. "Church and State in New Mexico, 1610–1650." *New Mexico Historical Review* 11(1–4)–12(1) (1936–1937).

———. "Troublous Times in New Mexico, 1659–1670." *New Mexico Historical Review* 12(2,4), 13(1), 15(3–4), 16(1–3) (1937–1941).

Schroeder, Albert H. "Rio Grande Ethnohistory." In *New Perspectives on the Pueblos*, 41–70. *See* Hieb.

Sekaquaptewa, Emory. "Hopi Indian Ceremonies." In *Seeing with a Native Eye: Essays on Native American Religion*, edited by Walter H. Capps, 35–43. New York: Harper and Row, 1976.

Simmons, Marc. "History of Pueblo–Spanish Relations to 1821." In *Handbook of North American Indians*, 178–93. *See* Basso.

Smith, Watson. *Kiva Mural Decorations at Awatovi and Kawaika-a, with a Survey of Other Wall Paintings in the Pueblo Southwest*. Papers of the Peabody Museum of American Archaeology and Ethnology, Harvard University, vol. 37. Cambridge, Mass., 1952.

Smith, Watson, and John M. Roberts. *Zuni Law: A Field of Values*. Papers of the Peabody Museum of American Archaeology and Ethnology, Harvard University, vol. 43, no. 1. Cambridge, Mass., 1954.

Smith, Watson, Richard B. Woodbury, and Nathalie F. S. Woodbury. *The Excavation of Hawikuh by Frederick Webb Hodge: Report of the Hendricks–Hodge Expedition 1917–1923*. Contributions from the Museum of the American Indian, Heye Foundation, vol. 20. New York, 1966.

Spicer, Edward H. *Cycles of Conquest: The Impact of Spain, Mexico, and the United States on the Indians of the Southwest, 1533–1960*. Tucson: University of Arizona Press, 1962.

Spier, Leslie. *Klamath Ethnography*. University of California Publications in American Archaeology and Ethnology, vol. 30, Berkeley, 1930.

———. "Elsie Clews Parsons." *American Anthropologist* 45(2) (1943): 244–51.

Stephen, Alexander M. *The Hopi Journals of Alexander M. Stephen*. Edited by Elsie C. Parsons. 2 vols. Columbia University Contributions to Anthropology, vol. 23. New York, 1936.

Stevenson, Matilda C. "The Religious Life of the Zuñi Child." In *Fifth Annual Report of Bureau of Ethnology, 1883–1884*, 533–55. Washington, D.C.: Government Printing Office, 1887.

———. "From 'The Zuni Scalp Ceremonial.'" In *The Congress of Women Held in the Woman's Building, World's Columbian Exposition, Chicago, U.S.A., 1893*, edited by Mary K. O. Eagle, 484–87. Philadelphia: S. I. Bell and Co., 1894.

———. "Zuñi Ancestral Gods and Masks." *American Anthropologist* 11(2) (1898): 33–40.

———. "The Zuñi Indians: Their Mythology, Esoteric Fraternities, and Ceremonies." In *Twenty-third Annual Report of the Bureau of American Ethnology, 1901–1902,* 1–608. Washington, D.C.: Government Printing Office, 1904.

———. "Ethnobotany of the Zuñi Indians." In *Thirtieth Annual Report of the Bureau of American Ethnology, 1908–1909,* 31–102. Washington, D.C.: Government Printing Office, 1915.

Steward, Julian H. *Ethnography of the Owens Valley Paiute.* University of California Publications in American Archaeology and Ethnology, vol. 33, pt. 3. Berkeley, 1933.

———. *Culture Element Distributions 13: Nevada Shoshoni.* University of California Anthropological Records, vol. 4, no. 2. Berkeley, 1941.

Stewart, Omer C. "Homosexuality among the American Indians and Other Native Peoples of the World." *Mattachine Review* 6(2) (1960): 13–19.

Stoller, Robert J. "Two Feminized Male American Indians." *Archives of Sexual Behavior* 5(6): 529–38.

Szasz, Margaret. *Education and the American Indian: The Road to Self-determination, 1928–1973.* Albuquerque: University of New Mexico Press, 1974.

Talayesva, Don C. *Sun Chief: The Autobiography of a Hopi Indian,* edited by Leo W. Simmons. New Haven: Yale University Press, 1942.

Tedlock, Barbara. "The Beautiful and the Dangerous: Zuni Ritual and Cosmology as an Aesthetic System." In *Conjunctions: Bi-annual Volumes of New Writing,* edited by Bradford Morrow, 246–65. Vol. 6. N.p., 1984.

Tedlock, Dennis. "An American Indian View of Death." In *Teachings from the American Earth: Indian Religion and Philosophy,* edited by Dennis Tedlock and Barbara Tedlock, 248–71. New York: Liveright, 1975.

———. *Finding the Center: Narrative Poetry of the Zuni Indians.* 1972. Reprint. Lincoln: University of Nebraska Press, 1978.

———. "Zuni Religion and World View." In *Handbook of North American Indians,* 499–508. *See* Basso.

———. *The Spoken Word and the Work of Interpretation.* Philadelphia: University of Pennsylvania Press, 1983.

Telling, Irving. "New Mexican Frontiers: A Social History of the Gallup Area 1881–1901." Ph.D. diss., Harvard University, 1952.

Ten Broeck, P. G. S. "Manners and Customs of the Moqui and Navajo Tribes of New Mexico." In *Information Respecting the History, Condition and Prospects of the Indian Tribes of the United States,* 72–91. *See*

Eaton.
Thompson, Mark. *Gay Spirit: Myth and Meaning.* New York: St. Martin's Press, 1987.
Timmons, Stuart. *The Trouble with Harry Hay: Founder of the Modern Gay Movement.* Boston: Alyson Publications, 1990.
Titiev, Mischa. *The Hopi Indians of Old Oraibi.* Ann Arbor: University of Michigan Press, 1972.
Trotter, George A. *From Feather, Blanket and Tepee.* New York: Vantage Press, 1955.
Tugwell, Rexford G. *Grover Cleveland.* New York: Macmillan Co., 1968.
Turner, Katharine C. *Red Men Calling on the Great White Father.* Norman: University of Oklahoma Press, 1951.
Turner, Victor W. *The Ritual Process: Structure and Anti-structure.* Chicago: Aldine Publishing Co., 1969.
Tyler, S. Lyman. *Spanish Laws Concerning Discoveries, Pacifications, and Settlements among the Indians.* Occasional Paper 17. Salt Lake City: American West Center, University of Utah, 1980.
———. "The Zuni Indians under the Laws of Spain, Mexico and the U.S." In *Zuni History,* 25–28. *See* Ladd, "Zuni Education."
Udall, Louise. *Me and Mine: The Life Story of Helen Sekaquaptewa.* Tucson: University of Arizona Press, 1969.
Ukestine, Danny. "Ancestral Homecoming." In *Experience Zuni, New Mexico,* 5. Zuni, N.M.: Zuni Area Chamber of Commerce, 1989.
Viola, Herman J. *Diplomats in Buckskin: A History of Indian Delegations in Washington City.* Washington, D.C.: Smithsonian Institution Press, 1981.
Vivian, R. Gwinn. "An Inquiry into Prehistoric Social Organization in Chaco Canyon, New Mexico." In *Reconstructing Prehistoric Pueblo Societies,* edited by William A. Longacre, 59–83. Albuquerque: University of New Mexico Press, 1970.
Vogt, Evon Z. "Intercultural Relations" and "Ecology and Economy." In *People of Rimrock,* 46–82, 160–190. *See* Kluckhohn.
Vogt, Evon Z., and Ethel M. Albert. "The 'Comparative Study of Values in Five Cultures' Project." In *People of Rimrock,* 1–33. *See* Kluckhohn.
Walker, Mitch. "Visionary Love: The Magickal Gay Spirit-Power." In *Gay Spirit,* 210–36. *See* Thompson.
Weeks, Jeffrey. "The Construction of Homosexuality." Chapter 6 in *Sex, Politics and Society: The Regulation of Sexuality since 1800.* London: Longman, 1981.
Westermarck, Edward. *The Origin and Development of Moral Ideas.* London: Macmillan, 1906.
White, Edmund. *States of Desire: Travels in Gay America.* New York: E. P.

Dutton, 1980.

White, Leslie A. "Anthropology 1964: Retrospect and Prospect." *American Anthropologist* 67(3) (1965): 629–37.

Whitehead, Harriet. "The Bow and the Burden Strap: A New Look at Institutionalized Homosexuality in Native North America." In *Sexual Meanings: The Cultural Construction of Gender and Sexuality*, edited by Sherry B. Ortner and Harriet Whitehead, 80–115. Cambridge: Cambridge University Press, 1981.

Whitham, Frederick L., and Robin M. Mathy. *Male Homosexuality in Four Societies: Brazil, Guatemala, the Philippines, and the United States.* New York: Praeger Publishers, 1986.

Whiting, John W. M., et al. "The Learning of Values." In *People of Rimrock*, 83–125. *See* Kluckhohn.

Williams, Walter. *The Spirit and the Flesh: Sexual Diversity in American Indian Culture.* Boston: Beacon Press, 1988.

Wilson, Edmund. *Red, Black, Blond and Olive, Studies in Four Civilizations: Zuñi, Haiti, Soviet Russia, Israel.* New York: Oxford University Press, 1956.

Winship, George P. "The Coronado Expedition 1540–1542." In *Fourteenth Annual Report of the Bureau of Ethnology, 1892–1893*, 329–613. Washington, D.C.: Government Printing Office, 1896.

Wittfogel, Karl A., and Esther S. Goldfrank. "Some Aspects of Pueblo Mythology and Society." *Journal of American Folk-Lore* 56 (1943): 17–30.

Woodbury, Richard B. "Zuni Prehistory and History to 1850." In *Handbook of North American Indians*, 467–73. *See* Basso.

Woodward, Arthur. "Frank Cushing—'First War-chief of Zuñi.'" *The Masterkey* 13(5) (1939): 172–79.

———. "Concerning Witches." *The Masterkey* 24(6) (1950): 183–88.

Wright, Barton, and Duane Dishta. *Kachinas of the Zuni.* Flagstaff: Northland Press, 1985.

Young, M. Jane. "Women, Reproduction, and Religion in Western Puebloan Society." *Journal of American Folklore* 100(398) (1987): 436–45.

———. *Signs from the Ancestors: Zuni Cultural Symbolism and Perceptions of Rock Art.* Albuquerque: University of New Mexico Press, 1988.

Index

'a:ho'i (living being), 12, 14, 128
Acoma, berdache of, 25, 26, 175, 251n2
Adair, John, 49, 103, 200, 201; Kasinelu and, 197; photograph by, 96; We'wha and, 44
'Adoshle, 36, 250n65
'A:dowa 'E'lashdok'i. *See* Corn Maidens
agents of assimilation, definition of, 42, 99
agriculture, 41, 154, 157, 158, 167, 229n36, 254n25; initiations of, 136; mythical origin of, 219; roles in, 19
'Ahayu:da. *See* War Gods
'Ahea'a, 134
'akna' a:ho"i. See cooked beings
'aktsek'i (young boy), 132
Alarcón, Hernando de, 172
Allen, Paula Gunn, xiv, 159; on women, 137; writing of, 204–6
All Pueblo Council, 184–86, 191–92; formation of, 181
Amejerado, Juan Felipe, 175
American Indian Defense Association (AIDA), 180, 186
Amugereados, Mariano, 26
amugereados. See *mujerado*
Anasazi, 16, 41, 228n27, 251n2
Ancient Society (Morgan), 67
anthropology: as fad, 67–68; impact at Zuni of, x-xiii; personality and, 160; women and, 60–61
Apaches, 30, 99, 110; raids by, 31; rites of, 249n52
'A:shiwi. *See* Zuni
assimilation, 42, 46, 98–99, 120, 176–79, 203; berdaches and, 202; campaign against, 181, 183, 187; education and, 199; forced, 112–13; IRA and, 182; religious freedom and, 184, 193–94; sexuality and, 180
Augur, Colon, 105–7, 109
Austin, Mary, 186
'a:wona:willab'ona ("The Ones Who Hold the Roads"), 141, 250n57

Badger People. See *donashi:kwe*
Balowahdiwa, 9, 127, 129
Bandelier, Adolph, 26, 177

bardajes. See berdaches
Bayadamu, 222
Bekwin (Sun Priest), 19
Beloved Twain, 218. *See also* Divine Ones
Benedict, Ruth, x-xi, xvi, xvii, 20, 21, 28, 101, 102, 110, 120, 163, 207, 208, 253n8; Dumaka and, 243n44; writing of, 27
berdache kachina. *See* Kolhamana
berdaches: archetype of, 161, 166–69; biases about, 4–5, 115, 194, 201–2, 211–12, 265n40, 265n43; clothes washing and, 47, 126, 170; definition of, 2, 5, 124–25, 212, 225n6; disappearance of, 173, 193–94, 198–203; English names for, 5, 124–25; female, 28, 158, 232n67, 251n72; female roles and, 125–26, 263n25; gay identity and, 210–11, 213–14; gender of, 144–46, 225n3; kinship terms for, 127, 242n32; modern, 97, 207, 214; multidimensional model of, 167–68, 213–14; prehistoric, 24, 25, 230n52; psychological development of, 32–33, 161–62; Pueblo names for, 5; rediscovery of, 204–6; role of, vii, x-xi, 22–28, 121–22, 164, 210–14, 229n36; sexuality of, 26–27, 153, 187, 204, 211–13, 260n55; shamans and, 24; Spaniards and, 172, 174–76; Spanish names for, 4–5; study of, 206–7; suppression of, 172–73, 199, 209; symbolism of, 210–11; women and, 152; Zuni conception of, x-xi, 5–6, 209, 213, 243n32. *See also* lhamana
beshatsilo:kwe (Bedbug People), 45
bichi:kwe (Dogwood People), 31
binanne (breath of life), 130, 143, 254n25
bisexuality, 201, 208
Black Corn people. *See* Kan'a:kwe
Black Crow people. *See* Kan'a:kwe
Black Gods. *See* Kan'a:kwe
Bourke, John G., 40
bow priests, 13, 98, 108, 111, 114, 118, 250n59, 255n37; arrest of, 109, 115, 119, 241n6; decline of, 120; initiation of, 142; in origin myth, 218; stature of, 32; witchcraft and, 102–4
Brant, Beth, xiv
Brosius, Samuel M., 182
Bryan, Mary, 185
bu"a, definition of, 164–65
Bunker, Robert, 29
Bunzel, Ruth, xi, 21, 22, 27, 34–35, 100, 119, 142, 154, 218, 242n32, 253n8; Dumaka and, 243n44
Bureau of American Ethnology (Bureau of Ethnology), 9, 61, 69, 225–26n2; expedition of, 8, 43
Bureau of Indian Affairs. *See* Office of Indian Affairs
burials, 24; description of, 123–24, 142–44; sex-specific, 230n52. *See also* death
Burke, Charles, 181–82, 186–89
Burns, Randy, 204, 205, 211
Bursum, Holm, 180
Bursum bill: campaign against, 180–81; IRA and, 185

Cameron, Barbara, 204
Campbell, Joseph, 165
Carib Indians, sodomy and, 171
Carlisle, John, 4, 124, 236n9; We'wha and, 56, 72
Carlisle, Mrs., 71, 124; We'wha and, 56

Carpenter, Edward, 207
Carr, Eugene, 100, 241n7
Carson, Kit, 39
Casteñeda, Pedro de, 172
ceremonies. *See* religious ceremonies
Cha'kwen 'Oka (Warrior Woman), 138–40, 144, 161, 162, 164, 166, 221–22, 229n36, 249n50, 251n2, 254n29, 254n30, 254n35, 255n47; ceremonies of, 249n49; counterparts of, 159; death of, 222; initiation by, 165; Mother Terrible and, 158–59
cha'le' (child), 32, 132
Chaco Canyon, 16, 19, 220, 228n27
Charles I, 171
child-rearing, 20; for berdaches, 32; Zuni approach to, 32–41, 159–62
childbirth, 141, 159; rites of, 129–31, 139
chimik'ana'kowa (origin myth), 217
Chodorow, Nancy, 160
Circular 1665. *See* dance order
civilization: savagery and, 68, 116, 122; Spanish view of, 174; stages of, 67–68, 116
clans, 13, 234n31
Cleveland, Grover, 4, 64, 66, 121, 191; We'wha and, 70–72
Cleveland, Rose, 60, 237n23
Clifford, James, xiii
clothes, symbolism of, 130, 145, 164–65, 200–201
clothes washing, 46–47, 126, 170
clowns, 1, 178–79. *See also* Koyemshi clowns
Code of Religious Offenses. *See* Religious Crimes Code
Collier, John, xvi, xvii, 239n49; activism of, 180–93; assimilation and, 183, 187; IRA and, 191; secret dance file and, 183, 189; vision of, 192–93; Zunis and, x
Comanches, 30
Committee of One Hundred, 184, 188
cooked beings (*'kna 'a:ho"i*), 128, 138, 145, 149, 156, 167, 219, 247n16. *See also* raw beings
Coolidge, Calvin, 190
corn: ritual uses of, 19, 54, 69, 130, 143; symbolism of, 15, 131–32, 134, 138, 140, 141, 153
Corn Maidens, 138, 144, 160, 222; cult of, 140, 249n51; mythological origin of, 219
Corn Mountain (Dowa Yalanne), 11, 17, 34, 50, 222; photograph of, 74
Coronado, Francisco Vásquez de, 16, 172, 173
Cotton Woman, 12
Council of the Gods, 1
cross-dressing, 2, 23, 125, 174, 212, 257n18; abandonment of, 198–201, 213; attitudes toward, 240n62. *See also* transvestism
Crow People. See *kakkakwe*
cultural relativism, xvii, 192, 208
Curtis, Edward S., 132, 151, 164, 189, 252n3, 252n8, 260n47
Cushing, Frank Hamilton, viii, xii-xiii, xvii, 7, 11–14, 17, 19, 25, 37, 40, 43, 46, 50, 54, 122, 131, 137, 140, 151, 153, 163, 208, 220, 252n8; Balowahdiwa and, 9, 127, 129; cooking of, 127–28; photograph of, 76; We'wha and, 126, 235n57; Zuni delegation and, xii, 54–55, 101–2

Dabb, Edith M., 183

dance order (Circular 1665): controversy over, 181–82, 184; IRA and, 182; religious freedom and, 186
dances, 1–2, 34, 35; kachina, 14, 175; stopping, 116; women's, 139
Dancing the Corn, description of, 140
death, 157, 219; rites of, 142–44; simulation of, 133, 248n33. *See also* burials
dehya [tehya], 22, 131
delabennane (folk tales), 217
Den'anikk'a, 134. *See also* Sayalhi"a
Denman, Leslie Van Ness, 196
deshkwi (sacred), 130, 134
dika:we'. See medicine societies
disease: impact of, 17, 31, 246n80; We'wha and, 31; witchcraft and, 103, 119
Dissette, Mary, 25, 33, 46, 47, 110, 117, 170, 178, 187, 188, 193–94, 260n55; dismissal of, 117–18, 246n80; interview of, 113–14; Kasinelu and, 195; Kwiwishdi and, 23–24; Marita and, 111–14; We'wha and, 71, 106, 231n61
divine-child archetype, 166–67
Divine Ones, 218, 220, 221. *See also* Beloved Twain
divorce, 20
Dodge, Mabel, 180
donashi:kwe (Badger People), 31, 45
Dumaka [Tumaka, To'maka], Nick "Zuni Nick," 100–101, 235n53, 241n7; description of, 243n44; Graham and, 100, 105; photograph of, 91; revenge of, 110; trial of, 104–11; witchcraft and, 101–2

Eakins, Thomas, 9
Ealy, Mrs., 43, 44; We'wha and, 46–47
Ealy, Ruth, 44
Ealy, Taylor F., 44–45, 100, 193; arrival of, 43; photograph of, 83
Earth Mother, 12, 39, 51, 133, 218, 221
education, 41–42; compulsory, 112–14, 116, 118, 199
Engels, Frederick, 67
epidemics. *See* disease
Evans, Mrs. A. H., 58

Fall, Albert, 180
farming. *See* agriculture
Faurote, May, 114–15, 193
fertility, 138, 139, 142, 161
Fewkes, J. Walter, 23, 26
Fort Wingate, 40, 100, 109
Freud, Sigmund, 159

Gatschet, Albert S., 61; We'wha and, 62
Gay American Indians (GAI), 205–7; founding of, 204; History Project of, xiv
gays: berdaches and, 210–14, 265n41; Indian, 203–6
gender roles, 98, 129, 165, 166, 170; alternative, vii, 22; berdaches and, 124–27; differentiation of, 124–25, 250n61, 250n65; mediation of, 141–42, 144, 168–69, 211, 213–14; social construction of, 207–8; symbols of, 132; Zuni conception of, 18–22, 127, 129, 146, 160, 201, 202, 218. *See also* men; third gender; women
General Federation of Women's Clubs, 188–89
Ghost Dance movement, 210
Gimbutas, Marija, 159

Goldman, Irving, 120
Gómara, López de, 173
Graham, Douglas D., 108, 110, 114, 246n90; Dumaka and, 100, 105, 241n7; photograph of, 91
Green, Deputy Marshal, 105
Guerra, Francisco, 172

hadikanne (Witch Society), 102
Hadotsi, 115
Halona:idiwana (Zuni), 11, 222
Hammaker, Jennie, 44, 50; photograph of, 83
Hammond, William A.: berdaches and, 25
Handbook of North American Indians (Smithsonian), 194
hanni (younger sibling), 33
Hawikku, 251n2, 256n14; burials at, 24
Hawkes, Jacquetta, xi
Hay, Harry, vii-viii
Heap, Mrs. David Porter, 56
hermaphrodite, 5, 49, 124, 125, 252n8; archetype of, 166–68; slang variations of, 25–26
heterosexuality, 20, 142, 208, 250n61, 253n18, 265–66n44
Hillers, John K., 8, 43; photographs by, 86–87, 238n30
Hirschfeld, Magnus, 124
'hlámon, 151, 153, 252n7
Hodge, Frederick, 186, 189
Hohokam, 16
homosexuality, vii, 5, 125, 168, 200–201, 203–4, 207–8, 210–12, 231n63, 256n13, 266n44; adolescent, 35; berdaches and, 187, 211 matrilineal society and, 161; medical model of, xi; mother complex and, 160; multidimensional model and, 213; suppression of, 172–73; Zuni, 203
Hopi: berdache of, 5, 25, 26, 33; kachina cult and, 227n27, 251n2; secret dance file and, 179
hova (Hopi), 5, 25, 251n2
Hrdlička, Aleš, 177
hunting, 13, 144, 154, 157, 164, 254n25; communal, 34; initiation of, 135–36
Huntt, George C., 109

'i:'bu'anaka (initiation), 128–29
'ikina (younger sister), 33
immorality, charges of, 114–16, 171, 174–80, 182–83, 256n13
Indian Petroglyph State Park, 25
Indian Rights Association (IRA), 23, 180, 188, 192; dance order and, 182; Dissette and, 187; secret dance file and, 183, 188, 191; True and, 184–85, 190–91
initiations, 132, 141–43, 145, 164–65; female, 137–39, 249n52; infant, 129–31; male, 134–36, 154, 163, 165, 250–51n68; origins of, 222; phases of, 128–29, 131, 133; symbols of, 129–31, 134, 141
Isleta, berdache at, 5, 200
'Itsebasha (Koyemshi clown), 148, 162, 163, 221; initiation of, 165

James, Darwin R., 61
James, George Wharton, 49, 51, 71, 107, 112; We'wha and, 29, 52
Johnson, William "Pussyfoot," 189–90, 192; secret dance file and, 187–88
Jung, C. G., 154–56, 158, 160, 166–67, 169; homosexuals and, 168; third gender and, 168

k'abin 'a:ho"i. See raw beings
Kachina Mother, 160, 163. *See also* Komokatsik
kachinas, 17, 21–22, 133; berdache, 24, 25, 28, 35, 148; children and, 34–37; gender symbolism on, viii, 253n8
kachina society, 13, 15, 130, 133, 152, 161, 227–28n27, 232n67; ceremonies of, 132; initiation for, 37, 131, 141; lhamanas and, 28, 144; origin of, 17, 222, 250n61; We'wha and, 38, 126; women and, 19, 232n67
Kachina Village, 151, 162
kakkakwe (Crow People), 154, 156
Kaklo, 133, 218; visit of, 37, 217
Kan'a:kwe (Black Gods), 16, 35, 157, 164, 220–22, 228n27, 229n36, 253n8, 266n11; ceremony of, 147–49, 158, 163, 165–66, 196, 252n3; costumes of, 148, 251–52n2; kachinas, 94, 147, 154, 251n2
Karsch, Ferdinand, 207
Kasinelu, 27, 124, 195–98, 200, 209, 262n8, 263n25; photograph of, 96
katsik'i (little girl), 132
katsotstsi (female berdache), 27–28, 232n67
Kearny, Stephen W., 30
Kenny, Maurice, xiv, 203–5
Kiasi, 102, 115
kihe (ceremonial friends), 201, 231n62
Kirmes, 63–66, 69, 121
kivas, 13, 17, 165, 175. *See also* kachina society
K'ohak 'Oka. *See* White Shell Woman
kokko (kachina gods), 21, 136, 141, 147, 221
Kokko 'A:'iya. *See* Sha'lako ceremony
kokko k'ohanna. See White Gods
Kokk'okshi, 21–22, 136, 142, 153, 163–65, 221; as firstborn, 151, 162, 164, 252–53n8
kokkokwe (kachina people), 154
Kokkwe'lashdok'i (Kachina Girl), 136, 151
k'okshi, 21, 37, 136, 156, 157, 164
kokwimu (Keres), 5, 251n2
Kolhamana (berdache kachina), 24–25, 35, 78, 147, 162–64, 166, 167, 169, 232n67, 235n60, 252n3, 254n29, 254n35, 255n47; birth of, 149–54, 220; drawing of, 95; initiation of, 165; Kasinelu as, 196; mask of, 94; photograph of, 94, 95; as role model, 165; We'wha as, 148, 196
Kolo:wisi, 38, 133, 134, 222
Komokatsik (Old Dance Woman), 151, 254n35. *See also* Kachina Mother
Koyemshi clowns, 1, 37, 114, 148–49, 153–54, 162, 166, 221; birth of, 151, 220; description of, 34; satire of, 163; as spirit guides, 165. *See also* clowns
Kroeber, Alfred, 20, 24, 124, 198; on berdaches, 125; Dumaka and, 243n44
kwidó (Tewa), 5
Kwiwishdi, 33, 47, 198, 200; description of, 23–24; development of, 209

Ladd, Edmund, 15, 18, 143
La Follette, Robert: on Cleveland, 70
Laguna: berdache of, 5, 25, 175, 199; kachina berdache of, 251n2
Lasbeke, 198–200, 209
Las Casas, Bartolomé de, 171, 174, 193
Lévi-Strauss, Claude, 157, 218, 247n16
Lha:hewe' ceremony, 139, 196, 249n49, 249n52
lhalha, definition of, 202–3, 263n23
lhamana, 5, 108, 163–64, 195, 232n1, 232n67, 235n60, 253n8; becoming, 22–23; burial of, 126; decline of, 197; definition of, 22–23, 202, 230n48, 252n7; female, 27–28; gender of, 125–26, 129; initiation of, 144–45; kinship terms and, 127; mythological origin of, 151, 220; number of, 231n63; psychological development of, 161–62; respect for, 202; sexuality of, 26–27; socioeconomic status of, 164; Zuni conception of, 213. *See also* berdaches
lhamanaye, 28, 146
lhewe:kwe (Sword People), 38
lhunide (Tewa), 5
Li An-Che, 36
liminality, 131, 133, 165; definition of, 128
Lindquist, G. E. E., 183, 184
Logan, John A., 58, 239n55
Lonergan, Philip T., 178–80, 192, 258n26
Long Walk, 40
López de Mendizábal, Bernardo, 175
Lummis, Charles, 53, 186
Lurie, Nancy, 49, 201, 237n24

McFeat, Tom, 18, 121
Macaw People, 149, 156
Manna, 23
Mallery, Garrick, 61
Marita (Melita), 244n46; trial of, 111–13, 244n49
marriage, 19–20, 35, 138; courtship and, 20
Marwig, Professor, 63, 65, 66
Marx, Karl, 67
Mason, Otis T., 61, 238n28
matrilineal society, 13, 19, 152, 161, 175, 177, 219, 229n36; roles in, 159–60
Matteson, Sumner: berdaches and, 26
Mead, Margaret, xi
medicine societies, 19, 45, 103, 132, 141, 142, 145, 228n27, 247n21; Dumaka and, 243n44; origin of, 220, 250n61
men: attitudes of, 22, 152; ceremonies for, 132–36; psychological development of, 144–54, 159–61; roles of, 18–22. *See also* gender roles
Middle Place, 1–2, 11, 99, 114, 149–50, 154, 156, 157, 166; search for, 15–16, 219–22
Midnight Sun, xiv
mik'abanne (female corn), 130, 140, 153
mili, 141, 143
military intervention, 111, 115, 117–18, 178

Mindeleff brothers, 61
missionaries, 9, 196; arrival of, 41–44; Christian Reformed, 198; Mormon, 42; Presbyterian, 24, 42, 45, 112
Mogollon, 16, 228n27
Mol'a:'iya (Melons Come), description of, 140
Moon Mother, 141
Morgan, Lewis Henry, 239n49; influence of, 67, 116
Morgan, Thomas J., 112–13
mother complex, 160, 168
Mother Rock, 50, 132
Mother Terrible, 160, 164; Cha'kwen 'Oka and, 159
mujerado, 5, 25, 26, 175, 230n54
multidimensional model, 213–14
mythology, 12, 149, 217–18; social development and, 16

Nancy, 27–28
National Museum, 61, 69
National Theatre, 64, 66
Navajos, 30, 34, 99, 110; defeat of, 39–40; raids by, 31–32; rites of, 249n46, 249n52
Nayuchi, 104, 111, 117, 195, 196, 198; arrest of, 109, 115, 116, 119; Dumaka and, 110
Neumann, Erich, 15
Newe:kwe (Galaxy Society), 157, 220–22
Nomase, arrest of, 115
Nordstrom, C. E., 112–17, 119, 120, 178, 180, 192

Oedipus complex, 160, 169
Office of Indian Affairs (Bureau of Indian Affairs), 98, 112, 116, 178, 188, 192; criticism of, 189; education and, 113, 114; regulation by, 176; secret dance file and, 179–80, 182; Zunis and, 41–42
Oñate, Juan de, 173
One Feather, Michael, 206
'onnane, 15, 32
origin myth, 15, 149, 156, 217–18, 228n27
Otero-Warren, Nina, 186, 188–89, 260n47
'otstsi' (manly), 28
Oviedo y Valdés, Gonsalo Fernández de, 171
Owlfeather, M., xiv, 205–6

Palle, José, 3, 38
Pandey, Triloki, xi-xii, 202; on Stevenson, 48–49
Parsons, Elsie Clews, xvii, 33, 36–37, 130, 131, 139, 142, 200, 208, 253n8; berdaches and, 26–27; Dumaka and, 243n44; Kasinelu and, 196–97; *katsotstsi'* and, 28; Lasbeke and, 198–99; on lhamanas, 125–26; True and, 226–27n10; We'wha and, 29; Zunis and, x
Patterns of Culture (Benedict), x, 27
Peace Policy, 42
Pearce, Roy Harvey, 68
Philip II, 174
Plummer, Kenneth: on berdaches, 207
pottery-making: commercialization of, 246n90; elements of, 39; modern, 203; We'wha and, 39, 50–51, 121, 126
Pottery Mound, 24–25, 78, 228n27
Powell, John Wesley, 61, 67, 239n49
prayer feathers, 4, 130, 133, 134

prayer sticks, 9, 64, 69–70, 71, 134, 140, 218
puberty: onset of, 137; rites of, 139, 249n46
Pueblo Indians: berdaches and, 5, 175; description of, 11; "progressive," 185–87; Spaniards and, 174–76; U.S. government and, 30, 32, 98, 113, 177; women, 227n15
Pueblo Revolt, 17, 175, 181

racism, 118–19, 193
rain priests, 13, 18, 19, 149, 150, 218
Raven People. See *kakkakwe*
raw beings (*k'abin 'a:ho"i*), 128, 130, 133. *See also* cooked beings
rawness, 145, 149, 156, 165, 219, 247n16; gender differentiation and, 250n65
religious ceremonies, 13, 128; children and, 34–35; dances of, 1 -2, 14, 175; government regulation of, 176–77, 181–82; men and, 18; women and, 19, 136–41
Religious Crimes Code, 176–77
religious freedom, 185; dance order and, 184, 186; protection of, 191–92
Rockefeller, John D., 185

Sacred Lake, 3, 143, 147, 151–52, 156, 160, 162–63, 220, 222, 254n25; kachinas of, 148, 157, 221, 251n2
Salimobiya, 133
Salt Woman, 12
Sandner, Donald, 15
San Felipe, berdache at, 5, 200
San Juan. *See* Tewa
Santa Ana, 186; berdache at, 5
Santa Clara, 184–86
Santo Domingo, 5, 26, 30–31
savagery: civilization and, 68, 116, 122; Morgan on, 67
Sayalhi"a, 133–35, 148, 162–63, 165–66, 221; initiation of, 165
scalp dance, 32, 142
Schneider, David, 160
secret dance file: controversy over, 179–93; description of, 179, 182, 186, 258–59n37; sexual politics and, 194
secret dances, 177–79, 185–86, 193, 258n26, 258n29
Sekaquaptewa, Emory, 135
self-control, 154, 157, 166
self-realization, 144, 156, 169, 206
Sepúlveda, Juan Ginés de, 171
sexuality: berdaches and, 26–27, 204, 211–13; forced changes in, 170, 174–77; initiations and, 142, 194; social constructionism and, 207–8; Spanish reports on, 171–72; Zuni approach to, 35, 146, 160, 201
sexual politics, 170–76; colonialism and, 194
Sha'lako ceremony, xv-xvi, 1–3, 14, 27, 99–100, 140, 250n59; criticism of, 114, 117; kachinas, 1, 2, 254–55n37
shamans: berdaches and, 24; at Zuni, 45, 104
Shiba:buli'ma, 220
Shiwanoka (Priestess), 19
Simpson, James H., 30–31
smallpox. *See* disease
Smithsonian Institution: Cushing and, 7; We'wha at, 61

Sniffen, Matthew K., 185, 188–90; work of, 182, 186
social constructionism, 207–8, 213–14; identity formation and, 208
sodomy, 5, 125, 178, 189, 208, 256n13; charges of, 187–88, 190; Spanish reports of, 171–74; Spanish suppression of, 172–73, 256n6
Spaniards: colonization by, 17–18, 29–30; berdaches and, 4–5, 172–73, 175; conquest by, 170–74; social regulation by, 173
Stephen, Alexander M.,25,109, 194
Stevenson, James, xii-xiii, 7–8, 43, 50, 53, 58, 235n60
Stevenson, Matilda Coxe "Tilly," vii, 11, 17, 19, 31, 35, 38, 40, 44, 45, 54, 70–71, 99–100, 106, 111, 135, 138–39, 144, 148, 230n49, 232n67, 235n60; berdaches and, 22–23, 26–27; cartoon of, 77; on Cushing, 9, 53; description of, 8–9; Dumaka and, 243n44; Kasinelu and, 195–96; Nayuche and, 119; origin myth and, 151, 164, 218, 220, 252–53n8; photograph of, 76; receptions by, 58–59; True and, 72–73, 226n10, 236n68; WAS and, 60–61, 236n2; We'wha and, 3–4, 29, 46–50, 55, 61, 62, 69, 120, 123, 194, 213, 225n3, 253n8
Stewart, Omer: Kasinelu and, 197–98; lhamanas and, 26
Sun Father, 128, 130, 131, 141, 159, 161, 163, 218, 219, 221, 254n37
suwe (younger brother), 33, 127, 242n32
Sweet, E. M., Jr., 179, 180, 181, 182, 192, 259n37
symbols: female, 131; gender-specific, 129–30; use of, 128–30, 132

tableaux vivants, description of, 63
Tafoya, Terry, 145, 162
Tedlock, Barbara, 14
Tedlock, Dennis, 22, 45, 131, 143, 217; "dialogical" anthropology and, xvii
Teller, Henry M., 58, 61
Tesuque. *See* Tewa
Tewa, berdache of, 5, 175, 257n18
third gender, 144–47, 149, 168, 207, 212, 263n25; benefits of, 145–46. *See also* gender roles
transsexualism, 5, 146, 160, 231–32n63, 263n25; definition of, 125
transvestism, 5, 124–25, 160, 264n40. *See also* cross-dressing
True, Clara D., 72–73, 194, 226–27n10, 236n68, 259n45; secret dance file and, 184–86; IRA and, 185; resignation of, 190–91; We'wha and, 191
Tsalatitse, 27
Tsanahe, Dick, 100, 105, 118, 246n79
tso'ya, 14
Turner, Victor, 128, 131, 142, 165

U'k, 27, 28
Ulrichs, Karl Heinrich, 207
United States government: conquest by, 30–31; Indian delegations and, 54; Peace Policy of, 42; policies of, 68, 98, 112–13, 118, 176–77, 181, 191–93; Pueblos

and, 113, 177; witchcraft trials and, 111, 119–20; at Zuni, 111, 115, 117–18, 178
Utes, 30, 226n5

Vanderwagen, Andrew, 116, 198

waffle gardens, description of, 12–13
waha (laughter), 142, 250n59
Ward, Lester F., 67–68; feminism and, 239n49
warfare, 31–32, 144, 154, 157, 220; symbols of, 135, 164
War Gods, 22, 141, 158, 161, 221, 229n36, 254n30
war of the gods, 154–58, 166, 220–22. *See also* Kan'a:kwe
warrior society. *See* bow priests
Warrior Woman. *See* Cha'kwen 'Oka
Washington, John M., 30
Washington, D.C.: society of, 56–59, 65–67
We'wha, ix-x, 25–28, 106, 165, 168, 191, 194, 195, 198, 200, 207, 209, 213, 225n2, 225n3, 232n1, 235n53, 253n8, 263n25; arrest of, 109; assimilation and, 98–99; childhood of, 32–33; contributions of, 120–22; crafts skills of, 39, 50–52, 121, 126; death of, 3–4, 111, 123–24, 234n29; description of, 2, 29, 46–48, 51–52, 196; domestic skills of, 38–40, 51–52; Dumaka and, 110–11; legacy of, 29, 121–22, 202; photographs of, 44, 48, 51, 61–62, 80–90, 92, 235n51, 238n30; religious roles of, 14, 48, 50–51, 54, 69–70, 120–21, 126, 148, 196; in Washington, 53–66, 69–73, 98, 126, 236n2
weaving, 18; photographs of, 85, 87–89; We'wha and, 39, 51–52, 55, 62, 121, 126
Welsh, Herbert, 182, 185, 187, 189, 190, 192–93
Westermarck, Edward, 207
whiskey, 101, 105, 108; impact of, 99–100
White Corn people, 154
White Gods, 148, 154
Whitehead, Harriet, 164, 212
White Shell Woman, 12, 138–39, 144
Williams, Walter, 206, 212, 265n41
Wilson, Edmund, xvi, 14, 71
winkte (Lakota), 206, 264n33
witchcraft: fear of, 101–4, 119, 219; trials, 103–13, 119; Zuni concept of, 45, 101–2, 120
Women's Anthropological Society (WAS), 66, 236n2; founding of, 60–61
women: attitudes toward, 22, 173; agriculture and, 12, 19, 139, 140; arts and, 18, 140; birth control, 20; ceremonial life of, 136–41; menstruation and, 137, 141, 158; roles of, 18–22, 140, 177; sexuality of, 20, 138–39, 213; training of, 38–39; whipping kachinas and, 138. *See also* gender roles
Wood Society, 220, 222
Wounded Knee, 107

ya:na (finished), 128
yaboda (male corn), 130, 140, 141
Young, M. Jane, 210, 229n47

Zuni: anthropologists and, x-xiii; artistry of, 13–14; berdaches and, 5–6; colonization and, 17–18; concept of time, 110; culture of, xvi, 11–17; defensive strategies of, 32; definition of, 225n1; emergence of, 15–17; isolation of, 11, 29–30, 41; Pueblo Revolt and, 17; theocracy of 13; U.S. government and, 98–99, 104–11
Zuni, Lina, 41, 100–101, 104–10, 119, 127, 242n32